Peepeyes

Peepeyes

Cause of Death: Unknown (DOA)

The True Crime Murder Mystery of Nell Tucker

DWAIN S. TUCKER

To order additional copies of this book, contact:
Xlibris Corporation
1-888-795-4274
www.Xlibris.com
Orders@Xlibris.com
93991

CONTENTS

Dedications

My dedication for this book is twofold, to two extraordinary women.

First, I dedicate this book to my beloved mother, Mary Judith Bond Tucker, who was clearly my lifetime best friend, who never let me down, who always chose me first even before herself, and loved me unconditionally. This is my tribute to a grand lady.

Second and lastly, I also dedicate this book to my beloved grandmother, Nell Annie Freeman Tucker, to me known simply as "Peepeyes." Her grace and dignity transcended the time and place from where she came. Her sweetness and gentility charmed all she met. Her love she freely and genuinely gave to her son, her grandchildren, and her relation. This is also my tribute to a lady of true class.

Nell (Freeman) Tucker and Judy (Bond) Tucker circa 1958

Preface

This book is not organized chronologically, although on a high conceptual scale, it does follow events roughly in the order they happened. Because some information was gained coincident in time with other information, I had to organize the book around topics or themes, such as putting all family interviews in one chapter, even though some of them occurred later than events in other chapters.

Some of the language in the book is a bit saucy at times, and some might even find some words used to be offensive. Because I repeat those words here doesn't mean I myself approve of those words—I do not. But I thought it important to be accurate to the words given me to fully portray the individuals described in this book. Therefore I didn't edit the words given to me from others; I just took them down like dictation, word for word, and reported them here. All these people described in this book should be taken in the context of from when and where they came. An individual using unpleasant terminology doesn't necessarily mean the person is a bad person, rather just a product of a place and time.

I don't believe I portrayed anyone in this book that is still living in a negative light, only in the accurate and balanced light of being a human being, as we all are. I tried to minimize my own personal opinions of people that I met or knew that appear in this book, because I didn't want that to color my writing of what they said.

It was never my intention to defame or hurt anyone with what is written here. I simply interviewed people, wrote down their stories, and reported it here. I make no representation that these stories are accurate beyond the veracity of the people that told them to me. Where I could I verified the stories with documentation from government and other sources. In some cases, if more than one person was the source of the information—that corroborates the story. But again, the information is only as accurate as the people that gave it to me.

Lastly, I hope those who read this book come away with an understanding of the emotional journey I went through during the investigation, as that really is the intent of the book. I wanted to describe an individual (myself) experiencing the discovery of how an extraordinary, bizarre mystery happened in a rather normal, Midwest family.

Dwain S. Tucker
Los Angeles, California
2006

Acknowledgments

With gratitude I acknowledge the following individuals for their editorial support and commentaries of encouragement on this project: Mischelle Mische, Bella Glozman, and JoAnna Jocelyn. I particularly want to acknowledge editorial input by Anne Carayon and cousin Debbie Schadt. Many thanks, my good friends.

I also wish to acknowledge and thank attorneys Dan Quisenberry, Esq.; Craig Englander, Esq.; and Kerry D. Smith, Esq.; for their legal advice.

Frank Leon Tucker, 1931-2005

Chapter 1

THE RUMOR

Tillie said that a few days after Nell and Leon got down to Florida on the evening of January 6, 1969, they got word that Nell had died of a heart attack. Grace told Tillie she didn't believe it and immediately said, "Leon killed 'er."

The phone rang around ten o'clock on a Saturday night, October 22, 2005. It was a family member. He said with a solemn voice that I recognized from a similar call some twenty-one months prior, "Dwain . . . Dad has passed on." My immediate reaction was "Oh my god," but in fact we had been expecting it for quite a while, so it wasn't a complete shock. The fact it was happening then was a small shock, since the family member had told me Dad was doing so much better just forty-eight hours earlier. The family member had e-mailed me one week before that Dad was in the hospital again with his failing heart, and that things looked serious. When I was reading that e-mail, I was on my last day of a Southeast Asian vacation and reading his e-mail in the Bangkok, Thailand, airport at a public Internet station. I called Dad's house on my cell phone, which miraculously worked in Thailand, after having checked the time at Dad's house and got the details. Basically the doctors said that Dad could die anytime or could last a year. I asked my family there at Dad's house if they wanted me to continue my flying after I reached Los Angeles, my scheduled destination, to come to Kentucky right away. I was told they would call me when I got home to Los Angeles, and we could see how things looked then.

When I got home to LA, I immediately called Dad's house and was told by family there that things were improving with Dad's condition. Dad was being discharged from the hospital in a day or two. By the end of that week, I was told things were looking up, and Dad was getting stronger. I already had scheduled a trip to see Dad in only two more weeks anyway, with airline tickets already purchased months prior. I was advised by family at Dad's house not to change the tickets to come earlier. It was therefore a small shock that Dad crashed so suddenly. At least I was told he did—I'll never know if that was the truth or not. I know that I was denied the chance to be there and hold his hand as he died, as family there with him did. I wanted that, having been similarly denied the chance to be there when my mother passed away in February 2004, also suddenly. Whether or not it was unavoidable circumstances or something else that denied me that moment, I'll likely never know.

I started making my plans to attend the funeral of my father, Frank Leon Tucker. It was to be less than a week away. The viewing would be on Thursday night in Kentucky, the funeral service would be Friday in Kentucky, and because of the long drive time, over five hours, the burial services graveside would be on Saturday. I would fly out on Tuesday night, overnight in St. Louis, and drive to Kentucky on Wednesday. I wanted to stop through Paducah on my way to Madisonville (where the services would take place) to visit Tillie Edwards, my father's first cousin on his mother's side, and Frank's lifelong close friend. Tillie is this woman in her early seventies, with a sometimes big hairstyle common to ladies of Kentucky, usually a broad smile on her face, very feminine in her comportment, and with a charming western Kentucky drawl. Tillie and Frank were raised more like brother and sister than first cousins. Frank trusted Tillie all his life with his deepest secrets. Tillie knew it all. And now that Frank was gone, I wanted to know it all—the good, the bad, and the ugly. I showed her some photos we had previously discovered in my grandma Nell's (Frank's mother) photo album that were not identified, as I didn't recognize the people. I hoped Tillie would help me identify who they were, and she did just that with most of the photos. Tillie's memory recall was amazing. Tillie was sharp as a tack and bright-eyed.

After sharing some commonly known memories of my father, Tillie suddenly dropped her ever-present wide smile and got serious. I wondered what could possibly be so serious as to wipe that permanent smile from Tillie's face. She said, "Didya know ya have a sister?" I flash-thought that maybe Tillie was getting a bit old and confused me with someone else. I said, "No, I don't have a sister, Tillie." She countered firmly without missing a beat, "Yes, ya do. Frankie had a daughter with his high-school sweetheart Nadine b'fore he married for the first time. Her name is Sharon. She lives in Cape Girardeau, Missouri. She's fifty-four yars old. I've arranged secret meetin's 'tween her, Nadine, and Frank for yars." I was shocked speechless. I never knew any of this.

I asked Tillie why Frank had kept it secret all these years. She said it was an agreement he had with Nadine. (One note of explanation: For privacy reasons, since it involves the virtue of a person still living, I had to change the real names of these two women to fictitious names, Nadine and Sharon, even though I only refer to them by their first names.) He wouldn't acknowledge or reveal Sharon was his daughter in exchange for not having to pay any child support payments, and Sharon would be raised as the daughter of Nadine's first husband. I suspect they changed Sharon's birth certificate to show Nadine's first husband as her father as that's what it shows today, even though from the storyline I was given, Nadine didn't meet this man until after Sharon was born, so he couldn't have been shown on the birth certificate at the time of birth. Having illegitimate children at that time, the early 1950s, in western Kentucky was still considered a major taboo. So a deep secret was born that my father would keep all his life and take with him to his grave, at least so he thought.

Frank and Tillie circa 1985

Tillie said Frank revealed the secret to her, so she could keep in touch with Nadine over the years and be a conduit of information back to him about his daughter, Sharon. When Frank and my mother, Judy, divorced in 1985, Frank began looking for another wife. He asked Tillie to arrange a meeting with Nadine and Sharon. Tillie set it up for a meeting at her bridal shop in Paducah, and then all four went to lunch together. Tillie was expecting the revealing of Sharon's real parentage to take place during the lunch, but it didn't. Tillie said she didn't know if Nadine and Frank had exchanged a few private words about it or not. Sharon was told that Frank was merely an old family friend. She had been raised believing Nadine's first husband was her real father. Tillie said Nadine told her that her husband always treated Sharon differently than he did their sons that came later, and Sharon always wondered why.

Frank and Nadine began dating a few times again after this 1985 meeting. One of those dates was actually a weekend-long out-of-town trip to Nashville. Nadine would later brag to her sisters about the "frilly little things," assumed to mean lingerie, she wore during her weekend with Frank in Nashville. Upon their return to Paducah, Nadine's husband had apparently discovered the infidelity and began divorce proceedings against Nadine. Nadine evidently began planning a long-sought and delayed life with Frank. After several dates, Frank told Tillie that there was something wrong with the situation, it wasn't the same as their high-school relationship some thirty years prior, and he couldn't marry Nadine now either. Imagine how furious Nadine would have been, being jilted by Frank two times in her lifetime. She told Tillie, as Tillie related to me, "I almost lost my house 'cause o' Frank this time."

I left Tillie's that day with a mind full of questions about what I didn't know about my father. He had so many secrets in his lifetime. Who could know what else I would find out? I shivered at the thought. This drove home for me the notion I had always suspected in the Tucker family—we had big secrets. Secrets like this can be kept for extremely long periods of time and never be leaked. The secrets of Watergate and the identity of Deep Throat weren't kept as well as the Tucker family kept our secrets.

The viewing the following evening in Madisonville was expectedly sad but normal as funeral viewings go. The following morning, just before the actual funeral ceremony, the fireworks began again. Frank had a son with his first wife, Maudine Celesta "Celeste" Pruitt, named Trent. After a roughly four-year marriage, Maudine and Frank divorced, and a bitter custody battle over Trent ensued. I'll detail the hideous divorce and custody battle in a later chapter. It ended with Maudine awarded custody and child support by an Arkansas court. Frank was awarded visitation rights, and the matter appeared to be settled.

Frank had some brief visits with Trent over the years following that, but there was such a great split and animosity between the families; eventually contact with Trent was lost. I hadn't seen him for thirty-five years prior to Frank's funeral. When he walked into the funeral home, accompanied by his uncle, Teddy Pruitt, Maudine's brother, I instantly recognized him. He just *had* to be a Tucker from his appearance.

Trent Tucker and Dwain Tucker at funeral of Frank Tucker, October 2005

One good thing came out of the funeral—Trent got to see what the Tucker family really was like, instead of just stories from others. Trent's uncle, Teddy Pruitt, said to Tillie at the wake following the funeral, "I told Trent that these people har' (referring to us, the Tuckers) are nothin' like what he's been told." Clearly, Teddy realized all the characterizations of the Tucker family that had been passed around in the Pruitt family over the years were completely wrong. We weren't these monsters or "low people," to quote Teddy, that the Pruitts had characterized us to be. And those wrong characterizations caused Trent to tragically miss out on knowing his other family—a family that wanted to know him—for thirty-five years.

At the viewing, a family member that was with my father Frank the day he died told me that Frank was seeing his mother, Nell, and my mother, Judy, both deceased, visiting him. The family member said that he entered the room where Frank was and heard him conversing normally to the other side of the room where there were two empty chairs. The family member asked Frank with whom he was talking, and Frank replied that he was talking to "Mom and Judy," who he said were sitting across the room from him. Spirituality and the occult have always been difficult for me to believe in, but I'm not so arrogant as to close my mind to the possibility that there is a lot we humans don't understand yet. I leave open the possibility that there is a hereafter, a place we go after we leave this world. I thought for a moment, perhaps those we love the most in our lifetimes come to us on our last day to show us the way, to calm us, so the transition to the next world isn't so frightening. I know scientists would explain that my father's heart was beginning to fail on his last day of life. As his blood flow slowed to his brain depriving it of necessary oxygen, the nerve endings in his brain began to fire and memories of his mother (Nell) and my mother (Judy) entered his mind. The apparitions of Nell and Judy were nothing more than hallucinations in my father's mind as he died slowly. That's the logical explanation. But I also leave open the possibility that perhaps another explanation was the truth of what he was seeing that day.

At a private moment during the funeral, after all other family had left the room and I was alone in the viewing room with my father's casket, I approached the casket to say something to my father I had been waiting forty-one years to say. I looked at his dead body, spoke out loud and in a normal volume, and said, "I forgive you." I paused, and then continued, "I know you always wanted to hear me say that to you, and I'm sorry I didn't say it to you while you were alive." That statement lifted a ton of burdens from me—four decades of resentment of my father stemming from an embarrassingly long list of horrendous grievances against him, all of which were justified. He wasn't a bad man, but he was far from a perfect man. His one great weakness was his inability to admit his wrongs in life, in a genuine way, not in a fake or planned way. Simply put—he had too much pride and lacked courage in this one area. It estranged him from Trent, caused him to never know his daughter Sharon, and caused a distance between him and me that was never bridged. We were cordial with each other, but never close as a father and son should be—and that was a shame, a huge waste of opportunity. So I forgave him for it—all of it—and moved on.

When the dust settled from all of that, I began to tell Tillie about some memories I had of my grandma Nell, Frank's mother. I said to her, "Did Dad ever tell you the story of how we gave my grandma Nell a nickname?" Tillie shook her head no with a glint of interest in her eye. I recounted the story for her. "When I was a baby, not fully verbal yet, my grandma Nell would come up to me and hold her hands together in front of her eyes like this." I demonstrated it for Tillie. I continued, "She would pull them apart quickly, and say, 'Peep Eyes! Peep Eyes!' She would just keep doing it over and over. I would laugh and laugh, and she just kept doing it to keep me laughing. I began to call her "Peepeyes." The nickname was pronounced like two words meshed together, "Peep" and "Eyes," as if saying "I's." I would call her this nickname every time she would enter the room, and everyone would laugh. I learned her name as "Peepeyes" rather than "Meemaw," which is what my brother called her and what all the kids in Kentucky called their grandmas. Everyone thought it was so cute that I called her that, so they all started calling her that in front of me to reinforce it, so I would learn her name was "Peepeyes." Then everyone started calling her that even when I wasn't around. Pretty soon people outside the family started calling her that. Before too long, it just became her permanent nickname from everyone. She loved it." Tillie smiled and seemed enraptured by the story. Tillie said she thought she had remembered hearing that nickname for her, but pointed out that she died soon after that time. It was true that Nell had died one month before I turned five years old.

I related to Tillie I only had two distinct memories of Nell. One was when she would sit on the kiddie train ride at Noble Park with me and ride it for hours. She worked the ticket booth at the park swimming pool, so they would give her hundreds of tickets for free, and we would ride all day. Another time I remember being at her house and admiring a ceramic elephant she had on a shelf. I asked her if I could have it, and Frank said quickly, "No, you can't! You put that back!" Peepeyes said with a big smile, "Yes, he can have that. Don't worry, Frankie, it's jus' a little thing from the dime store. Didn't cost nearly nuthin'." I continued to Tillie, "Do you know I still have that ceramic elephant today, some thirty-seven years later?" Tillie said with a warm smile, "Well, I'll be darned."

Since I had brought up the subject of my grandma, Nell, it jogged Tillie's memory about a rumor that had haunted the Tucker family for more than three decades. Tillie began to recount a story for me that I had heard a few times before, but not in such detail. I patiently listened, not really interested at first. She told the story of how she believed my grandfather Elbert Leon Tucker, known as "Leon," had actually murdered my grandmother, Nell Annie (Freeman) Tucker. This ugly rumor had surfaced at pretty much every Tucker family gathering I had ever been. It was discussed at my grandfather Leon's funeral in June 1987, at a Tucker family reunion at the Old Concrete Church and Cemetery (also known as Carter's Mill Cemetery) near Symsonia, Kentucky, sometime when I was in my teens, and now at Frank's funeral here in 2005. My mother Judy had discussed it with me several times, always with a serious tone, like it wasn't idle chatter. Whenever our family would visit some of the Tucker cousins, the rumor would come up. They would always be looking at us like we must know the inside story and weren't telling it, therefore we must be a part of whatever wrong that happened, or at least part of the cover-up. The raised eyebrows sent our direction always bothered me.

Tillie told me that Leon and Nell went down to Florida around Christmas in 1968. Nell told her sister, Grace, who was Tillie's mother, that she didn't want to go, and sniffed that Leon was up to something because he was acting strange. Tillie said Nell and Grace made a plan that Nell would send to her a postcard with the *i* in her last name (Grace's married name was Martinez) dotted with a circle instead of a dot. If Grace received that card, that meant Nell felt that she was in trouble and needed help. This postcard warning was the best they could do since in the late sixties, there were no cell phones; and at remote campgrounds, there were no payphones either. Tillie said when it came time to leave, Nell still didn't want to go, and that Leon came into Grace's house where Nell was at, laid a shotgun down on the coffee table, and basically ordered Nell into the car so they could go.

Leon and Nell in previous years had always headed to a campground on Lake Okeechobee, located where the Kissimmee River empties into Lake Okeechobee. Leon especially liked it because it was not crowded, off the beaten path, and the fishing was therefore good on that section of the lake. Tillie said that a few days after Nell and Leon got down to Florida, on the evening of January 6, 1969, they got word that Nell had died of a heart attack. Grace told Tillie she didn't believe it and immediately said, "Leon killed 'er." Tillie told me the next day after they got the notification, she intercepted from Grace's mailbox a postcard addressed to Grace from Nell in Florida. The postcard just said they had arrived OK, and the *i* was dotted with a circle instead of a dot. Tillie said she thought the sight of that would cause her own mother, Grace, to have a heart attack. She took the postcard over to the Paducah police along with the story of how it was a signal. Someone from their office called down to the police in Okeechobee, Florida. The police searched the campsite and Leon's camper.

I asked Tillie if they ever found anything in the investigation. She shook her head no with a sense of sorrow on her face. I remembered that my mother Judy had told me years earlier that somehow she knew the investigation revealed an empty medication bottle found in the trailer. The empty medication bottle was for a prescription that had been refilled immediately before going on the Florida trip. By the number of days of usage between the refill date and the date of her death, the bottle could not possibly have been empty. The police found this notable enough to write it down in their notes. No clear indication of foul play had been found at the campsite, so no criminal charges were ever filed.

Tillie said Leon told everyone at Nell's funeral about how she died. He said Nell had been eating fresh citrus and had begun to have bad chest pains in the car on the way to a seafood restaurant about fifteen miles from the campground. Leon said he raced toward a hospital. She arrived at the hospital still alive and was begging for help in the emergency room as they were treating her. She died at the hospital, according to Leon's story he told the family at the funeral. Grace didn't believe the story and called the hospital in Okeechobee, Florida. She spoke with a doctor that had been on duty that night in the emergency room and had treated Nell. He said Nell arrived at the hospital already dead, and the body appeared to have been dead for over five hours. This, Tillie said, was Leon's lie. If Leon lied, Tillie concluded, then he was guilty. He had killed her.

When Tillie was telling me this, I began to remember the night our family got the word that Peepeyes had died. We were living at 1530 N. Forty-sixth Street in East St. Louis at the time. It was the middle of the evening, and Judy called Frank to the phone, saying it was Leon calling. We always called my grandpa Leon by the name "Papaw" instead of "Grandpa" or "Granddad." It's a Kentucky culture thing. Grandmas were called "Meemaw" also, except in our case, we had adopted the name "Peepeyes." As Frank picked up the phone, I remember Judy jokingly calling out loudly so Leon could hear through the phone, "Remind him to bring us back some oranges!" Frank answered the phone, speaking in his familiar Kentucky drawl, "Yeah, Daddy, how's things goin' down thar in Florida. Ya catchin' any fish?" I saw the smile drop from his face as he heard a serious tone from Leon. Frank's brow furrowed. Leon told him his mother had died. Frank raised his hand to cover his eyes and exclaimed, "Oh me no!" He then told Judy that Peepeyes had died in Florida, and Judy expressed her shock. This is probably the hardest news anyone can hear, that his or her mother has died. I remember it was the first and one of the only times I would ever see my father cry, and he wept copiously before composing himself to get the details from Leon.

Leon told Frank the same story he would later tell to the other family members at Nell's funeral—that she died at the emergency room. I distinctly remember, even at my tender age just shy of five years old, that this was the story Frank told me of how she died. He would reiterate that story to me in later years, not knowing anything else.

In the months after Nell's funeral, Leon would return to Kentucky to sell and box up Nell's property. Nell was living in a house she rented from her sister Ila Mae at the time she died. Tillie told me that her mother had conducted her own investigation into Nell's death and had contacted the local commonwealth attorney's office (Kentucky's version of the district attorney) in Paducah. She became convinced that Leon had killed Nell and had decided to take justice into her own hands. Tillie said that Grace knew Leon had lunch every day that he was in Paducah at the Farmer's Market. Grace waited for him there one day with a pistol, intending to shoot him. But Leon was lucky that day. He had already decided to leave early for East St. Louis, and Grace missed her chance.

I knew that Leon had been living with his girlfriend, or so we thought she was at the time, Audie C. (Marshall-Reed) Hayden, known as "Audrey," in East St. Louis for many years prior to Nell's death. It was a widely known but never discussed secret in our family that Leon was a bigamist, if not in law, at least in practice. He had two households set up. One was with Audrey in East St. Louis where he worked most of the year doing construction work. The other was with Nell in Paducah, where both had family roots. Several weekends a month and whenever he wasn't working, he would drive down to Paducah to be with Nell then return to Audrey in East St. Louis after.

Tillie had lost her characteristic smile, and tears welled up in her eyes as she finished telling me the details she knew of the rumor of Nell's murder. I could tell this wasn't some gleeful, fun gossip she was passing around, but something she truly, heartfelt believed. She was deeply fond of her aunt Nell when she was alive, and it obviously hurt Tillie to her core to believe Leon murdered Nell.

The conclusion of Frank's funeral was the graveside burial ceremony the next day after the viewing. They weren't on the same day because of the long travel distance, greater than five hours, to the burial site in the Smith-Kirby Cemetery, Chesterfield, Illinois. Trent did not attend the graveside burial ceremony. I guess we were just lucky enough to get him to come to the viewing and ceremony at the funeral home. After the graveside burial, I invited all those that attended, perhaps thirty people, to a nearby restaurant in Carlinville for a meal on me—sort of a pseudowake. Everyone came, and we reminisced about Frank and other family members. I didn't know what to believe about the story of Nell's death after the conclusion of this funeral for Frank.

Flying back to California, I began to get irritated that this rumor just kept coming up at each family event. It was a stain on my immediate family's reputation. Anyone wouldn't like it that there was the stigma of murder in your immediate family. I began to think that even in the future at the funerals of my siblings, or my own funeral, or future Tucker family reunions, this ugly rumor would resurface again and again. I decided I wanted to look into it and put it to rest once and for all. I believed at that point it was nothing more than an unfounded rumor started by naturally suspicious and superstitious people. These family members, her sister Grace and her niece Tillie, dearly loved my grandma Nell. I thought they just couldn't come to terms with Nell's loss and invented this murder theory to deflect their unbearable grief by turning it into anger. I thought if I looked into the story and gathered whatever evidence might still exist, I could come up with evidence to prove this rumor false.

After all, the suggestion that Leon could have been a murderer and killed his own wife just didn't make sense to me at all. That was totally inconsistent and uncharacteristic of the man I knew Leon to be. The man I generally remembered my grandfather to be was this gentle old man with a quirky sense of humor, sometimes aggravating, but never violent. Life and old age had kicked the fight out of him, and he seemed to me to be simply passive. He was a man who loved fishing, gardening, camping, hunting, and going to church. He wasn't even a yelling-type man. The rumor just didn't fit.

A few years before Frank died, he gave me Leon's pocket watch that Leon had always carried, with an engraving of initials and dates on the back. It was a wonderful keepsake of a man that I missed and wanted always to remember. Even though my memories of Leon were balanced, some good, some not so good, at the time of Frank's funeral, I still had never seen or heard anything that would make me believe Leon was capable of murder. That's why I initially thought this rumor of him killing Nell was just preposterous. However, my belief wasn't going to stop this rumor from resurrecting itself at every family gathering. The only thing that would stop this rumor was to put it to rest. If I investigated this rumor, I could exonerate Leon once and for all from any suspicion about Nell's death. Armed with the evidence I uncovered in my investigation, when in the future this ugly rumor resurfaced, I could say, "That rumor is false. Here's the proof I found showing that Nell died of natural causes. Leon had nothing to do with it." This was my mission. I began a journey that I couldn't be sure where it would end, but I was determined to find the answer.

*   *   *

Chapter 2

THE MEMORIES

Leon was renowned in the extended Tucker family as the best storyteller. His deep, gravelly voice made it seem like actor Lorne Greene was narrating the story, so it was always entertaining . . . Those are some of my best memories of Leon.

I decided the best way to start my investigation was to write down everything I remembered about Leon, whom I called "Papaw," and from those memories, it might give me a clue where to proceed next. My specific memories of Leon were mostly positive ones. Here are just a few of them. I remember when I was very young, perhaps three or four years of age, we were visiting with Leon in Florida, likely on Lake Okeechobee. Leon was peeling fresh peaches for me with his pocketknife. He had picked up a crate of peaches in Georgia on the way down to Florida. They were huge, cold, sweet, juicy, soft, and absolutely delicious. I loved them so much, I kept saying, "Mo mo pee pee Papaw?" That was the best I could manage at asking for more peaches at my almost preverbal age. Judy and Frank told me Leon would just laugh and kept peeling the peaches for me as long as I would keep eating them. I ate so many of them that I could only pass peach juice for days after.

Some of my memories of Leon are more mixed. Once, when I was perhaps seven or eight, we were behind Leon's house on Husband Road in Paducah. Leon somehow was pitting my older sibling and I against each other in some kind of contest that I don't exactly remember what it was, perhaps a throwing contest. When I couldn't throw (or perform at whatever the basis of the contest was) as well as my older sibling, Leon commented to Frank, "That one (pointing to me) is not as good as that one (pointing to my older sibling.)" Judy overhead this in the house and stuck her head out the backdoor and yelled, "Frank, I don't want them pitted against each other. Dwain is smaller and younger. It's wrong to make him compete against someone bigger and older than he is." She was, of course, entirely correct in her parenting. Leon gave Frank a sour look that clearly said, "Son, ya ain't mindin' ya woman (meaning he wasn't controlling his woman)." Nothing would make Leon more irritated, not mad, just irritated, than a mouthy, Northern-type woman. But Frank, typical to his nature all his life, would not stand up to Leon. Off of Leon's cue, Frank just said to Judy, "Go on into the house, Judy. I'll take care of things out har'." She repeated her plea, and Frank repeated his direction for her to let him handle it. Of course, letting him handle it meant Frank would do nothing about Leon's wrong-headed adventure, figuring "Dwain will forget 'bout it. It's jus' this one time." Well, it didn't scar me for life or anything like that, but I didn't forget about it.

Remembering Leon's look that day, signaling to Frank his displeasure at Judy's comment, it reminds me of something else Judy told me once. When I became an adult, Judy once told me that when she initially married Frank, Leon didn't like her. Leon had evidently made a pass at her, and she rebuffed him, as naturally any woman would rebuff their father-in-law's advance. After she did that, Leon went to Frank and said, "Son . . . why . . . ya didn't marry ya'self a Southern girl!" Leon disliked opinionated women who would open their mouths from time to time. To him that was the difference between a Northern and Southern type woman. Neither Nell nor Audrey ever spoke up to him, and he got used to that. From what I hear, it's the reason why he didn't like Nadine, Frank's high-school sweetheart, and refused to let Frank marry her when she got pregnant. Nadine, despite being from the South, evidently was opinionated and not shy about it.

Another memory of Leon I have was from a trip I took as a young man during my college years to visit him on my own. It would have been 1984 or 1985, as he passed away soon after in 1987. During the trip, Leon assumed I was visiting him because I wanted something, like to be included in his will. Leon always thought cynically of people, that they wouldn't do something for familial love, but always for an angle for self gain. That's because that's the way he lived his entire life and dealt with others, including family members. So he naturally thought others would be doing that toward him as well. I called him to tell him I had a weekend free and wanted to drive down to see him for two days. He agreed. My motivation was to see my grandfather, because I knew he was closing in on his final years, because I loved him, and also because quite honestly I pitied him. I knew he didn't have many visitors, and I imagined he spent most of his days sitting in his chair, looking at the television. I thought a visit by his grandson might pick his spirits up. I hadn't seen him in a year or so. Since becoming an adult, I no longer accompanied Frank on his Kentucky visits every other month.

During my visit, at one point, Leon gave me his cynical smile again, like he was going to discuss the real reason for my visit and said, "Now, I don't have as much money as ya'll think I do." He basically was insinuating that I was visiting him because he thought I wanted some of his money. He also insinuated the rest of us, my parents and sibling, were seeking the same thing from him—money. I told him I didn't care how much money he had, a lot or none at all. I didn't want any of it, and that wasn't the reason I was visiting him. He quickly accepted that, or acted like he did at least. Whether he actually did or not, I'll never know. I knew then and always had known that I would not be in Leon's will anyway. At most, Audrey, Frank, and perhaps Audrey's children,

Elbert Leon Tucker, 1911-1987

Harold and Frances, would be in his will. But his assumption and sort of accusation underscored for me how Leon viewed the world and the people in it, including his own family members. Everything was about money. He genuinely thought all human interaction, even inside families, was angled around money.

During this 1985 visit, Leon and I discussed income taxes, probably from some story appearing on the television news that we watched together. I lamented how I had to pay taxes now that I was earning my own money, and he said he had stopped filing his tax returns altogether years earlier. I told Leon that he still had to file tax returns and pay income taxes even though he was retired, and that the IRS isn't going to believe some excuse like, "I'm jus' an old man and I didn't know." I found out later from Frank that Leon had gotten spooked by my comments to him, and after I left, he went to the tax offices in Paducah and paid up his back taxes, to the tune of around $10,000 in back taxes and penalties.

Leon thought everyone in the world was an idiot, except him. He would take me around his house, making sure I knew where the light switches were and how to turn them off. I would think to myself, "Duh, you mean you flip it down, Papaw, and the lights go off? Wow—what'll they think of next?" He would show me how to close his doors, so they clicked closed. I'm not kidding. He was so freaked out about his electric bill that he insisted on showing me how to do these simple tasks that any imbecile could do. I remember him telling me to piss in the toilet once, saying some of Audrey's grandkids had visited recently and had pissed in the corner of the bathroom instead of the toilet. I thought to myself, "What—were they Guinea bushmen?—or Amazon tribesmen? Had they never seen a toilet before?" I rather think Leon just made that up to have a reason to tell me how to use the toilet.

Leon's control freak behavior extended to telling me how to eat as well. Nobody except Frank wanted to eat the game meat Leon had caught and cooked, which were mainly deer, squirrels, and rabbits. Leon tricked me into eating deer once, saying it was beef. I thought as I ate it that it tasted funny, but guessed he had just cooked the beef with a southern spice. He proudly told me afterward, "Now you've eaten deer." He wanted to prove to me I could eat it by tricking me, and I was pissed. I never again ate meat at his house unless I saw the packaging. He missed the point. I knew I could eat the deer meat. I just didn't want to eat the damn deer meat! Nor did I care to eat squirrel, which I considered too closely related to rats. Squirrels are in the rodent family, but that fact seemed to escape Leon and Frank. I think because squirrels were plentiful in the forests and easy to kill, they made for a cheap supply of meat.

When Leon and Frank would get the squirrels home, they would skin them by pulling them out of their hides like a plastic wrapper being pulled off of a slice of cheese, making this horrible tearing sound, like two pieces of Velcro being ripped apart. The squirrels would be beheaded and gutted. Then the headless and skinned little corpses would be floating in this big pan of water on the back stoop, I suppose to tenderize the meat before cooking. It was a revolting sight. Then Leon would deep fry them like chicken and serve them up for dinner. Audrey always knew to fix Judy and me a hamburger meatloaf, as we wanted nothing to do with the chicken-fried rodents.

Leon made a visit to our house in Cahokia, Illinois, (712 St. Maud Street) one time. We had a wild, baby rabbit running around our house. We had discovered a nest of baby rabbits in the backyard while mowing the lawn, and accidentally ran over the nest with the lawnmower. All the baby rabbits were killed except one, which we named Sidecar, named that because he sucked on the baby bottle nipple we would feed him milk with out of the side of his mouth. We gave Sidecar free run of the house rather than caging him, and he left little rabbit pellets everywhere. We fed him and raised him for several weeks, and he was growing in size. When Leon visited, he declared that we couldn't raise Sidecar because he was a wild rabbit. Frank disagreed, although he told Leon we intended to set Sidecar free just as soon as we finished raising him to at least a juvenile size. When we went out to the store, leaving Leon alone in the house, he intentionally left a side door to our house open, so Sidecar got out. Up to that point, we had made a point to keep the doors closed so he couldn't, at least until we got him raised to near adulthood. As a baby rabbit, he couldn't have made it on his own in the wild, so letting him out before he was reasonably grown meant sure death for him. But Leon didn't care—he didn't want us to prove him wrong and successfully raise Sidecar. That was Leon, insisting on having his way whether it was his business or not.

At other times I remember Leon regaling us of the stories of his life, such as how he used to work at a cooper shop, which made wooden barrels, in Paducah for eighteen cents a day in pay. The Paducah cooperage shop was nicknamed the "Penitentiary" by the men that worked there because of the brutality of the work environment, such as long hours of grueling labor and harsh treatment by supervisors.[1] Leon would tell us of how hard times were when he was a young man, and it would keep us all enthralled. He'd tell us of how he quit school in the third grade to begin working an adult's job. Leon was renowned in the extended Tucker family as the best storyteller. His deep, gravelly voice made it seem like actor Lorne Greene was narrating the story, so it was always entertaining. He'd love to walk us around his garden to show us which vegetables were "comin' in good this yar." Those are some of my best memories of Leon.

*   *   *

Chapter 3

THE JOURNEY

When I got the death certificate, it was perhaps the most shocking thing I had ever read. There, blaring off the page in big letters, larger than any other writing on the page, in the box for "Cause of Death," showed "UNKNOWN (DOA)."

I didn't know really where to begin searching for evidence in an event that occurred almost thirty-seven years prior. I thought the first step was to write down what I knew myself, from my own recall from over the years. The only thing I could remember at first that wasn't part of the story Tillie had told me was regarding a call Frank received that night it all happened. Shortly after Frank had received the call from Leon, telling him Nell had died, he received another call from Florida. I didn't witness the call at the time, but Frank told me about it years later. This time, it was a call from the hospital in Okeechobee. They were calling to ask if Frank wanted an autopsy of Nell's remains. They were calling because Leon had refused to allow an autopsy. They wanted to give Frank the opportunity to request one, since as an immediate family member to Nell, he could make the request, overriding Leon's decision against an autopsy. Frank said he made the decision not to authorize the autopsy because he couldn't bear the thought of his mother being "cut up like that," referring to the process of autopsy where a body is dissected. This process prevents an open-casket funeral later unless extensive reconstruction by the funeral directors is performed, or at least Frank thought so.

I remember when Frank was telling me this, he was solemn, not only because he was talking about his dead mother, but also because he knew what it meant. He had an uneasiness on his face that wasn't just sorrow for his dead mother. It was immediately obvious to me that if a hospital was calling a son for permission to do an autopsy over the objections of a spouse, there must be some serious suspicion. The suspicion was that an autopsy was needed to reveal something that should be known, such as evidence of foul play. That was kind of a no-brainer. I'm not sure Tillie even knew that Frank had the chance to request an autopsy of his mother's remains before they were embalmed, but refused. I remember my mother, Judy, commenting years later that she thought Frank refused not because of his reticence about Nell's remains being dissected, but because he was afraid of going against his father, Leon.

We were always told by Leon that Nell had died of a heart attack. I thought the first line of investigation should be to seek any medical records existing of the event in 1969. Through the Vital Chek (sic) network, a private company, linked with the State of Florida's Vital Records Office, I ordered Nell's death certificate, even paying the extra cost of having it sent via FedEx overnight. I was eager to see what it said, confident it would provide the documentation I needed to prove this murder rumor false.

When I got the death certificate, it was perhaps the most shocking thing I had ever read. There, blaring off the page in big letters, larger than any other writing on the page, in the box for "Cause of Death," showed "Unknown (DOA)." Unknown? Say what? How can you have a cause of death on a death certificate say "unknown"? I had a strong feeling of dread when I saw that. It gave me the shivers. For a brief moment, I almost decided to stop the investigation here, because I really didn't want to find more. But I reminded myself of the decision I made to find the truth, good or bad, and pressed on.

Another anomaly I saw on the death certificate was where the box asked the question "Was Autopsy Performed." The box was checked for "No," I thought, "What do you have to do in that county to warrant an autopsy—show up covered in blood?" Seems to me if you have people show up with a body at a hospital emergency room with no apparent cause of death, you'd force the point for an autopsy even over family objections to legally establish without a doubt the cause of death. Short of doing that, you had to just take the word of the people with the dead body in their arms.

I noted that the date of birth had been crossed out and changed. What was crossed out was "August 10, 1910," and above it typed "7/16/19." The box for her age at the time of death showed "49." That immediately raised flags to me, since I knew she was fifty-eight years old at the time she died. I broke out some photos I had of her and Leon's joint headstone, and it showed her birth year to be 1910. That simply had to be true, since my father was born in January 1931. If Nell was born in 1919 as her death certificate indicated, then she was all of eleven years old when she gave birth to Frank. That was kind of a laughable red flag that something was awry here.

The address for the informant, Leon, was shown to be "1225 N. 52th Street, E. St. Louis, Ill." Despite getting the letters following the street name wrong, it should have been "52nd" instead of "52th," I noticed this was not the Paducah address where Nell was living at the time of her death. Leon was having the death certificate sent to his East St. Louis address, and that was strange. He had to be planning on being back in East St. Louis shortly after the funeral. I verified later on by pulling the property records for that address in East St. Louis that Leon did indeed own that property from 1957 to 1974. I would later see the East St. Louis city directories showing Leon at that address starting in 1955, so perhaps Leon rented the property for a few years before buying it. Audrey lived in East St. Louis during this time period. The time period ended in 1974, coincidentally when I remember Leon and Audrey moving from East

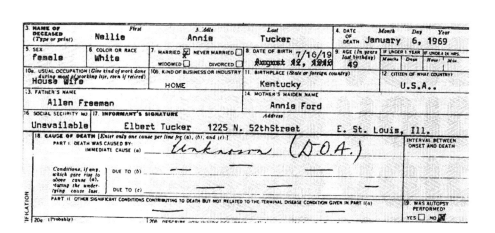

Excerpt from Nell Tucker's death certificate

St. Louis to Paducah for their retirement years after they had built a new home there at 1735 Husband Road. They departed East St. Louis for Paducah in November 1974, never to return (except visits to Audrey's children).

At the bottom of the death certificate, it showed the doctor that signed the certificate was Dr. Steve R. Johnston. I began searching for Dr. Johnston, hoping he might still be alive and could shed some light on these anomalies on the death certificate, and perhaps answer some questions I had about the night Nell died. I first called Okeechobee General Hospital in Okeechobee, Florida, which an Internet search revealed was now called the Columbia Raulerson Hospital, having been purchased by a private organization in 1979. They were also in a different location now. The original location of the hospital, in 1969, was now housing the Okeechobee County Planning and Building Department. Raulerson said that their records from that long ago had been destroyed or transferred to the Board of County Commissioners. I phoned the Board of County Commissioners; they searched for any records and found nothing on my grandmother's time at Okeechobee General Hospital in 1969. They also couldn't give me any leads on Dr. Johnston, only that he wasn't at their hospital anymore. I called the licensing board for the State of Florida for physicians and still couldn't find a Dr. Johnston. I feared he left the state or was dead. Even a nationwide phone number search for a Dr. Steve Johnston didn't lead me to the one I was looking for, although I did find another doctor with the same name. His name isn't that unusual, so it's not surprising there was at least one more doctor in the U.S. with the same name. I would find more on Dr. Johnston later on when I located his daughters, a stepson, and a nurse that worked with him, which I will include later.

I contacted the Okeechobee County Planning and Development Department that now occupies the former site of the hospital Nell was taken to in 1969. One of their employees, Diana, offered to "ask around the office" to the old-timers who were there if they knew where the files where from the old hospital days. She also offered to let me "take a look around" the building when I visited Okeechobee in a trip I had planned for a month later. Ultimately, she could find nothing more for me than to tell me the general area of the building where the old emergency room used to be. I describe my visit to this building in a later chapter.

Back to examining Nell's death certificate, I next noticed that the funeral home that had removed Nell's remains from the hospital the next day, on January 7, 1969, for embalming was the Yates Funeral Home in Okeechobee, Florida. A phone number search didn't yield a funeral home in Okeechobee by that name, but there was one in nearby Ft. Pierce, on the Atlantic coast side of Florida. I called them, and they acknowledged that they used to own a funeral home in Okeechobee but had closed it many years ago. Joseph W. Yates was the funeral director that had signed Nell's death certificate in 1969, and he was still alive. He was an older man in his sixties, so therefore must have been a young man in his twenties or thirties in 1969. I began to speak with Mr. Yates, and he didn't initially remember the Nell Tucker case. I asked him to retrieve his funeral services file on my grandmother's case and copy it for me, which he readily agreed to do.

He began to examine the file and read through the notes inside. After a few more moments, he asked me, "Was this a full-figured woman with pale, white skin and dark black hair?" I told him that matched her description. He then asked, "Was she and her husband camping at a campground out on Lake Okeechobee." I said yes with rising excitement, glad that I had found someone who remembered my grandmother's case from that long ago. He said, "Yes, yes, now I remember this woman." I first asked Mr. Yates about Dr. Johnston, if he knew how I could get a hold of him. He told me that Dr. Johnston was very old at the time in 1969 when this event occurred, and died a short time later. So that was going to be a dead end—contacting the doctor that saw Nell's remains. But Mr. Yates might be the next best thing, since he embalmed her remains.

I related to Mr. Yates what anomalies I found on the death certificate, and he asked that I fax him a copy. He said he understood why I had suspicions, considering the unknown cause of death on the certificate. I questioned him about the lack of an autopsy coupled with an unknown cause of death. But he said that wasn't uncommon at the time in Florida, since many retired folk from northern states came to Florida for vacation during this time and still do today. Many of these elderly people die in Florida, and it costs a significant amount of money to provide autopsies at state and local government expense for people who are citizens of other states and pay no state or local taxes beyond sales taxes for what they buy in the state. He said if someone showed up at an emergency room with a dead body, barring any specific reason not to believe them, such as some physical sign on the body itself, their story of what happened to the dead person would be believed. Nowadays, Mr. Yates stated, Florida law would require an autopsy, or a police investigation would automatically be triggered if an unknown cause of death were the case with a DOA (dead on arrival) body that showed up at a hospital emergency room. I was dismayed by Mr. Yates' description of how callous Floridians at that time could be to allow an unknown cause of death to go uninvestigated just because they feared the cost of it. I thought, "Couldn't they charge the State of Kentucky (Nell's home state) for it?"

I asked Mr. Yates if he noted anything unusual with Nell's remains when he examined them for embalming. I specifically asked how long she had been dead at the time he retrieved the body. He said without hesitating, "She was fresh. There was no problem with the embalming." This would seem to contradict the doctor that spoke to Grace at the time the event occurred, who said she had been dead for five hours when her body arrived at the hospital emergency room. Who knew who was right on this point? Would a funeral director know more than a doctor about how long a body had been dead? Mr. Yates continued by telling me that as he was undressing her body to begin the embalming and he removed her brassiere, he found that she had a secret pocket sewn into one of the cups and had hidden inside the pocket about $200 in ten- and twenty-dollar bills. He found that very odd, and his voice when describing it to me was sort of sheepish, like he was revealing something that gave him pause.

Mr. Yates said, "Being an honest young man, I drove out to the campground on Highway 78 on Lake Okeechobee, found her husband, Mr. Tucker, and gave him the money. I told him where I found it, and he said to me, 'I knew she 'as a hidin' money on me, I jus' didn't know whar.' He then told me the story of what happened the night before—"that they were on their way to a seafood restaurant, she began having chest pains and died just as they arrived at the hospital emergency room." I immediately recognized this differed from the story Leon had told everyone at Nell's funeral, which was that Nell arrived at the emergency room alive and died inside while receiving treatment. There were now three versions of how and when Nell died: Leon's first version to Frank and the family, Leon's second version to the funeral director, and the doctor's story to Grace. It seemed logical to me that Leon knew he couldn't lie to the funeral director about Nell arriving at the hospital still alive. The funeral director had already been told by the hospital staff that Nell was a DOA. So Leon would have had to alter the story slightly for Mr. Yates.

I next discussed with Mr. Yates the anomaly on the death certificate regarding the date of birth. After he had received the faxed copy of the death certificate I sent to him, I called him again, and we resumed our previous discussion. He could not explain why the date had been changed, or by who. I asked him for what purpose would someone want to change the date of a birth on a death certificate. His immediate response, again without missing a beat, was, "Well, insurance fraud for one." Mr. Yates told me that a person who had taken out life insurance on someone might state they were younger than they actually were to get a lower premium rate, or even to get the policy issued in the first place. "People didn't live as long in the sixties as they do today. Getting insurance on a forty-nine-year-old woman might be easier going than getting life insurance on a fifty-eight-year-old woman," he said. When the insured person died and the beneficiary would submit the claim on the policy, a death certificate would have to accompany that claim. The date of birth on the death certificate would have to match the date of birth on the initial application for insurance, or the policy would be deemed as issued based on fraudulent information and not be paid. Mr. Yates also suggested that not only life insurance could be involved, but also credit-life on car loans or house loans might be a motivation to lie about someone's age on a death certificate.

My mind was reeling with all that Mr. Yates was telling me. I knew that Nell didn't have many assets at the time of her death, and definitely would not have lied about her own age to get life insurance or credit-life on loans. I searched my mind and could not think of a single alternate reason why someone would want to change the date of birth on a death certificate. Mr. Yates continued, "You wouldn't change that date for no good reason, like vanity or something similar. You would have to go through such trouble with the State of Florida getting that date changed that you would definitely have to have a compelling reason driving you to do it."

Mr. Yates and I discussed his file on the funeral services he provided for Nell, which he had copied the entire contents and mailed me a copy. He pointed to a copy of the air bill for the shipping of Nell's remains in a casket from Palm Beach, Florida, to Evansville, Indiana, to be received by representatives of Kennedy Funeral Home in Paducah, Kentucky on January 7, 1969, the day after she died. He remarked how cheap it was at that time to ship the casket that distance, which was a mere $67.33. The total bill for services, including the metal casket, embalming, burial gown, transportation, and general services, totaled only $781.33. He noted there was notation in the file that Nell had died of a heart attack, which was the first documentation I had found that someone at the time was talking heart attack as the cause of death. Leon had to have been the source of this information to Mr. Yates for him to write it down in his file, and not the hospital. If the hospital believed she died of a heart attack, then it would have showed that on her death certificate as the cause of death. It didn't, rather showing the cause of death to be "unknown."

He said the date of birth in the notes, August 12, 1909, didn't match either of the birth dates, original or the changed one, on the death certificate. There was a notation in his file notes indicating age of decedent of fifty-eight years. This at least was closer to her actual age at death of fifty-eight rather than what the death certificate said of forty-nine. This raised even more questions about that. It at least documented that conflicting dates were being given at the time. Leon was the only person in Florida at the time that could be providing this information. Could it be that he was just mixing up the dates in his own mind? He was, after all, fifty-seven years old at the time. It was possible, but not enough to make his wife out to be forty-nine years old instead of fifty-eight years old. He definitely knew she wasn't forty-nine. At the date of her death, January 6, 1969, Nell and Leon had been married one day shy of forty years. The date of their marriage was January 7, 1929. He knew she wasn't ten years old when he married her.

I called the Okeechobee County Sheriff's Office and asked if they had anything on record about the investigation at the campground that Tillie had described to me. They looked for the records but called me back with the disappointing finding that their records were destroyed beyond approximately twenty years back in time. I asked them if an investigation at the campground were undertaken, would it have been the sheriff's office or the Okeechobee City Police that would have performed it. The sheriff's office confirmed for me that it would have been under their jurisdiction, and the city police wouldn't have been involved. I next called the Okee-Tantie Campground, nearest campground to where the incident occurred. I asked if they had any records of the event in 1969. They told me the campground had switched hands between government agencies and private owners several times over the years, and at that time in 1969, the campground would have been under the control of the South Florida Water Management District (SFWMD). I called their office (SFWMD) for a search of their files for anything they had on the incident. They did an extensive search for me, but it yielded nothing.

I called several libraries, one in Okeechobee and the other in Palm Beach, and asked if they had any newspaper articles on the death of a tourist woman at a campground on Lake Okeechobee. Both libraries couldn't find anything within the week following the death in January 1969. The librarian at the Okeechobee library told me their newspaper was only a once a week printing, and the edition published the week following the death didn't have any articles on the event. I knew Nell's obituary was published in her hometown newspaper, the *Paducah Sun*. But even the daily newspaper in Palm Beach, Florida, didn't have a news article on it, which surprised the librarian, as she said a death of that kind would likely have made the papers.

Having checked for hospital records, sheriff's office records, campground records, funeral director's records, and newspaper microfilms, I thought I had explored all avenues in Florida for information about Nell's death. I had gathered all that could be gathered—or so I thought. The focus of the next phase of my investigation would turn toward the family.

*　*　*

Chapter 4

THE TUCKERS

Bert told me that the Tucker boys, at least the younger three of them, Remus (known as "Reem"), Robert (known as "Rob"), and Leon, were the "meanest men you'd ever come across."

After conducting this major investigation on the phone to Florida, I started trying to identify family members that might still be alive that might have some recollection of the event in 1969. I found a wealth of family I never knew I had. Since my mother Judy had died in February 2004, I had been starting a family tree investigation, learning the craft or science, whichever it was, of genealogy along the way. I noticed in my mother's photo albums that there were many pictures of people I didn't recognize. Why I didn't sit down with her before she died and ask her to help me identify all of them and also record her life history, I'll never know. It was a major gaffe on my part. I began to meet with family members on my mother's side of the family, the Bonds and the Dawsons, in hopes they could help me identify the people in the pictures and fill in some family history I neglected to get from my mother before she passed on.

Seeing how difficult this was, in 2004, I splurged and bought a video camera for the sole purpose of videotaping my father, Frank. I wanted to get him down on tape talking about the family history and his own life history. When I did that during an October 2004 visit to Frank's home in Madisonville, Kentucky, I noticed that Frank had degraded in mental clarity to the point where he talked in circles about the family genealogy. I had to be happy with just getting him down on video, his voice, his facial expressions, and some of his memories of his lifetime. Of course, Frank was known to embellish his own life history as well as the family genealogy, so he wasn't a great resource for accurate information on the family tree. Tillie had filled me in previously on the Freeman family tree, as she is a member of that family also. Frank possessed a few photo albums that were owned by Nell, his mother. I didn't sit down with him and identify all of the pictures, as I'm sure he would have known all of them. I regret that now. After he passed away in October 2005, I ended up having to do the same thing as I did with Judy's photos the year before. Even before Frank died, I began visiting the Tucker and Freeman family relatives still alive, in hopes they could not only help identify some of the people in Nell's photos, but also fill me in on the family history and genealogy. It wasn't until after Frank's death and Tillie reminding me of the dark family secret of Nell's death that my interviews of the Tucker family members I was meeting would include questions about Nell's death. I didn't know to ask about it before that time.

The only cousin of my father's that I knew of on the Tucker side was a man named Corbett Tucker, called "Son" because his father was named Corbett also. Evidently the culture of western Kentucky didn't use the word "Junior" for a son of the same name as the father, but rather "Son." Son Tucker's wife was named Mildred, and she was the sister of Tillie. Son and Mildred had socialized with my parents over the years, and we had black-and-white pictures of them on a picnic trip to a river region in our photo albums, apparently sometime in the sixties. When I called to see if Son and Mildred had any recollections they'd be willing to share, they were both very ill and not willing to talk very long. Son was in his early eighties, and Mildred in her late seventies. I hoped to contact them sometime in the future when they would be more willing to talk, but now wasn't the time to press the point. Mildred did recommend that I talk to Bert Mitchell, a cousin on the Tucker side to Frank. She told me he lived "up near East St. Louis," but didn't know the exact city.

With an Internet search, I found Bert in Caseyville, just outside of East St. Louis, and called to introduce myself. He remembered who Frank was instantly and seemed somewhat welcoming to meet me. I mailed him some photos of our family members and asked him if I could come to meet him the next time I was in Illinois. He agreed. My first visit to Bert's house on Valley Drive in Caseyville was in the spring of 2005, before Frank's death and the beginning of my investigation into Nell's death. I was surprised he had so many pictures of my ancestors and a complete history of the Tucker family in his eight-two-year-old memory. Bert was literally a walking history book. I clearly had hit the jackpot. Bert was this slight of build older gentleman with a western Kentucky drawl that immediately reminded me of Leon's speech pattern.

Bert had a gravitas to his presence and tenor to his voice that made me want to listen closely. He also had a lowered-eyelid look coupled with a slow nodding of the head when I would answer one of his questions to me like he almost didn't believe me. I knew he did believe me, but that was a characteristic trait of the Tucker men. They all did that, Leon, Frank, all of the Tucker men I had met did that, almost on automatic. It was like they didn't want to reveal to you they believed you so you wouldn't be overconfident that you had their trust yet. He questioned me on my motivations for visiting him and why I was asking him about the family history. I told him it was to fill in the blanks my parents hadn't on the family photos and genealogy. He seemed to accept that.

Bert Mitchell, 1922-2006

George W. Tucker with Ruth (Keeling) Tucker. Left is daughter Lizzie,
right is daughter Annie, in George's lap is daughter Nettie,
in Ruth's lap is daughter Vera, circa 1895

Bert began a slow but steady regaling of the Tucker family history, and I avidly wrote it down as quickly as possible. I didn't know it at the time, but these notes would become enormously valuable in my later investigation of Nell's death. Bert told me how my great-grandfather, George W. Tucker was settled in Kentucky by his father, Levi. George W. Tucker had married two women. His first wife, whose name is believed to have been Mary Ann Eders (some in the family believe her name was Jane Pierce), died in childbirth of their third child, with the child apparently dying as well. George's second wife, Ruth Keeling, and he had more children for a total of thirteen, ten of whom survived to adulthood. Ruth Keeling took George's two daughters from the previous marriage, Annie and Lizzie, to raise as her own when she married George.

Out of the ten Tucker children that survived to adulthood, there were six girls: (1) Annie, who married into the Stevenson family; (2) Lizzie (pronounced "Lye-zey"), who married into the Taylor family; (3) Vera, who married into the Burgess family; (4) Robie (pronounced "Roh-bee"), who married into the Mitchell family; (5) Nettie, who married into the Brooks family; and (6) Versie, who married into the Nowak family. There were four boys that survived to adulthood: (1) Corbett, (2) Remus, (3) Robert, and (4) my grandfather, Elbert Leon, known just as "Leon." I began to notice the people of western Kentucky at this time sometimes used their first name as a formal name for legal purposes or marriage only, and their middle names were their common names by which they would be known. Bert's level of recall of specific details was truly amazing. He could remember maiden names of the women that married into the Tucker family, all the children's names, and most years of when people married, died, and when children were born.

Bert told me that the Tucker boys, at least the younger three of them, Remus (known as "Reem"), Robert (known as "Rob"), and Leon were the "meanest men you'd ever come across." Reem was a bootlegger that could outrun (in his car) police cars chasing him. Reem also sold used cars and drove racecars at racetracks. He used to toughen his hands up for fighting by beating them on a steel washing pan. He died by being cut in half at a racetrack in 1958 when a racing car veered off course and hit him as he stood watching it from the side. He had married a woman named Martha Frick, and they had two daughters, Ruth and Virginia. Virginia was nicknamed "Dink" for some inexplicable reason. Reem's wife, Martha, divorced him for another man, George Meredith, and she tried to get George to kill Reem. Reem beat the stuffing out of George and then paid for his hospital bill. George never came after Reem again. They are all three buried next to each other at the Old Concrete Cemetery near Symsonia, Kentucky, with Martha strategically positioned between the two men she married.

The four brothers would fight each other often. Bert said once Reem, Rob, and Leon got into their heads, they were going over to Corbett's house to beat on him. Corbett was warned by someone ahead of the three men getting to his house. Supposedly, Corbett stood in the doorway of his house with a shotgun in his hands and said to his brothers, "Now I ain't done nuthin' to y'all. But if y'all try to come through this har' door, I'm a gonna kill every one o' ya's." And Bert was sure he would have to.

Remus Tucker

Corbett and Daisy Tucker

Left to right: Leon, Robert, and Remus Tucker, sometime in the 1930's

Leon's brother Rob had married a woman named Gertrude, and had two sons. Both died in infancy. One died at or near birth, but one lived two years and died from eating raw peas. His mother Gertrude didn't stop him from eating them despite warnings by others in the family watching it all. She was quoted as saying at the time, "Well, if he ain't got 'nough sense not to eat raw peas then he deserves to get sick." He was only two years old and didn't know any better because he hadn't been taught about them. Eating raw peas being dangerous certainly isn't an instinctual thing humans know, and it was stupid of Gert to think that. The child sickened that night, a doctor was called, but couldn't save him. He died the next day. Rob initially blamed Gertrude for the death, saying to her, "Well, Gert, you've killed our son." They remained married to each other for the rest of their lives, as divorce in the early 1940s in western Kentucky was unthinkable. They never had any more children, and Rob buried his two infant sons next to his parents, George and Ruth Tucker, in the Old Concrete Church Cemetery (also called Carter's Mill Cemetery) in Symsonia.

Reem, despite being the smallest of the four brothers, was the fiercest fighter, sort of like a wolverine. Reem was nicknamed "Bad Eye," because he had one lazy eye. Leon, my grandfather, had several inches of height and probably forty pounds of weight over Reem, but still couldn't best him. Reem was beating on Leon once so bad that Leon got out a pocketknife and slashed Reem's stomach wide open. Reem said to him, "Now Leon—I'm a gonna go down t' the hospital an' git sewed up. When I git back, I'm gonna beat ya till ya pee ya pants." And he did just that. Leon told Bert he peed his pants just to get Reem to stop beating on him. There was definitely a pecking order among these brothers, with constant fights to establish dominance and their place in that pecking order, much like a pack of wild dogs would do. This even extended up until their retirement years, minus the violence. I can remember when I was just a small kid, going to Rob's house with Leon and Frank. Rob wouldn't even let us into the house, but met with us in the driveway, all of us standing while visiting. Rob had that familiar lowered eyelid, cynical smirk, slightly nodding head look when talking to Leon. I could see Leon even change his body language around Rob, like he was playing up to him, trying to get his approval by showing him his grandsons. Around just our family, Leon always behaved like Rob was behaving to him right then, with overconfidence at being the alpha male, or the male higher on the totem pole. But with Rob, Leon was acting like a subordinate, like he was talking with his boss. Rob was his older brother, but that's all. Rob died in 1976 of a heart attack raking leaves in his own front yard.

Robert and Gertrude Tucker

Leon Tucker in World War II

Bert told me that Leon had killed three men in his lifetime that Bert knew of for sure. Reem had killed three men also. Rob had killed two men. One of the men Leon killed was a hobo. Another was a man Leon killed in a bar, and the man's family didn't know it was Leon who killed him. Leon ended up being a pallbearer at the funeral of the man he had killed. Bert even knew the service history of my grandfather, when my own father didn't, or at least had never told me about it. Bert said in World War II, in Germany, Leon was manning a machine gunner's nest, and the German shells were getting closer, landing either side of the nest. Clearly, the Germans were fine-tuning their aiming to try to take out the gunner's nest. When one shell landed in their nest and exploded, Leon supposedly was knocked out from the concussion and woke up injured in a military hospital. He was sent home as injured sometime in 1945.

I asked Bert what his memories of my grandmother Nell were. He said, "Nell wasn't a strong woman. She was sickly. She was up at the tuberculosis sanitarium at Fairview Heights for several yars." I later learned those were the war years, while Leon was overseas fighting in Europe in World War II. I would later call the St. Clair County Health Department and ask them to search their records on this point. They found an old register of the patient names with admission and discharge dates for each, and located my grandmother's record. They sent me documentation to prove Nell Tucker was admitted on April 27, 1944, and discharged on July 3, 1946. She was quarantined for 797 days, approximately two years and two months. In those days they called tuberculosis by a more common name, which was "consumption." This came from the way tuberculosis acts, by forming fibrous growths in the lungs and literally consuming the lungs, making the victim incapable of breathing. It really was a horrible way to slowly die. Nell's father, Allen Freeman, died of consumption/tuberculosis in Paducah in May 1947, some ten months after Nell was released from the sanitarium, herself cured of the disease.

Bert told me that was the time when Leon hooked up with his second wife, Audie C. (Marshall) Reed, known as "Audrey." Reed was her first married name, but by the time Audrey met Leon, she was living under her second married name, Hayden. Oddly, Audrey kept her listing in the East St. Louis city directory reading "Audrey Hayden" all the way from the early 1940s through 1969. After that, her and Leon's relationship could be out in the open because Nell had died in 1969. Audrey was a blond woman with a couple of kids, Harold and Frances, from a previous marriage to a man named Michael Reed. She was divorced from Reed when Leon and her started a romance during this period of time. Apparently Leon thought Nell would die in the sanitarium, and he would need a new wife. Only he didn't wait for Nell to die first before looking for the new wife. Bert told me that the doctors treating Nell had pronounced several times that the "end was near," and summoned her siblings and parents from Kentucky. Only Nell didn't die at this time and slowly improved, eventually well enough to be discharged.

Nell Tucker in the sanitarium

Abandoned ruins of Hunter Meat Packing, East St. Louis, 2006

Bert was a little off by only a few years of pinpointing when Leon began dating Audrey. In fact, the East St. Louis city directories fill in some of when Leon likely met Audrey. Leon worked for Hunter Meat Packing in East St. Louis in 1941-1942. Audrey was also working there at that time, having divorced her first husband Mike Reed for being a heavy drinker and suicidal, and remarried to a man named Joe Hayden. According to Audrey's daughter, Frances, the marriage to Joe Hayden lasted less than a year because he was violent. Divorce records actually have Audrey saying Joe Hayden abandoned her after about a year and a half of marriage. Audrey however kept the last name Hayden for the next thirty years or more, at least publicly, until after Nell died. I would find out later why she did this, but I'll explain that in a later chapter. Leon definitely met and started a relationship with Audrey before leaving for basic training in World War II in early 1943, as he wrote her love letters and sent her gifts during his time as an enlisted man.

This presented a problem for Leon. His relationship with Audrey was going strong when Nell was discharged from the tuberculosis sanitarium in Fairview Heights, Illinois, and she returned to her and Leon's house in East St. Louis. It wasn't long after that, according to Bert, that Leon moved Nell back down to Paducah and returned to East St. Louis alone to be with Audrey. Frank would tell me about the times when Nell was in the tuberculosis sanitarium and he was thirteen to fifteen years old, he would take a bus for five hours from Paducah to Fairview Heights and then walk several miles from the bus station just to stand outside the tuberculosis sanitarium and wave up to a window where Nell would be waiting. She would waive back, and that was the closest they could come to a visit. At that time, tuberculosis was thought to be a highly contagious disease, requiring total isolation. Frank was living with other family relation at that time, drifting from household to household, whoever would take him in for a while. Nell was in the sanitarium, and Leon was fighting in Europe in World War II, so Frank was alone during these years at a still somewhat tender age.

Bert showed me many pictures of these ancestors just described and agreed to allow me to scan the pictures when I returned again in the future with a portable computer and a portable scanner. When I left that day, I realized I had certainly won the lotto of information on the Tucker family. With Bert's detailed description of the family tree, I could trace down Tucker cousins of my father's. Some of these people I had never met, or if I had met them, it would have been when I was a baby. I might have been in their presence at family funerals or the one Tucker family reunion I remembered being held at the Old Concrete Church near Symsonia sometime in my teens.

The Tucker family reunions would always be held at that location because the cemetery behind the church is where a lot of the family ancestors are buried, including the matriarch and patriarch of this branch of the Tuckers, George W. and Ruth (Keeling) Tucker. George W. Tucker died in 1936, but Ruth (Keeling) Tucker lived on to 1957. A lot of Ruth's family (the Keelings) are buried in this small cemetery also. One could call the location the origin point for this branch of the Tuckers, as the old Tucker family farm was only a few miles away. The church is no longer there, having been taken by a

51

tornado years ago, and not rebuilt. But the cemetery remains, well tended, with a sign also calling it the Carter's Mill Cemetery because of an old mill that used to be nearby. New burials are no longer allowed there except for those who already own plots.

Of all the names Bert was giving me of my Tucker kin, I honestly hardly recognized any of them. Therefore, Bert's recollections greatly aided and organized for me my next phase of investigation. I would interview as many Tucker cousins as I could find. The task was to be daunting.

*　　*　　*

Chapter 5

THE COUSINS

"I heard Leon smothered 'er with a pilla' (pillow). He then drove 'round for five 'ars (hours) with a dead body in the car . . ."

My approach to searching for the Tucker cousins was outlined by Bert Mitchell's family tree oration. I knew that some of them would know nothing, and some of them would know something. I also would expect that some of them would be willing to talk to me and relate what they knew of this family secret, and others would be reticent to talk to me about it. Analogous to how police keep a code of silence for each other, Tucker men have this bizarre allegiance to each other, not wanting to reveal anything bad against another Tucker. My father had a particularly strong case of this allegiance, always wanting to spin the facts like the Tucker's were more than they were, if not perfect. Well, they were far from perfect, more like a normal family with good apples and bad apples. Only in the Tucker family, the bad apples stood out from the rest, glaringly, in my opinion. Breaking through this Tucker allegiance was proving harder than I thought.

I knew some of the cousins would remember tidbits of the story I was seeking, but time and word of mouth would have changed the stories. Only people with firsthand knowledge of the events could be trusted to know the most accurate version, and to my knowledge, none existed. The only people with my grandparents at the campsite in Florida, so I initially thought at least, were their nephew and his wife, Walter and Dollie Stevenson. Walter and Dollie's son, Eddie, and his wife, Linda, were also there. Because Leon's older sister Annie, Walter's mother, was so much older than him (thirty-five years), Leon and Walter were close in age, despite Leon being Walter's uncle. Walter was actually five years older than his Uncle Leon. They were raised together as kids, and Walter had a strong bond and allegiance to Leon. Finding the Stevenson clan was the hardest task, so I started my search for the Tucker cousins with the ones that were easier to find.

Leon's sisters; Versie (Tucker) Nowak & Robie (Tucker) Mitchell.
Behind Robie is her husband James

MITCHELLS: My grandfather Leon's older sister Roba (Robie) married into the Mitchell family, and her children still living in 2006 were Bertie, Elizabeth, Jim, and Bert. Robie died in 1983. I already knew Bert Mitchell, and just after my father died, I visited him again in November 2005. Bert welcomed me into his home again, and this time I brought with me my laptop computer with a portable scanner to scan Bert's photos of my great-grandparents, George and Ruth Tucker, as well as any other photos of Tuckers that he had. He had many, and he was more than willing to share them with me. After completing the scanning, I sat down with Bert to prompt him for more of his Tucker storytelling. Bert was nearing death at this point, and he even said to me he was "tired of living." I think all the medical treatments he was receiving were making life a struggle for him every day, and this wears anyone out over time. It wore my mother out also, and she gave up as well. I asked Bert point-blank about the rumor I had heard that "Leon had done away with Nell, that he may have killed her." Bert stopped his storytelling cold, dead in his tracks, fell silent for perhaps ten seconds, looked at me in the eye, and said very slowly with raised eyebrows and a slow, serious emphasis, "Who told you that?" I told him that many people had told me, but it was mainly Tillie. He knew who Tillie was, despite Tillie being in the Freeman family, Nell's family, and not the Tuckers.

Bert thought for a minute after I told him who had told me of the infamous "Nell's murder rumor." He finally turned to me with a face half of disgust and half resignation, and said, "Well, all I can say is, I heard the same thing." I didn't say anything, not wanting to prompt him, but to just let him tell his story the way he wanted. I realized it was difficult for him to break the Tucker men code of allegiance and reveal this. But he was talking to a Tucker man (me), and these people, the people involved, were all gone now, and Nell was my grandmother after all, so I think Bert realized or made the decision I had a right to know what he knew. He continued after pausing for a moment of silent reflection, "I heard Leon smothered 'er with a pilla' (pillow). He then drove 'round for five 'ars (hours) with a dead body in the car (before taking her to the hospital)."

I was stunned that he knew details of what had happened, rather than just the big picture, like Tillie. Clearly, someone had filled in the blanks for Bert on the story, and I was curious who that was. I asked Bert how he knew the story and who had told it to him. His immediate response was to pull the cloak of secrecy and allegiance to the Tucker men code over the story again. He recoiled, "I don't remember how I heard that." I didn't believe him. Bert was an incredibly sharp man, even at his advanced age of eighty-two; his memory was razor sharp and detailed. It was a lifelong hobby for Bert—to memorize the family stories in detail, so he could recount them later on, making himself the family historian. The look on his face clearly told me he did remember how he had heard the story of Nell's death, but for some reason, he didn't want to tell me. It was almost a look of fear or shame on his face, I couldn't tell which, when he denied remembering who told him the story.

I speculated that perhaps Bert felt guilty about it. Not because he had any involvement at all with Nell's murder, but because he knew the story and didn't tell anyone. He had just spoken with my father (and Bert's first cousin), Frank, a few months prior after I had given him Frank's number. Through all the contact he had with Frank over the years, he never told him about this story. Perhaps he felt I might blow up at him if he admitted to me how he knew the story details, particularly if they came from a source that should have been revealed years earlier. Much to my sadness, Bert passed away in January 2006, just a few months after we had met for the last time. But I didn't know at that point that Bert's words and further knowledge of the story details would find me again, at a later date.

Of the other Mitchell cousins still alive, I had lunch one day with three of them, Elizabeth (Mitchell) Walsh, Bertie (Mitchell) Gillison, and Jim Mitchell. Jim was seventy-one years old at the time I spoke with him and was the youngest of his siblings. Jim told me that Leon had once been run out of Paducah by the police, actually chased across the bridge over the Ohio River into Illinois, and told he'd be arrested if he stepped a foot back into Kentucky again. Evidently Leon was either picking too many fights or mixed up into too many crooked deals. Jim told me that my father, Frank, rose in the East St. Louis Masonic Lodge to the highest level, a thirty-second-degree Mason, and then went on to become a Shriner. Jim said that Leon was also in the Masons, but got "blackballed," which meant being kicked out of the lodge, for pulling too many crooked deals on the other members, which probably included just plain thievery. This term, "blackballed," came from when the members would vote to expel another member, they would drop a small, black ball into the ballot box. Jim said everyone in the family in East St. Louis at the time knew of Leon's relationship to Audrey, and that he kept Nell down in Paducah and would see her on weekends or vacations.

Jim told me Leon used to drive up on sidewalks to aim his car at "blacks" walking on the sidewalks—he hated them that much. I knew my grandfather was a racist, most of the southern whites from that generation were, but I never thought he was violently racist. It might have had something to do with the union issues. It was true that the union whites of East St. Louis at the time thought the African-Americans were taking work away from them. The meat-packing houses of East St. Louis in the early 1900s were importing African-Americans from Mississippi that were willing to work for lower wages than the union members, usually whites, already living in East St. Louis. This caused periodic race riots. Up until perhaps the Los Angeles race riots of 1992, which I witnessed firsthand living in Los Angeles at that time, the worst race riot in U.S. history occurred in East St. Louis in 1917,[12] with scores of deaths from beatings, lynchings, burnings, etc . . . The general consensus of the Mitchell cousins was that they knew Leon to be "one mean son-of-a-bitch" in his youth, but that he softened when he got in his older, retired years. None of them knew any details about Nell's death in Florida in 1969.

Jim Mitchell told me of a road trip he took with my parents, Frank and Judy. I believe he said they were headed toward the clubhouse at Grand Tower on Rattlesnake Ferry Road. He said they ran out of gas. On the side of the road, Frank told Jim to turn around so he wouldn't see the signal Frank was going to use. Then Frank made a Masonic signal with his hands and arms, and flagged down a passing motorist. This likely was the "Grand Masonic Hailing Sign of Distress,"[2] made by raising both arms above his head like a bank robbery stickup situation, palms forward. He might have even lowered them in three stages, pivoting the forearms at the elbow until they are perpendicular with the floor, palms down, as the motorist passed them.

Evidently a passing motorist who happened to be a Mason recognized the signals and stomped on his brake, bringing his car to a screeching stop. Jim told Frank that he needed to go with the guy back to a gas station to get gas, but Frank wanted to stay with Judy instead, so he sent Jim. Jim said the motorist was asking him a bunch of strange questions, clearly probing how much he knew of the Masons. But Jim didn't know the answers, since he was just a beginner Mason. The Masons have all these secret hand gestures, signals, questions, and responses so that they can communicate with each other and those around them have no idea what they are saying. I remember Frank once told me he could carry on a conversation with another Mason without ever opening his mouth. He could just use casual body language, facial gestures, or hand gestures, and nobody around them would even know they were conversing.

The motorist likely asked Jim questions like, "I see that you are a traveling man." Jim's response would have needed to be, "I am. I travel from west to east and from east to west again." Hearing that correct Masonic response, the motorist would have next asked, "Why did you leave the west and travel to the east?" Jim would have needed to respond, "In search of that which was lost."[2] That would suffice and confirm to the motorist that Jim was a Mason just like Frank was. But Jim didn't know these correct responses, being brand new to the Masons, probably as an Entered Apprentice (first degree) or Fellowcraft (second degree).[3] Evidently the motorist wasn't happy with Jim's lack of knowledge of the correct responses to his questions, so he abandoned Jim at the gas station. After getting a can of gas, Jim had to get another motorist to give him a ride back to the car where Judy and Frank were waiting.

Burgesses: My grandfather Leon's older sister Vera married into the Burgess family, and some of her descendants still living in 2006 that I could find were daughter Louise (Burgess) Price in Mayfield, Kentucky, and grandkids Tom Burgess, Vera (Burgess) Mitchell, Eugene Burgess, and Richard Burgess. Louise (Burgess) Price was too elderly to remember anything of use for me. I met with Tom Burgess in March 2006 at his son's home in Palmdale, California. He told me that Leon and his father, Elmer Ardie Burgess, known by "Ardie," were very close friends. Ardie and Leon built clubhouses next to each other at Grand Tower, Illinois, on Rattlesnake Ferry Road. Tom told me he saw Leon show up at their house with Audrey many times over the years when he was young, in the 1940s, in East St. Louis, again verifying to me that Leon was seeing Audrey even at this early time. Tom said Leon could never leave Audrey because he was afraid of her twin brother, Claud, who was in a position of power in the Local 100 construction union in East St. Louis. Tom said Leon feared losing access to construction work in East St. Louis, the only work Leon could get. Claud might also have controlled the "enforcer gang" at the Local 100 union, or had access to using it.

Vera (Tucker) Burgess with husband Harrison and their son Elmer Ardie

It was tough for me to believe Leon feared physical danger from any man. Then again, with Claud being in the labor union of East St. Louis at the time, the potential for physical danger was real. Evidently the construction labor unions of East St. Louis in the middle 1900s were heavily influenced by organized crime. My father Frank told me that very fact, saying they were "one and the same thing." Leon would therefore be in a position to know what the unions were capable of—meaning that if he left Audrey, Claud might very well have made Leon pay dearly for it.

Tom Burgess told me he had heard the story of how Nell died from his father, Ardie. Ardie heard it directly from Leon, so it was only a variation of the early story Leon was passing around to the family—that Nell ate some citrus in Florida and had a heart attack. Tom remembered going raccoon hunting with Leon and Frank many times, with Leon burning carbide to smoke out the raccoons from the tree trunks. Leon would also use the carbide in a tin on his hat to shine a light in the trees, looking for the reflection of raccoon eyes to spot them. Tom told me of the time that Leon thought Ardie's son, Elmer G. Burgess had broken into his clubhouse at Grand Tower, when he hadn't, and slapped Elmer G. hard across the face. When Ardie heard about that, he drove down to Grand Tower with a pistol. Ardie put the pistol in the back of his pants and went around back of the clubhouse to talk to Leon. Evidently, Ardie got an apology for the slapping out of Leon, but was prepared to fight him, to the point of using guns if necessary.

Tom Burgess had told me that Versie, Leon's sister, had been drinking buddies with Leon when they were young. Once at their sister Robie's house, a drunk Versie and Leon got into a fight, and Versie called Leon a "son of a bitch." Evidently Leon was confronting Versie because she had been telling Nell about Leon seeing Audrey, and it got back to Leon. Nothing made Leon madder than when someone would stick their nose into his business. Leon beat Versie up bad, including putting her head through a wall, according to Tom Burgess. This would have been in the early days of their time in East St. Louis. Tom said Robie pulled a gun on Leon to get him to leave. This is the second of Leon's siblings to have pulled a gun on him, his brother Corbett having been the first. After that, whenever Leon would get drunk, he would go hunting for Versie to exact further revenge. Tom Burgess also told me that Leon with Audrey, and Versie with her husband Frank, went down to work on the clubhouse at Grand Tower, Illinois. Tom said Versie witnessed Leon and Audrey have a fight on the roof of the clubhouse when they were working on it, and Leon pushed Audrey off the roof, almost killing her.

Another cousin in the Burgess family is Robert Stoner, son of Aileen Burgess, and grandson to Vera (Tucker) Burgess. He would be a grandnephew to Leon. I met with him in 2006 at his log cabin-style home he had built himself in the countryside near Prairie Du Rocher, Illinois. He was sixty-nine years old at the time. He remembered fishing with Leon when he was a young man on the Burgess family farm near Fancy Farm, Kentucky. Leon would want them all to go fishing at nighttime because that's when the catfish are biting the most. They would walk along the banks of a long river, using sticks and tree branches as fishing rods, and push them into the ground, hanging over the water, then move on. After walking several miles and installing perhaps a hundred fishing rods, they would camp for an hour and share stories around a campfire. Leon was supposedly a masterful storyteller, keeping everyone enthralled and entertained. Then they would "run the rods," going back down the river to check their fishing rods, to find most of them had fish on them. They would camp again downstream, then repeat the process, "running the rods" perhaps four times a night, and stay out until dawn. Many other relatives told me of how Leon would hunt all night by himself sometimes, never afraid of the dark or the wilderness.

Robert would join Leon at Ardie Burgess' clubhouse at Grand Tower on occasions, and met his wife Shirley there, as she came from the small town of Howardton (just a collection of three or four houses really) at the end of Rattlesnake Ferry Road. Robert said he thought he remembered Leon being "hard on Nell, not good to her," but wouldn't elaborate or be more specific. His tone of voice was lowered and grave, like he was ashamed of what he was saying, fearful he might hurt my feelings if he told me fully what he knew. I suspected he knew Leon was violent with Nell, perhaps had seen it himself, and those word choices were his way of softly telling me. Robert also worked in East St. Louis during the years Leon and the rest of the Tuckers were there, but didn't work with Leon in construction.

In a later phone call with him, I pressed Robert on the details of what he meant about Leon not being good to Nell. Robert told me of another time that many of the Tucker cousins were out at Grandma Ruth (Keeling) Tucker's house outside Paducah. It must have been around 1950, since Robert thought that my father Frank was "in his late teens." Frank was born in January 1931, so this dated this event to 1949 or 1950. Many of the Burgesses were there, and Leon was there with Nell. Frank showed up, and evidently Leon was furious that Frank had stayed out all night with his buddies. The two men began verbally fighting at the top of their lungs. Frank was evidently testing his pecking order status with Leon, being that Frank was entering adulthood now. Robert said the argument escalated to the point of Nell trying to get between the two men. Nell was trying to get Leon to calm down. Leon shoved Nell hard out of the way, so he could keep going at Frank. That's when all the other men there jumped on Leon. The Burgess men grabbed Leon, forced him to sit down on the porch to calm down. Robert said, and these are his exact words, "Leon was like two different people." Robert said when Leon would get mad, he would go over the top, red-faced, and blind furious. Only brute force by big men restraining Leon could get him to calm down.

This made sense to me, because my father Frank was sometimes like that also. Nothing made a Tucker man madder than one of their children talking back to them. With an audience around watching also, Leon losing face by his son standing up to him in front of all these Tucker cousins and his mother (Ruth (Keeling) Tucker) would have made Leon white-hot mad. Robert said at other times, when they would go fishing, Leon was jovial and fun to be around, especially because of his great storytelling ability. Robert distinctly remembers the two different Leons he saw. Robert said the furious version of Leon made you "not want to be where you were at" when you saw it.

Uvil and Stella Taylor with Leon and Nell in Florida 1959.
Photo taken by Nell—her handwriting identifies those in the
picture and dates the photo on the upper margin

TAYLORS: A very distant cousin, a descendant of my great-grandfather's brother Jim Tucker, Uvil (pronounced "Yoo-Vil") Taylor and his wife, Stella, were frequent vacation partners with Leon and Nell. Uvil's and Stella's names were mentioned in the notes of Bill Yates at Yates Funeral Home in Florida as the contact people for reaching Leon in Paducah. Many photos in Nell's albums were of Uvil and Stella with Leon and Nell in Florida. My father used to tell me stories of how cheap Uvil was—how he ate eggs for breakfast, lunch, and dinner because they were cheap. I remember Leon once telling Frank how Uvil would pretend to search his pockets for change and announce he didn't have any to get his car passengers to pay for the parking meter. Later, Leon would see that he did have the change needed earlier, but just wanted someone else to pay the meter. I desperately tried to find some of Uvil and Stella's descendants, confident they would know something of the story of Nell's death. Their son Robert had already passed on by the time I began my search, but their daughter Wanda (Taylor) Fennel was still alive and living in Paducah. I phoned her to get the story of what her parents might have told her.

Wanda was seventy-six years old at the time I spoke with her, and after a few moments of talking, her memory began to liven about the people I was talking to her about, Leon, Nell, and Frank. She said she remembered her father and Leon used to go raccoon hunting a lot, and the families were close. The story she recounted about hearing of Nell's death was the same one Leon spread around, that she died of eating oranges, and that somehow triggered a heart attack. When I told her that some people questioned that story and suspected Leon might have had something to do with Nell's death, Wanda lowered her voice and almost whispered, like telling a secret, "I wouldn't put it passed 'im." She had heard he was a violent man in younger years, and that he was violent toward Nell also. She remembered my father, "Frankie" she called him, and that he was redheaded. She said they used to play together as kids. She also remembered Audrey, Leon's second wife, and that she had heard the rumors of Leon being with Audrey for years prior to Nell's death.

Wanda's husband, James Fennel, was home when I visited Wanda on Hovekamp Road in Paducah in May 2006. I gave her some photos from Nell's photo album of her parents, Stella and Uvil Taylor, some of which she said she had never seen before. She reciprocated by giving me pictures of Nell from her photos albums. James Fennel had left Wanda behind in Paducah and worked with Leon up in East St. Louis doing construction during the 1950s. It was common for men in Paducah at that time to leave their wives behind with family in Paducah, while they went to work in East St. Louis, sending money back to Paducah to support their wives and children. Wanda regaled me of tales of when the men would come home from hunting, they would cook the squirrels they had shot that day. She said she particularly liked eating the squirrel brains. Both Wanda and James remembered Leon as being someone no one wanted to mess with, as he was very violent. But I got the feeling the culture of their family didn't allow Wanda and James to be candid about negative things, and they wanted to only talk about positive things. So I didn't feel I got the full story from them as to what they really knew about Leon.

Versie (Tucker) Nowak

NOWAKS: My grandfather Leon's older sister Versie married into the Nowak family. Versie died in 1988. Her daughter, Katherine (Nowak) Taylor, lives in East Carondelet, Illinois, just south of East St. Louis. I visited with Katherine in person in March 2006. Her memory was spotty on these issues to where her standard response to any questions on the Tuckers was "I can't remember." She did screw up her face and act disgusted when I mentioned my grandfather Leon. Evidently his reputation pierced the lack of memory such that she retained at least a general yet strongly negative opinion of him.

Bert Mitchell's friend Scott Sumida sent me an audio CD of a taped conversation between Leon's sisters Versie and Robie years earlier. They were both deceased at the time I got the CD. On the tape, Versie said she thought Leon had changed a lot in his older years, that he used to be "so mean" when he was younger. Once when Leon had gotten into going to church, he softened. Robie disagreed Leon had changed at all and said so with disgust in her tone of voice. Versie said Leon would repeatedly punch her in the back and then spit on her when they were both kids. Versie said Leon and she used to be given ten cents to press the pants and shine the shoes of their older brothers. She would save hers in a can hidden on a rafter under the house. Leon would spend his at the movie theater and on candy as fast as he earned it. She said Leon stole her stash, about three dollars in dimes, and their mother Ruth (Keeling) Tucker made him pay it back to her out of future earnings.

Versie told the story of Leon coming home all cut up really bad one night from a fight at the tavern in the small village of Hardmoney, Kentucky. That night, Leon told his mother that he had been in a car wreck to explain his injuries, but his car wasn't damaged at all, so everyone knew it was from a bar fight. Leon had been beaten with a corked whisky bottle and knifed as well. It was from a fight with his Keeling cousins—most likely Hard Keeling. This was further evidence that the Keelings of western Kentucky hated the Tucker family, despite two of their daughters marrying Tucker men. Versie said the grudge between the two families started with a Keeling picnic crashed by some Tucker and Stevenson men numbering eight. The Keelings told them not to come into the picnic, that they were not welcome. The Tucker and Stevenson men, who included Corbett, Remus, and Rob Tucker, as well as Arlie and Walter Stevenson, began to tear up the picnic completely. When someone on the Keeling side pulled a gun, the Stevenson men ran for cover, and Remus pulled his own gun and shot Coon Keeling (nickname) through the neck. Thus, similarly to the infamous Hatfields and McCoys, a family feud was born, between the Tuckers and the Keelings of western Kentucky. Leon getting cut up by Hard Keeling years later in the tavern at Hardmoney was how the Keeling-Tucker feud touched my end of the family. Years later, it was suggested that Hard Keeling may have been killed by Leon, and Leon ended up being a pallbearer at his funeral. This was the man Bert Mitchell was referring to that Leon had killed and carried his casket at his funeral.

Versie said her mother was a hard-edged woman, once taking off with a wood-chopping ax after her husband George when he wouldn't stop beating their three oldest sons. He was beating them one day for not chopping the wood fast enough, and when she told him to stop and he didn't, she chased him through the woods with an ax. It's this uncontrollable temper that these people had that I would later see show up in my grandfather Leon and my own father, Frank. It had to be a genetic personality trait passed down from generation to generation. I've not seen it in myself yet—perhaps I was spared. Versie said on the tape that she witnessed her father George Tucker beating Leon one day with Leon's head pinned between George's knees. He would beat all of them that way. He twisted Leon's neck and beat him until he began vomiting.

Versie's daughter, Betty (Nowak) Stamps, was still alive in 2006, and I spoke with her by phone. Her husband, Marion Stamps, appeared to have the better memory of the two and told me many stories of Leon and Frank Tucker. He worked with them on construction projects in East St. Louis. He said he was in the car with Frank around 1956 when he went to Maudine's place in East St. Louis, right after she left him, to steal Trent. Marion said Frank walked out of the house with Trent, put him in the car, and had to fight one of the Pruitt men that came out of the house to prevent him from taking Trent. According to Marion, a fistfight happened, and Frank "kicked the tar" out of the Pruitt man then drove off with Trent. Maudine called the police, and the police found Frank with Trent. They took Trent back to Maudine, who apparently at that point had legal custody of him.

Marion said he saw Leon hit a man in the face with a shovel on a construction job where Leon was enforcing that it be union work only, and this electrical lineman was nonunion. Marion said his wife told him of the instance where her mother, Versie, was almost beat to death by Leon after Versie had told Leon's wife, Nell, about Leon dating Audrey. Betty was in the living room of their home at the time, just a small child, and watched Leon beat up Versie. In the commotion, Leon knocked Betty down by accident. He stopped beating on Versie, and softly said, "I'm sorry, darlin'." Leon picked up Betty, calmly put her in a chair, and then went back to beating on Versie, putting her head through a wall. Marion said he knew that Leon had met Audrey around the time that Nell was in the tuberculosis sanitarium (1944-1946), and started a long-term relationship with her. She said Frank certainly knew about it and didn't seem to mind, although he admitted that Frank was so scared of Leon like everyone was, he wouldn't have said anything about Leon seeing Audrey even if he wanted to.

Marion said he visited the Tuckers in Kentucky often, and remembers visiting Leon and Versie's mother, Ruth (Keeling) Tucker, at her home near Paducah. Marion said Ruth Tucker could pull tobacco off the plant and chew it on the spot, but he (Marion) couldn't do it because it burned too badly. Marion said he knew that Leon had a mean streak in him and acted crazy angry at times. Betty also verified that Leon wasn't "someone you'd want to meet in a dark alley."

TILLIE & MILDRED: On one of my last visits to Tillie in Paducah, she told me she was also there at her mother Grace's house at the time when Leon and Nell left Paducah for Florida that year. According to Tillie, Leon was cleaning his shotgun out in front of Grace's house, knowing Nell was inside still refusing to go on the trip. Leon came into the house, laid the gun down on the coffee table, and forced Nell to go. Nell told Grace, "I don't believe I'm gonna see ya again. I don't think I'm gonna come back from this trip." Nell was crying as she got into Leon's car, according to Tillie. If this story was true, this was tantamount to kidnapping, albeit being his own wife. Tillie said Nell was definitely forced to go against her will.

Tillie said that Nell had visited Barnes Hospital in St. Louis twelve days before she left on the trip to Florida and was given a clean bill of health. Using this lead, I contacted Barnes Hospital in St. Louis to retrieve any medical records they had and was told that they didn't keep records beyond thirty years—a dead end. Tillie said Grace shared her Valium tablets with Nell, but Tillie didn't know of any other medications she was on at the time of her death. This contradicted other cousins who said she definitely was on medications—for what ailments they didn't know. Being fifty-eight years old at the time, I can reasonably assume Nell was on some medications as most women of her age would be. Tillie told me that her mother also had the habit of hiding money in her brassiere as Nell had. But Nell keeping that hidden money secret from Leon was different than what Grace would have done, who would not have kept it secret from her husband.

Tillie said Leon's story when he arrived with Nell at the hospital was that Nell was complaining of the chest pain while at the hospital, and died while at the hospital. This directly contradicts the death certificate which clearly shows "DOA," or "dead on arrival." Leon also told others that she died in the car "just before getting to the hospital." There clearly was a lie somewhere here. Tillie told me that John Barker was the McCracken County (Kentucky) Coroner at the time, and because of a social relationship with him, he agreed to look into Nell's death for her. Tillie didn't hear what he had found, if anything. I contacted John Barker in Paducah in 2006. He was now working at Milner and Orr Funeral Home in Paducah. He had no specific recollection of Nell's case, being so long ago, but he directed me to the Roth Funeral Home, saying that any files he would have would be "in the basement" there. I called the people at Roth Funeral Home, and they agreed to look for me. I didn't have high hopes they would find anything. They ultimately couldn't find the records I sought. Tillie told me that Leon blew up a bridge in East St. Louis once because it was built with nonunion labor. This corroborates the previous information that I had that Leon was an "enforcer" for the union in East St. Louis. Tillie told me that her sister Grace had called "Pood" Roberts, head of the union in East St. Louis at the time, to tell him of her suspicions that Leon had murdered Nell, but Tillie couldn't tell me if anything was done about it.

Last Sunday Night in 1968.
Made in Tillie's Living room
on 3200 Kentucky Avenue.
Oh Oh how I did love her.
She was so dear to my heart.

One of the last photos ever taken of Nell (on the right), approximately one week
before she died. Grace typed her feelings on the photo in the upper right.

On one of my last visits with Tillie about this research into Nell's death, Tillie gave me a gift that touched me greatly. She gave me a blue cloth clown doll—a handicraft that Nell had made while in the tuberculosis sanitarium in 1944, and gave to Tillie. Tillie had always had the doll on her bed for the roughly sixty years since it was given to her. This meant the doll had great emotional meaning to Tillie. The fact she would give it to me was quite significant, and I was humbled by the gift. I, of course, will treasure and preserve this important piece of Tucker family history for the next generation.

Mildred was willing to talk to me at length on the phone. Mildred told me the day Leon and Nell left for the fatal Florida trip, Leon came to Grace's house with a shotgun. Mildred said she was there at the time with Tillie, Nell, and Grace, and witnessed it firsthand. Leon laid the shotgun on the coffee table and forced Nell to leave with him. Nell was crying when she left because she didn't want to go. After learning of Nell's death, Mildred's mother (who was also Nell's sister) took the story to Albert Jones, the commonwealth attorney in Paducah at the time, to investigate it. Mildred was confident Leon had married Audrey long before Nell had died.

From Mildred's and Tillie's combined memory, Nell tried to divorce Leon right after she got out of the tuberculosis sanitarium and discovered that Leon had married Audrey. She hired Paducah attorney, Joe Freeland, and served Leon with divorce papers while he was in East St. Louis. Leon returned to Paducah quickly and put a shotgun blast through Ila Mae's (Nell's sister) door trying to scare Nell into calling off the divorce. He knew that if in the divorce it would come out he was a bigamist, he might get criminally charged for that. I pursued trying to find any legal file on Nell's divorce action from Joe Freeland and found that he had died in 2004 in Nashville, Tennessee. I spoke with his widow, Murray, on the phone, but she was advanced in years, so I doubted I would get much of value from her, especially since I was of no relation to her. I sent a letter with questions to her through her children, thinking that might be more productive, but I heard no response, so this was a dead end.

Some general memories Mildred had about Leon were that once Leon was fighting with Audrey and knocked her off a roof of a clubhouse they were working on at Grand Tower, and Versie was there at the time. This was a second source for this story, Tom Burgess being the other. Mildred said Leon was a thief—that he stole an expensive clock from Grace, Nell's sister. She also said that Leon set fire to a house on Yarbro Lane he had built because he had mistakenly built it on a lot he didn't own. He owned the lot next to it. I remember Frank telling me this exact same story once, about Leon burning a house he had just built so the landowner, old Mr. Yarbro, wouldn't get it.

TUCKERS: Corbett Tucker's son, Owen, still lived in Paducah, now owning the house on Husband Road formerly owned by Rob Tucker, his uncle and Leon's and Corbett's brother. He bought the house right after Rob Tucker died, and Rob's wife Gert wanted to leave Paducah for St. Louis to be near her family. Owen asked Gert at Rob's funeral for the first chance at the place, and Gert gave him that. Owen was seventy-six years old when I met him in 2006, but clear of mind. His family nicknamed him "Blue" when he was a young man, because his hair was whitish blond naturally, and he swam in the public swimming pool so much that the blue coloring they put in the water colored his hair blue. Owen's memories of Leon were mixed, some good, and some not so good. He remembered Leon had been in a knife fight once in East St. Louis, driven down to Kentucky by Audrey, and left at his mother's house in Paducah. He lay in a bed for two weeks, recovering from his wounds, with Owen's sister, Dorothy Tucker, nursing him back to health. Once back on his feet, he left Paducah for East St. Louis without so much as a thank you to Dorothy for her efforts.

Owen said his father Corbett considered Leon an "outlaw," always getting on the wrong side of the law. Owen remembered a story of Leon tying Audrey to a tree when over at the clubhouse in Grand Tower and shooting an apple off her head. He heard the story from Leon's best friend, Eloy Overstreet. Eloy was a big nightclub owner in Paducah, with gambling taking place at his clubs. That's how he met Leon, as Leon frequented those places. Eloy told Owen that he said to Leon, "Don't do it, Leon. Don't do it. You're gonna kill that woman." And Leon replied to Eloy, "Nah, I know what I'm a doin'." Evidently Leon was drunk at the time when he did it, but this story verified the shooting an apple off of Audrey's head story that had circulated in our family over the years. Eloy told Owen he thought Leon was crazy, literally. I suspect this individual named Eloy was the infamous "Eli" that I heard Leon and Frank refer to all the time. Every time they would encounter someone in traffic that they thought was driving bad and irritating them, they would call them an "Eli" in a disparaging way. Perhaps Leon had a falling out with Eloy (his formal name) at some point and thus earning his nickname a lifetime of scorn with Leon, transferring to Frank. Owen said something profound, and it resonated with me. He said he thought Leon's way of thinking didn't grow with the times, that he was trapped in the "old way of thinkin'." He said he had heard how Nell died down in Florida but never believed the official story. Knowing Leon, Owen believed Leon killed Nell for insurance money. He said he had heard as much but didn't remember where he had heard it.

Son and Owen Tucker's sister, Bertie Lee (Tucker) Howe, was also alive and still living in Paducah in 2006. I contacted her, but she said she had left Paducah after getting married young and missed out on seeing much of Leon's antics, only hearing of them secondhand. Leon's older brother Rob had two sons that didn't survive to adulthood. Remus was Leon's older brother as well, and Remus had two daughters both deceased before I began this investigation. Leon's older sister Nettie married into the Brooks family and had three children that have not been located to this date. Leon's older sister Lizzie married into the Taylor family, and I haven't located any of their descendants to this date. Tillie remembers "Aunt Lizzie," saying she was the "ugliest woman ya eva' saw, but boy could she cook!" Uvil Taylor and his descendants listed above are a different Taylor family than Lizzie Tucker married into.

Lizzie (Tucker) Taylor & husband Lum

STEVENSONS: Leon's older sister Annie married into the Stevenson family. Annie died in 1958 at the age of eighty-two. Being so much older than Leon (thirty-five years), none of Annie's children are still living, but some of her grandchildren were still living in 2006 that I could locate. They were the children of Annie's son Walter, who was also Leon's best friend from childhood and throughout his life. Walter's children with his wife Dollie that I could locate in 2006 were Eddie, Charles, Glenda, Ethel Lee, Freeda, Dorothy, and Shirley. It was particularly important that I speak with all the living Stevenson children of Walter and Dollie Stevenson, as Walter and Dollie were witnesses at the campground in Florida in 1969 when Nell died. Since Walter died in 1975, and Dollie died in 1979, their children would be the closest things I could get to eyewitness accounts of what happened to Nell.

Dorothy (Stevenson) Richardson was alive and living in Paducah. For a reason I don't wish to reveal for respect for her privacy, I was unable to communicate with her. Shirley (Stevenson) Donovan, now living in southern Illinois, told me that Leon would have huge scars on his belly from where he had been cut wide open in knife fights with African-Americans in East St. Louis at the time. She said he was once cut so bad that he had to use his hand to hold his guts inside until he could get to a hospital.

Shirley was sixty-eight years old when I interviewed her by phone, so I tried not to upset her, but didn't entirely succeed. I could hear her voice get tight when the subject turned to Nell's death in Florida in 1969. She actually said, "We shouldn't be talkin' 'bout this stuff," but then continued without a prompt from me. I need to paraphrase a bit of what she said to me to protect her comments regarding her own parents, which are of no concern to this story, and I wish to respect her privacy on that. She finally admitted she felt that Leon had taken Nell to Florida to do away with her. She said Leon was drunk when he attacked Nell. She never believed the "Nell died from eating oranges" story, scoffing at it as ridiculous.

Ethyl Lee (Stevenson) Phelps was eighty-two years old when I spoke with her, but still sharp of memory, and living in Calvert City, Kentucky. I asked her about Nell's death, and she remembers that Nell had a citrus allergy, and when she was eating tangelos, it reacted with her medication and shut down her heart. She didn't believe the story of Leon having anything to do with it. She said Nell died in Dollie's arms at the campground. That differs from the account of Leon saying she died at the hospital begging for help, and differs from several other accounts, like Dorothy McNeal's account that Nell died in the trailer. Ethyl said she was afraid of Leon in a general way, but doesn't remember why. She said she remembered a couple of lascivious looks coming from Leon at an ice-cream social event at Possom Trot, Kentucky, and a joking remark from Leon to her father, Walter, that Leon wanted to take her home with him. She was only fifteen years old at the time. Ethyl also heard that Leon was violent with Nell. She said she knew Leon beat his sister Versie almost to death, which coincides with the previous sources on that story. Ethyl remembers Leon being banned from Paducah by the police, which coincides with other sources on that story also.

Tucker sisters Annie (Tucker) Stevenson & Vera (Tucker) Burgess. Annie's mouth is puffed outward because she chewed tobacco and carried it in her lower lip

A young Walter Stevenson and his hunting dog

Charles Stevenson was also living in Calvert City, Kentucky, when I spoke with him, first by phone, and then he invited me to come visit him in person. When he began recalling what he knew about Nell's death, he said Nell was on medications. He said she was only supposed to eat cooked food, but was eating these tangelos, and they caused her to have a reaction leading to a heart attack. It sounded like a similar story that Walter and Dollie would have passed around among their kids when they returned from Florida. He said in this initial telephone interview with me that he didn't think Leon had anything to do with Nell's death, but admitted he only heard secondhand what he knew about it. I knew that Charles was close to Leon in his younger years, staying with him in Leon's house in East St. Louis when Charles went up there from Kentucky to find work.

Next I met with Charles Stevenson in his home near Calvert City, Kentucky, just a stone's throw from his brother Eddie's home. Charles seemed to welcome me into his house like old family, even though he likely had never laid eyes on me before. If he had seen me before, it would have been when I was a small child. But because I was Leon's grandson, that was enough to establish a family bond between us. Charles worked with Leon in East St. Louis on construction during the years of 1955-1957. He established that time period from the time he got married. He said he used to stay in the trailer Leon had on his lot at 1225 W. Fifty-second Street. He remembered my father Frank, "Frankie" to Charles, built a small house in the rear of Leon's lot behind his trailer, and was living there with his first wife Maudine and son Trent. Before that, Frank, Charles, and Uvil Taylor all shared Leon's trailer, while Leon stayed over on Forty-second Street at Audrey's house.

Charles remembered Leon telling him he was injured in World War II by a German .80 caliber shell that blew his buddy to pieces, and almost killed him. Leon told Charles he was left for dead by the first round of rescuers, and then picked up by the team that comes through to pick up the dead bodies, but found Leon still alive. Leon was sent to a hospital in England for many months and was told he would never walk again. But Leon recovered and was never sent back into combat again. Leon told all of these war details to Charles, and Charles was retelling them to me.

Leon admitted to Charles to having killed three men in his lifetime. One of the men Leon admitted to killing was named Ted Snooks. Charles remembers going fishing with Leon, and Leon using one of the old-type hand crank telephone machines that generated an electrical current. He would lower the wires into the water, crank the machine, and it would electrocute or stun the fish within thirty or so feet of the boat. The fish would float to the surface, dead or stunned, or sometimes jump out of the water and up on to the bank of the lake or river they were in. Charles said Leon would catch raccoons alive and sell them to the state of Kentucky for $7.50 a head because Kentucky was trying to reestablish the raccoon in the state. It had been over hunted, and the population of the animal in the state was too low for a viable population. This came perhaps from considering the need for genetic diversity or the position of the raccoon, "coons" as the Kentuckians would call them, in the ecological balance of the state's forests.

Charles told me he had also gone down many times to the campground in Florida on Lake Okeechobee with Leon, before and after Nell had died there, but wasn't there in 1969. Charles said Leon was a union enforcer for the Local 100 Laborer's union in East St. Louis. Leon was once told five nonunion workers were working on a bridge on the Mississippi River, and went down there to stop the work. He used a shovel to fight all five of them, shoving the sharp end of the shovel into one man's face and beating another one with the broken handle of the shovel he had just broken over another man. Charles didn't know if Leon killed anyone that day, but it evidently was serious enough Leon had to get out of East St. Louis for a while. Leon went down to Paducah for a few months until it all blew over. That was Leon's habit, Charles said. He would get in trouble in one place and take off for someplace else; either East St. Louis, Paducah, or Florida, until the police stopped looking for him.

Charles said Leon would take Nell to Florida, then come back, drop Nell off in Paducah, pick up Audrey in East St. Louis, and take her down to Florida immediately after. Charles said Leon was a thief, always selling tools he had stolen from his employer's worksite or from people he visited. He said he stole Claud "Smitty" Marshall's (Audrey's brother) boots, sold them to Walter Stevenson, and when Claud made such a ruckus about his stolen boots, Leon stole them back from Walter to give back to Claud. But he kept the money he got for them. Leon would take a truckload of strawberries from the Stevenson farm in Kentucky, without payment, and sell them in East St. Louis for fifty cents a box, and keep the money.

Charles told me of the huge fight between Leon and his older brother Reem. He said Reem stole some gas from Leon, Leon stole it back, and filled Reem's gas tank with water. As payback, Reem got three men to "whoop" (slang for "whip," meaning to beat up) Leon, two of which were Ben and George Griffy. Leon "whooped" two out of the three men and was beating on the third one when Reem knifed him in the back under the shoulder blade. Leon cut Reem's stomach open that day and then ran off because he knew Reem would fight him until one of them was dead. Charles said Leon had fistfights with a union boss named Joe Abernathy, and later with Audrey's son Harold Reed. Joe Abernathy evidently almost killed Leon, but Leon almost killed Harold.

Charles initially over the phone said he didn't think Leon had anything to do with Nell's death. However, in person, when he saw that I would not have my feelings hurt if he revealed what he truly believed, conceded that "it looked bad for Leon at the time," meaning that people at the time suspected Leon was responsible. He said he had asked his father, Walter, if he thought Leon had anything to do with Nell's death. Charles said Walter told him he "didn't think Leon had anything to do with it." The lack of certainty in Walter's statement left open the possibility that even Walter thought Leon might have had a role in Nell's death. Charles finished his comments about the subject by saying that if Leon had something to do with Nell's death, certainly Walter and Dollie had no knowledge of it. It was understandable that Charles would want to defend his parents' reputation.

Eddie Stevenson was also living near Calvert City, Kentucky, when I spoke with him, first by phone, and then he also invited me to come visit him in person as his brother Charles had. So I began thinking about organizing another trip to Kentucky to see the Stevensons in person. I knew people were more likely to reveal details when you were face to face with them rather than just a voice on the phone. Eddie said he and his wife were with Leon and Nell, as well as Walter and Dollie, at the campground in Florida in 1969 when Nell died. He said they still go to that campground nowadays for fishing. He said he felt confident that Leon "took Nell down there to die." Eddie said he knew that Leon was "fixin' to retire," and knew that Leon couldn't retire and bring Audrey to Paducah. Paducah was a relatively small town, and a religious one also, and therefore his brothers Rob and Corbett wouldn't have accepted him if he tried to set up a second wife in a second house in Paducah, since Nell was already living there.

Eddie said Leon stole a lot, not just a little, but a lot. Eddie said he knew Leon couldn't divorce Audrey or Nell, either one, because both knew about the other, and Leon might get in trouble with the law for being married to two women at the same time. He needed to get rid of one of his wives before retiring. Eddie said he thinks Leon "did something with Nell's pills" to cause her to have the heart attack, then didn't get help in time for her and let her die. He said, "It all fits . . ." meaning the evidence he saw and the conclusions he drew from it. This was the first independent corroboration that I got from an eyewitness on the scene at the campground in Florida in 1969. I knew I was hearing the most important information I had come across to that date in my investigation. I started making plans to visit Eddie in person to get all the details.

In May 2006, I visited Eddie on his farm near Calvert City. He had bought the farm of his parents, Walter and Dollie, and met me at the end of his driveway on his four-wheeler with a joke when I asked him if he was Eddie Stevenson. He said, "If you're a bill collector, I'm not." We sat on his front porch, and he pointed down the road to the old brick home of his parents, Walter and Dollie. He was fifty-nine years old at the time I spoke with him, making him twenty-two years old in 1969 when Nell died in Florida, and he was there witness to it. Eddie is an amiable fellow, hard not to like, with his joking and plain-speaking nature. He warned me before he began talking about Leon, Eddie got a serious, raised-eyebrow look on his face, and said, "Now I'm gonna tell ya true, OK?" This sounded like a warning that I was about to hear negative things about Leon. I told Eddie to tell me the whole truth—the good, the bad, and the ugly. I wanted to know it all about Leon. Eddie told me that his brother-in-law, Earnest Collins, husband to his sister Freeda, was once nosing into Leon's affairs a little too closely for Leon's comfort. Leon had so many deals going at once, all of them with some angle of illegality to them, it would not have been hard getting something on Leon if Ernie was starting looking for it. Leon found out about Ernie's prying and began to try to arrange with Walter to con Ernie into going hunting with Leon alone. Leon was planning a "hunting accident" for Ernie, and would have gotten away with it without any witnesses around. But Leon made the mistake of telling Walter first. Because Ernie was married to Walter's daughter, Freeda, Walter told Leon he wouldn't allow him to kill Ernie. Eddie said no one had ever told Freeda or Ernie about this story. Ernie died in a car accident a few years ago.

In his early twenties, Eddie said he went up to East St. Louis to find work after Leon told him he could get him construction work there. When he got there, Leon demanded Eddie pay him "doby money," which is basically a bribe to the construction foreman to pick him for his crew that day. The doby money was to be paid to the Local 100 union as dues, but Leon would keep it for himself. Eddie suspected Leon was picking out the worst jobs for him to do, trying to drive him out of East St. Louis for some reason Eddie couldn't figure out. After a short period in East St. Louis, Eddie went back down to Kentucky.

During my visit with him, Eddie expanded in detail on Leon's habit of theft. Eddie said Leon wouldn't just steal from strangers or employers, but from family members. Eddie said Leon couldn't control his urge to steal, saying, "He couldn't help it." When the Stevenson men would go hunting with Leon, Leon would steal shells from the other hunters' supplies when they weren't looking. Eddie said when Leon would come out to the Stevenson farm, he would go into the houses of the Stevensons even if they weren't home. He'd jimmy the door open somehow, mosey around for anything he wanted, and leave the garbage can on the tabletop as a signal he had been in the house. Because he was related to them, somehow Leon thought he had their permission to enter without them there, when they had never told him he could. Once, in East St. Louis, Eddie said Audrey had collected some money donations for the poor and kept it in her dresser. Leon took the money, but then came up to Eddie and his buddies to tell them they were suspected of taking it and had to replace it. At the time they were living alternately in Leon's trailer on Fifty-second Street and Audrey's house on Forty-second Street. Because Leon and Audrey controlled where they lived at, they felt they might have to replace the money even though they hadn't taken the money in the first place. While they considered what they should do, Audrey came up to them, after Leon had left, and told them she knew Leon had taken the money himself. Eddie said that Audrey told them, "Don't worry, boys. I know Tucker took it. He's done this to me before." Eddie said Audrey always called Leon by his last name, "Tucker."

Eddie said Leon was seen once stealing lumber from the Interstate 24 Highway construction project that bisected the Stevenson farm near Calvert City, Kentucky. He said they saw someone down the hill at the construction site running like a very young man would, extremely fast, loading up the lumber in his truck, so as not to get caught stealing it. They at first thought it couldn't be Leon since he was too old to be running like that. But then they looked closer and saw incredibly that it was Leon. His adrenalin must have been pumping, giving him the extra speed to do the stealing quickly and not get caught. Eddie said Leon once came to his farm when he wasn't home and stole his chainsaw and several gas cans, filling the cans with Eddie's gas as well.

Eddie said he knew that Leon was violent, not just toward men, but women also. He said Audrey told them that Leon had once beaten her up so bad it knocked her out. She awoke to find herself in a boat in the middle of a lake, with Leon rowing the boat.

Leon intended to throw her body overboard so she would drown while unconscious, and it would look like an accidental drowning. Evidently Leon suspected he had killed Audrey, or that she would die soon from his beating of her that went too far. Only because she woke up before he dumped her in the lake did he not go through with it. Leon used to keep a .38 caliber pistol and a crescent wrench under the driver's seat of his car for combat at any moment. Once when visiting the Stevenson farm, Leon was boasting he had " . . . jus' whooped me a nigger." The Stevensons gave him doubting looks, so Leon went back to his car, got the crescent wrench, and showed them blood and "nigger hide" on it. Leon would ask Audrey to carry the .38 pistol and a knife in her purse when they would go to a nightclub. Once in a nightclub, when a fight broke out between Leon and someone else, Audrey saw someone coming for Leon from behind his back with a knife. Audrey yelled out, "Tucker! He's a gonna cut on ya!" She then threw him his knife from her purse. Audrey was one tough old woman, said Eddie, but he thought she was a "good person" and liked her. Eddie asked me if I had ever seen Leon without his clothes on. I said I hadn't, at least not to my memory. He said if I had, I would have seen Leon's body covered with huge scars from all the knife fights he had been in over the years.

Eddie said about the Florida trip in 1969, that he and his wife Linda, along with his parents Walter and Dollie, had arrived before Leon and Nell. Leon and Nell arrived in the first week of January after stopping off at Ft. Meade at the home of one of their mutual cousins, Robert Stevenson. Robert Stevenson owned some vacant land there that had citrus groves growing on them. Leon had purchased one of them years before from Robert's father Larkin, intending to use it as a home building spot for his retirement. They picked up tangelos there at the lot Leon owned, according to Eddie, and brought them with them to Okeechobee. Eddie said the campground lots they always went to were (at the time) free public camping spots on Federal Land on the banks of the Kissimmee River immediately before it dumps into Lake Okeechobee. The camping spots were wedged between the river and a private campground then called Joe and Wanda's Fish Camp. That describes a location directly opposite of the Okee-Tantie Campground, and upstream of the bridge over the Kissimmee River, and on the east bank of the river. Eddie said it was just an unorganized area, not a formal campground, and people would just park their trailers next to the river with no hookups (power, water, or sewer) for the campers.

Leon had a favorite, specific spot on the Kissimmee River adjacent to the lake that he always liked to return to whenever he went to Lake Okeechobee for fishing. When he arrived that late December 1968 or early January 1969, he saw that an old man had taken the spot next to his favorite spot and also had set up a tent on Leon's favorite spot. Leon told the old man to move his tent, that he couldn't save it for people who hadn't arrived yet, which the man said he was doing. The man refused, so Leon backed his trailer up over the tent, smashing it beneath his wheels. The man ran over and told Leon he would remove the tent if Leon pulled forward off of it. Eddie thought there was going to be a fistfight over this, but he guessed the old man was smart enough to realize he shouldn't mess with Leon.

Leon and Nell in Florida with a fresh catch

Eddie reiterated to me when we spoke on his porch that he saw Walter and Leon carry Nell out of the camper, but he couldn't be sure if she was dead already or not. He said he didn't remember, or maybe he did and just didn't want to tell me. I sensed some protectiveness of the details on this point, because the story involved his parents at this point. Perhaps Eddie wanted to make sure he didn't implicate his parents in any way, which I could understand. He also said he couldn't remember if the police came to the campsite in the next days or not, again an ambiguity that could have been protectiveness.

Eddie said when Leon left Florida for Nell's funeral, he left his trailer behind, and later returned with Audrey about five or six days later. His wife of forty years, Nell, just died, and he was continuing with his vacation anyway, without interruption, with his second wife, Audrey. Eddie's wife Linda helped him remember that when Leon returned with Audrey to the campsite, he insisted the entire group move upstream a mile or so. Leon didn't want to be around the same people, the other campers at the campsite, that saw him leave with one dead woman and return with a second live woman. Eddie said Leon felt uncomfortable about how that looked to others. After many years of watching Leon pull his antics around the Stevensons, Eddie said the family grew tired of worrying that their property would be taken and houses invaded by Leon, so they finally began cutting contact with him. Eddie said the family stopped asking him around. Whether he was formally told not to visit them anymore he wouldn't say.

When Leon would come out to the Stevenson's farm, he would say to Eddie loud enough for Walter to hear, "Son? Ain't ya got that stock fed yet?" He'd say it in a plaintive, criticizing way, like Eddie was being a slacker, when in fact he wasn't. Eddie could do a perfect impression of Leon's voice, which made me smile when I heard it. It was like hearing Leon alive again. Eddie would raise his voice through the word "son," starting low and ending high, just like Leon would, stretching out the middle vowel long, like Leon did. It almost sounded like Leon would be calling out to someone, a male, that was at a distance, and Leon was summoning his attention. I remember that Leon always referred to any man younger than him as "son," including me.

Freeda Sue (Stevenson) Collins was also living in Calvert City, Kentucky, at the time of my investigation. I spoke first via e-mail with her daughter Barbara (Collins) Stevenson (husband no relation to mother's family) who was doing her own genealogy research on the Stevenson family. We first compared notes on our common family heritage and helped each other fill in our family trees with the missing parts we both needed. She asked her mother for me a list of questions, basically what she remembered about the 1969 death of Nell in Florida, and general memories of Leon and Nell. Barbara e-mailed me back a wealth of comments from her mother. Freeda said Leon was a moocher, always coming to the Stevenson house and having Walter load up his car trunk with meats and vegetables from their own farm.

She said Leon would come to their house on weekends sometimes with Nell, but sometimes with a girlfriend, and the girlfriend most common was Audrey. Freeda thought that Leon could not get Nell to agree to terms for a divorce, so he was not kind to her. Nell was fully aware of Leon's girlfriends. Dollie Stevenson, a devout Southern Baptist woman, didn't appreciate it when Leon would show up at her house with a girlfriend, and wouldn't let them out of Leon's car, even when it was Audrey. Over time since Audrey became the regular with Leon, she was allowed out of the car, but not encouraged to be there. Freeda believed that Leon had done something to Nell in Florida to cause her a heart attack, or at least not gotten help in time, because he wanted free from her to retire with Audrey in Paducah. Freeda and her husband, Ernie, visited several times with Leon and Audrey after they (Leon and Audrey) had built their home for their retirement at 1735 Husband Road in Paducah.

I spoke with Freeda later by telephone in 2006. She was sixty-five years old at the time. She seemed reluctant to talk about Nell's death directly to me, saying it was just rumors. I had run into this before, where people were afraid to say something directly to me about my grandfather, fearing they would offend me or hurt my feelings, like it was bad manners. I had to assure her that it was OK to say anything to me about him, that "all these people are gone, so it doesn't matter now. Nothing will change my memory of my grandfather anyway." Freeda believed it was possible Leon messed with Nell's medications in Florida. She confirmed that Leon knew Audrey as far back as before World War II, and used to bring her to Walter and Dollie's farm long before Nell's death in 1969. She said her mother Dollie told her once that Audrey had told her the story of how she and Nell met on a bus in East St. Louis. Audrey told Dollie that she used to ride the same bus as Nell did in East St. Louis for a long time. The two women didn't even know each other until one day they sat next to each other by accident. They began talking about their men, Audrey about her boyfriend, and Nell about her husband, until they realized, to each other's horror, that they were both talking about the same man.

Freeda said Leon liked Audrey because she was a plain woman that would do dirty work, such as dressing and cleaning squirrels Leon had shot and clean fish Leon had caught, where Nell wouldn't do these tasks. Audrey worked as a meat packer, so handling animals in this manner was nothing new to her. Nell was a proper lady that kept her nails done, her hair done, and always dressed nice, so she wouldn't do those unpleasant chores like Audrey would. Freeda called Nell "Leon's Sunday woman," and called Audrey "Leon's everyday woman." Freeda's memories seemed to coincide with Eddie's the best, at least about the rumors of Nell's death.

Another son of Annie (Tucker) Stevenson's children was Tommy Stevenson, who together with his wife Ollie (Russell) had seven children: Frances (Brown), Thomas "Tinker," Edison "Doodle," James, Milton, Clifton, and Rudell. I located six that were still alive in 2006 and spoke with Frances a couple of times on the phone as the contact for several of them. Frances remembers Leon and Nell visiting her parents when she was a little girl, and remembers Nell bringing her paper dolls she had made for her. She said her mother Ollie would have remembered a lot about Leon, but unfortunately had suffered strokes and was confined to a nursing home with little to no memory left by the time I contact Frances in the summer of 2006. Ollie later died toward the end of 2006. I missed out on getting Ollie's memories by about a year or two. Frances said her brothers "Tinker" and "Doodle" didn't remember anything specific about Leon and Nell. James Stevenson did have some memories of Leon and Nell, especially a raccoon-hunting story that Leon told when he visited their family.

James said Leon told of when he would go raccoon hunting near Grand Tower, catching them alive and turning them in for cash reward in Kentucky. Kentucky was trying to repopulate its forests with raccoons, which had been over hunted there. James said Leon would sometimes employ an African-American man as an assistant or bearer. Leon would take a "coon" hunting dog (trained for hunting) with him to chase down the raccoons and "tree" them, meaning chase them up a tree. But the dog couldn't climb the tree to shake the raccoon loose. If Leon did the climbing, he couldn't get down to the ground fast enough to catch the raccoon before it ran away. Leon needed a hunting assistant. So Leon hired this African-American man. When the dog would "tree" a raccoon, the assistant would climb the tree and shake the branch that had the raccoon on it until it dropped to the ground. The dog would pin the raccoon to the ground so it couldn't run away, and Leon would then grab the raccoon with his hand and put it in the sack. The assistant would carry the sack like a bearer. Leon told James that he used a light mounted on his forehead with a small electric wire leading down to a battery on his belt. Once, when Leon bent over to grab a raccoon, the wire came loose from the battery, and the light went off. Leon grabbed the raccoon in the darkness and put it in the sack.

The hunting party went on in search of the next raccoon. Leon started calling out to the dog to find another raccoon. The African-American assistant said to Leon, "Mr. Tucker, every time you call out to that dog, this sack jumps." They looked in the sack, and in the darkness (since the light on his head had went out), Leon had grabbed the dog instead of the raccoon and put the dog in the sack with the raccoons they had already caught. That story made everyone laugh at the Stevenson's house. It was one of many of Leon's great stories he could tell, keeping everyone entertained.

This raccoon-hunting story jogged my own memory of Leon's hunting prowess, and the few times I would go squirrel hunting (with rifles) with Leon and Frank when I was very young. I remember once Leon shooting a squirrel out of a tree, but the squirrel wasn't dead yet when they found it on the ground, so Leon stepped on the squirrel's head to finish it off. Leon also had built elaborate rabbit traps, which were these long, wooden boxes, with a trap door at one end. They worked by the movement of the rabbit at the far inside end of the box, tripping a handle extending to the trap door at the entrance. Leon would place the rabbit traps in the woods and cover them with leaves. Leon somehow knew that rabbits were attracted to a dark opening that resembled a hole in the ground. I remember Leon telling me never to worry about reaching into the trap to get the rabbit because "a rabbit will never bite you." I wasn't sure I believed that, but I took him at his word, since he was the expert at hunting and trapping. He may have just said that to quell any fears I might have at reaching into the dark box to blindly grab the rabbit.

MISCELLANEOUS TUCKER COUSINS: I had concluded the interviews with all the Tucker cousins I could find, written this entire manuscript, and put the book aside to concentrate on getting it published. Then, out of the blue in 2008, I started being contacted by more Tucker cousins I didn't know existed. I had used Ancestry.com to construct my family tree and uploaded it to that Web site. Others who were similarly constructing their own family trees viewed mine, got information from it, and then contacted me. Several of these distant cousins contacted me from both of my parents' sides of the family. One of these that I located through this avenue, albeit through a few more people involved, was Joyce Cole. Joyce is a lifelong resident of Paducah, Kentucky, and descended from James Young Tucker, her great-grandfather, who was brother to my great-grandfather, George W. Tucker.

Joyce knew Leon and Nell both from their days when they would attend her church, the Eastside Holiness Church on Husband Road in Paducah. Nell would attend with her sister Grace during the 1950s and 1960s when she was living in Paducah alone. Leon was living with Audrey in East St. Louis at the time. Leon would attend Eastside Holiness in later years, the 1970s and 1980s, when he was married to Audrey. Joyce said she knew Nell very well and thought very highly of her, saying she was a deeply religious person and always finely dressed—usually with clothes from Paducah's finest department stores. She said Nell would sometimes talk to her about Leon, and that she knew Leon was living with Audrey in East St. Louis. Nell told Joyce that she thought Audrey and Leon had already married as well, and that's why Leon didn't want Nell in East St. Louis with him. Joyce said she thought Nell loved Leon, but didn't quite understand why she didn't divorce him.

Joyce then told me something she initially was reluctant to remember regarding the time of Nell's death. She said just before the 1969 Christmas trip to Florida, Nell told many of her church friends that she didn't want to go. Nell told them she had a dream about the trip and was convinced "the Lord" had told her not to go to Florida with Leon this time, for if she did, she would not return. Joyce said that many in her church begged and pleaded with Nell not to go on the trip to Florida with Leon, but Nell said she had no choice. Leon wanted her to go, and she had to do what Leon wanted. Many at Eastside Holiness suspected foul play had happened in Florida, with Nell predicting her own death, and then it happening just as she had predicted. This coordinates with what Tillie told me that Nell had told her and Grace before the fateful trip—that she didn't think she would return from it alive. Joyce's story, however, was the first I had heard of Nell saying she had a premonition of her own death, and that she felt God had warned her.

One additional thought came to me after listening to Joyce's recollections of Nell's focus on her church, that this coordinates with what I saw in her photo album, which I possess. Nell had many black-and-white photos of all her church friends, and with help

83

from distant Tucker and Keeling cousins, Joyce Cole and Jessie Noe, I had identified the people in most of the photos. Jessie is a descendant of Virginia Keeling Tucker, sister to Leon's mother, Ruth Keeling Tucker. He's actually a double cousin, as Virginia Keeling Tucker married James Young Tucker, brother to Leon's father, George W. Tucker. Both Tucker brothers married two Keeling sisters, doubling the family connection of Jessie to me. It became evident that nearly all of the congregation of the Eastside Holiness Church in Paducah during this time period (1940s-1960s) were related to each other. Leon and Nell both had kin there—Tuckers and Keelings on Leon's side, and Freemans on Nell's side. Being that the church was more than just for religious worship but was the center of social activity for these people, this heavy family presence at their church made for a difficult situation for Nell and Leon regarding divorce. Previously I thought that Nell was reluctant to divorce Leon because of his violent behavior, but I thought in addition Nell might not want to be divorced in front of her entire social circle and family. Paducah was at this time, and remains so today, a very religious city. Divorce at this time was scandalous, whereas today it is more casual and commonplace. This social pressure on Nell might have inhibited her from seeking a divorce from Leon.

Another cousin that I located through Jessie Noe was Wilma Keeling Holmes, also of Paducah. She is a cousin through the family tree branch emanating from my great-grandmother Ruth Keeling Tucker. Wilma descends from Ruth's brother Joe Keeling. Wilma is twin sister to Pete Keeling, the pastor of the Eastside Holiness Church, and close friend of Leon's. When I spoke with Wilma, she was eighty-six years old and clear of memory—remembering Nell "very well." She backed up most of what Joyce Cole said about Nell, but added that she knew that Audrey was "afraid of Leon" and that Leon was "not good" to Audrey. "Not good" to her was code that I recognized from other Kentucky relation. This was their way of saying Leon was violent to Audrey. They couldn't bring themselves to say the actual words like "wife-beater," they consider this to be bad manners, but the code phrase of "not good to her" clearly conveys the message. Wilma also said she knew of a fistfight between Hard Keeling (undoubtedly a Keeling cousin to Leon) and Leon. Wilma said Leon lost that fight, and I knew what this meant. Any fight Leon would have lost would have only been because he was either cut so badly that he was bleeding to death or was beaten unconscious. Wilma said Leon changed in his later years, becoming peaceful and churchgoing—a huge change from his younger "rascal" years.

A granddaughter of Leon's brother Remus Tucker that I located also through Ancestry.com was Debbie Schadt of Louisville, Kentucky. She is the daughter of Virginia "Dink" Tucker (deceased), who was the daughter of Remus Tucker. Debbie said her cousin Barbara, daughter of Ruth Tucker Eggleston (deceased), also daughter of Remus Tucker, had told her that Leon had threatened to kill Nell if she ever tried to divorce him. She heard the story from her mother, Ruth, who used to run a shoe store business in Paducah with her cousin Bertie Lee Tucker Howe. Bertie Lee was also the niece of Leon, being the daughter of Leon's brother Corbett Tucker Sr.

Wilma (Keeling) Holmes at left in front of Eastside Holiness Church in Paducah approximately in the 1950's. Photo from Nell Tucker's photo collection.

Adam Bond in 2006

BONDS: An additional source on Leon and Frank as union enforcers was my first cousin, Adam Bond, from my mother's (Judy's) side of the family. Adam is the son of Judy's brother, Donald Bond. The families, the Tuckers and the Bonds, were close during the East St. Louis years of the 1960s and 1970s. Adam was raised with me more as a brother than a cousin. Adam's first memory of Leon was how he would taunt us preschool age boys by pretending he only had enough money to buy ice cream for two of us three young boys, and we had to choose who wasn't going to get the ice cream. Adam remembers him feeling bad he had already gotten his ice cream, and offering me some of his so I wouldn't be left out. Then Leon would laugh and announce we were all getting our own individual ice creams, leaving Adam feeling foolish. That was classic Leon behavior—he loved to make a fool of someone, even little kids.

In a darker memory, Adam remembers his family discussing seeing Frank pull up to Leon's house one time with the bloody body of a man lying in the back of his station wagon. He picked up Leon, and they both took off together to either dispose of the dead body or, if the man was still alive, dump him somewhere. Somehow they knew it was union enforcement work by Frank and Leon that they saw in that instance. This story might coordinate with a story Frank himself told me sometime during the years we lived in Morrisonville (approximately 1976 to 1985). In a rare moment of candor, Frank admitted to me he had once "killed a man," and that was the reason why we moved out of the East St. Louis area—so Frank wouldn't get in trouble for it with the police, or receive any backlash from it locally. If this isn't the same killing that Adam remembers, then perhaps Frank was involved in more than one killing.

CONCLUSION: I listened to all of these stories from the Tucker cousins about men apparently I never knew—at least the whole picture of them. Leon Tucker was only a gentle man in my presence—albeit during his older, retirement years. My father never told me anything about Leon being violent when he was younger. I used all of these stories from the Tucker cousins to help complete the picture of my family heritage, the side people didn't want me to know about. It had been hidden from me on purpose—of that I am sure. If I hadn't gone looking for it, prying and digging, pulling it out of reluctant family members in some cases, this side of the Tucker heritage would have been lost to time.

Learning of these stories helped me understand that Leon Tucker could indeed have done what I was investigating about him—that being violent murder. I previously thought that was far-fetched. But after hearing of all these instances of violent behavior, coming from many different sources, I began to believe he had such capability for violence in him. If it were just one source saying this, I might be able to discount that, but not so many sources, all saying the same thing through different stories or different instances. It was pretty overwhelming evidence.

*   *   *

Chapter 6

THE WIVES

He reached into the casket, touched the hand of Judy's remains, and said softly, "Thank you, Judy, for twenty-eight years o' marriage. They were the best years o' my life."

The women that have married into the Tucker family have been a varied lot. I had to write a separate chapter for the wives of the Tucker men, as they didn't quite fit into the chapter on the Tucker cousins.

NELL: This is the correct chapter to introduce a brief overview of Nell's background. Nell was born Nell Annie Freeman on July 16, 1910, in Graves County, Kentucky. There was no city of birth specified on her birth certificate as she was born on her family's farm in a rural area. Nell was born to Allen Freeman and Annie (Ford) Freeman. Allen and Annie had four children, three girls and a boy. Ila Mae Freeman was Nell's older sister by only two years. Grace Lily Freeman was Nell's younger sister by only two years. Their baby brother was Ernest Melvin Freeman, younger than Nell by seven years. Allen and Annie were fourteen years apart in age, Allen being older. Allen was thirty-eight years old when Nell was born, and Annie was a young twenty-four-year-old. Allen had been married twice before Annie and had a mysterious, long-lost son named Arnold Brooks. We've never been able to locate any descendants of Arnold Brooks, and only knew that he lived in the Washington state area, where Allen Freeman had traveled to marry Arnold's mother in the late 1800s. Whether he bore the Freeman name is also unknown. Tillie had only limited information on this half-brother to Nell. Allen and Annie would later divorce after their children were grown, and neither would remarry. Annie returned to her maiden name of Ford upon divorcing. Both are buried within a few yards of each other in Clark's River Cemetery in Symsonia—Annie buried next to her parents, Allen buried next to the unmarked grave of his first wife. Allen died in 1947 of tuberculosis, or "consumption" as they called it in those days, and Annie died the following year.

Nell's parents: Allen Freeman & Annie (Ford) Freeman

Nell as a young girl

Nell (left) & her sister Grace in flapper chic in
Paducah sometime in the late 1920's

Nell (left) & cousins at her childhood home

Frank told me that Nell had described her youth as very backward country life, with her being ashamed that at times she didn't have shoes on her feet. That may have been an exaggeration on Frank's part. To Frank, making Nell's background sound meager and hard seemed noble. I say this because that description doesn't match the photos of Nell's youth that were given to me by Tillie. It does show that she grew up in an old wooden house that appeared unpainted in the black-and-white photos. But Nell always appeared adequately dressed in clean, untattered clothes, was well combed and groomed, and most certainly always had shoes on her feet. They may have been poor farmers, but they had dignity.

In Nell's later years of youth, she is shown in the photos dressed fashionably in the "flapper" style, it being the "Roaring Twenties" (1920s). One might even say she looked affluent in her stylish dress and hat, posing with attitude on the city streets of Paducah with her sister Grace. She was clearly the prettiest of the three Freeman sisters. It's no surprise how she caught the eye of Leon Tucker. Leon and Nell married in McCracken County near Paducah on January 7, 1929, when Leon was seventeen years old and Nell was eighteen years old. Their only child, Frank, was born two years later on January 3, 1931. Nell's forty-year marriage to Leon is described in other chapters.

AUDREY: To compile a description of Audrey, Leon's second wife, I first approached Frances (Reed) Lemanski, Audrey's daughter. She wasn't a Tucker wife herself, but the closest thing I could get to interviewing the actual Tucker wife I wanted to speak with—which was Audrey. Audrey was actually named Audie (maiden name Audie Cordelia Marshall). Audrey was a nickname. She was born in 1909 to William Marshall and Idella (Riley) Marshall in western Kentucky. Audrey died in December 1999, just two weeks before the Millennium New Year's, at the age of ninety years old, in a nursing home in Belleville, Illinois. She is buried alone, no direct family next to her, in a cemetery in Belleville.

I tracked Frances, Audrey's daughter, down with the help of Ancestry.com Web site. Also Bert Mitchell knew her, being they only lived about a mile apart. I met with Frances at her home in Caseyville, Illinois, several times in 2006. She was seventy-nine years old at that time, and the stereotypical old lady, with a soft voice, soft demeanor—all the toughness from her young years now gone. I couldn't feel any animosity toward her since she was just a harmless old lady now. Frances welcomed me into her home, actually glad to see me like I was old family. Any animosity she might feel toward the Tuckers was gone, and she just wanted to reminisce with me. She gave me Leon's military dog tags from World War II, along with some military citations, military photos, and the register from his funeral. She said she would search for the marriage certificate of Leon and Audrey's, as she was sure she had it "tucked away somewhere." I noticed Frances had terrific recall of details of Leon and Audrey's history together. She even admitted that she was "a bit of a witch . . . in my younger years." That made me feel a little more at ease with her—at least she recognized that she hadn't always been an angel to our family.

Leon and Audrey circa 1980

Frances began reminiscing with me by first telling me of Audrey's history. Later, to get a full picture of Audrey's marriage history, I pulled the divorce records from St. Clair County Circuit Court for Audrey's first two divorces. I'll combine both references, Frances recollections and the official record, to reconstruct Audrey's life. Frances said Audrey's first husband was Michael Reed, the father of Harold and Frances. She married him in July 1925, and Frances was born in February 1927. Harold followed in April 1928, and after only a few years of marriage, either Audrey left Michael Reed or he left her, which is unclear. Their divorce documents from St. Clair County show that Audrey claimed Michael Reed abandoned her and their children in February 1933. She evidently stayed married to him, on paper at least, for six more years, until January 1939, when St. Clair County Circuit Court records show their divorce. Audrey made no allegations of violence in her divorce papers, just abandonment. Frances said Michael Reed was not violent toward Audrey, but was a heavy drinker. Evidently Michael Reed didn't contest the divorce or Audrey's claim of abandonment since it recorded that officially on their divorce decree. Michael Reed died in 1946 at the relatively young age of forty-three years old.

Audrey likely went for the divorce at that time, in 1939, because she wanted to marry another man. Audrey's next husband, Joe Hayden, married her in August 1940. Joe Hayden evidently turned violent, and that second marriage only lasted about a year and a half. Frances told me of a time where Joe Hayden kicked Audrey in the stomach so hard Frances thought it would have killed her. This kick happened in front of Frances and a high school friend she had brought home with her for lunch. Joe Hayden abandoned Audrey in December 1942, so claimed Audrey in her divorce application. The East St. Louis city directory shows Audrey married to Joe Hayden by 1941, and stopped listing him at her address by 1945. But there was no city directory for me to check in 1942, 1943, or 1944, likely due to World War II, so the divorce document showing Audrey's claim of abandonment in 1942 seems to be the only record of when Joe Hayden left the picture. It is known that Audrey and Leon began dating around 1941 or 1942, so it's likely that Joe Hayden was out of the picture even before the December 1942 date Audrey claimed he abandoned her.

Audrey's divorce of Joe Hayden didn't happen until July 1969. She remained legally married to him for almost thirty years, despite him being gone for around twenty-nine of those years. She didn't even know where Joe Hayden lived at the time, and divorced him in absentia. She claimed the last address she had for him was in Indianapolis, Indiana. The court made her run a newspaper ad announcing the divorce to give him a chance to respond, and the court sent notice to the address Audrey provided to them, in Indianapolis. The letter was returned as "no such street number." Audrey may have made up the address, or it may have been true, who knows? Frances told the U.S. Government, after Audrey retired and was in a nursing home near the end of her life, that they knew that Joe Hayden had died in Mayfield, Kentucky, in the middle 1980s. The court in St. Clair County had no choice but to grant Audrey the divorce she sought.

Frances (Reed) Lemanski in 2006

Oddly enough, when I tried to find the marriage certificate for Audrey's marriage to Joe Hayden in Mayfield (Graves County), Kentucky, (where Audrey said in her divorce documents the marriage took place) with the date Audrey provided in her divorce documents, August 18, 1940, they had no record of it. They suggested I check neighboring counties. I had previously checked McCracken, Marshall, and Ballard counties with no record found there either. The county clerk's office in Mayfield suggested I check Carlisle County, as their county seat, Bardwell, was closest to Fancy Farm. Some of the Tucker cousins, the Burgesses, were from Fancy Farm as well. Upon searching, Carlisle County found no record of the marriage either. I couldn't understand why Audrey may have lied about it on her divorce papers. What motivation would she have to lie about it? I wasn't going to search the entire state of Kentucky county by county to find Audrey's second marriage record, it wasn't important enough. It was just important to verify that what Audrey put down on her divorce documents may not have been accurate, for some unknown reason. Why Joe and Audrey married in Kentucky is beyond my understanding. Frances, Audrey's daughter, says that Audrey and Joe never lived in Kentucky during their marriage, so perhaps Audrey and Joe were just visiting their parents there at the time, and decided to get married there on the spur of the moment. What county they got their marriage license in remains a mystery.

Audrey needed the divorce from Joe Hayden in July 1969 since she wanted to marry Leon, at least legitimately. Nell was gone by then, and the road was cleared for Leon and Audrey to legitimize their relationship, or at least be married in the open. This might have been because Joe Hayden was still alive in 1969, didn't die until about 1985, and might have brought their bigamy to light if she had married Leon without divorcing him first and he got word of it. Who knows why Audrey would have stayed married to Joe Hayden all those years while living with Leon? Perhaps Audrey didn't want to lose the insurance rights over Joe Hayden. Those would be hers as his legal wife, or perhaps for the tax benefits—only Audrey could have answered why it took her so long to divorce Joe Hayden. It did raise the specter of one thing unusual—Leon was married to another woman and living with Audrey, Audrey was married to another man and living with Leon, for roughly thirty years prior to them marrying each other, at least formally. Audrey knew that Leon was married, maybe not at first when the relationship started, but definitely later she knew, because she accidentally met Nell, Leon's wife. It is unknown if Leon knew of Audrey's continuing marriage to Hayden while Leon and Audrey lived together for roughly thirty years. She may have told him she was already divorced, when she wasn't. This story got more bizarre the more I investigated it.

Frances next told me about her brother Harold's death in 1989. My father, Frank, always hated Harold, thought he was slimy. Harold had been injured in a construction accident sometime in the late 1980s, and had won a personal injury settlement of around $300,000. He said he was going to use it to pay back his mother Audrey $25,000 he had borrowed from her. Harold's wife, Gloria, boiled over in anger when she heard Harold intended to pay the borrowed money back to his mother, Audrey. Shortly before receiving the money, Harold was found shot through the head in his bedroom. Gloria claimed it was a suicide, and the coroner's inquest ruled it as such, since only Gloria was allowed to testify. Audrey and Frances were not allowed to testify. Both Audrey and Frances were convinced Harold did not kill himself, but rather Gloria killed him or arranged to have it done.

They reasoned why would he kill himself if he was coming into a lot of money in a few days? That argument made sense to me also. Gloria tried to reason that suicidal tendencies ran in the family, since Harold's father Michael Reed had tried to commit suicide with oven gas unsuccessfully. Leaving the coroner's inquest that day, when Frances and Audrey tried to speak to Gloria on the courthouse steps, Gloria began to beat Audrey with her purse, swinging at her side to side, until the courthouse guards came out and told them to disperse or they would be arrested. Gloria had Harold's remains cremated immediately after the coroner's inquest was over. Frances thought it was to hide any evidence any future autopsy might reveal. No autopsy was performed, and no police investigation was ever conducted into Harold Reed's death, just a coroner's inquest. Frances said Gloria remarried several times after Harold died in 1987. Gloria died around 2005, living in Ohio at the time. Frances said she was glad Gloria moved out of Illinois because she "hated her guts." Gloria and Audrey would eventually be buried in the same Belleville cemetery, a few years and a few hundred feet apart.

Frances told me that a drunken Leon once took the car keys of her future husband, Ed Lemanski, and drove his car into a telephone pole, smashing up the front of it. This one story helps me date how far back Leon and Audrey were a couple. If Frances was nineteen years old when she got married, and this story took place just before she got married, and Frances was born in 1927, then this story had to have taken place in 1946. That proved that Leon was seeing Audrey at least as far back as 1946. Frances told me it was even further than that, since Leon had sent items and mail while he was in the military to Audrey. That put Leon and Audrey's relationship back as far as early 1943, since that is when Leon was drafted into the army.

I discovered paper documentation that in 1951 Leon was living with Audrey, not just memories from people who knew them then. Leon owned property at 1225 N. Fifty-second Street in East St. Louis and kept a trailer on it. According to the East St. Louis city directory for the previous year, 1950, no address was listed for "Leon Tucker" elsewhere in East St. Louis, and his place on Fifty-second Street was being occupied by a man named Charles Payne. That name would surface again in 1969 as the man residing at that residence. Leon still owned it, wouldn't sell it until later years, but was allowing someone else to live there, presumably a friend to whom he rented it. Frank listed his home address with the University of Kentucky as 1132 N. Forty-second Street in East St. Louis in 1951, which was Audrey's house. Frank's college transcript from 1951 was the paper proof I needed to establish Leon and Audrey's cohabitation as far back as 1951. The college tuition bills were sent to that address because Leon was paying those, and Frank knew that Leon was living there with Audrey. That situation had to be with Frank's full knowledge and without apparent objection. That was established by the fact he would send his mail there. If he objected to Leon living with another woman in East St. Louis while his mother (and Leon's legal wife) lived alone in Paducah, then he certainly wouldn't have had his mail sent to the "other woman's" house. Since Leon was paying for some of Frank's college expenses, Frank couldn't have objected even if he had wanted to.

I suspect Leon most probably met Audrey during the 1941 to 1942 time frame. Both worked at Hunter Meat Packing during this time period. It's a reasonable assumption they met there at that time. Frances thought they might have met through Claud Marshall, Audrey's twin brother, who worked with Leon in the Local 100 Laborer's Union. Leon definitely knew Audrey by 1943 when he left for basic training in the military, as he began to send her notes and gifts. Since Audrey's marriage to Joe Hayden didn't last more than a year in the earliest part of the 1940s, she would have been available to meet Leon during this time frame.

I asked Frances if she knew of the story of Leon tying Audrey to an apple tree and shooting an apple of her head. She said she didn't witness that herself, but believed it to be true, since her mother told it to her. I asked her why would Audrey stay with a man that would do that to her, and she said because Audrey genuinely loved Leon. To Audrey, Leon was such a good-looking man when he was young, bigger-than-life, manly, masculine, and very strong, both physically and personality-wise. To Audrey, such a man was hard to resist, even if he was violent at times. Frances said Leon was violent with Audrey, leaving her eyes blackened sometimes. Frances told me the police came to her house once and asked her if she was Audrey's daughter. She said she was, and they told her she needed to pick up Audrey at the local hospital. Audrey had been found on the side of the road. She had been beaten up badly, thrown out of a moving car, and left for dead. Frances knew Leon had done it.

One of my last visits with Frances was in late June 2006. She welcomed me into her house, this time with her daughter Vicki Rose joining us. This time she gave me two souvenir pillowcases from Ft. Shelby, Mississippi, where she says Leon was stationed in 1943 as part of basic training in a tank division. It matched the group photo she had given me earlier of that tank battalion, which apparently showed Leon in the picture, even though I have yet to find any documentation of his service there from the military. One of the pillowcases was a love letter of sorts, with a saying printed on it begging his girlfriend to write to him. The fact that Leon sent these to Audrey in 1943 clearly indicates Leon and Audrey were a couple by this time.

In this June 2006 visit, Frances told me she had a specific memory of Audrey attending Nell's funeral in 1969, and that Audrey kept "something" from it, most likely a prayer card that is commonly given out to those attending a funeral. On the prayer card is the deceased's name, birth and death dates, and a Christian prayer. Frances was positive she'd seen that in her mother's possessions, and was going to look for it to give to me. It surprised me that Audrey would attend Nell's funeral and then keep a souvenir from it all her life. Frances remembers taking Audrey to the bus station in East St. Louis many times to send her to Paducah when Leon called for her to come down there. This time, in 1969, after hearing of Nell's death, it fits that Audrey, if she wasn't already down in

Florida waiting, would have traveled from East St. Louis to Paducah by bus to attend Nell's funeral. If Audrey was already in Florida when Nell died, she traveled back from Florida to Paducah with Leon for Nell's funeral. Immediately after Nell's funeral, Audrey went with Leon to Okeechobee, Florida, to finish Leon's January fishing vacation. This is known from a firsthand witness in Okeechobee, Eddie Stevenson.

Frances also said she would continue to look for the marriage record of Leon and Audrey. She couldn't be sure where the marriage took place, and neither could her daughter, Vicki (Lemanski) Rose. But they both knew it didn't take place in St. Clair County, Illinois, or they would have attended the wedding. They both said the wedding must have been a justice of the peace wedding, rather than a church ceremony. During our visit I think Vicki figured out something from the context of what I was saying that she didn't know previously—Leon hadn't divorced his first wife when he was with Audrey. Vicki asked me with this wide-eyed, raised-eyebrow look of suspicion and foreboding on her face, "You mean Tucker never divorced Nell?" I quietly said no, like I was revealing something I knew she didn't want to hear. Why, I don't know, it was her grandmother, not her, that was involved in it. She called Leon "Tucker" as Audrey always did.

Evidently, Leon and Audrey had told her kids that Leon was divorced. Obviously they saw Leon living with Audrey, so for "looks" purposes they had to tell the grandkids that Leon was divorced. Living together unmarried was bad enough, but living with a married man would have raised too many eyebrows. Audrey certainly knew Leon was married, and I suspect Frances and Harold knew as well. But the grandchildren didn't have any business knowing. I'm quite certain they were never told and made the assumption Leon was divorced, or perhaps Leon and Audrey actually lied to them about it. Vicki looked pained and embarrassed when I told her Leon never divorced Nell. I tried to put her at ease by discussing how the people of that time thought of divorce as gargantuan—*way* more serious than its thought of nowadays. I told her not to worry about it—it couldn't matter now since all the players were now gone.

I told Frances and Vicki I had searched for the marriage record in the two obvious places, McCracken County, Kentucky, and St. Clair County, Illinois, with no results. Frances and I discussed the possibility that the marriage took place at Grand Tower, Illinois, or perhaps in Florida, both vacation destinations for Leon and Audrey. Those were my next steps in the search for the elusive marriage record. I began to ponder if the marriage record was being hidden from me intentionally for some reason, like the marriage of Leon and Audrey occurred before Nell's death, establishing bigamy. I couldn't know until the marriage record was found. I decided I'd also try contacting the Social Security Administration to see when Audrey's last name was changed to "Tucker," and what documents were submitted to make that name change.

The Social Security Administration wrote back to me. The first several letters seeking the specific information yielded the wrong information being sent to me. With persistence, finally, I got the right information sent to me. According to their records, Audrey changed her name on her file with them from Audie Hayden to Audie Tucker on January 13, 1973. They said that Audrey would have been required to show proof, such as a marriage certificate or driver's license, to justify the name change on her Social Security account. But I already knew that she had taken the Tucker name years earlier from the Florida property records of the Ft. Meade vacant lot that she and Leon owned together. On the sales record from that property, Leon sold that property back to the Stevenson family on April 10, 1971, and that record showed the name Audrey Tucker, with her signature. So Leon and Audrey's marriage had to have taken place prior to that date. I still had no proof though that it occurred prior to Nell's death on January 6, 1969. Why was this marriage record so hard to find?

If Leon and Audrey married legally after Nell died, then it's logical they would have married where it was the simplest and quickest for them, in either East St. Louis (St. Clair County, Illinois) where they lived at the time, or in Paducah (McCracken County, Kentucky) where they intended to build their retirement home. They would have had no motivation to go far away to marry, and they weren't the traveling kind, except to Florida so Leon could fish on Lake Okeechobee. I checked St. Clair County, McCracken County, and three bordering counties to McCracken; Marshall, Graves, and Ballard counties. No record found. I checked St. Louis city and St. Louis County in Missouri, and then did a statewide search of all of Missouri for the record. No record found. I contacted Jackson County, Illinois, which contains Grand Tower. No record found. I checked the entire state of Mississippi, as I was told that people got married in Mississippi easily during the 1900s so many out-of-state people traveled great distances to get married there. My own father, Frank Tucker, eloped with his first wife, Maudine Pruitt, to get married in Mississippi. No record found. I checked the entire state of Florida, with four combinations of their formal names (Elbert and Audie) and common names (Leon and Audrey). No record found. I checked with the Office of Vital Records in Louisville, Kentucky, for a statewide search of all counties in Kentucky. They could perform such a search from 1958 forward in time, but not before 1958. No record found. So at least I knew that Leon and Audrey were not married in Kentucky anytime after 1957. Before 1958, I would have to check county by county in Kentucky.

Obviously, since I had checked all of the easy places for Leon and Audrey to have married, this told me that Leon and Audrey were married in a place difficult to get to for them, thus requiring effort. That effort had to be exerted for a reason. I theorized that reason could have been because they were concealing something they didn't want anyone to know, like marrying before Nell died, thus establishing bigamy. It made sense if I made that assumption. I always wondered why Audrey stayed with Leon for roughly thirty years before Nell died. Would any woman stay with a man that long on the promise he would someday marry her when his wife died? Exactly what was the attraction that kept Audrey on the hook all those years? Leon wasn't a rich man, wasn't particularly handsome in my opinion (Frances said Audrey thought Leon was handsome), and was known to be hyper-violent at times. He nearly beat Audrey to death several times. Why did she stay with him all those years if he hadn't married her yet? I began searching Illinois records county by county, trying to find this perplexing marriage record.

Quite by accident, and being simultaneously climactic and anticlimactic for different reasons, in October 2006 I finally located the marriage record, and it raised as many questions as it answered. I found it by searching county by county in Illinois, writing to each county clerk for the searching, and also writing to the Illinois State Archives for a statewide search of their limited records, which were not complete (1964 to present only). Both Randolph County in southwestern Illinois and the Illinois State Archives responded on the same day and had located the record. Leon married Audrey on September 19, 1969, some nine months after Nell's death in January 1969. So at least by this record, Leon and Audrey were not bigamists in the formal, legal sense. This does not address their roughly thirty-year cohabitation prior to this marriage, clearly establishing a common-law marriage. Most states respect a common-law marriage after a cohabitation of a man and a woman of about seven years. I could prove that Leon was living with Audrey from 1951 onward with paper documentation. Frank's college transcript address in 1951 was Leon's legal address at Audrey's because he was paying Frank's college bills. Family memories date the beginning of Leon and Audrey's cohabitation to 1941 or 1942, but at the very latest 1946 when Leon returned from World War II. This cohabitation establishing a common-law marriage could have easily been proven in court, thus making it impossible for Leon to allow Nell to divorce him.

The marriage record finally being located was anticlimactic in that I was expecting to find that Leon had married Audrey much earlier, most probably 1946 when Leon was notified by the tuberculosis sanitarium that Nell was likely dying. Tillie remembered that her entire family believed Leon had married Audrey at that time since he wasn't by Nell's bedside as she was dying, or so they thought she was. Nell, of course, didn't die at that time, but her doctor's thought she would and told Leon that, so Leon would have believed Nell was dying. It's conceivable if he was waiting for that to happen to marry Audrey, he would have chosen this time to rush off and marry Audrey. Perhaps Leon in a moment of clarity realized he simply couldn't marry Audrey legally until Nell died, as this marriage record appears to indicate.

Leon and Audrey's marriage was apparently a wedding in front of a justice of the peace in the small town of Chester, which is located on Highway 3 about two-thirds of the distance to Grand Tower from East St. Louis. It's approximately sixty miles and a ninety-minute drive from East St. Louis to Chester. Chester is about thirty-three miles from Grand Tower, and a forty-five-minute drive. Since Highway 3 winds through some small towns, one can't drive as fast as on an interstate, thus explaining the longer drive time than normal for these distances. It's logical Leon and Audrey would have married in Chester on their way to or from Grand Tower. Why they elected to marry there instead of East St. Louis where it would have been much easier remains a mystery. They certainly had the legal right to marry at that time since Nell was dead, so there was no motivation for the secrecy or the distant marriage location. Perhaps they got married on a spur of the moment in an impulsive, spontaneous act? Since both were in their late fifties at that time and had been together for roughly thirty years, it's hard for me to believe they were swept away with romance.

There had to be a reason why Leon and Audrey married in Chester at that time, and not in East St. Louis. Vicki Rose thought it might have been because Audrey's brother Claud retired there where his in-laws were at, and Audrey went there to visit from time to time. That sounded a bit weak as the excuse why someone would travel a great distance to get married there. That might prove too hard a mystery for me to solve. The State Archives sent me a certified, stamped Verification of Marriage, but Randolph County would only send me a letter verifying the date of the marriage, not a copy of the actual certificate. Randolph County said I had to wait fifty years after the marriage for a certificate copy for nonlegal purposes, despite all the parties being deceased. That made no sense to me and sounded like an anal, bureaucratic rule. The Veteran's Administration finally sent me a copy of the marriage certificate, which was in their file of claims submitted by Audrey after Leon died.

Regarding Leon and Audrey's elusive marriage license, in total I probably spent the better part of the year, many hours writing letters, and probably over $500 in fees searching for this marriage record. It was sitting in an obscure location; a small, rural Illinois county, where neither Leon nor Audrey were born, had ever lived, ever worked, ever owned property, or ever vacationed at. How could anybody know to look there for it? It could only be uncovered by accident or in a county-by-county statewide search of Illinois. My determination to find it paid off by uncovering what obviously Leon and Audrey made great efforts to conceal. This was an addition to the long list of mysteries of Leon Tucker's life. Leon always had a plan for everything—did nothing on a whim. There was a reason for this Chester marriage—the date and the location—of that I was sure.

How did I feel now that I had found the record after all this searching? I felt relieved that Leon hadn't actually, legally married Audrey prior to Nell dying, at least by the records I had found to date. If Leon had married Audrey earlier, and this later marriage was a "clean-up" type marriage to make the legal documents appear proper, I couldn't know this unless I found another record of an earlier marriage. An earlier marriage would explain why Audrey stayed with him all those decades. This 1969 marriage would have been done to create the necessary paperwork for Leon and Audrey to apply for Social Security benefits as a married couple, and file taxes jointly as a married couple. They couldn't have done those things with a marriage document that predated Nell's death. Somebody somewhere in a government office (e.g. Social Security, IRS, etc.) might have noticed the date on any earlier marriage certificate that was dated prior to Nell's death in January 1969, so Leon and Audrey needed a marriage certificate after that date. Such unwanted attention to their first marriage date might have generated a visit by law enforcement. Leon and Audrey would have needed to marry (again) in 1969 so Leon could continue to file income tax returns as a married man. As a widower, he would pay a higher rate of taxes by losing the exemption of a spouse.

Of course this is all speculation unless an earlier marriage document could be found. At this point in time, Frances and her children were not producing it for me, whether intentionally or by lack of interest in searching for it. I couldn't be sure of which was the case. I stopped looking for the proof of an earlier marriage after I received this 1969 marriage certification. It wasn't worth the effort. But even if I assumed this 1969 marriage was their only marriage, it didn't erase their common-law marriage, just legitimized it by "putting it on the books." Leon and Audrey were still bigamists, in my opinion and the opinions of others in my family (Tillie, Mildred, etc.). I've proven they were married to separate people when they began their long-term relationship and cohabitation in the early 1940s that lasted until 1969, when they formally married. Some would argue that this made Audrey only a "mistress." But full-time cohabitation including a sexual relationship beyond seven years in most states establishes a common-law marriage, and clearly Audrey and Leon's relationship qualified.

After getting all I could from Frances's recollections of Audrey and Leon, it triggered many of my own memories of Audrey. I can remember at the time of Leon's death in 1987, she was telling people just before he died, "I'm gonna decide where that man is buried." Nell had already been buried at Mt. Kenton Cemetery in Paducah, and the joint headstone already showed Leon's name with no death date yet. On the back of the stone are the inscriptions and grave sites of Leon's brother Rob and his wife Gert. It was always known Leon wanted to be buried there next to Nell and his brother Rob. But Audrey was saying she wanted to bury him somewhere else where she could be next to him. She didn't get her wish.

Just before Leon died in 1987, Frances was at the hospital, Lourdes Hospital in Paducah, saying to the doctors, "Don't do anything to keep him alive." Leon was dying of blood clots and general cardiac failure and was unconscious. Frank heard about this comment Frances made and was infuriated. He told her it wasn't her father, she wasn't blood related to him, and had no business discussing with Leon's physician what treatment he was to receive. It was, in fact, Audrey's right as Leon's wife to make those medical decisions, and perhaps Frank had a right to influence those choices as Leon's son, but Frances definitely had no say in the matter. Apparently she didn't understand that. Frank always hated Frances, and you could see from the looks and the body language the feeling was mutual. Frances would have been approximately sixty years old at the time of Leon's death.

I remember at Leon's funeral, which I attended, Frances insisted that her family ride with Audrey in the funeral home's limousine, instead of Frank, Leon's son, riding in it with Audrey. Frank drove himself that day to the cemetery. At the conclusion of the funeral ceremony, I saw Audrey lean into the casket and kiss Leon's forehead, and she was crying. It showed me she really did love him, which some in our family had doubted. Frank was fighting to control his tears, not wanting to express them in public. He wasn't successful in controlling all of them. A singer from the chorus at the Eastside Holiness Church in Paducah, the church Leon attended and where the funeral ceremony was conducted, sang the gospel hymn "Crossing the River Jordan" for Leon. It was his favorite song from church services. The song tells of passing into eternity and going to God. The register from Leon's funeral visitation shows Bert Mitchell being the first signature, which was his nature. Bert felt such a strong identification with his Tucker heritage, he attended all of the funerals and other family events of all of his Tucker cousins. Bert was always the first to arrive and the last to leave, making sure not to miss talking with anybody and everybody that attended.

Originally Leon had a will drawn up, leaving all of his assets to his son, my father, Frank, and nothing to Harold and Frances. Audrey would leave her assets to them, and that would be the fair distribution of their assets. Audrey had her own money and pensions from her work at Hunter's Meat Packing plant in East St. Louis. To my knowledge Leon and Audrey's financial assets were never co-mingled with the exception of their house in Paducah. Audrey always used to say, "I matched Leon dollar for dollar on that house we built on Husband Road." No one believed it. Everyone knew that Leon had the larger stake in the house. With Leon in a declining health condition, Audrey knew it was her time to make her move. She left Leon. She abandoned him alone in Paducah and moved in with her kids near East St. Louis. She knew Leon wasn't in any state to be left alone and couldn't fend for himself. Without her, he would have had to go into a nursing home. She knew this was her trump card, as most Tucker men can't stand to be alone and are deathly afraid of nursing homes. She got her way. Leon rewrote his will, leaving all his assets to Audrey "for life," with the stipulation that after Audrey died, all of their mutual assets would be split three ways, one third to Audrey's son, Harold Reed, one third to Audrey's daughter, Frances (Reed) Lemanski, and one third to my father, Frank Tucker.

Sometime after the showdown over the will, Frank and our family were going to visit Leon and Audrey again. We made visits to them about once every other month. It was a five-hour drive from our home in central Illinois to Paducah where Leon and Audrey lived, so it couldn't have been just a day trip. It had to be a weekend-long visit. When we arrived, we had the unpleasant surprise that Audrey had quickly gotten her son Harold and his family down there as well (they lived close to East St. Louis at the time, a three-hour drive to Paducah). Apparently Audrey didn't want to be there alone with us Tuckers all there at the same time. She particularly didn't want Leon to be alone with Frank. She figured Frank would get Leon off alone and talk him into changing the will again, but couldn't do that if Harold stuck to Leon like a Siamese twin. Frank was trapped, we all were, and we at least had to stay the night because it was too late in the day to head back for home. Staying in a motel that night in Paducah would look like an insult to Leon, so we had to stay the night at his house, despite not wanting to be around Harold and his family.

We weren't snobs about Harold and his family. There was good reason for not wanting their company. Frank always felt Harold "put shit on for him," in Frank's words, meaning taunted Frank or talked about things he knew would bother Frank, intentionally trying to irritate him. Both men clearly didn't like each other. In Leon's kitchen, I remember Harold smiling big and saying, "Well, Frankie, everythin' ya ever touched turned to shit, didn' it?" It was a joke on Frank's job, said in a joking manner as cover for Harold's real intent, which was to needle Frank in the side. At the time, Frank was a supervisor of a wastewater treatment plant, a leading position at a large public municipality, which was at least as much or even more respectable than anything Harold could show for himself in his lifetime. Harold was a construction laborer, and not even a leader at that. Leon laughed along at Frank's (his son's) expense, agreeing with Harold, and paraphrased the statement again. Leon was pretending to support and agree with Harold so that he could ingratiate himself to Harold. Why? I don't know. I speculate it was for peace purposes between him and Audrey, since they had just went through the short separation over the specifics of Leon's will.

Right after Harold and Leon said their insulting jibe to Frank, Judy (Frank's wife) jumped to his defense. She said, "That's not true, Harold and Leon, Frank has made a big success of himself!" That was true—he had. Frank was at that point in time making significantly more money than Leon or Harold would ever make in their lifetimes. He was in a leader position that neither Leon nor Harold would equal in their lifetimes. Showing class and maturity, Frank just softly hushed Judy, letting them have their laugh at his expense. That night since all the beds in the house were taken by the adult couples, all the kids had to sleep in Leon's Shasta camper parked in the backyard. This was the same camper Nell had died inside in Florida in 1969. I didn't know that at the time, but it gives me chills now to remember that.

The following morning things ignited. Previous to this weekend, Frank had offered to buy a small fishing boat from Leon, but Leon refused. During this later visit, Leon was giving it to Harold for free, and Frank saw that. It made Frank furious. But rather than explode on the spot, Frank just calmly told Judy and his teenage kids, including me, to get in the car. Frank then told them we were leaving just to go shopping in Paducah and would be back, but Gloria, Harold's wife, suspected we were leaving for good. She even came to the door to plead with Frank not to leave. We drove the five hours home. We weren't home more than thirty minutes before Leon called on the phone, worried about where we were. Frank told him we were home already. It was the first and only time I would ever hear Frank lose his temper with Leon. He yelled into the phone, "Ya gave that boat to Harold for nuthin' when I offered to buy it from ya! Ya ain't never loved me! No, I ain't after ya money! Thar's other people after ya money—that's for damn sure!" From the context of what I was hearing Frank say, I could surmise that Leon said on the phone to Frank something like, "I thought ya's after ma' money." To Leon, money was the motivation for everything. There couldn't be a family love motivation for why Frank wanted to visit with his father—it had to be because Frank wanted his money. This situation similarly and eerily repeated itself years later when I would visit Leon on my own, with Leon suggesting that my motivation for visiting him, my grandfather, was because I wanted his money. In this phone call this day, Frank was standing up to Leon for perhaps the first time ever, from the safety of 220 miles away. Leon and Frank patched things up later on, but things were never the same between them. On subsequent visits, Audrey never pulled that trick again of having her kids down there visiting at the same time we visited.

Even though Leon had signed a will leaving all his assets to Audrey "for life" with a three-way split to follow Audrey's death between Frances, Harold, and Frank, Leon still had a private agreement with Frank for a direct transfer of some money he had in a bank in Paducah. I think Leon thought Audrey didn't know about these accounts. He was wrong. The owner of the certificates was Leon, but he designated it "POD Frank Tucker" meaning "payable upon death to Frank Tucker." With that designation, the money was to be transferred outside of a will. It sidestepped any probate of an estate of Leon's assets after his death. The Certificates of Deposit were entirely typewritten in all the entry locations and signed by the bank. Where Frank Tucker's name was at, indicating the payee upon the death of the owner, Elbert (Leon) Tucker, Frank's name was hand-crossed off, and handwritten next to it was the name "Audrey Tucker." This whole thing was fishy, with the crossing off and substitution of names in handwriting. It stank to high heaven.

Just prior to Leon's death, he had been losing his clarity of mind for about a year. Frank had sued in McCracken County Court for guardianship of him, not trusting that Audrey would take care of him. Also if Audrey had been appointed his guardian, which she was seeking to be as would be expected being his wife, Audrey could then pass all of their assets to her kids from her first marriage, Harold and Frances. She could do this asset transfer even before Leon died, and there would then be nothing on the books as mutual assets of Leon and Audrey's when Leon died. The three-way split feature of Leon's will would therefore be null and void, since the assets wouldn't exist at the time of Leon's death. Frank feared he would lose everything that was destined for him from Leon's assets. Frank eventually had to drop his lawsuit for guardianship of Leon, because Leon ordered him to. Audrey called our house one day and put Leon on the phone with Frank. Leon said to Frank, "Audrey is all upset, son. Jus' call it off." Then Audrey got on the phone with Frank and yelled, "Do ya har that, Frankie? That's yer Paw tellin' ya that!" Frank had no choice but to comply. Audrey knew she had to pull out all the stops because the end game was near, the stakes were the highest, and she had to go for it if she intended to win. She played hardball.

After Leon died, Audrey was still so furious at Frank for suing to get guardianship of Leon, that she didn't let Frank have anything of Leon's belongings, not even the smallest of mementos—absolutely nothing. We didn't hear that Audrey had died (in 1999) until a few years after it had happened, and we were never contacted about any of her (and Leon's) assets that were due to come to Frank. I actually have a copy of Leon's will and could pursue collection of that "one-third" due to Frank, but decided to table all of that until I finished my interviews with Frances. I'd decide later on if it was worth pursuing or not. I needed to concentrate on one thing at a time.

After Leon died in June 1987, Audrey sold the house on Husband Road in Paducah and moved back to Caseyville, Illinois, just outside of East St. Louis, to be near all of her children and grandchildren that lived there. That made sense for her. Less than three years after Leon's death, Frances got Audrey to sign over to her a complete power of attorney in March 1990, covering all financial and medical matters. Two years later, Frances placed Audrey in a nursing home in Caseyville in March 1992. Audrey died there in the nursing home in December 1999.

Much to my surprise, Joe Reed, Audrey's grandson and Harold Reed's son, contacted me one day out of the blue. Apparently he worked with Walter Abernathy at the Local 100 Laborer's Union, and I had spoken with Walter a month or so prior about Leon Tucker (Leon). He told Joe that "Big Tuck's grandson was looking for stories on him" and suggested Joe give me a call. Joe remembered me, and I remembered him, from when we were kids and occasionally both families would be visiting Leon and Audrey's house at the same time. He was one of the Reed kids that I actually bunked in Leon's tiny Shasta camper together with, separate beds of course, during one of those visits.

Harold and Gloria Reed originally had three boys and two girls that I knew of. Two of the boys were dead, dying young from accidents, leaving Joe and the two girls, Carrie and Tammy, still alive. Joe was two years older than me, forty-four years old when I spoke with him in 2006. He confirmed for me that Leon and Audrey met each other at Hunter's Meat Packing in East St. Louis in the early 1940s and dated for roughly thirty years until Leon's wife (and my grandmother) Nell died in 1969. He said Leon used to live in a shack behind Audrey's house on Forty-second Street in East St. Louis, leaving his trailer on the lot he owned on Fifty-second Street open for Frank or the Tucker cousins to use. I rather think the "shack" story was cover Leon and Audrey told their grandkids to keep from looking immoral by living together unmarried.

Joe had a lot of details of how Leon was injured in World War II, and when he told them to me, it jogged my own memory of Leon telling me the same stories. I hadn't remembered them before Joe said them to me. Leon told us he went through Omaha Beach in Normandy shortly after D-day, and everyone else in his landing boat died. He fought all the way across France and ended up getting shot in the knee outside Aachen, Germany, just before the Battle of the Bulge at the same location began. This specific injury, getting shot in the knee, markedly differed from the story the Tucker cousins told me that Leon had told them how he was injured in World War II, which was by a German .80 shell blowing up in his machine gunner's nest. At the time I thought perhaps a combination of the two stories is what really happened. They aren't entirely mutually exclusive stories.

Joe told me his father Harold told him he fought Leon once so long that it ended up with a knife pulled by one and a gun pulled by the other, and Audrey stepping between them to get them to stop before one of them would be killed. I doubted this story since Harold was so small in stature and Leon so big and brawny, Leon could have snapped Harold like a twig. But Harold was fast because he was small, so I don't doubt he could outrun Leon to escape his fury. I seriously doubt he held his own with Leon in a fight though, because Leon could have swatted him like a fly with minimal effort. From as much experience at fighting all his life that Leon had, there were few men that could hold their own with him. I think this was more probably some exaggeration on Harold's part telling the story to his son, and perhaps Audrey stepped in to save her son's life before Leon, seeing blood red, killed him. Charles Stevenson witnessed this fight between Harold and Leon, and said Leon almost killed Harold that day.

Joe recounted how he used to go hunting with Leon, Frank, and others near Grand Tower, at areas with such colorful names as Oakwood Bottoms, Wolf Lake, and Turkey Bayou. Joe remembered that in the Local 100 Laborer's Union he and Leon worked, "doby money" was paid by each worker to the union hall to keep it going, and then the "busman's fare" was what each worker paid to the "business agent," or "BA," or to the job foreman, whoever booked the workers for the job. The busman's fare was basically a bribe to get the work, or a "commission," if you want to call it that.

Joe recounted for me when he and Leon, along with his father Harold, my father Frank, and a few others would go "frogging" near Grand Tower, which meant hunting for frogs. Also called "frog giggin'," this was the process of flashing a light in the eyes of frogs after dark, and that would cause them to freeze in place. You could then just reach down and pick them up. The light hypnotized the frogs. Joe said the game wardens were frequently around, enforcing the limit of six frogs per hunter, but Leon often found a way around this limit. He would have cages for the frogs hidden near the riverfront, and not camp near the cages. Joe said Leon would have sometimes two hundred frogs in the cages. Sometimes the cages would be empty when they would come back to get their catches, because snakes would have eaten all the captive frogs. So many snakes would be around the cages it sometimes was impossible for Leon to approach the cages to get the frogs. Joe said he loved the taste of deep-fried frog legs or frog backs.

From Joe I got the contact information for his two sisters, Tammy (Reed) Grubbs and Carrie (Reed) Bell. I spoke with Tammy by phone to her home in Florida, and despite being the oldest of the remaining siblings, she couldn't remember much about Leon and Audrey, or if she did remember, wasn't willing to share it. She did verify that her side of Audrey's descendant family broke with the other side, the Lemanskis, over Harold's death and the accusations flying back and forth about how he died. I had better luck reaching Carrie Bell in Illinois, who despite being the youngest of all of Harold's children, seemed to remember quite a lot.

She said she had been Leon's favorite when she and her siblings were growing up in the sixties and seventies, with Leon nicknaming her "Baby Girl." She remembers that she always thought Leon was her real grandfather until she was about sixteen years old, when her mother finally told her he wasn't. Being born in 1966, she never knew a time when Leon wasn't in Audrey's life. She remembered that her mother, Gloria, had spoken often about Leon and Audrey being together before World War II, in the early 1940s. She said Leon was always kind with her and taught her how to jug fish and shoot rifles, activities usually reserved for boys. She remembers on one of the fishing trips to the Land between the Lakes in Kentucky, she wanted to use the outhouse, but a possum was inside, and Leon, whom she also called "Papaw," got it out for her. She said Leon named a tree he had planted at his Paducah home after Carrie, and she returned the favor by naming one of her twin sons Brenden Leon. The children of Harold and Gloria always referred to Audrey as "Deedee," a nickname much like my nickname for Nell being "Peepeyes."

Carrie remembered Leon and her father Harold along with Larry Green shooting their rifles at "blacks" in East St. Louis for "fun." Carrie also remembers an incident where Harold got into a fight at a bar near East St. Louis called the Waterhole, and hit someone in the head with a barstool. The police were called, Harold was arrested on the spot, and handcuffed. Before the police could take him away, Leon was called by a friend, and arrived at the Waterhole. He argued with the policeman, who happened to be an African-American. He demanded that he let Harold go and let him take him home. Finally, Leon's temper broke, and he screamed at the black policeman, "Why ya liver-lipped, lily-suckin', son-of-a-bitchin' nigger!" Evidently the policeman assessed he had a crazy white man standing in front of him, probably more trouble than the situation was worth to him, so he took the handcuffs off of Harold and let him go. Carrie remembers this incident in particular since she was in the car when Leon went to get Harold that night. From her age estimate, this event is roughly placed around 1974. From that day on, Harold remembered that phrase of Leon's, and repeated over and over.

AUDRA: The next Tucker wife I spoke with was Audra Lance, my father Frank's third wife. Lance was her first married name, her maiden name was Audra Nichols, daughter of James Nichols and Beedie (Merritt) Nichols, of southern Illinois. Audra married Frank on August 31, 1986, in Paducah. My parents, Frank and Judy, had only divorced one year earlier. Tillie would later tell me Frank went prowling for a new wife immediately, and tried to start things back up with his high-school sweetheart, Nadine, in Paducah. Despite having an illegitimate daughter with her, he decided not to marry Nadine again in 1985 or 1986, because, as Tillie quoted him as saying, "something is not right there," referring to Nadine. So he asked Tillie if there was someone else she knew of that Frank could date. She suggested Audra, a friend of hers, and introduced them.

I interviewed Audra first by phone in spring 2006, and then made an appointment to visit her at her home in Red Bud, Illinois. Frank and Audra divorced in 2003 (filed 2002), and divorces are never pleasant, so it surprised me she was willing to talk to me. Frank and Audra were married approximately sixteen years. A family member had sort of done her dirty by not telling her that Frank had died in October 2005. I wasn't responsible for notifying the family of Frank's death as I had done that when Judy had died in 2004. It wasn't my turn at this unpleasant task this time around. Despite the divorce, she was married to Frank for sixteen years, so in my opinion, she at least deserved to be notified of his death. So I had that unenviable task of notifying Audra when I called her to interview her about her memories of Frank and Leon. She cried a little when I told her that Frank had died some four months prior, and exclaimed, "Why didn't somebody tell me? I would have been there (at the funeral)!"

Audra Lance, Frank Tucker's third and last wife

In my first phone call with Audra, I got straight to the point, never knowing when she would cut off the conversation. I asked her to verify a story that Tillie had told me. Tillie had told me that Audra had told her about a trip to Florida she and Frank had taken in the 1990s. Audra verified the story and said when they (she and Frank) were down in Florida vacationing, Frank made a point to go out of his way over to Lake Okeechobee to the campground where his mother had died. Audra said he looked around it like he was looking for something in particular, but she didn't know what. Audra said she guessed he was trying to verify some of what Leon had told him had happened the night Nell died in 1969.

Next, Audra said they went over to the hospital in Okeechobee town. She said Frank got out of their car, intending on going in to retrieve whatever records existed of Nell's time at the hospital when she died. Audra said Frank stopped at the front door and just stood there smoking his cigarettes for about an hour without moving. She said he came back to the car, never having gone into the building. At the car, he had a white, ashen look on his face and said, "I don't want to know this. If my father killed my mother, I don't want to know it." Audra felt it was too much for Frank to know if his father killed his mother—it would have hurt him too badly, perhaps even killed him to know it. Audra said from time to time he would "do more" investigation on the issue, but always stopped short of finding the actual evidence. She was sure he was afraid to learn the truth, yet periodically felt compelled to pursue it. She said he said to her once, "I don't know why I didn't look into this at the time it all happened."

Talking with Audra this day jogged my memory of a conversation I hadn't previously remembered that I had with Frank. It was during my college years, and after Leon had died, so that puts the conversation somewhere between June 1987 and May 1989. I don't remember how the subject came up, but we were talking about how Nell died. He told me he had looked into her death somewhat, but decided he didn't want to know the truth, whatever that was. He told me if he had looked into it before Leon had died and found out the rumors were true, he was afraid of how he would have reacted. "I'd 'ave had to kill 'im," he said, "I'd 'ave went to jail for it. But it'd 'ave been worth it—'cause that was *my* mother (he put emphasis on "my")." He had a combination look of anger and hurt on his face when he said this—a look that was unfamiliar to me—such that it imprinted on my memory. That's why I could remember the conversation now. He meant it too—he would have had to shoot Leon. So in his mind, it was better that he didn't know for sure the truth. Even after Leon's death, it would have been too much to know, perhaps literally driving him crazy, to learn his father had killed his mother.

It also explained to me why Leon didn't confess to me that day he and I stood over Nell's grave in approximately 1985. The look on Leon's face that day I understood better now when I linked with this memory of Frank discussing how he would react to finding out the truth. At the time I didn't know what the look on Leon's face meant, but the look was like he had something he wanted to tell me, but he was keeping himself from saying it. Now I understood why Leon couldn't tell me what he wanted to tell me—because he knew it would get back to Frank. He could reasonably foresee what Frank's response would be. He couldn't risk that.

These memories and stories from Audra told me that even my father thought it was possible that Leon had killed Nell. Frank knew Leon better than anybody on the planet. If he actually thought Leon was capable of doing this to the point he would investigate it, then that told me I should also believe it was possible Leon could have done it. Previously, I didn't think it was possible for the man I knew Leon to be to have done this crime. But Frank knew him better, knew him his whole life, and saw a lot more than I did. I only saw Leon's older years.

I decided it was worth it to visit Audra in person at her home in Red Bud, Illinois, to see if she could remember more of Frank's efforts, and just in general, her recollections of the sixteen years she was married to Frank. The visit with Audra was going pleasantly to my surprise. She even fixed me a home-cooked meal of roast beef, and fresh-baked an apple pie just for me. I was touched, and I developed some respect for her. She may have wanted something from me, or just was being genuinely nice to me, I couldn't tell. She did ask me for a copy of Frank's death certificate so she could file for some type of benefit from his state government retirement account in Illinois. I told her the account had already been refunded into Frank's estate, but she said that agency notified her that the ex-spouse of Frank's was due some type of benefit independent of the general account. I didn't know if I believed that or not, so I didn't give her a copy of Frank's death certificate. Access to that death certificate was limited to family members by law, and Audra didn't qualify anymore. But she could likely get a copy from some avenue, so I let her do that on her own. Despite the suspiciousness of the retirement benefits issue, I decided to give her the benefit of the doubt that day.

Tillie and I speculated months later that Audra likely wanted the death certificate to claim the life insurance she had on Frank. During their marriage, Audra sold insurance for extra money, not full time, but part time. Frank knew at that time Audra had taken out an insurance policy on Frank, but he forgot about it at the time of their divorce. It never came up. So if Audra had kept up the payments on it, even though she and Frank were divorced, she would still be entitled to that insurance payout on Frank's death. It made sense—that's likely why she wanted the death certificate.

Audra said when she and Frank visited with Leon shortly before he died, in 1986 or 1987, that Leon scared her. She would suddenly find him looking at her when she didn't think he was—like he was thinking something about her. It made her uneasy. She said she remembered seeing Audrey, Leon's wife, being scared of him also. When Leon asked Audrey to fix something specific for dinner, Audra offered to help Audrey, but Audrey refused her offer. Audra saw Audrey's hands shaking while she cooked, and it looked like fear causing them to shake rather than old age. Audra reiterated to me that she believed Frank thought "foul play" had been at work in Nell's death in 1969.

Just before I left Audra's that day, I shared some photos of the funeral and Frank in life with Audra. She got teary-eyed when she looked at the funeral pictures. She admitted a friend in Madisonville, Kentucky, had told her two weeks after the funeral that Frank had died, which would have meant she knew as far back as November 2005. I first had called her to interview her in March 2006 and told her of Frank's death. In that call she reacted like it was the first time she had heard it and cried. Now I didn't know if that earlier reaction was fake, or this new information was wrong, or what to believe, since both could not be true. She couldn't have heard of Frank's death in November 2005, and then reacting like she heard it for the first time in March 2006. I honestly didn't know if Audra was being straight with me or not about her knowledge of Frank's death and when she found out. But about the matters regarding Leon and one other personal thing she said Frank had said about me, which was unkind, I rather think those stories of Audra's were true. She would have had no reason to lie about those.

In one of my last visits with Audra in September 2006, I dropped off a copy of a video that we found in my father's things after he died. It was a video of his and Audra's wedding in 1986. In it, Leon and Audrey appeared, as well as Audra's own mother, now deceased. Their marriage took place in August 1986, so it was less than one year before Leon died in June 1987. He looked surprisingly fit and clear-headed in the video, moving about the room with his eyes darting around as they always did—like he was looking for something familiar. He and Audrey posed with the wedding couple for photos. These photos are perhaps the last images we have of Leon alive. After Leon and Audrey moved through the reception line and greeted the newlywed couple, it is seen that Audrey whispers something to Leon, like "you forgot to . . ." Leon then maneuvers back to kiss the bride on the cheek and embrace her, like a formal welcome into the Tucker family. It is also seen how Audrey sort of maneuvers Leon into position for the posing of family pictures and rests her hand on his shoulder. This may have been the early signs of Leon's mental deterioration that came upon him in his last year, ending in a custody battle between Frank and Audrey for Leon's power of attorney.

MAUDINE: Maudine Celesta "Celeste" Pruitt was the first wife of my father, Frank Tucker. (There appears to be some difference of opinion about the spelling of Maudine's other name, so I provided both.) She was the daughter of Jess Pruitt and Inez (Low) Pruitt of Etowah, Arkansas. She died in 1992, so I couldn't speak with her directly, which I wished I could have. So I would have to be satisfied with speaking with her family instead. Frank and Maudine married on December 19, 1953, in Hernando, Mississippi, when he was twenty-two years old and she was just seventeen years old. They knew each other for about a year before. It couldn't have been more than a year because Frank had just left his girlfriend Nadine in Paducah because Leon didn't like Nadine and refused to allow Frank to marry her. Nadine was pregnant and gave birth to Frank's daughter, Sharon, in January 1953. Along about this time or late in 1952, Frank met and started dating Maudine in East St. Louis. Maudine was staying with an aunt in Belleville and met Frank there. Frank and Maudine eloped to Mississippi to get married since, at that time, getting married there was easy, no questions asked.

Frank and Audra's wedding, attended by Leon and Audrey

Their first child, a premature girl that didn't survive, Cynthia, is a bit of an enigma to both families since no one can remember exactly where she is buried. Most believe she is buried in Paducah, but which cemetery, no one can recall. Their second child, a son named Trent, followed in July 1955. Frank gave Trent his father's name, Leon, as a middle name. A divorce was begun the following year in 1956, and a bitter custody battle started in 1957. Somewhere around this time, Frank made an attempt to steal back Trent from Maudine, who had physical custody if not legal custody of him when she left Frank. This was witnessed by Marion Stamps, who is the husband of Betty (Nowak) Stamps, herself a first cousin to Frank. Frank resorted to fisticuffs with one of the Pruitt men over Trent that day when stealing him, won the battle, and left with Trent. But Maudine reported Frank to the police. The police found Frank and returned Trent to Maudine.

Leon once told the Stevensons that Maudine had tried to seduce him, as recounted to me by Eddie Stevenson. Leon said that Maudine had "tried to pull me down on top of her." None of the Stevensons believed it. Why on earth would a very young girl still in her teens, newlywed to Frank, be trying to seduce middle-aged Leon? The Stevensons knew that Leon was just expressing his own crude desires for Maudine, only reversing the direction of the advances to make himself look good. Eddie Stevenson thought that Leon's improper advances toward Maudine were probably one of the reasons that Frank and Maudine's marriage began to fail.

To discover the details of the events of Frank and Maudine's marriage and divorce, and their possible involvement of Leon and Nell Tucker, I had to first go to Trent. He was reluctant to talk about it, saying he didn't think he knew much of the specifics other than to say generally that "Leon was mean to my mother." Instead, he referred me to his aunt Peggy, Maudine's younger sister, to get the detailed history. I hit the jackpot with Peggy (Pruitt) Sheffield, as she talked for an hour and a half to me over the phone, giving me all the details, which she completely remembered down to the nitty-gritty. I was prepared to hear a very ugly story from Peggy, because I knew there was great animosity between the families—so much so it caused a break between Frank and Trent that was never bridged before Frank died in October 2005. To my surprise, Peggy was perfectly cordial with me, like she was talking with an old friend, and recounted all of the stories without holding back any of the unsavory details. A few days after speaking with Peggy, I spoke with her and Maudine's brother, Jim Pruitt. He also recounted some other stories that Peggy didn't know, and confirmed others she did know. I'll recount what each told me together rather than separately to try to stay chronological.

Peggy said that Frank and Maudine were introduced by Captola Range, who was Maudine's aunt. I smiled when I heard that name, thinking it is one of those grand old names they used to give to women back in the early 1900s, names that are completely gone now. Captola was still alive and living in Belleville, Illinois, in 2006, so I got her number from Peggy and contacted her as well. I'll include her memories mixed in with Peggy's and Jim's.

Frank and Maudine circa 1954. Handwriting on the picture is Nell's.

Peggy and Captola said at first Frank and Maudine's marriage seemed a good one. When Frank and Maudine would visit her family in Arkansas, Frank would show up with Christmas gifts for everyone. They would all be impressed with Frank's new cars each time he visited, and that Frank was always very charming. Nell and Leon were frequent visitors to the Pruitts in Arkansas, with Leon bonding with Maudine's father, Jess, by going hunting and fishing with him on Big Lake in northeast Arkansas. But then something changed in Frank and Maudine's marriage. Peggy said Frank was a violent man and very jealous, always accusing Maudine of flirting with other men. He would get angry when other men noticed her without Maudine doing anything, Peggy said, to attract their interest. From the photos we have of her, I could tell Maudine was an extremely beautiful woman, with dark hair, big green eyes, and a round face, similar to a young Ava Gardner, in my opinion. It would have been normal for her to attract the attention of men whether she tried to or not. I began to see a pattern in my father's life. He apparently liked women that resembled his mother, Nell. Nadine resembled Nell, and so did Maudine, as well as my own mother, Judy Bond. All four women had dark hair and similar facial features.

Peggy said Frank struck Maudine while she was pregnant, and at other times. She said when Trent was born in July 1955, Maudine almost bled to death from the birth, but still felt compelled to leave Frank within a month of the birth and stay with her aunt Captola in Belleville, just outside of East St. Louis. Captola remembered Frank talking to Maudine on the front lawn of her house and convincing her to return home with him. Peggy said Maudine's mother, Inez, came to visit Maudine and Frank in East St. Louis, where they were living in a garage converted to a bungalow behind Leon's trailer at 1225 N. Fifty-second Street in East St. Louis. Inez helped Maudine rearrange the living room furniture one day while Frank was at work. When Frank came home and saw the house rearranged, he became enraged and ordered Inez out of the house. This story sounded a bit incomplete to me, because I found it hard to believe that Frank would have become enraged over something so picayune, and ordered his mother-in-law out of the house. That sounded exaggerated or made-up. There are probably elements here that are missing to the story that Peggy didn't tell me or didn't know herself, since she wasn't there herself to see it and was getting the story secondhand from her mother.

Peggy said Maudine left Frank in East St. Louis and returned home to Etowah, Arkansas, with Trent. Frank went to visit Maudine and Trent in Arkansas in June of 1956 when Trent was only eleven months old. Peggy said Frank didn't like what he saw in Etowah, it being a very small village of perhaps fifty people. The living conditions were poor, and Peggy said she sensed Frank decided he didn't want his son raised in those conditions. So Frank stole Trent and returned to East St. Louis. Frank had told me once that after he took Trent, he went to Chicago to live so that Maudine and her family wouldn't know where he was and try to take Trent back again. I found in Nell's photo album one photo of Trent as a toddler on a beach in Chicago (known from Nell's handwriting on the border of the photo), so that documents this part of the story.

However, what dates this Chicago time occurred between is unclear, since so much of what was going on between Frank and Maudine was in East St. Louis during 1956.

Maudine filed for divorce and custody of Trent once Frank left with Trent. Frank joined Maudine's divorce action in a countersuit against her, and sought full custody of Trent as well. The custody hearing portion of the divorce was evidently very acrimonious. Peggy said Maudine was hit broadside, totally unprepared, with allegations she knew nothing about. Peggy said Frank had taken very intimate photos of Maudine while they were married, and showed them in court to besmirch her virtue. Frank had someone testify that he had seen Maudine soliciting. I found that hard to believe when Peggy said that to me. I know child-custody battles are horrible, and both sides make up stuff to throw at the other side, since the stakes are so high.

If Frank actually did that, made those strong allegations against Maudine, it would have been too much—over the top—crossing a line of decency. That's why I doubted it when I heard it. But I wasn't there, and Peggy was, so how can I dispute it? These events being fifty years ago, and both Frank and Maudine now dead, why would Peggy lie about it now? But then again, if you repeat a story, even a false one, to yourself enough times over the years, it begins to seem like the truth to you. This might have been an exaggeration on Peggy's part, or it could have been the truth, I might never know.

Also using reason and common sense, if Frank had actually taken those intimate photos of Maudine, then why would he show them in court? If they besmirched her virtue for posing for them, they did the same thing to Frank for having taken them in the first place, correct? So Frank would be hurting himself, as well as Maudine, by showing them in court. It didn't make any sense. This is a hole in the logic of what Peggy was telling me, and made me doubt that it was the true story. Frank wasn't here to tell me his side of the story, such as if the photos came from some other source and not taken by him, or even if they never existed at all.

What I did find odd about the subject of intimate photos is that when I went through Nell's, Frank's, and Judy's old photo albums, I didn't find any intimate photos of Maudine, but I did find them of Frank. Apparently Frank when he was a young, unmarried man in the early 1950s had posed for beefcake photos that appeared in bodybuilder magazines of that time. They were the early versions of muscle magazines that appear today, and were usually collected by men, not women. He posed in a posing strap, much like what we could call a G-string thong today. He showed everything in the photos shy of genitalia, including his buttocks, and was posing suggestively in the photos. So if Frank had posed for these photos and allowed them to be published, he certainly had no business pointing a finger at Maudine for posing for similar photos, if that even happened at all. To try to find out the truth, I sought from the St. Clair County Circuit Court records the divorce filings and legal documents still on file there regarding Maudine and Frank's divorce and custody battle from 1956 to 1957. They sent me a copy of the complete file. It revealed a lot.

Frank posing beefcake-style in the early 1950's.

The first thing I noted, was that at no time in the legal documents did Frank ever allege that Maudine was soliciting, nor was there any evidence of intimate photos of Maudine to suggest she wasn't a fit parent for Trent. There was an allegation by Frank of repeated adultery by Maudine and statements that he had repeatedly forgiven her conditional that she continue their marriage, cohabitation, and co-parenting of Trent. Frank's filing said Maudine left anyway, voiding that forgiveness. Frank also alleged Maudine repeatedly abandoned Trent to the care of others for extended periods of time. Maudine's own filings state that Frank was violent to her on three occasions, and that she left him in January 1956. Frank disputed this, saying they together left East St. Louis to move together to Paducah that January 1956 for Frank to pursue work as a railroad conductor. Frank said in his filing that Maudine didn't leave their cohabitation until April 1956. In February 1956, between those two disputed dates, Frank's filing states Frank found Trent in the care of a "nine-year-old girl at 2:00 AM . . . while the plaintiff was out with another man." I can only assume this nine-year-old girl might have been one of Maudine's younger sisters, Peggy or Patsy. Frank took the baby at that point because he felt Maudine had abandoned him. Maudine countered by filing for a temporary custody order in St. Clair County, Illinois, which was granted. But evidently Frank talked her out of that, and they resumed living together in Paducah for about two more months. Maudine left for the final time in April 1956.

Maudine's filings in this divorce involved Leon Tucker also, since he was co-owner of the 1225 N. Fifty-second Street, East St. Louis property that Maudine and Frank shared. Nell's name appears nowhere in any of the documents, suggesting to me that Leon and Nell were not living together at this time and may have been informally separated. Nowhere in Maudine's filings are there any allegations against Leon of any cruel treatment toward her, as suggested by Trent. Since he was a baby at the time, Trent could only know these cruelty allegations by what was told to him by his mother or Pruitt relation, and if this cruel treatment by Leon to Maudine were serious, she certainly would have mentioned it in her filings to the court. She didn't shy away from saying Frank was cruel to her, so she wouldn't have shied away from saying Leon had also been cruel to her if it was serious. She did not mention Leon at all, so I have to assume it wasn't serious beyond normal family interactions, which are not always pleasant. I don't doubt Leon was highly suspicious of Maudine when Frank's and her troubles began. Leon was always highly suspicious of all women and never treated any woman with respect or trust, so Maudine wouldn't have been any exception to that.

But because Maudine tried to get the Fifty-second Street property awarded to her in the divorce, Leon had to get his own lawyer, and made his own filings in the matter, some of which actually went against his own son, Frank. He said Frank never paid any part of the property they co-owned, and the co-ownership was just established so Frank could spend his money converting the garage into a bungalow for Maudine and him to share in the back of the property. Leon asked that Frank be ordered to buy him out of the property, or he be allowed to buy Frank out of it, as well as any interest Maudine would be awarded.

The filings by Maudine's lawyer seem to indicate that Leon was the corroborating witness that Maudine had repeatedly committed adultery, and they suggested he was unreliable. But what Leon testified to was that he saw Maudine in a car driven by another man in Paducah. Maudine countered in her filing that it might have been her father driving the car that Leon saw. As I cannot know who is telling the truth on this point, one thing is clear. Maudine riding in a car with another man is hardly proof of adultery. No other evidence of Maudine committing adultery was offered, at least in the court filings sent to me. What was said in court during the custody hearings is not documented in the filings sent to me, so I can't speculate on that beyond what Peggy told me. I now doubt what Peggy told me was the whole and accurate truth, and rather think it is the truth she truly believes from repeating it so many times over the years. Her allegations Frank took intimate photos of Maudine and accused her of soliciting appear to be exaggerations from the lack of documentation to back it up. These exaggerations from 1956 and perhaps in subsequent years were likely told to Trent, perhaps to poison his mind against Frank. That is also common in child-custody battles.

Peggy said Frank also testified in the custody proceedings that the living conditions in Etowah, Arkansas, (where Maudine lived) were very poor, rural, and backward, and that wasn't as good an environment and an education that Trent would get living in East St. Louis with Frank. Trent himself backed up this point to me, that he also thought the living conditions in Etowah were backward and poor, and that it "angered" him that his mother had to grow up in that environment. Nell attended the custody hearing, according to Peggy. Frank's filings said Maudine had taken residence in Memphis, Tennessee, for work, and had left Trent with her parents in Arkansas for care.

Peggy said the judge decided in favor of Frank and awarded him full custody of Trent, with visitation rights awarded to Maudine. I don't find that supported in the documents sent me from the court files, only a temporary order giving Maudine custody in February 1956. But the documents sent to me appear to be lacking the final court order, so Peggy's version on this could be the truth. Peggy remembers Maudine's family was with her at the hearing, and they all cussed out Nell and Frank in the courtroom. She said they told Frank and Nell they intended to get Trent back, and then Frank and Nell would "never see Trent again." How prophetic that was for them to say that, because that's pretty much exactly what happened. Frank began dating my mother, Judy Bond, also from East St. Louis, sometime in 1957. In July of the previous summer, 1957, Maudine and her family came to East St. Louis to give Trent a birthday party in the park. Peggy said Frank took Trent in the middle of the party because his new girlfriend Judy was throwing him a party at her house also, with Nell to also be there. The photos of this birthday party at Judy's, with Nell and Frank there, showed up in Nell's and Judy's photo albums. This apparently angered the Pruitts that they didn't get to finish their birthday party for Trent.

At sometime in 1957, Frank, Trent, Nell, and Leon were back in Paducah for a time period. The Pruitts got word from mutual friends that they were there and told them Frank was unemployed at the time. The Pruitts planned a trip to Paducah to steal Trent back. Jim Pruitt said that he, Maudine, and their father, Jess, went over to Paducah and waited outside an unemployment office for Frank to come by to pick up his unemployment check. That Frank was unemployed in Paducah is backed up with his filing to the court, where he stated he was unemployed, saying he was unable to pay for Maudine's legal costs and perhaps child support. I found this odd, since Frank was one of the most capable and ingenious men I have ever known. He was never unemployed in his lifetime that I knew him before retirement, and could easily find work as a day laborer just from his physical abilities. Therefore, this period of time in Paducah where he was unemployed may have been by choice, to artificially create the appearance that he was broke and couldn't afford to pay Maudine's legal bills or child support. It didn't seem like a smart move to make, because what judge would award custody of an infant to an unemployed single man? Perhaps the unemployment was genuine and not manufactured, but I'm suspicious of it, from my knowing Frank's nature.

During their trip to Paducah, the Pruitts planned to steal Trent out of Frank's car when Frank went into the unemployment office. When they saw Frank drive up, he was looking around expecting them, probably tipped off by the same mutual friend that was playing both sides. He left without going into the building and called the police on the Pruitts. Frank had a preexisting police order, a "warrant out for gunmen," as Jim Pruitt says. The police found them, interviewed them, found out it was a custody matter, and let them go on their way. They went back to Arkansas empty-handed. Jim says they had no guns with them. This story loosely follows the story Bert Mitchell told me of the Pruitts sending a gang of armed men to Paducah to try to steal Trent back. Whether they had guns or not, I cannot know, Jim says they didn't.

Later that year (1957), perhaps because of the Pruitts' attempt in Paducah at stealing Trent, all of the Tuckers, Leon, Nell, Frank, and Trent, moved back to East St. Louis, and Frank resumed seeing Judy. Maybe they felt the greater distance from Arkansas made it less likely the Pruitts would try again to steal Trent back. But Maudine still had a legal visitation order, so at Christmas time in 1957, Maudine made arrangements to see Trent on Christmas Day. The agreement was she would see Trent at Leon's trailer at 1225 N. Fifty-second Street in East St. Louis. Nell and Leon would be caring for Trent that day. Frank was not present. Frank was courting his next wife, my mother, Judy, at this time in 1957, and so was likely spending Christmas at her house with her parents, Glen and Ruth Bond. Glen and Ruth Bond lived at 1602 N. Park Drive in East St. Louis at that time.

My own mother, Judy, had told me that she knew that Nell had been partially siding with Maudine about the custody battle with Trent. Frank was living in his own apartment on the other side of East St. Louis, and Nell had taken an apartment nearby, living there by herself. Nell wanted to babysit Trent during the day, while Frank worked, and didn't want strangers, like a day care center, watching him. Being closer to Frank's residence allowed him to drop Trent off with Nell before going to work at the Local 100 Laborer's Union doing construction work.

Nell with Trent, October 1957.
Nell's handwriting is at top, and the photo is dated at left.

Leon was likely living with Audrey during parts of 1957. Leon evidently rented out his trailer to George Hubert, according to the East St. Louis city directory. George's name shows up at that address in the 1957 city directory, and Leon's does not. Frank's name is suspiciously absent from the East St. Louis city directory in 1957, having been listed in the previous and following editions. This was probably because Frank was gone to Chicago in part of 1956 when the survey was done for the following year's directory. Frank didn't list the address on the other side of town for the year he was there, likely not wanting to make it easy for the Pruitts to find out where he and Trent were living.

At Christmas time in 1957, Leon and Nell needed somewhere for Maudine to visit them, so they played house at their trailer on Fifty-second Street, probably to create the illusion they were a happy couple living there, basically for "looks." Frank was not there, but Trent was when Maudine and her sister Peggy arrived on Christmas Day, 1957, at the trailer, driving up in a brand new car. Peggy said she was only fifteen years old at the time and had no driver's license. Here's where Nell's peculiar behavior comes in. Peggy said that she thought Nell was "trying to play both sides against the middle." Whenever she could get out of earshot of Leon, she would signal and whisper to Maudine that she thought she should have Trent. She didn't believe Trent should be without his mother, but she wanted to see Trent also. Perhaps Nell believed Maudine would one day regain custody of Trent, and Nell wanted to maintain a good standing with Maudine so she could continue to see Trent if that happened. But Nell feared Leon, so she couldn't make her comments to Maudine in Leon's presence. Trent was a mere two and a half years old at that time. Peggy told Maudine if she got a chance to get away with Trent, not to worry about her, she'd find a way to her aunt Captola's in Belleville on her own.

So then the fireworks began again. Maudine and Peggy had come up with the intention of stealing Trent back and were looking for the right moment. But with Leon in the room, they knew they didn't stand a chance. He was a big, strong man, and intimidating as hell. During their visit with Trent, they gave him a cocker spaniel puppy as his Christmas present. They kept looking at Nell for a signal it was a good moment to bolt with Trent. When Leon got up to go to the bathroom, Maudine figured this was her chance. She waited until Leon got started with this "business," then grabbed Trent and ran for the door. Nell jumped up and started screaming for Leon, "They're taking the baby! They're taking the baby!" Leon came running out of the bathroom with his pants down around his ankles heading for the door after Maudine. Peggy was still in the trailer, and she jumped on Leon's back. Leon carried her on his back out the door, grabbed a handful of her hair, and pulled it out trying to get her off of him. She finally was shaken off of his back, and by this time, Maudine had started her car, with Trent inside with her. She floored the gas pedal and tried to drive off, but Leon jumped on the hood of the car, trying to grab something. He could only grab the antenna and fell off to the side, breaking the antenna off in the process. Maudine got away, almost cleanly.

Now at this point is where the stories differ. A Tucker cousin, Jim Mitchell, had told me that Maudine had "run over" Leon when he tried to block the driveway. Of course, the Pruitts' version of this event would be that Leon jumped on the hood of the car, but the Tuckers' version was that she ran him down. Who can say what the truth was? There is only one witness to this event still alive, Peggy. But she has a biased position, in favor of her sister, so I can never know what the actual truth was. In any event, Peggy ran across the street to a neighbor's house—complete strangers to her, and basically asked for asylum until she could get a taxicab to Captola's. She explained to them it was a child-custody matter, and they allowed her in, despite it being Christmas Day. Leon and Nell came across to the house and demanded she tell them where Maudine was taking Trent. She obviously refused to tell them. She eventually got to Captola's in Belleville. I would suppose the cocker spaniel puppy they had brought with them for Trent's Christmas gift was left behind at Nell's and Leon's. It is logical there would have been no time in the ruckus to grab it while they were making off with Trent.

Peggy said she found out later that Maudine drove out into the country east of East St. Louis, rather than what most would think as the smarter move, to cross the Eads Bridge over to St. Louis and get out of the state of Illinois. Maudine parked the car, a brand new one, at a stranger's house in the country, asked them if she could leave it with them along with the keys, and called a taxicab. Maudine took Trent by taxicab across the bridge to St. Louis and to the airport. She called Captola's and told them where she had stashed the car. At first I wondered why Maudine couldn't have driven the car to St. Louis and leave it at the airport? A little more thought revealed the answer.

Captola told Peggy to take a taxicab to where Maudine left the car and drive it back to her house, even though Peggy was just fifteen years old and didn't have a driver's license. Peggy retrieved the car. By the time she got back to Captola's in Belleville, the police were waiting. Leon had filed a police report on a hit-and-run by Maudine. There was a statewide warrant out for the car and for Maudine. Maudine, even at her young age of twenty-two years old, was smart enough to realize Leon would likely call the police on her. She knew there would be a warrant out for her arrest, and the license plate on the car she was driving would have given her away. So she headed for the country to stash the car there and took a taxicab to the airport instead. The bridges across the Mississippi River to St. Louis would have been the perfect choke point for the police to catch her also, so she was smart not to immediately dash from Leon's trailer to the bridges to St. Louis and the safety of Missouri.

When Peggy and Captola told the police it was a child-custody matter, not a true hit-and-run situation, the police relented and left them alone. That is common in child custody disputes—at least it was at this time in the 1950s. The police rarely enforced the law to the letter when child-custody disputes were involved. They realized people did things like this when children were at stake. Maudine boarded a flight in St. Louis to Memphis, her family picked her up at the Memphis airport, and before nightfall, she and Trent were walking up the sidewalk of her parents' house in Osceola, Arkansas (they had since moved there from Etowah). Trent would never be in Frank's custody again. Maudine would apply for custody in Arkansas. States rarely go against their own citizens in favor of people from other states in child-custody matters, and gave

Maudine full custody in April 1958. Frank was given some visitation rights and ordered to pay child support.

Her other general memories were that Leon was a "scoundrel," in her words. She said he treated Nell, Frank, and Maudine badly. Maudine told Peggy that Leon had "another woman" on the side, and this undoubtedly was Audrey. She said Maudine told her that Leon was heavily involved with organized crime, that the Local 100 Laborer's Union in East St. Louis at that time, in the 1950s, was heavily controlled by organized crime, and that Leon was in the middle of all of it. This corroborates what Jim Mitchell told me about the union and Leon's involvement in it. Peggy said Maudine knew about Sharon, Frank's daughter with his high-school girlfriend that he never married.

Peggy said she remembered seeing Frank next when he and his new wife, Judy, came to visit Trent in Osceola. She said she thought Judy was very pretty. Peggy said in future years when Frank or Leon and Nell would come to visit Trent in Osceola, and if Maudine wasn't home or there weren't enough men in the house to ensure protection of Trent, she would dash out the back door with Trent. This corroborates what Frank told me, that several times when he would go to visit Trent in Arkansas, the Pruitts would not let Frank see him. While the Pruitts would complain that Frank wouldn't be paying his child support, Frank would complain they wouldn't be observing Frank's visitation rights. Both were withholding what they had to force the other side to give in. So it was an impasse—with Trent being the loser from both angles. Peggy said Maudine moved to Houston, Texas, when Trent was around five years old, looking for work. Peggy said Maudine changed her name she was known by to a variation on her middle name, "Celeste."

This may have been the time when, in 1961, Frank filed in an Arkansas court for custody of Trent. He stated in his filing that he had remarried (to Judy) and established a proper home for Trent, that Maudine's family was preventing Frank from his court-ordered visitation of Trent, and that Maudine had left Trent in the care of her mother, Inez Pruitt, and was living elsewhere. Presumably Maudine was living in Houston at this time, working. It made sense if Maudine wasn't caring for Trent herself and left him with her parents, being that he was six years old at this time, Frank might have been the better parent to be raising him. Maudine's response was that she asked the court to force Frank to pay for her relocation back to Arkansas to contest his action, to the tune of $750, a tidy sum at that time (1961) for middle-class people. The action by Frank failed, and he didn't regain custody of Trent, probably because it meant Trent would leave the jurisdiction of the Arkansas court and be transferred to the jurisdiction of the court in St. Clair County, Illinois. Courts rarely want to give up control over minors. If Frank had lived within the jurisdiction of the Arkansas court, he might have stood a chance at regaining custody of Trent.

There were visits in later years by Frank, Nell, and Leon with Trent as I found photos of the visits with a pre-teenage Trent in Osceola in Nell's photo albums. Trent was thirteen years old when Nell died in 1969. Peggy said Maudine was notified of Nell's funeral, and couldn't decide if she should send Trent to the funeral in Paducah or not. To our family recollections, Trent did not attend his grandmother's funeral. I was at the funeral of Leon in 1987, and I know he didn't attend that either. He may not have been notified of Leon's death—I don't know. He did know about Leon's death when I spoke with him on the phone in the middle 1990s, so somehow word got to him about it.

Trent himself told me that he has a memory of visiting briefly, for just an evening, in East St. Louis with Frank and Judy around 1970. Maudine was traveling north through the area and dropped off Trent for a visit with Frank while she visited Captola in Belleville. This is the only time I have a memory of seeing Trent when I was a child. We were living at 1530 N. Forty-sixth Street in East St. Louis, and I remember seeing Trent as he was leaving. He looked down at me playing on the living room floor. I was only five or six years old at the time. He smiled lightly, and then kind of said with a closed mouth, "Humph," like a general expression saying, "So that's my little half-brother." I didn't see him again for thirty-five years (except for one brief, impersonal phone call and one short, impersonal letter) until I invited him to attend our father's funeral in 2005. After remarrying to David Griffith in 1964 and having two daughters, Maudine passed away in 1992, and is buried near Fairfield Bay, Arkansas.

In the brief phone call in the middle 1990s, initiated by me to Trent, I asked him if he wanted to have contact with Frank. He said he "thought things were better left as they were," but that Frank was welcome to write to him. I knew that statement meant that there would be no contact between them, since Frank was not a letter-writer. I related Trent's comments to Frank word for word, not editing nor softening any of it. In 1997, when Frank and Audra were traveling across country in their camper toward California for a visit with me, Frank said he stopped in Albuquerque, New Mexico, and tried to call Trent. He knew that's where he lived because I provided him with Trent's phone number and address. The number was disconnected, with no forwarding number provided. Frank took that personally, thinking Trent had intentionally changed his phone number to avoid receiving a call from him. I told Frank at the time not to interpret it that way, since there are many reasons why people would change their number, even if they still lived at the same address.

Frank left Albuquerque that day without attempting further to contact Trent, such as stopping by his house. He said he was too afraid of the possible negative reception to surprise Trent like that. I asked Trent about this incident at Frank's funeral in 2005, and Trent said that he had briefly changed his number while he moved to another house in Albuquerque, and didn't have a forwarding telephone number attached to the old one for only about a week's time. As a bizarre twist of incredible odds to this story, the one short week during decades of estrangement that Frank attempted to contact Trent was the one week that Trent was without a home telephone number, and Frank interpreted that wrongly. Trent appeared shocked at this revelation at Frank's funeral, realizing the gravity of the missed opportunity. He apparently had thought Frank never cared enough to try to contact him.

Sometime in 2004, when I saw Frank beginning his final decline toward death, I contacted Trent again by letter and told him of Frank's declining health. Trent responded several months later with a very brief, impersonal letter but did include some photocopied photos of his life over the years, which were welcome. He didn't indicate any desire for contact with Frank, or me for that matter, in his letter, so I couldn't press further about it. I didn't even know if I should pass the photos on to Frank, as the letter didn't specifically ask me to do that. If I passed those photos on to Frank and Trent hadn't wanted me to do that, rather keep them private just to me, I thought I might anger Trent and alienate him from me as well. At Frank's funeral in 2005, Trent asked me if I had passed those photos on to Frank the year before. I said I hadn't, not knowing for sure if I had his permission to do that. The lack of clear communication in this situation caused a lot of misunderstandings and misdirected efforts, even if the intentions were pure.

At the funeral, Trent was acting like he didn't know things were this serious about Frank's health, and he asked why he wasn't contacted sooner. But I reminded him I had contacted him the previous year about Frank's declining health, and again sent him a letter just a few days prior to Frank's death, telling him the end was near. Unfortunately, my last letter to him didn't arrive prior to Frank's death. No one knew Frank would die that soon when things began to look grave, or I would have used an overnight letter service for my letter to Trent.

This had to be fate. It was like circumstances were in collusion to prevent Frank and Trent from ever having contact before Frank died, as if scripted this way by a fiction writer. Unfortunately, it was all nonfiction. Looking back over the sum total of Frank and Trent's unusual father-son relationship, I saw a pattern of missed opportunities, disinformation, lies, exaggerations, wrong assumptions (on both parts), and freakish bad luck. Considering the fifty-year odyssey that began in 1955 with Trent's birth and ended in 2005 at Frank's funeral, I don't think the bizarre twists of this story could have been worse if both parties had worked hard to make it so. It was like flipping a coin fifty times in a row, calling "heads" each flip, and losing every time.

NADINE: I would have liked to write a few paragraphs on Frank's high-school sweetheart, Nadine. She wasn't a formal Tucker wife, but she should have been. If Leon hadn't interfered with Frank's desire to marry the then pregnant Nadine, Nadine would have become a Tucker wife. I couldn't interview Nadine for this investigation as she was not open to talking about the history of her and Frank's relationship, and their daughter Sharon. When I contacted her about this matter, she actually denied even knowing Frank at all, saying she just remembered him "vaguely from high school. He was a few years behind me I think." This is understandable, considering the circumstances and values held by the people of the time era these events took place in. Unwed births were scandalous during that time period. Today they are commonplace and acceptable, or at least tolerated. So if Nadine felt so strongly about keeping this matter from the deep past secret, then I had to respect her wishes. I did feel the story as it involved my father Frank's life was important to tell to understand the high level of control Leon had over Frank.

Frank in his football days at Paducah's Tilghman High School

In deciding to pursue the Nadine-Frank story, I was also deciding to pursue finding my half-sister, Sharon. I knew I wanted to locate her and make contact, but didn't know how to do it or what I would say if I found her. Tillie told me she didn't know Frank was her father, so I thought to myself, "How in the world do you tell someone their father isn't who they think he is?" With an extensive Internet search utilizing various Web sites (I won't detail exactly how for her privacy), I located Sharon in late 2005. I phoned her just to confirm she was the daughter of Nadine, and it was odd talking briefly with her on the phone. I didn't tell her who I was in the first phone call. I knew I wanted to mail her a carefully worded letter to explain all that I had learned about our shared history rather than discuss it in an out-of-the-blue telephone call. I told her in the initial phone call that I was the son of a man whom her mother had dated in high school, and we had photos of her mother we wanted to send to her. She agreed to let me send them to her and gave me her mailing address.

I sent her my letter, explaining what I had learned from Tillie, and asked her if she thought it might be true. I didn't hear anything for about two months, figuring I might have opened Pandora's box. She finally e-mailed me back with the greeting at the top, "Hi Bro!" She had contacted her aunts, and they confirmed for her that she was Frank's daughter. They told her the history she never knew about the events around the time she was born, and of Frank and Leon. She was told that Leon was an "enforcer" for the labor unions in East St. Louis, was a violent man, and prevented Frank from marrying Nadine. She was told unflattering things about both Leon and Frank. What is to follow is basically the story she was told mixed with the information I know to be true from our own family recollections of this period of Frank's life.

The time was 1952. Nadine would have become pregnant in March 1952, probably discovering it by late spring. Frank was already studying at the University of Kentucky at Lexington since September 1951. Frank told me he played football for their team, the Kentucky Wildcats, under famed coach Paul "Bear" Bryant. I checked the 1951 yearbook, *The Kentuckian*, for the University of Kentucky, and didn't see his picture on the team, but it being his first year, he might not have shown up in the team photos yet. His transcript does show "Inter Football" both semesters he studied there at the University of Kentucky. Because of his talents, Frank told us years later, the professional football team Green Bay Packers were interested in Frank for a career in professional football. Only an injury would keep him from taking them up on the offer. I have no way of verifying any of that, it all came from Frank, and may have been exaggeration, but I'll give him the benefit of the doubt. It was likely Frank's poor academic record that would eventually cause him to leave the University of Kentucky after only two semesters and transfer to Murray State University in Kentucky starting in January 1953. He would later leave Murray State as well after two full years of study and before finishing a degree, again for a poor academic record. He would be at Murray State through 1954. The top of his Murray State transcript has handwritten "Probation" without any explanation of what that means, academic or disciplinary probation.

Judy's parents, Glen and Ruth Bond

But in 1952, Frank's football career, and any chance of finishing college with a degree, would evaporate if he had to leave school, marry Nadine, and get a job to provide for her and their child. Leon didn't like Nadine for unknown reasons, but they can be reasonably guessed. As previously stated, Nadine was outspoken, and Leon hated mouthy women. Leon surmised that Frank's chances of getting a good start in life were encumbered by the then pregnant Nadine. Leon told Frank he would cut him off from any more financial support for his college studies if he married Nadine. So in obviously a selfish moment, Frank made the fateful decision to abandon Nadine. According to Nadine's sisters, who related the story to Sharon, Nadine went to Louisville, Kentucky, to a home for unwed mothers before she began "showing." Her parents never knew she was pregnant. She told them she was going to Louisville to accept a clerical job offer. There in Louisville, Nadine had the baby in January 1953. She left the baby behind in foster care and returned to Paducah. Only the pressure from her sisters would force her to return to Louisville in a few months to retrieve the infant girl. Upon returning to Paducah with infant Sharon, Nadine would marry a man, Billy Joe, she had only dated a few times prior to marrying, and changed Sharon's birth certificate to show Billy Joe as Sharon's father, not Frank. Frank would never know his daughter, Sharon, except for one brief, incognito meeting some thirty years later, arranged by Tillie.

According to Sharon, she felt the man whom she thought was her natural father never treated her the same as her brothers who were born later, and she always wondered why. Discovering in late 2005 that her actual, biological father was Frank was a shock to her, but answered many questions as well. She never got to know Frank, only discovering him shortly after he died. Sharon also revealed that Frank and Billy Joe actually knew each other at the time of her birth, and evidently hated each other, probably over the Nadine and Sharon situation. Considering all the above history in deciding whether or not to include this story in the book, I had to balance the need to tell Frank's story with the desire to respect Nadine and Sharon's privacy. That is why I chose to change the names of Nadine and Sharon in this book.

JUDY: Mary Judith Bond, known simply as "Judy," my mother, was the daughter of Glen Bond and Ruth (Dawson) Bond. She married Frank on August 2, 1958, in East St. Louis. They began having children in 1961, briefly divorced in 1963, and then remarried each other in Hernando, Mississippi, on August 27, 1963. This was the same location Frank had married his first wife, Maudine, at in 1953, almost ten years earlier. From what I've heard from several relatives, many people would travel great distances to get married in Mississippi as it was a "no questions asked" marriage state. I asked Tillie about this remarriage, and she was aware of it. She said Mississippi didn't require blood tests. A couple could get married quickly by just appearing at the courthouse, and that's why a lot of people eloped to Mississippi. It's a good thing Frank and Judy decided to get back together, because if they hadn't, I wouldn't be here to write this book. I was born the following February 1964, approximately six months after they remarried. Obviously, Judy discovered she was pregnant again, while she and Frank were post-divorce dating in the summer of 1963, and they decided to remarry to legitimize their new offspring that was on the way.

I'm guessing, from my knowledge of the man, that Frank also didn't like the idea of paying child support to Judy on their first child while simultaneously trying to make an independent life for himself. He was already obligated for one child-support payment to Maudine for their son, Trent. When Judy got pregnant again, meaning his child-support payments to Judy would double, the financial motivation to remarry Judy must have been strong. Besides, Frank was striking out three for three with women and having children—not a good track record. Nadine had Frank's child after he abandoned her at Leon's insistence, Maudine had Frank's child and divorced him, and now Judy had Frank's child and divorced him as well. A clear pattern was developing in Frank's life. This sounds like it was a serious moment of self-reflection for Frank—for any man in similar circumstances.

Finding the Mississippi record of Frank and Judy's second marriage reminded me of an instance where Judy let it slip about their brief divorced period. It was some time in the 1980s when we lived in Morrisonville. Frank looked panicked and plaintively asked to Judy, "Must our lives be an open book to them (the children)?" For some strange reason, Frank had shame about this brief divorced period and wanted to keep it a deep secret. I think I discovered why Frank wanted to keep this first divorce from Judy secret, at least secret from his children with Judy. Judy's first divorce filing was in April 1963, less than five years after they were married in August 1958, and charged Frank with spousal abuse. Specifically, Judy charged that Frank in two instances, May and July of 1962, physically attacked her, leaving her with "bruises and contusions." Judy also charged Frank with pursuing a "course of conduct well calculated to render the life of the plaintiff (Judy) miserable and hazardous to life and limb," which basically meant extreme mental cruelty. Judy's filing said that in March 1963, Frank threatened more violence toward Judy, and she left him at that time. If I interpret the divorce documents correctly, in exchange for no alimony payments, Frank did not contest the divorce or even deny Judy's charges of violence. The divorce went through quickly with the reasons for the divorce being stated as Frank's violence and cruelty. That was an amazing thing for Frank to allow to be recorded on a public document. It certainly negated any future political career Frank might pursue to have exercised violence toward a woman recorded on a public record. This documented spousal abuse is likely what Frank felt shame about and wanted to keep secret from his children.

Judy and Frank Tucker circa 1978

My guess is at this time neither Judy nor Frank had money to pay for divorce lawyers. Frank was being ordered by the court to pay not only for his own attorney but also pay for Judy's attorney as well. For Frank, this was a big incentive to settle quickly with Judy. He was ordered to pay child support to Judy on their infant child. Apparently Judy and Frank continued to date after they were divorced, Judy became pregnant again, and Frank decided he had to remarry Judy. Judy, facing life with two children on her own, probably felt compelled to remarry Frank also. Both of them were likely remarrying out of financial necessity if not out of love. It reminded me of a statement Frank made to me decades later, in the early 1990s sometime. I made the comment to him that I thought the high divorce rate noted in the newspapers at the time (greater than fifty percent of all marriages failing) was because people were marrying for the wrong reasons, such as for money. I philosophically asserted, and perhaps naively asserted, that people should only marry for love and compatibility. Frank replied with a knowing look of life experience on his face, "You're gonna realize one day that a lot o' marriage *is* 'bout money." He stressed the word "is" in that sentence. Apparently things worked better the second time around for Judy and Frank. Ignoring the brief divorced period (under a year in 1963), Judy and Frank's marriage spanned twenty-eight years, from 1958 to 1985.

Pondering this brief divorce period and remarriage date, I wondered if it explained a long family mystery to me. I had always wondered why Frank was distant from me when I was growing up, always showing partiality toward my older sibling. Everyone saw it—Judy, cousins, friends—everyone. It wasn't just my imagination. Frank had a resentment of me that caused him to basically ignore me from my earliest memories as a toddler. When angered, he would get angrier with me than anyone else in the family, and his anger usually was greater than the circumstance generating it, whatever it was. The additional anger that was greater than warranted from the instance at hand likely came from his residual resentment of me overall. As a baby or a toddler, certainly I couldn't have done something at that point to deserve that treatment. It had to come from something inside Frank. I wondered if Frank felt forced to remarry Judy when she became pregnant in the summer of 1963. If he didn't really want to remarry Judy but felt forced to, it may have caused that resentment of me. Frank always hated to be forced to do anything. Frank may have felt he couldn't afford child-support payments on three children, one with Maudine and two with Judy, so remarrying Judy negated one of those financial burdens.

There is no doubt that Frank loved Judy since they were together for more than twenty-eight years, long after the financial obligation for raising their children was over. Indeed, it wasn't Frank who sought both of their divorces. Judy filed both divorces, in 1963 and 1985. Frank wanted to remain married to Judy in 1985 when she divorced him—that became clear in later years as he said as much. But in 1963, when choosing whether or not to remarry her, Frank may have felt he had no other choice, financially. I suspect that may have been the reason why he resented me from birth onward. That resentment caused a distance between Frank and me that was never bridged for forty years until he died in 2005.

Judy's recollections of her life with Frank are interspersed throughout the other chapters in this book. She had specific recollections of Frank, Nell, Leon, and even Trent over the years that she would rarely talk about. But unfortunately, she died in 2004 before I had a chance to interview her with specific questions about what I uncovered in my investigation into Nell's death. I know she knew a lot more than she revealed to me.

Even after her last divorce from Frank, she was reluctant to reveal something negative about Frank to me, because she didn't want me to think negatively about him. She did tell me about the times Leon made inappropriate sexual advances toward her, recounted in another chapter. This eerily is reminiscent of Leon's surly comments about Maudine. It validates that Leon likely made improper advances to both of Frank's first two wives. It raised the specter of why Leon didn't like Nadine, Frank's high-school girlfriend whom he wanted to marry, and Leon wouldn't let him. Judy knew of Nell's signaling to Maudine that she thought Maudine should have shared custody of Trent. Perhaps Nell even discussed this with Judy when Judy was dating Frank in 1957?

Judy's own experience of violence from Frank coordinated with the allegations brought by Maudine in her divorce filings and the statements of Maudine's family. It made it ring true to me when I read it in the divorce filings and hearing it from Peggy Sheffield (Maudine's sister). Tillie told me that Leon was violent with Nell, and Frances told me that Leon was violent with Audrey. That's putting it mildly—Leon almost beat Audrey to death multiple times. Leon had either left Audrey for dead or thought he had killed her and was trying to dispose of her body when either she was found or she woke up in time to stop him. So violence toward women was apparently not uncommon at all among my ancestors. The stories of how violent George Tucker, Leon's father, was toward his children also validated that family commonality. I have to admit, hearing all this violence in my family history made me sick to think about it.

Frank once broke Judy's nose early in their marriage. One evening during the East St. Louis years, Frank called Don Bond, Judy's brother, and said, "Judy's hurt. You better come over." Don took Judy to the hospital. Frank, of course, couldn't go, because he would have been arrested for battery. This lack of bravery by Frank was breathtaking. Later on, Don Bond would threaten Frank to his face that he would kill him if he ever hit Judy again. This would be the only time Don would ever stand up to Frank, since Frank outweighed Don by about half of his weight. This story came from a distant family member, whose name I don't recall, at Don Bond's funeral in 1997 in St. Louis. A first cousin of mine, Adam Bond, who is Don's son, also confirmed this story of Frank breaking Judy's nose. Adam remembers his father telling him about it. I asked my mother, Judy, after Don's funeral about this story, and she quietly nodded her head affirmatively, confirming it. She said to me, "You're not supposed to know about that." It appeared to me she was half-ashamed I knew of this story. Apparently it was a deeply held secret. She said she didn't want me to think of my father like that, so she never told me the story. She showed class by caring more about how I saw my father than protecting herself.

Judy Bond before she married Frank, circa 1950

Donald Bond, Judy's brother, sometime in the early 1950's

I believed this story to be true, about Don defending Judy, because it coordinated with a story Frank himself told me about Don coming to defend Judy, at least her virtue, once before. When Frank and Judy were dating in 1958, Frank took Judy along with his cousin Jim Mitchell down to the clubhouse/cabin owned by Tucker cousins, the Burgesses, in Grand Tower, Illinois. Leon was a frequent user of the place also. Jim Mitchell verified this story for me when I spoke with him in 2006, adding the detail about the encounter with a Freemason who aided them when their car ran out of gas (Jim's story is detailed in another chapter). Don heard about Frank taking his unmarried, older sister Judy to this cabin for a weekend getaway without a chaperon, and he didn't like how it reflected on his sister's virtue. Don gathered two of his buddies and drove down to Grand Tower, intending to beat up Frank. Since Don was smaller than Frank, he would need help if he was going to whip (meaning defeat) Frank. When they got there, Frank's smiling and jovial nature coupled with Judy's apparent willingness to be there and being unharmed prevented fisticuffs from breaking out among the men.

Another instance of violence toward Judy from Frank was when I was sixteen years old, around 1980. Our family was living in Morrisonville, Illinois, at the time. I saw firsthand my father Frank's violence toward my mother. They were arguing in the house, and Judy left to get in her car and leave. Frank followed her out and got in the passenger side of the car. He had this sick and reddened face that was screwed up tight like a fist. I was standing in the front yard, watching the whole scene. I saw Frank punch Judy in the side of the face, and her head ricocheted off the driver's window. She yelled out, "My god, Frank!" His only reply was "Then come back inside and take what you deserve!" She remained silent, just crying, terrified to look at him, just looking down. After a few moments, Frank got out of the car, walked inside fuming, satisfied he had gotten his victory of the last word. Judy drove off crying. I just stood there frozen the whole time, praying no one I knew drove by or the neighbors weren't watching. I still feel guilt about this incident even today. I wonder if I had ran up and tried to stop him if it would have done any good, or just enraged him further and gotten her an even worse beating, and some blows for me as well. Should I have tried to defend my mother? Where do I go for absolution?

Frank was even occasionally violent to the family pet. We had a beautiful, lovable golden retriever named "Trouble" when we lived in Cahokia and Morrisonville. He lived for seventeen years, which was very unusual for a large dog. Frank insisted we call him that name after he was wetting everywhere in the house as a puppy. We got him just as we were leaving East St. Louis for Cahokia. Many years later after I had grown up, moved away to college, and just before Judy and Frank would divorce for the last time, Frank injured Trouble in a disciplinary moment. Trouble occasionally had the odd habit, as many dogs do, of being half-asleep when he would awaken from sleep. He would growl and bare his teeth at us, sometimes while simultaneously wagging his tail and dropping his ears, as if happy. He had such confused emotions in this half-sleep state we knew just to leave him alone until he awoke fully. It's from where the old adage "better to let sleeping dogs lay" comes.

Trouble Tucker, our beloved golden retriever

When I came home from college at Christmas time, I noticed Trouble walking funny, like his back end couldn't be controlled anymore. When walking around a corner, his back end would keep going, and he would wipe out, falling down usually. I asked Judy what was the problem, and she said Trouble pulled muscles and hurt a disc, according to the veterinarian, when they were washing him in the bathtub once. Trouble was known to fidget a lot in the bathtub, he hated baths, so I bought this excuse. Also, certain breeds of golden retrievers are known to have a genetic defect that causes degeneration of hip joints in their older years. We hadn't seen any indication of this in Trouble despite him being well past ten years of age at that point. But when Frank and Judy told me this accidental injury story, I had no reason to doubt it.

Many years later, Judy confessed to me that the story was a lie, made up by Frank and supported by Judy, to cover what really happened. Evidently, when Trouble awoke in this half-sleep once, he growled at Frank. In the stress of the separation he and Judy were going through at the time, Frank picked up a thick piece of wood and threw it at Trouble, saying "Goddamn ya! Ya don't bite the hand that feeds ya!" Frank was lashing out at whatever opposition he got from anybody.

It seemed familiar to me. I could just picture him doing that in my mind when Judy told me that, as it was totally in his character and demeanor to do that. The wood strike injured Trouble permanently in the back end. They took him to the veterinarian when they saw he was seriously injured. Frank and Judy couldn't tell the veterinarian the true story, since the veterinarian would report it as cruelty to animals, and Trouble might have been taken away from our family. So Judy agreed to support Frank's lie rather than lose Trouble. As it turned out, Judy took Trouble with her when she moved out of the Morrisonville house to divorce Frank for the last time. Trouble lived a few more years in Judy's care, finally succumbing to a stroke in 1988. He is buried in a pet cemetery in Springfield, Illinois, with a granite headstone engraved "Trouble Tucker." He deserved nothing less—he was an amazing pooch.

These incidents of violence described in all the above stories about the wives, and even a pet, of the Tucker men made me see a very clear pattern. It gave it credibility when all of it is compared against each other. I felt so detached from these events because I've never felt the urge to be violent toward a woman, no matter how angry I've gotten. I just couldn't relate to how this type of behavior made sense to these Tucker men. If it was a behavior passed down from generation to generation, taught from father to son, then it was definitely stopping with my generation—at least with me.

In Judy's 1985 divorce filing, she claimed "extreme mental cruelty" by Frank as the grounds for the divorce. It was just a legal requirement that she had to choose one of the requisite grounds for divorce in Illinois at that time. Illinois is one of a few states that had held to the fault-based grounds for divorce, but had recently added "no-fault" grounds, known as irreconcilable differences. Perhaps her lawyer didn't know that the year prior to Judy's 1985 filing, in 1984, Illinois added the "irreconcilable differences" grounds to Illinois divorce law? Perhaps Judy was told that she had to choose from one of the previously allowable grounds for Illinois divorce prior to 1984? From that previous list, Judy chose the grounds with the least negative connotation to Frank. Judy certainly could have justifiably claimed a great deal more with the history of violence by Frank toward Judy. But showing class and realizing her divorce filing was a public document and not wanting to harm Frank's public name, she kept violence out of it, and simply cited the bare minimum required for a divorce—extreme mental cruelty. Just as she had sought to protect Frank's reputation with me by not telling me of his violence toward her, she sought to protect his public reputation as well.

Judy's second divorce filing was in November 1985. I remember receiving a call from her at that time that she was leaving Frank. I was living away in Champaign/Urbana, Illinois, during my first semester at the University of Illinois. Frank and Judy's divorce was finalized by early spring 1986. Frank wasted no time at all searching for wife number three, asking Tillie to introduce him to one of her single lady friends in Paducah. Tillie introduced Frank to Audra Lance, and they began dating before Frank's divorce was final. Frank did not know Audra prior to Judy leaving him in the fall of 1985—of that I'm totally positive. Tillie additionally verified the time frame of the introduction of Frank to Audra. Frank and Audra's wedding followed in August 1986, less than six months after his divorce from Judy was final, and less than a year from when Judy left him. Just as Leon had married Audrey less than a year after Nell died, Frank remarried in under a year after the divorce from Judy. The old adage held true—nothing terrified a Tucker man more than the thought of being alone.

Judy did not know of Frank's first child, Sharon, with his high-school sweetheart, Nadine. I believe if she knew this she would have said something to me over the years, particularly after she and Frank divorced again in 1985. Judy spoke to me once about her suspicions about Nell's death, recounted in detail in another chapter. I sensed over the years that Leon came to respect Judy's strength, and tried not to confront her, particularly after Frank and she began having children. I guess he figured he was partially the cause of Frank's first two children (Sharon and Trent) being chased out of his life, so he shouldn't chase this third woman away from Frank or he would never get a chance to see any of his grandchildren at all. After the 1985 divorce, Judy never remarried, and passed away in 2004.

It was never in doubt that Frank was deeply in love with Judy, and remained so until the day he died. He plainly said so many times. He said about Judy, "That was *my* woman," with emphasis on the "my," as if to say she was the great love of his life. It hurt him deeply when Judy divorced him for the final time in 1985. When attending the viewing of Judy's funeral in 2004, Frank was already decrepit from old age, as he neared his own death the following year. At the viewing, I helped him approach her casket, and he wept openly and loudly, saying, "Ohhhhhh! Ohhhhhh!" Such a display of emotion was very unusual for a normally self-repressed, masculine man. The only other time I had seen him cry so openly in my lifetime was when his mother Nell died in 1969, and Leon notified him by phone. At Judy's funeral, he stood next to her casket, him leaning on a cane, with me supporting his arm and handing him a handkerchief to wipe his wet face and runny nose. He reached into the casket, touched the hand of Judy's remains, and said softly, "Thank you, Judy, for twenty-eight years o' marriage. They were the best years o' my life." Judy's remains were buried the following day, next to her parents, Ruth and Glen, and brother, Don, in Chesterfield, Illinois. A Roman Catholic priest officiated at the graveside ceremony. A bagpiper, wearing a Scottish kilt and full bagpiper regalia, played the gospel hymn "Amazing Grace" for Judy at her burial ceremony, slowly fading out on the last bars of the song as the bagpiper walked away, signifying Judy's departure. Frank did not attend the graveside ceremony. Frank died the following year and, as he requested, was buried near his beloved Judy.

*   *   *

Bagpiper (Steve Scaife) at Judy's funeral

Chapter 7

THE OFFICES

The next bit of information on the SGO records really floored me. I couldn't believe what I was reading.

There were various offices I had to write to and obtain information during the course of this investigation. Since they weren't family members, I didn't feel I could include that information under the previous chapters, so I put it all here in a separate chapter.

STATE'S ATTORNEY: In March 2006, I called the Ft. Pierce, Florida medical examiner's office, and spoke with one of their investigators, Merv Waldren. He stated there was little likelihood of any evidence in Nell's remains after this long of a time of any physical assault causing her death, such as strangulation or smothering. He said it was possible that if she was strangled, and there was no sign of it on the body such that it was missed by the physicians examining her remains at the time and missed by the funeral director, the hyoid bone in the neck might have been broken during the strangulation, and that would show up on an X-ray of her remains now. It was possible if flesh remained, such as bone marrow, that a heavy-metals toxicology test might reveal if she was poisoned by heavy metals, such as arsenic. He recommended that I call the state's attorney covering the Okeechobee area and see if they had any interest in a murder investigation. If they had any interest, they might be willing to pursue having the body exhumed and shipped back to Florida for an autopsy, and his office would be willing to do the autopsy at that time. Alternate to that, his office would be willing to look at any official autopsy results from a medical examiner in Paducah, not a private autopsy from a hired pathologist. Even with that, they could not guarantee that they would change the cause of death on her death certificate. If they felt confident in the results from a government medical examiner's findings in Paducah, they might be willing to change the cause of death based on that.

Based on the recommendation from the medical examiner's office, I contacted the state's attorney's office in Florida for the region covering Okeechobee. His name was Ashley Albright, assistant state attorney. I wrote to him and included a copy of Nell's death certificate as evidence. I detailed for him why I believed Nell was likely murdered, what I felt justified the exhumation and autopsy, and asked for his assistance. What I mainly needed from him was his help in getting the autopsy underway, and to identify for me any additional sources of information I might check in Florida. I basically wanted him to start the investigation into Nell's death that should have been done in 1969, but I wanted him to start it now, in 2006. I wanted his assistance also in convincing the medical examiner's office in Ft. Pierce to change the cause of death on the death certificate from "unknown (DOA)" to "homicide."

Mr. Albright called me after receiving my letter and asked me a few questions about the matter. He mainly focused on the fact that all the parties involved in the event are now deceased. I told him that a few witnesses, namely Tillie Edwards and Eddie Stevenson, were still alive. He probed with a few questions designed to reveal if I had any other motivations for wanting to pursue this matter, such as estate or property issues regarding Nell's assets. I told him "no," there were no issues of money involved at all. He told me he would get back to me after researching a few things.

A few days later I got a very short letter, only one paragraph, from Mr. Albright. It said because Leon was deceased, and the statute of limitations on "other crimes," which he did not specify, had run out, there was nothing else he could investigate. Basically, I was being waved away—as if saying, "You may have discovered a crime, but I have no interest in it." I was appalled at the behavior of Okeechobee's public servants. First, Nell dies under clearly dubious circumstances, and her body is brought to a hospital dead on arrival. The doctor there doesn't follow Florida law and require an autopsy, rather inexplicably signs her death certificate with cause of death "unknown (DOA)." The local police do only a cursory investigation into her death, and that was done only because Grace, Nell's sister, insisted. Faced with all the evidence I had summarized for the local prosecutor, Mr. Albright, the State of Florida was once again dismissing Nell's death as inconsequential, or not worth investigating. Evidently, her death certificate showing an unknown cause of death was not significant to Mr. Albright, because he couldn't prosecute somebody for her murder being that all the principal parties in the event were already deceased. It was apparent things hadn't changed much from 1969 to 2006 as far as Okeechobee public service goes, in my opinion. Quite frankly, this lack of interest in Nell's case disgusted me.

LIFE INSURANCE: When preparing the documents necessary to seek the permit for the exhumation and autopsy, I quite by accident took a closer look at Nell's birth certificate. Nell had obtained her birth certificate in a "delayed birth certificate" form, in 1968 at the age of fifty-eight years old. She had never been issued a birth certificate before because the rural area of Kentucky she came from, Graves County in 1910, didn't keep such birth records. She got the county to create a birth record for her by submitting three forms of proof of her age. The first document of proof she submitted was an affidavit from Thomas Fike, the eighty-six-year-old (in 1968) father-in-law of her sister, Ila Mae (Freeman) Fike. Thomas Fike evidently knew Nell all her life. The second document of proof was a school census record from the McCracken County school system. The third document of proof hit me like a sand-filled sock when I saw it on the page. It indicated a life insurance policy with Prudential Life, initially taken out in 1937, but still active in 1968. The policy number was shown for me to pursue with Prudential, which I did. Owen Tucker, nephew to Leon and Nell, had told me in 2006 that he thought Leon had killed Nell for "life insurance," but couldn't tell me where he heard that. Previously I thought no one had any records existing of what kind of insurance Nell might have had in 1969. This indication on Nell's delayed birth certificate, complete with policy number, was my first lead with this issue.

I contemplated the whole big picture regarding the insurance and delayed birth certificate for a moment, and it began to give me the chills. Why on earth was Nell pursuing her birth certificate for the first time in her life at the ripe old age of fifty-eight? She was still more than three years away from the earliest date she could retire and draw Social Security. Why was she pursuing it only three months prior to her death? Of course there could be reasons I could never know at this late date, but one reason that makes sense is that Leon wanted it. For some inexplicable reason, he was bugging her to get it. Perhaps he thought he might need it to claim the life insurance policy later on. Perhaps he knew that the life insurance he had on Nell didn't reflect her true age, and a birth certificate might screw up claiming the policy after Nell's death? In this case, he would need a copy of it to alter it before submitting it. Otherwise, the insurance company might seek a copy on their own, if Leon didn't provide a copy. Then they'd discover Nell's true age, possibly invalidate the policy, and refuse to pay it. This is one theory, and just a theory.

The fact that Nell listed the Prudential policy proves that she was life insured at or at least near the time of her death, and that she had the policy out for some reason, not tucked away in a drawer and forgotten. Could Leon have been reviewing the insurance policy on Nell's life within three months of her death and asking her to get her delayed birth certificate issued for some reason? Does this correlate to the fact that the birth date on Nell's death certificate is wrong, by approximately ten years, stating she was forty-nine years old when she died instead of her correct age of fifty-eight years old? It began to give me an eerie sense of foreboding. Could Leon have actually been planning Nell's death more than three months prior to it happening in January 1969? This activity regarding the delayed birth certificate and reviewing of life insurance policies was going on in late September 1968. Was this just a creepy coincidence?

There have been so many coincidences in this whole story of Nell's death; I began to feel it wasn't credible anymore to call them coincidences. If these events were truly random and unrelated, then there wouldn't be so many coincidences. One or two coincidences might be possible to believe, but dozens aren't. I pondered whether Nell had placed the insurance policy number on her delayed birth certificate intentionally, like a flag or a clue left behind for a descendant or other family member to find later on. Was it a signal, one in a long trail of breadcrumbs, from Nell to others who would view the document later on, as if saying, "Hey, look further into this, and here's the policy number." It was just plain odd that she would use a life insurance policy as one of the documents to prove her birth date.

Furthermore, why would someone be buying life insurance, on a woman's life, when you were only eight years into the marriage, and Nell was only twenty-nine years old (in 1937 when the policy was issued) and in apparent perfect health? I could perhaps see Leon having insurance on his own life, because should he have died suddenly he would have left behind a wife and young son unable to survive in a time and place still recovering from the Great Depression. Leon and Nell were dirt-poor during these years, arriving in East St. Louis in 1936 with only twenty-five cents in Leon's pocket. They lived in a shack with a dirt floor for a year until they could earn enough to establish themselves in a regular rental place. That clearly told me they would have no money extra for buying life insurance on Nell's life—clearly not a necessity in such a subsistence-living situation. Why then would Leon purchase life insurance on Nell when they could barely afford a roof over their heads? Could Leon have been planning to murder Nell for the life insurance payout as far back as 1937? I had to allow for the possibility since no other apparent explanation is logical, considering all the factors. Almost with reluctance, I wrote to Prudential to ask them if they could find the file on this insurance policy, dreading to see what it would reveal.

Another route I took to get the insurance information was to try getting a copy of the evidence Nell submitted to the state of Kentucky to get her delayed birth certificate. They had to have kept a copy of that on file. When I contacted the Office of Vital Records in Frankfort, Kentucky, they were being quite firm about their rules. The information I was requesting was "sealed" and could only be released under a court order. I thought that was just plain ridiculous. Nell was deceased, I was her next living descendant, so why would there be a problem for me getting copies of that evidence? They followed their rules and refused to give in, directing me instead to petition a court in Paducah to get the court order necessary. I did that, writing to Judge Cynthia Sanderson of the McCracken County Circuit Court—Family Court Division, and asked her to issue the necessary court order for the release of copies of the sealed documents to me. Her legal assistant initially refused to help me, I think misunderstanding what I was wanting and why. After some persistence, I finally got Judge Sanderson to sign the court order for the release of Nell's sealed documents. I forwarded it on to Frankfort's Vital Records Office.

What came back from the Vital Records Office in Frankfort was disappointing. After all the trouble of getting the court order, all they sent me was a copy of the Affidavit of Thomas Fike and the school record. I phoned them and asked why they didn't send me the insurance document as well. They said they didn't have it, it wasn't attached to the delayed birth certificate. They said at the time in 1968 Nell likely just showed the insurance document or mailed it in with a request to have it mailed back, which it would have been. There were no Xerox machines at that time, so they likely didn't keep a copy of it, and returned the original to Nell. After a long search by Prudential Life Insurance, they failed to find the record of the 1937 policy either. They searched for the record both by year, location, policy number, and Nell's name, and couldn't find it. It was just too old to be found. I was at a dead end pursuing this insurance record. I would never know what it showed. I could only know from the delayed birth certificate that Nell had life insurance at the time she died, purchased by Leon in 1937, and could safely assume it was payable to Leon.

MILITARY: I contacted the U.S. Military, Personnel Records, in St. Louis to retrieve my grandfather's army service record, hoping it might illuminate something of what my grandfather was going through in World War II. I thought it might help me reconstruct what happened during those years, or at least pin down what time frame he was gone from East St. Louis. The first response from the National Personnel Records Center was that there was a catastrophic fire at their main records storage center in St. Louis on July 12, 1973. They stated that most of the army's personnel records for the period of 1912 through 1959 were lost in that fire. That time frame included the years that my grandfather served. I thought I had hit a dead end.

But then they responded later that they had other sources of information kept at other locations, and some of his service record might be recoverable. However, it was not possible to recover a complete service record from these sources. What they did find in their searching was a collection of computer magnetic tapes created by the National Research Council, a private organization, from admissions punch cards prepared by the Office of the Surgeon General, Department of the Army. The tapes contained information for the years of 1942-1945 and 1950-1954 on a large sampling of patients admitted to army medical treatment facilities during those time periods. The Office of the Surgeon General (SGO) records were confidential, with no names appearing on them, and the individual records were identified by the member's service number only—basically identified by their dog tag numbers. If Audrey's daughter, Frances Lemanski, hadn't given me Leon's dog tags that showed his service number on it, I doubt I could have even recovered this meager amount of records.

Much to my happy surprise, they found information on two admissions by my grandfather to army hospitals, one in the European war theater in November 1944, and the other in a stateside hospital in July 1945. I knew that my grandfather was mustered out of Camp Shelby, near Hattiesburg, Mississippi, in March 1943 to join the Antitank Company of the 339th Infantry of the U.S. Army. I knew this from the army photo given to me by Frances Lemanski. The army said he formally entered active service on January 18, 1944. Sometime between leaving his training in Mississippi in 1943 and being shipped out to England in 1944 to wait for D-day, Leon visited Kentucky or East St. Louis. I know this because we have a photo of Leon in his uniform posing with his then teenage son, Frank, my father. Frances Lemanski gave me a photo of Leon posing with several other uniformed men, all heavily inebriated in the photo, at a bar in New York City. I can assume his army transport home from Europe stopped in New York City waiting for a train home. The photo was still in the souvenir cardboard

150

Leon (far right) at Bartley Madden's in New York circa 1944

frame from the bar, which apparently sold them to enlisted men who drank at their establishment for one dollar each. The handwriting with the photo indicates 1945 as the date. The bar, Bartley Madden's Bar and Grill at 307 West Forty-seventh Street in Manhattan, just off of Times Square, apparently would mail the photos home to family for the soldiers. The Blarney Stone Pub today in 2006 occupies the site of the former Bartley Madden's. Leon had the bar send this souvenir photo to Audrey in East St. Louis, further proving Audrey and Leon's relationship existed prior to his leaving for military service in 1943. A similar photo (different pose but taken at the same place and time) was sent to Nell in Paducah as well, as I found that photo minus the souvenir frame in her collection of photos.

My father told me Leon's unit was sent to England to be part of the D-day invasion. My father told me that Leon landed at Normandy five days after D-day, and had to step over the dead bodies of soldiers killed in previous days while climbing the cliffs of Normandy. The army hadn't had time or opportunity to remove the bodies yet in the heat of battle. According to my father, Leon fought all the way across France and into Germany. I remember Leon once telling me, in one of the rare instances that he would be willing to talk about the war, that he bought eggs from a German lady on her farm that they were fighting near. She taught him the German name for eggs, which he remembered incorrectly. Bert Mitchell told me that Leon had told him the story of how he was injured in the war, which was in a machine gun foxhole that the Germans were targeting with mortar fire. This must have been in October or November of 1944, since Leon entered a U.S. Army hospital in Europe in November 1944. His age was thirty-three years old on his entry, and the SGO record said he was an "invalid," assumed to mean injured sufficiently that he had lost the ability to walk. It had to be between November 15 and 30, 1944, since Leon's birthday was on November 15, 1944, when he became thirty-three years old.

The next bit of information on the SGO records really floored me. I couldn't believe what I was reading. Their records showed they examined Leon for "history of prior disease," meaning some affliction that he had prior to active military service. The first diagnosis on the SGO record stated "emotional instability (including inadequate personality, schizoid, cycloid, prepsychotic, etc.)." This just stunned me to read that. Evidently Leon stayed in this European theater war hospital until June 1945, before being sent home to a stateside hospital. The record at this first hospital says he stayed there 238 days. The math doesn't add up on that since there aren't 238 days between November 1944 and June 1945, more like 180 days approximately. But perhaps the 238 represents days before the November 1944 entry date as well—I'll never know. There are no more clarifying documents to find. The document makes no mention of his war injuries from being injured in battle. There is room on the form for "second" and "third diagnosis," but these are left blank. This raised the specter to me that perhaps the injuries Leon told everyone he got in battle were fictitious. Maybe he was never injured in battle, but was diagnosed with mental illnesses instead, and made up the stories being injured in battle out of shame of the truth. Knowing Leon's temperament,

TYPE OF CASE: J   Disease
TYPE OF ADMISSION: x   Readmission case, Same diagnosis, EPTS (Existed Prior To entry on active military
                                     Service)

FIRST DIAGNOSIS: 4632   Emotional instability, cycloid, inadequate personality, prepsychotic, schizoid
                                     Not Found

Excerpt from Leon's military hospital discharge report

I can easily imagine him getting into fights in the military with anyone that even looked him in the eye. Frequent fighting might have gotten Leon sent to the hospital for mental examination.

The next record showed Leon being admitted in July 1945 to a regional military hospital at Ft. Sheridan in Illinois, a northern Chicago suburb located on Lake Michigan. The SGO record showed Leon being readmitted on the same diagnosis as before, calling it an "EPTS (Existed Prior To entry on active military Service)." This meant that Leon's mental illness didn't come from his exposures to battle and witnessing the horrors of war, or from his physical injuries sustained in the war. The second SGO record showed Leon being diagnosed as "emotional instability, cycloid, inadequate personality, prepsychotic, schizoid." The "circumstances" line on the report indicated "not a traumatism." This meant the mental illness they had diagnosed in Leon didn't come from some traumatic event, such as being injured in war.

These records just amazed me—my mouth was agape reading them. No one in my family had ever heard anything about this before. Leon didn't share these diagnoses with anybody in his family, not even his two wives or son. One can easily assume why Leon didn't reveal these facts to anyone—out of shame at being diagnosed severely mentally ill. Knowing Leon's personality, he probably scoffed at it as nonsense, or "bullshit" as he would say, and gave it not a second thought. As I processed this information in my mind, I couldn't understand why no one in our family had ever seen this before. If the army could twice diagnose, from two different sets of doctors at two different hospitals, that Leon had severe mental illness, then why didn't anyone in the family, for all his life, ever see it? Leon was honorably discharged on July 16, 1945, for "Inaptness." Inaptness meant that Leon was inept and wasn't capable of functioning in the army to any benefit of theirs. Rather than return him to active duty with these mental issues, the army evidently chose to honorably discharge him.

Thinking about the various diagnoses one by one, the word "schizoid" in the dictionary means "of, relating to, or having a personality disorder marked by extreme shyness, flat affect, reclusiveness, discomfort with others, and an inability to form close relationships" and "of, relating to, or suggestive of schizophrenia."[4] The word schizophrenia I had heard in jokes before, as well as the word schizoid, but I never really knew what the actual definitions and characteristics of these conditions were. The dictionary defines schizophrenia as "any of a group of psychotic disorders usually characterized by withdrawal from reality, illogical patterns of thinking, delusions, and hallucinations, and accompanied in varying degrees by other emotional, behavioral, or intellectual disturbances. Schizophrenia is often associated with dopamine imbalances in the brain and defects of the frontal lobe and may have an underlying genetic cause."[4] The definition goes on to say that schizophrenia is "a psychotic disorder characterized by loss of contact with the environment, by noticeable deterioration in the level of functioning in everyday life, and by disintegration of personality expressed as disorder of feeling, thought (as in hallucinations and delusions), and conduct called also dementia praecox."[4]

I had a sickening feeling welling inside as I continued to read these definitions of what my grandfather Leon had been twice diagnosed with by army doctors. The word "dementia" in the definition of schizophrenia I knew, because my mother experienced that near the end of her life following a severe stroke experienced during heart surgery. I witnessed the sort of fantasy world people live in who experience dementia. Another term on the SGO records was "inadequate personality," and the dictionary defines that as "a personality disturbance characterized by an inability to cope with the social, emotional, occupational, and intellectual demands of life."[4]

Another term on the SGO records was "cycloid." This term is defined as "afflicted with or relating to cyclothymia," which is to say "relating to, having, or being a personality characterized by alternating high and low moods," further defined as "a mild affective disorder characterized by alternating periods of elevated and depressed mood."[4] This made me think of manic depression, as this is characteristic of alternating elevated and depressed moods. Of course, manic depression wasn't discovered until later years, and at this time, couldn't have been diagnosed beyond this earlier term cyclothymia. I knew about manic depression, having an aunt on my mother's side, who was no blood relation but married into our family, being diagnosed as manic-depressive in her later years. She was institutionalized for manic depression until lithium medication got it under control, and she could live a normal life again outside an institution.

Another term on the SGO records was "prepsychotic." This term is defined as "relating to the period prior to the onset of psychosis" and "of or being a mental state or condition having the potential to elicit a psychotic episode."[4] I started to get light-headed as I read these definitions, like I was nearing fainting. The blood was moving to my feet so I could run from what I didn't want to be seeing with my own eyes. I just couldn't believe Leon was this sick. For God's sake, even a layperson like myself knew that someone with psychosis was very mentally ill. The definition of psychosis was "a severe mental disorder, with or without organic damage, characterized by derangement of personality and loss of contact with reality and causing deterioration of normal social functioning."[4]

Surely these diagnoses could not be the result of the doctors just misunderstanding a country-raised Kentuckian such as my grandfather. Surely these doctors had encountered country folk before and knew the cultural differences between how people expressed themselves and thought patterns in different regions of the U.S. These could not be misdiagnoses by the doctors who saw Leon. If the first diagnosis in Europe was wrong, surely the second diagnosis at the stateside hospital would have uncovered the previous error. If both were in error, surely they wouldn't have made the same, identical error. I had to reluctantly believe what the SGO documents were telling me was true. Leon, at this time in 1944 to 1945, was severely mentally ill and had been so before being drafted. Clearly Leon needed mental help, to be institutionalized, or at least receive major therapy and treatment, rather than living freely in East St. Louis and leading a family. These army hospital diagnoses of Leon would prove to be the only time Leon would have received mental examination in his lifetime, at least to anyone's knowledge. No mention of Leon and mental illness was ever made to me by any of the family—the

Tucker cousins. Left untreated, it is logical that Leon carried this mental illness with him for the rest of his life, as these mental afflictions do not heal themselves.

It now explained why Leon never wanted to talk about the war years when we would ask him about it. We would have to wait for rare times when he would volunteer a tidbit of a story, usually prompted by something he saw on television that would trigger a memory, such as a World War II movie. He didn't want to talk about the war years because it might cause him to slip up and reveal the army doctors' diagnoses of his mental illness. I'm convinced he kept this absolutely secret from everyone, including his two wives and his son, for the remainder of his life.

After I received the SGO documents, and why it didn't all come together in the same shipment I don't know, but the Veterans Affairs Department (VA) sent me a copy of Leon's "Enlisted Record and Report of Honorable Discharge." The previous office, National Personal Records, had said the SGO documents were all they could find on Leon, but this other office, the VA, apparently could find more, to my pleasant surprise. The discharge report they sent me was a bombshell—it revealed a lot. The discharge report was basically a summary of his entry and exit from the army, with all the pertinent facts necessary for both actions. First, it said Leon had been living at 1844 Bridge Street in Paducah at the time of his induction in 1943. I sent away for the property record on that address for the years of World War II to see who owned that house at that time. The property appeared to be a rental property at the time, not owned by any relative. This may have been Nell's address in Paducah at this time. During the war years she would not have wanted to stay in East St. Louis by herself and would have preferred to be in Paducah near her parents and siblings.

The discharge report also said that Leon had been inducted on December 23, 1943, at Ft. Sheridan, Illinois, which was located on the north shore of Lake Michigan just north of Chicago. At the time of his induction, Leon was five feet ten and a half inches tall, weighed 195 pounds, and had two legal dependents, obviously counting Nell (Peepeyes) and my father, Frank. It didn't list their names, so he could have been counting Audrey—who knows? His date of entry into active service was January 18, 1944, some twenty-seven days after being inducted. The discharge report said Leon was on "inactive status" from December 28, 1943, to January 17, 1944, which was likely the time Leon came home to visit Frank and Nell, as well as Audrey. These dates conflict with the photo from March 1943 that Audrey's daughter Frances gave me, showing Leon as part of a tank company at Ft. Shelby in Mississippi. It clearly is Leon in the picture, or at least we both thought it was. Perhaps it isn't him in the picture, since he is at a distance in the photo, or if it is him, perhaps Leon received advance training earlier in March 1943 before formally being inducted into the army in December. I don't know how this exactly comes together, because the form the VA sent me didn't mention anything about this earlier service in Mississippi. Perhaps the Mississippi training was some form of basic training or reserve training prior to being formally inducted. Frances was certain that her mother Audrey never dated anyone else during the war years, she was Leon's alone, so it had to be Leon in the photo.

Frank and Leon Tucker circa 1944

The discharge report said Leon was registered with Selective Service in St. Clair County in Illinois under the address he and Nell shared in East St. Louis, which was 5009 Bunkum Road. The form said Leon was trained as a rifleman for combat infantry. His decorations were an Overseas Service Bar and a European-African-Middle Eastern Theatre ribbon. No purple heart was mentioned here, as had previously been rumored in our family. This was because of what the discharge report showed below the decorations. It clearly said in the box titled "Wounds Received In Action" that Leon had "None." This fact conflicts entirely with what Leon had told our family and Bert Mitchell, as well as I'm sure the extended Tucker family. Leon told us he was injured in World War II in the battle of Aachen (a city in Germany)—that he was injured when a mortar shell exploded in his foxhole. He said he woke up in an army hospital, not able to walk, and had to recuperate for many months in a hospital in England. He said the doctors there told him he'd never be able to walk again, but he fought through the pain and regained his ability to walk prior to being discharged. This discharge report proved Leon had never been injured in World War II at all.

Leon lied about all of that—that whole story of being injured in Europe was one big fat lie from start to finish. Leon was obviously ashamed of the truth and covered it up with this made-up story. The truth was Leon spent all or most of that time from November 1944 until July 1945, when he was discharged, in army hospitals being treated for mental illnesses. It disheartened me greatly to read this on the discharge report. I had always hoped at least a little of Leon's heroic tales from World War II were true. Now I had found the proof they were lies. They were not even exaggerations. They were just plain lies. It saddened me greatly.

The discharge report said that Leon had departed the U.S. for the "ETO," which meant the "European Theatre of Operations," on August 24, 1944, and arrived on September 1, 1944. Leon said on the ship over to England he was so seasick he had to find the absolute bottom of the ship, strap a hammock between two posts, and sleep in it to get any peaceful rest from the constant rocking of the ship. If Leon arrived in Europe in September 1, 1944, his tale of passing through Omaha Beach only a few days after D-day was a lie also. D-day was on June 6, 1944, and Leon was still at Ft. Sheridan, Illinois, at that time, according to the form from the VA. The discharge report said Leon served nine months and eight days in "Continental Service" and seven months and twenty days in "Foreign Service." Leon left Europe on March 31, 1945, bound for the U.S., and arrived April 13, 1945. The two-week transit obviously meant Leon came home by ship. VE day, Victory in Europe day, wasn't until May 8, 1945, so Leon left Europe before the war in Europe was over.

If Leon arrived in Europe on September 1, 1944, and was admitted into an Army hospital in Europe for mental illnesses somewhere between November 15 and 30, 1944, then Leon could have seen two and a half months of combat. From the last half of November 1944 until March 31, 1945, Leon was in the army hospital in Europe. When transferred home, the gap of time between mid-April 1945 and when Leon was admitted to an army hospital at Ft. Sheridan for mental illnesses (June 1945) was about forty-five days. This likely was time for Leon to visit home in East St. Louis, or maybe it was time spent at Ft. Sheridan. Leon's Infantry Regiment, the 110th, was known to be at Ft. Sheridan preparing for the battle for Japan at this time. The discharge report said Leon was given an honorable discharge in July 1945 under the Army Regulation 615-369, which is for "Inaptness." This regulation was created in July 1944 so that the army could rid itself of men it could not use because their mental or physical abilities were not sufficient for the tasks a soldier needed to perform. Leon definitely had the physical abilities to be a soldier, being a strong man with a high tolerance for pain. Therefore, the "inaptness" had to refer to Leon's mental capacity. Evidently, Leon couldn't perform with his mental illnesses afflicting him, so the army wanted him out. The discharge report said Leon was "not eligible for reenlistment."

At the bottom of the discharge report, it said Leon had achieved five years of grammar school, and no higher education. Leon had always told us he had quit school in the third grade, so this was a mild exaggeration or confusion by Leon. Or maybe he was held back a few years for not achieving passing grades? I know we have a school photo of Leon at the Farley Elementary School on Old Benton Road in Paducah, from 1924 to 25. From his birth year of 1911, this would put Leon at least thirteen years of age in the photo, which normally would put someone in ninth grade or junior high school. Who knows then truly how much schooling Leon had? The discharge report concluded by stating, for pay purposes, that Leon served his country one year, six months, and eighteen days, most of which was in army hospitals being treated for mental illnesses. At least two and a half months of it could have been Leon seeing combat. Any combat time deserves my respect, and I give that respect to Leon for fighting in a tough war, something I've never had to do.

The discharge report bore Leon's signature and thumbprint at the bottom, validating it. To connect the two sets of documents, the SGO documents and the discharge report, to see if they validated each other, I noted that both showed Leon at Ft. Sheridan, and both showed honorable discharge in July 1945 (before the war in Japan ended) for "Inaptness." Any doubts I had that perhaps the SGO documents weren't Leon's, since they only bore his service number and not his name for confidentiality purposes, were dispelled. The VA also sent me a copy of Leon's honorable discharge certificate, which Audrey's daughter Frances had already given me the original. However, this copy from the VA also bore some additional information, that Leon was part of the L110th Infantry (meaning "L" Company of the 110th Infantry Regiment), and was honorably discharged at Ft. Sheridan, Illinois, on July 16, 1945. Immediately following this discharge, Leon returned home to Audrey in East St. Louis.

Since Frances offered me a copy of the discharge report, this proved that Audrey had seen the proof that Leon had never been injured in battle. This made me wonder how much Audrey knew of Leon's lies about his wartime service. She may have not known it before he died. But when ordering his military headstone for his grave after he died, she discovered the truth. Frances didn't offer me a copy of the army hospital records showing Leon's treatments for mental illnesses, so it's possible Audrey never knew that. It is probable Leon's two wives and his son never knew Leon was diagnosed mentally ill. I could be the first person in Leon's family to ever know that. It is known that Frank once told a coworker that he knew his father wasn't discharged honorably from the military. Frank told this to Aloysius "Pete" Langheim, a coworker from his Taylorville, Illinois, days. I spoke with Pete in 2006 when he was eighty-four years old and still spry of voice and clear of memory. If Frank did say this about Leon to Pete, he was factually wrong. Leon did get an actual honorable discharge, albeit for a less than honorable reason, "inaptness," resulting in Leon being designated as "unable to reenlist." It's possible Frank may have seen the discharge report at some point. It's doubtful that Frank knew of Leon's stays in the military mental hospitals unless Leon disclosed this to him, which is highly unlikely. This is because the military mental hospital stays do not appear anywhere on the discharge report, which is likely the only thing Frank might have seen.

The Veteran's Administration (VA) kept searching for more of Leon's military records at my behest, and found a file of claims put in by Audrey after Leon died. Evidently Audrey, and later her daughter Frances, using a power of attorney (POA) over Audrey, tried to apply for Leon's military pension and health benefits. It was first denied because Audrey couldn't prove she had divorced her second husband, Joe Hayden, before marrying Leon. Frances guessed the Hayden marriage was in Mayfield, Kentucky, in 1939, with a divorce in Indianapolis, Indiana, at an unknown later date. I checked Graves County (Mayfield), and they had no record of the Hayden marriage, nor did St. Clair County in Illinois, and nor did McCracken County (Paducah) in Kentucky. I gave up searching for it at that point. After the exhaustive search for the record of Leon and Audrey's marriage, I wasn't about to repeat that for Audrey's second marriage record. It wasn't important enough to have the dates on it exactly. In another chapter, I detail the divorce record for Audrey's marriage to Joe Hayden, which incredibly didn't take place until 1969 when she wanted to marry Leon legitimately.

It was interesting that the VA was demanding to see documentation of the Hayden divorce before they would approve any benefits for Audrey. Originally Frances and Audrey tried to keep this Hayden marriage off the books, and just acknowledged the Michael Reed and Leon Tucker marriages. They said the Reed marriage ended with Michael Reed dying in 1946, and they provided a copy of his death certificate. Frances and Audrey originally didn't mention the Hayden marriage at all, evidently because they couldn't document its ending and figured the VA wouldn't find out about it. They figured wrong. A good axiom for dealing with the U.S. Federal Government is "Never lie to them." They find it out eventually. It was kind of a giveaway that Audrey's last name when she married Leon was "Hayden" (not her maiden name of "Marshall" or first married name of "Reed"), meaning she had to have gotten married a second time between the Reed and Tucker marriages. Only a complete oaf at the VA would overlook this obvious inconsistency.

I'm guessing it never occurred to Frances that all she had to do was write to the Circuit Clerk of St. Clair County in Belleville, Illinois, and retrieve the divorce file from Audrey's 1969 divorce of Joe Hayden in absentia. This suggests that perhaps Frances never knew that her mother divorced Joe Hayden that year. Perhaps Frances always thought her mother divorced Joe Hayden decades earlier, when he abandoned her, in 1942. Perhaps that's what Audrey told Frances, so it never occurred to her to check the county's records for it all the way out to 1969. If Frances looked for the divorce documents in the 1940s era and in Indianapolis, she would have looked in the wrong place and time. Records weren't computerized then like they are now. Searching blindly at that time would have been far more time consuming than nowadays with the quick searching capabilities of computers. This computer searching assisted me greatly in my investigation. Had Frances searched for the divorce record, she would have made the same shocking discovery I made about the 1969 divorce, which her letters to the VA suggest she did not know about. When I asked Frances about this 1969 divorce when I spoke with her in 2006, she said she had no knowledge of it.

The VA wrote back to Audrey through Frances, her POA, insisting they would have to provide proof of how the Hayden marriage ended. Joe Hayden died in Kentucky sometime in the 1980s (according to Frances), so they couldn't even ask him for the information or a copy of the divorce document. The VA also wanted proof of how Leon's marriage to Nell ended. I doubt Frances or Audrey had a copy of Nell's death certificate, and with Leon dead, had no access to getting one from the State of Florida. Only Frank had access to it at that point. Frank hated Audrey—Audrey hated Frank—so there was no point in Audrey or Frances contacting Frank for a copy of Nell's death certificate. Eventually, after additionally being disqualified because Audrey's pension income was too high for assistance, they gave up pursuing Leon's military pension and health benefits.

* * *

Chapter 8

THE VISIT

Charles said that Leon once said to him, "I got me a drug that'll stop a heart, an' they'd be no trace of it later on."

I made plans in the spring of 2006 to visit the death scene in Florida. I selected July 3-5 for a visit to Florida, as the July 4, holiday didn't mean much to me anymore with both of my parents now gone. Checking the airfares to the two closest major airports to Okeechobee, Ft. Lauderdale and Orlando, I selected the significantly better airfare, which was to Ft. Lauderdale. My half-brother Trent lived in Orlando, and I almost wanted to visit with him, but we had just reunited about nine months prior (in Kentucky), and though we were e-mailing occasionally to get to know each other slowly, he hadn't extended an invitation to me to visit him in Orlando as I had extended to him to visit me in Los Angeles. So I thought I should skip visiting Trent for this visit to Florida, not wanting to crowd him too soon after reuniting with him at Frank's funeral the previous October.

The purpose for the trip to Florida I wouldn't have wanted to reveal to him anyway. I needed almost the entire three days because of the drive time from Ft. Lauderdale to Okeechobee, from Okeechobee to Ft. Meade, and returning to Ft. Lauderdale. I also needed a few hours each in Okeechobee and Ft. Meade for investigating, photo taking, and to meet with the Stevensons (in Ft. Meade). So there really wasn't any time for a visit with Trent even if I had felt the welcome mat was out, which I wasn't sure it was. So I got up my nerve and called Trent. He seemed to be open to the idea of meeting on July 4 in Ft. Meade, but said also he was working that day and would have to "arrange things." I took that as meaning he needed to think about it. So I decided I'd call him closer to the actual day and give him one more chance.

The purpose of the Okeechobee visit would be to touch base at the campground on Lake Okeechobee—to actually stand where it all took place some thirty-seven years ago. I felt I needed to do it, just to close the loop on this investigation. First, I wanted to photo-document the campsite area. I wanted to photograph the old Okeechobee General Hospital, now transformed into the Okeechobee County Planning and Development

Department offices. I wanted to time the drive from the campground to the hospital, then drive around Okeechobee briefly to get a "feel" for the city, and last, I wanted to visit the grave of Dr. Steven R. Johnston in Evergreen Cemetery, located northeast of Okeechobee. Why I wanted to visit his grave, I'm not sure, but it's something I felt compelled to do. Again, it was like touching base at a point in history for this whole mystery.

Lake Okeechobee had become in the early 1900s a huge fishing export spot, where enormous hauls of catfish were taken from the lake and exported to the Midwest, notably St. Louis.[5] This is likely where Leon got the idea to go fishing on Lake Okeechobee. Leon loved to fish all his life, mainly in small rivers, creeks, and on the twin lakes of Kentucky Lake and Lake Barkley in Kentucky. His main type of fish he went for were catfish and black crappie, which were in plentiful supply in Lake Okeechobee.[5] Leon likely heard during his early years around East St. Louis that huge hauls of catfish were coming out of Lake Okeechobee, and he wanted to get in on it himself.

Living was cheap in East St. Louis in those years, and Leon made good money in construction. He could take off for a month during January each year, head down to Lake Okeechobee with one of his wives, alternating wives each year or taking one wife for a couple of weeks, coming back up to the Midwest and then taking the other wife down to Florida for the remainder of the month. Leon had picked out a free camping area on the north shore of Lake Okeechobee right where the Kissimmee River dumps into the lake that he would return to each year. I wanted to see that campsite for myself, hoping to find some insight into what the attraction was for Leon to this location. I had some evidence from Nell's photo album, which I possessed, that Leon and Nell would also go to other campgrounds around Okeechobee. Tom Lykes Trailer Court in Palmdale, Florida, just a few miles off the western shore of the lake is where Leon and Nell camped on February 18, 1964, just five days after the birth of their grandson Dwain (this author). I wondered if they even knew on that day that I had been born, since they didn't call back to check on people in Kentucky and Illinois except once every couple of weeks or so. The item providing this date was a sort of "Hi, I met you here" note from another couple they met at that campground. Nell filled in the form, dated it, and kept it in her album. There are also photos of Leon and Nell at Clewiston, Florida, on the southwest side of the lake, from 1967, perhaps one or two years (depending on the month in 1967, which wasn't indicated) before she would die in Okeechobee.

The purpose of the Ft. Meade visit would be to meet with the Stevensons who lived there, mainly Irene Stevenson and her daughters, who were alive at the time when Leon and Nell stopped through there for a brief stay on their way to Okeechobee in January 1969. I also wanted to see the plot of land that Leon had owned in Ft. Meade at the time in 1969, and drive around the small city to get a "feel" for it. I extended an invitation for my half-brother Trent to drive the hour and a half down from Orlando, where he lives, to meet with me at a restaurant there in Ft. Meade and have a short visit with him. He initially said he would be working that day, but then said to call him closer to the time I was going to be there, and we'd "work something out." I wasn't entirely sure the invitation was welcome, so I had to rethink my strategy at that point.

I arrived into Ft. Lauderdale on the evening of Monday, July 3, 2006, after having attended a Bond family reunion (my mother's family) in Illinois the prior Saturday. I took off for the two-hour drive to Okeechobee at six o'clock the following morning, knowing I had a full day of driving ahead of me. I got to Okeechobee right at eight o'clock in the morning on schedule and began my exploration. I took the road south on the northwestern edge of Lake Okeechobee toward the Kissimmee River, and found the Okee-Tantie Campground & Marina at 10430 State Route 78 West.

I drove around the area, looking for the "hole" that Eddie Stevenson had described to me as Leon's favorite camping spot. This being July, and very hot in temperatures, there were only a handful of campers in the area. It was largely empty. Winter months I would expect are Okee-Tantie's busy time. I found the name "Okee-Tantie" to be an odd one, so I looked it up. "Okee-" obviously came from Okeechobee, and the "-Tantie" part came from the original name of Okeechobee town, which was "Tantie," named after Tantie Huckabee,[6] one of the first schoolteachers in the town once it had been settled in the late 1800s.

Because the area had changed so much since 1969, it was unlikely I would find the free camping spot that Leon and Nell were at when she died. The area to the upstream side of the bridge over the Kissimmee River is built up as a permanent trailer court now. So I satisfied myself with driving around Okee-Tantie, and up on the banks of the Kissimmee River. I realized I had to be standing very near the spot that my grandmother, Nell Annie Tucker, died some thirty-seven years prior. I got somber for a moment, almost like paying my respects at a grave site. I took photos all over the area to document what I saw, and then started out to time the distance of the drive from the Okee-Tantie Campground to Okeechobee town. It took only seven or eight minutes to reach the town. With the confusion of panic that night in January 1969, I could reasonably add another ten or fifteen minutes to that total as Leon tried to find the hospital. The total transit time from the campground to the hospital could not have been more than twenty-three to twenty-five minutes total, with the most likely time being between fifteen and twenty minutes. It most certainly did not take five hours to drive the distance, which is the missing time in question from when Leon and the Stevensons left the campground with Nell's body in the car to when they showed up at the Okeechobee General Hospital.

The site of the Okeechobee General Hospital today is now the Okeechobee County Planning and Development Department, located at 499 NW Fifth Avenue in downtown Okeechobee next door to the sheriff's office, just four blocks away to the northwest from the main intersection of Okeechobee. Okeechobee is still today a very small town, approximately five thousand citizens, not more than twenty blocks in any direction, with most of the city concentrated in the center eight to ten blocks around the main intersection of town. One can imagine thirty-seven years ago, in 1969, that the town was even smaller.

Site of former Okeechobee General Hospital

I took photos of the old Okeechobee General Hospital, and again felt a somberness coming over me, realizing this is where Dr. Steven Johnston examined Nell's remains, with Leon refusing to allow an autopsy of the remains, in violation of Florida law. From this location is where Leon placed the call to my father Frank in East St. Louis to notify him his mother had died. At this location is where Bill Yates of Yates Funeral Home picked up Nell's remains and spoke with Leon about what arrangements he wanted for Nell's remains and their transport home to Kentucky. It was a Saturday, and the offices were closed, so I couldn't go inside. I made a promise to myself that my next visit to Okeechobee, if there were to be one, would be on a workday when the building would be open, so I could explore inside.

I next visited the Evergreen Cemetery and the grave site of Dr. Steven R. Johnston. It was an above ground granite mausoleum, not uncommon in Florida. The Florida sand and high water tables don't always make for the best situation for below ground burials. Dr. Johnston's last wife Christine, his fifth wife, was still alive in 2006, and has an empty, adjoining mausoleum next to Dr. Johnston. The face of the mausoleum lacked the two features I had hoped it might have on it, a photo of Dr. Johnston (sometimes family members mount in stone a portrait-type photo of the deceased) or a Masonic symbol. Sometimes Masons have the Masonic symbol placed on their gravestones, as a sibling had insisted that we place on our father's grave. I don't know why, but I felt I needed to touch base at Dr. Johnston's grave site, since he likely took with him to his grave the answer to the riddle of Nell's death. He certainly knew the answer as to why no autopsy was performed, or insisted upon over Leon's objections, to comply with Florida law. He being a licensed physician of many years experience, I refuse to believe he didn't know it was Florida law that an autopsy was required in a death where the cause was undetermined. He certainly knew the answer as to why he wrote "unknown" as the cause of Nell's death, rather than "natural causes." That was the key to the riddle, right there. I would never know what Dr. Johnston knew.

This being July 4, Independence Day, I knew that all of the government offices would be closed, so there was no point in trying to stop by the local library. I had previously written to them, and their searches of local newspaper files had produced no fruit for my investigation. The day before arriving in Okeechobee, I had called Pearl Godwin, the now elderly nurse who was at Okeechobee General Hospital in the 1960s. I asked her if she had any additional information for me she had discovered since I spoke with her weeks earlier. If she did, I would have stopped by to pick it up while I was in Okeechobee. Much to my disappointment, she had no further information on the whereabouts of the old medical files from the Okeechobee General Hospital. My hopes would continue to lie with the Okeechobee Historical Society, to whom I wrote about the old medical files, hoping they might help me locate them. After two hours in Okeechobee, it was time to keep to my schedule and head off northwest toward Ft. Meade, and the Stevenson family there. I felt a bit wistful as I departed Okeechobee. Somehow, I knew I was leaving behind a little bit of my family history in that small Florida town.

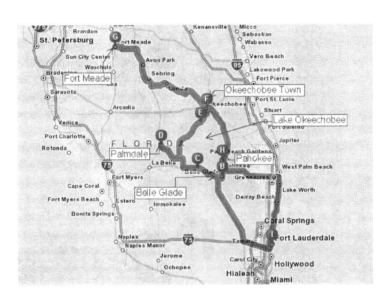

Route of Florida trip 2006

As I drove to Ft. Meade I second-guessed my decision not to call Trent (half-brother) to invite him a second time to meet me in Ft. Meade. I made the decision not to call Trent again the day before I would be going to Ft. Meade because I wasn't sure what I was walking into there. I had never been to that town before, so I didn't really know if they had a decent place to meet someone at, like a nice café or restaurant. Also, Trent knew what date I was going to be there, I had e-mailed him that information, and he didn't extend any interest in my direction via e-mail as the date closed in. I took a guess that perhaps my invitation wasn't welcome, and I didn't want to put him on the spot with a telephone call. No one likes to be rude to someone, and I didn't want to put him in that situation. I thought it was sort of odd that history was repeating itself. My father was always afraid to call Trent over the thirty-five years of their separation for fear his call wasn't welcome, and I suspected Trent was feeling the same thing on his end. They were both afraid of each other. Now I was feeling that same situation with Trent as my father had as well, and wondered if Trent was feeling the same thing again also with me. But I had already made the effort to reach out to Trent, so I made a reasonable assumption that if he had any interest in seeing me, he would make some kind of attempt to reach back in my direction. That "reach back" wasn't present prior to my visit to Ft. Meade, so I thought it was best I not call him again, at least about this visit.

I arrived in Ft. Meade a little early for my visit with the Stevenson family that still lives there. So I used that time to visit the parcel of land, still a vacant lot in 2006, which was owned by Leon Tucker during the 1960s. Larkin "L.A." Stevenson had sold the land to Leon in February 1959, and it had a mixed citrus grove on it—mainly oranges. After Nell's death in 1969, Leon sold the parcel back to the Stevensons in April 1971, specifically to Joleen (Stevenson) Harden and her husband Joseph Kenneth Harden. The nominal price of only $10 was the selling price both times the property was bought and sold by Leon. Evidently this was done to minimize the property taxes if the recorded value of the property was only $10, but obviously the property was worth more than that. I'm sure what the property was actually worth was privately paid to and from Leon, the $10 payment was just for the official record.

As an interesting side note, the sale in April 1971 was witnessed by Frank and Judy Tucker, my parents. Both signed the warranty deed as witnesses. They must have been vacationing with Leon and Audrey in Florida that year. I most certainly was along with them, as I would have been seven years old at that time but have no memory of it. Audrey was definitely married to Leon by this time, since her name appears as his wife on the document, and she had to sign it also under the name "Audrey Tucker," as she would have a legal interest in any of Leon's property as his wife. Joleen's husband Kenny uprooted the citrus trees over the ensuing years, and the lot nowadays has just some old trees, perhaps oak, on it along with grass—no fruit trees at all. Joleen had told me previously on the phone that she and her husband Kenny planned to build their retirement home on that lot, having refused many offers for it over the years.

I photographed the lot and walked around it a bit, feeling nostalgic as I walked the ground my grandparents had owned at one time.

Ft. Meade is a sleepy little town about the same size as Okeechobee, approximately five thousand citizens. I arrived at Irene Stevenson's in Ft. Meade around noon, my scheduled meeting time with her. A Stevenson cousin, Freeda (Stevenson) Collin's daughter, Barbara Stevenson (Barbara had married another Stevenson, not in her family), who lived a two-hour drive away from Ft. Meade in Cocoa, Florida, joined me at Irene's at that time to question her on Stevenson family history. Irene Stevenson, seventy-seven years old, met with us first. At first she didn't seem to remember much about either family history, but with specific memory prompts from Barbara and me, she seemed to remember more. She remembered the story of Leon Tucker saving her daughter Joleen's life once at the public swimming pool in Ft. Meade. Joleen reiterated this story when she joined us, saying she was "about ten years old" at the time. Since she was fifty-five years old when she was meeting with us in July 2006, this placed the event approximately at 1961. Evidently Joleen was drowning for some reason in the pool. Leon, seeing her in distress, jumped in and pulled her out. Irene and Joleen didn't seem to remember how Leon would bring Nell or Audrey through Ft. Meade on their way to Okeechobee at different times, but did remember both women. They had no specific recollection of the time when Nell died in 1969. They did have a photo of Leon when he was approximately eight or nine years old, holding some wooden crafts he had whittled, and they allowed me to scan the photo along with others. Joleen said she was fond of "Uncle Leon," as she called him, and agreed he was charming. Joleen still had the deed documents from when Leon was sold the land they now owned in Ft. Meade, and then sold it back to them in 1971. She agreed to copy it for me and send it to me.

I left Ft. Meade that day, not sure I had accomplished too awful much, but glad I touched base at another point in the story of Nell's death. Nell and Leon would have stopped through Ft. Meade to visit with the Stevensons on January 3 or 4, 1969, on their way to Okeechobee. It is unlikely Leon would have stopped again through Ft. Meade on his way north after Nell's death, perhaps on January 8, 1969, as he needed to get to Paducah as quickly as possible. Leon would have stopped again in Ft. Meade in about a week later with Audrey in his car, perhaps on January 13 or 14, 1969. He was headed back toward Okeechobee to finish his January fishing. He had left his trailer at Okeechobee with the Stevensons, who remained there and did not drive north with Leon to attend Nell's funeral. They remained behind to hold the camping spots. As I write this chapter, I feel the callousness of that situation, the Stevensons not attending Nell's funeral after having known her closely for forty years and being witnesses to her death, and Leon returning to Florida to continue his January fishing vacation with wife number two, Audrey, immediately after Nell's funeral. It's a little hard to understand how that could have made sense to them (Leon and the Stevensons). I suppose it is possible that the Stevensons offered to join Leon in a trip back to Kentucky for Nell's funeral, but Leon told them he'd rather them stay in Okeechobee to hold the camping spots for the group, and guard all the campers.

Leon Tucker as a young boy showing crafts he had whittled
while visiting his Stevenson cousins in the late 1910's

I left Florida the next day to return to Los Angeles and contemplated what I had learned in Florida on the flight home. I had confirmed with my own eyes that the drive from the campground on Lake Okeechobee was not more than fifteen to twenty minutes to the Okeechobee General Hospital. As small as the town was, there simply was no credible explanation for the long time gap, some five hours, between Leon leaving the campground with Nell's body and arriving at the hospital. Seeing the sites firsthand—the Okee-Tantie Campground and camping areas near the Kissimmee River, the site of the former Okeechobee General Hospital, Dr. Steven Johnston's grave site, the lot of land formerly owned by Leon in Ft. Meade, and the Stevenson's house in Ft. Meade—made the whole story of Nell and Leon in Florida in 1969 gel into reality for me. It wasn't just a story anymore—it actually happened.

As an addendum to this story of this first visit to Okeechobee, at the conclusion of the trip. I e-mailed Trent when I got home to L.A. I told him I didn't call him for the meeting in Ft. Meade because I thought he would be working and didn't know what to expect in Ft. Meade anyway. That was all true. He e-mailed me back that he was indeed working that day, July 4, being one of their biggest sales days in his industry of timeshare vacations. He wouldn't have been free to meet with me. But he did indicate I was welcome to call him later to interview him about the family history. So in a way, he did reach back after all—and I was glad he did.

Not satisfied that I had gotten all that I needed from Okeechobee, I planned another visit there in September 2006. I wanted this time to drive around the western side of Lake Okeechobee, visiting towns that appeared in Nell's photos from the 1960s. Specifically, Belle Glade, Clewiston, and Palmdale were on my list, and I wanted to try to pinpoint exactly where the trailer was located in January 1969 when Nell died. With prints of aerial photography of the area that I would show to Eddie Stevenson, I hoped to pinpoint exactly where the trailer was located for this second trip to Okeechobee. I hoped to go on a business day this time around, so I could actually go inside the Okeechobee Planning and Development Department's office building. I wanted to see if I could locate the old emergency room.

In September 2006, I visited again with Frances and Audra near East St. Louis, and I stopped through Paducah to visit again with Tillie Edwards and Eddie Stevenson. I began to sense that something was up with the Stevenson clan, as most were refusing to allow me to visit them. I think most of them began to feel uncomfortable that I was asking so many questions about Nell's death—too many perhaps, in their opinions. Eddie still allowed me to visit him, and we talked for three hours at his dinner table. Eddie revealed to me something that shocked and surprised me. He said his brother Charles, whom I had visited with in his home earlier in the year, recently had confided in Eddie something Leon had once told to him. Charles said that Leon once said to him, "I got me a drug that will stop a heart, an' they'd be no trace of it later on." This shocked Charles, so much so that he put it away in his memory for permanent keeping. I was surprised that Charles didn't tell me this himself when I visited with him earlier that year. But I sensed during that visit that Charles was holding back—that he didn't want to tell me things negative against my grandfather Leon for fear of hurting my feelings. To Charles, I sensed that would be bad manners to say something against Leon to me, despite my assurances to him that I wanted to hear it all, "the good, the bad, and the ugly." But Eddie felt it was important for me to know everything there was to know, and I thanked him for that.

After all, I reminded Eddie, Leon was long gone, and so was Audrey—so was everyone remotely connected in any way to Nell's death. So there wasn't any reason to keep secret any of the story now. Even Walter and Dollie Stevenson, Eddie's and Charles's parents, were long gone, and they were merely witnesses and bystanders to the event. So certainly there was nothing of any threat to anyone now about discussing the details of Nell's death. But the rest of the Stevensons apparently felt differently from Eddie and stopped returning my telephone messages and started refusing to meet with me. So I had to be satisfied that I had gotten all of the story from the Stevenson clan that I was going to get, despite the fact I felt there was more to know from them. Before I left Eddie's that night, he pointed on the aerial photographs I had sent to him previously to the exact spot that Leon and Nell's trailer had been parked the night Nell died. This was valuable information for me to locate the spot when I visited Florida in a few more days.

Continuing on my September 2006 trip, I drove down through the foot of Missouri and crossed into northeast Arkansas. I visited the tiny town of Etowah, the hometown of Frank's first wife, Maudine. The sign said the town had a population of around two hundred, but I find that hard to believe considering the size of the town. The town consisted of nothing more than a collection of perhaps twenty trailers and old wooden homes, all of them in a state of disrepair and disintegration. Unless ten people lived in each of these houses or trailers, the population on the sign had to include some of the rural area around the town. What I saw driving through that day allows me to safely say this—Etowah is about as poor as it gets. I can easily see now why Frank said in his divorce documents that Etowah was too backward of a place for his son Trent to be raised. As I drove through the town, a dog was sleeping in the middle of the dirt road that I had to drive around, as it wouldn't do anything but yawn at me. Other dogs that were free of any tethers surrounded my car, howling, barking, and baring teeth menacingly. This was definitely "Hee-haw, Arkansas," as we used to joke. I drove over to Osceola, Arkansas, where the Pruitts later lived, and found a much more normal city, with businesses, schools, and an affluent neighborhood on the west side as well as a poorer neighborhood close to the Mississippi riverfront. This is where Trent would have attended high school, so I was relieved he had a decent upbringing here.

Aerial photo of campsite location.
Lake Okeechobee is just out of the picture to the bottom.

Infant Sally Rose with probable slave caretaker Sarah circa 1850

I continued my journey to Memphis, arriving almost at nightfall. I made a quickie tour of the highlights of Memphis, having never been there before. I buzzed passed the Lorraine Motel National Civil Rights Historical site, where Dr. Martin Luther King Jr. was assassinated, passed the Memphis Pyramid arena, passed Graceland with Elvis's plane "Lisa Marie" visible from the road, and passed Beale Street where supposedly blues music partially originated. The next day I started out for my exploration of Arkansas by stopping first through Little Rock and doing a quickie tour of the William J. Clinton Presidential Library and a drive by of the Central High School National Civil Rights Historical site. My main motivation for exploring Arkansas was to see the farm owned by my great-great-grandfather Levi Tucker. A copy of a will (Thomas Chapman's) recorded in the records of Graves County, Kentucky, revealed much about Levi's history at this time.

Levi Tucker (born in 1833) married Sarah Chapman (born 1840) in Kentucky sometime around 1854, when she would have been only fourteen years old. He had been raised in the house of her father, Thomas Chapman. Thomas Chapman was married to Levi's mother, Melissa Gibson Tucker, after the death of Levi's father (d. 1947), Levi Sr. Levi (Jr.) married his stepsister, Sarah, and upon the death of her father, Thomas, in 1855, Levi received an inheritance of money and "one Negro slave." This is the first documentation I've found that one of my ancestors ever owned a slave. It wasn't for long though as the civil war came about in 1862 with the first phase of the Emancipation Proclamation. Kentucky would be a Union state in the civil war, but Arkansas was a confederate state, thus ownership of this slave might have continued until the fall of the confederacy. As a side note, I have found one family photo of a woman of African race with an ancestor on my grandmother Nell's side of the Tucker family. The young woman is holding an infant, who was my great-great-grandmother Sally Rose. Sally Rose was my grandmother Nell (Freeman) Tucker's grandmother. Sally Rose was born in 1850, which dates this photo to near that time. This predates the civil war, so very likely the young woman holding the infant Sally Rose was a slave.

On July 2, 1860, Levi Tucker bought eighty acres of land in Arkansas from the federal government and emigrated from Kentucky with his pregnant wife Sarah, one infant son named James, and presumably with the slave he had inherited. They set up their farm near what is now called Kentucky Valley Road near the city of Romance. Local historians have told me that the area was settled by many immigrants from Kentucky, and that they had wanted to call their new village "Kentucky," but the local government wouldn't allow it. They settled on Romance and named their road past their farms Kentucky Valley Road. Driving by the land in September 2006, I felt a weird connection back in history some 156 years, to my great-great-grandfather (Leon's grandfather).

Locals in the area that I contacted, mainly Jim McKay, told me that this property was what everyone still called "the Tucker farm." According to Jim, when he was growing up in the area, that meadow, totally enclosed by trees, contained an old shack that was once the Tucker farmhouse. The shack was nowadays used by hunters to get out of the elements and bunk overnight while hunting in the area. He pointed on a map where I should go to view the farm.

Romance, Arkansas in the mid 1800's

Levi Tucker's house in Romance, Arkansas (built circa 1860)

Though it didn't happen on this 2006 trip, it's the right point to insert an update from 2009. I missed finding the Tucker farm on the 2006 trip, mistaking Jim McKay's directions, taking me to the next farm past the Tucker farm, and thinking that was it. In 2009 I made another trip to the site, and this time, had success. Having contacted the current-day local caretaker of the Tucker farm, Dennis Murray, he gave me directions to Foster Road, and up a muddy offshoot road, just before a bridge over a creek, I found the old Tucker farm. Just as Jim McKay said, and Dennis Murray reiterated, the old Tucker farmhouse that Levi Tucker built was still there, barely standing. Deterioration with time had it leaning backward, gutted, but still clearly an 1800s era farmhouse with a dirt floor and two rooms, a sleeping loft above those two rooms, and an adjacent covered area for horses.

Sarah Tucker evidently died in childbirth of their third child. Levi, unable to farm and raise two small boys, took both boys, James and George (my great-grandfather), back to Kentucky to live with their aunt Molly. "Molly" was a nickname for Mary—Aunt Molly was Mary Ann (Tucker) Edwards, Levi's sister. Levi gave his sister a bag of $500 in gold coins, mostly twenty-dollar pieces, to pay for her raising his two sons. Evidently, Mary Ann (Tucker) Edwards hid the gold coins in a closet and left them there, a secret only known to her all her life. On her death bed, in 1906, she told her children where the bag of gold coins was hidden. They looked for it, found it, and it was reported in the local paper[18] about the mysterious "bag of gold." No one knew at the time where the gold came from, but pairing the two stories together, Levi's descendants, knowing he gave Molly the bag of gold, and her descendants finding it after her death, connects the two stories and validates it as true.

Levi returned to Arkansas to his farm, and family lore has him dying August 6, 1881, from a gunshot wound in a bar somewhere in Arkansas. What happened to the farm at that point is unknown. It may have been confiscated for back taxes as nothing was ever handed to Levi's sons in Kentucky. After touching my past in 2006, I proceeded northward through Arkansas toward Missouri.

I passed through the city of Fairfield Bay, Arkansas, where in the adjacent village of Edgemont is the grave of my father's first wife, Maudine. She had remarried to David Griffith, who was still alive at this point. I visited her grave in Woodland Memorial Park and, when standing over her grave, spoke aloud to her that I wished I could have met her before she had passed away. She likely knew so much of the Tucker family history, at least the East St. Louis years. I continued on northward through the Missouri Ozarks, staying overnight in the cheesy city of Branson. Branson impressed me as a poor man's Las Vegas. With not enough money to gamble, a poor man could only afford to see country music shows and eat at barbeque joints. The neon lights of the main strip of Branson reminded me of gambling towns. Completing a grand circle by returning to St. Louis, I searched the city and county records for any marriage record of Leon and Audrey's that existed there, and found nothing. I flew to Florida next for my next phase of investigating.

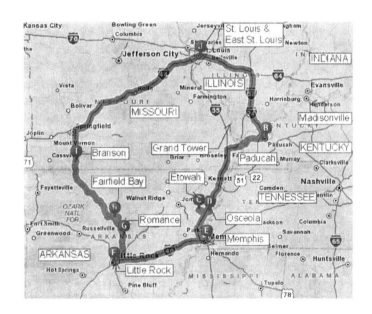

Route of Arkansas trip 2006

Leon and Nell's campsite location viewed from the
Highway 78 bridge over the Kissimmee River

Again with Ft. Lauderdale as my base, and again deciding not to bother Trent, I set off for another exploration of Okeechobee, retracing Leon and Nell's vacation trips. This time I drove first to West Palm Beach, then west to Belle Harbor, on the southern tip of Lake Okeechobee. On the way I passed the West Palm Beach Airport where Nell's embalmed and casketed remains were flown home to Kentucky from in 1969. I proceeded westerly around the lake, through Clewiston, where some of Nell's photos were taken. All the way around the lake is a dike of perhaps twenty feet in height, called the Herbert Hoover Dike, after the president that commissioned it. This was to allow the cities around the dike to not suffer repeated flooding every time a hurricane came through and pushed the lake out of its banks. I drove away from the lake on the western edge about sixteen miles to reach what the map showed as the village of Palmdale. Leon and Nell had stayed at a campground there. When I arrived, the sign said "Palmdale," but I saw no village. I only saw a collection of houses off the road, and one roadside alligator attraction called "Gatorama." The only site that looked like it used to be a privately owned campground was nothing more than dirt road, Shady Acre Road NW, leading to a poorly maintained site. This whole town was reminiscent of what I had just seen in Etowah, Arkansas. A new state-run campground was nearby on the edge of Palmdale. It can be assumed that when it was constructed, the privately owned campground was run out of business.

I was not unhappy to say good-bye to Palmdale and got back on my trek northwesterly around Lake Okeechobee. I approached Buckhead Ridge, the nearest village to the campsite where Nell died. The place where Leon and Nell, Walter and Dollie Stevenson, and Eddie and Linda Stevenson camped that time in 1969, according to Eddie Stevenson, was a spot of riverbank owned by the federal government wedged between the Kissimmee River and what was then Joe and Wanda's Fishcamp, a privately-run business. The Fishcamp is now gone, replaced by a federal boat launch and recreation area. It doesn't appear camping is allowed on the site now, and it consists mainly of a large parking area for boat rigs and a building of metal siding. It is located on a side road, SW Ninety-ninth Drive, and is called the C. Scott Driver Jr. Recreation Area operated by the Board of Okeechobee County and South Florida Water Management District. The location is immediately upstream from the bridge crossing the Kissimmee River and immediately across the highway from Okee-Tantie Campground.

The spot where Eddie pointed that Leon and Nell's camper was parked was halfway between the bridge and the canal heading into the boat launch of the recreation area. I approached that spot, having to walk around a closed and locked gate, and stood on the spot. I spoke aloud to Nell, as if I were standing on her grave, "I'm sorry this happened to you, Peepeyes. I wish he hadn't done this. I wish someone could have saved you. But I'll set things right now. I promise." I took some more photos on the bridge facing toward the camping spot. I drove up the SW Ninety-ninth Drive a bit to the spot where Eddie Stevenson said the group moved when Leon returned to Okeechobee with Audrey in the car. He returned after burying Nell in Kentucky, and

181

since he was returning with another woman, Leon wanted the group to move to a new spot so the other campers around them wouldn't raise eyebrows. He had to have known it would have been a shocking display—his breathtaking lack of grieving over the death of his wife of forty years. Apparently showing this in front of the Stevensons didn't matter to Leon, only in front of strangers.

I moved on to Okeechobee town and stopped again by the former site of the Okeechobee General Hospital. This was a Friday this time, my previous visit had been on a holiday, and the office was closed. The site is now a local government office housing several different government entities. Lettering on one of the glass doors revealed that the local state's attorney, Ashley Albright, whom I had just written to regarding Nell's death, had his office in the building as well. He had declined to investigate Nell's death entirely, and I had half a mind to drop into his office unexpectedly and tell him what I thought about that. But I resisted, stayed professional, and asked if I could see the site of the former emergency room. They said it didn't resemble anything like an emergency room, just an office space, and so there was no point. But they did point me to the outside of the back where the emergency room doors and ramp were at, which still existed. I went back there and photographed it, thinking of Nell, already dead, being brought here in 1969 by Leon, with Walter and Dollie Stevenson along in the car.

After completing my tasks in Okeechobee, I proceeded southeasterly around the east side of Lake Okeechobee. I passed through the town of Pahokee, which was also depicted in Nell's photos from the 1960s. I completed the loop around the lake back in Belle Harbor. Leaving Florida this time, I felt I had completed the investigation of the campsite and had learned all that could be learned there regarding Nell's death in Florida.

*   *   *

Former entrance to the Emergency Room of the Okeechobee
General Hospital in 1969. The ramp up to the door is still there.

Chapter 9

THE REVELATION

"Son, I'm a gonna be a dyin' soon. They's somethin' been on my mind,
an' I wanna get it off my conscience. I want someone to know this 'fore I die."

At this point in my investigation, I made another visit to Tillie (Dotson) Edwards, Frank's cousin on the Freeman side, and Nell's niece, and she provided some new, shocking information. She related to me something told to her by her sister, Mildred (Dotson) Tucker, of Bert Mitchell's final call to Mildred's husband, Son Tucker, just before Bert died in January 2006. Leon's older brother Corbett had two sons still alive in 2006, Corbett Jr. (called simply "Son") and Owen, both living in Paducah. Son Tucker had married Tillie's sister Mildred, and they had no children. Mildred later confirmed with me directly that Bert said he knew how Nell's murder happened in a phone call to Son just before Bert died. Mildred quoted Bert as saying to Son, "Son, I'm a gonna be a dyin' soon. They's somethin' been on my mind, an' I wanna get it off my conscience. I want someone to know this 'fore I die." He then told Son he had been visiting Leon in Paducah a few years before Leon died, placing it approximately in 1985. Leon evidently knew he was nearing his own death and wanted to clear his own conscience. Bert said Leon confessed to him that he had smothered Nell to death in Florida, and that Walter and Dollie Stevenson helped move the body after the murder had taken place. Bert said Leon told him they drove around for five hours with the dead body in the car, figuring out what story to tell when they finally got to the hospital, which was only a short distance from the campground.

Tillie said she thought that Leon had also confessed to his pastor at the Eastside Holiness Church in Paducah, Pete Keeling. She thought this because of the manner in which Pete spoke of Leon's desire for a late-life atonement for his earlier "wayward ways." Pete Keeling had died by the time I began my investigation, but I spoke with his widow, Grace, in 2006, and she of course didn't know anything specific about Nell's death. Pete never revealed anything to her about what he meant about Leon's earlier "wayward ways." Of course, as a pastor, he wouldn't reveal anything Leon had confessed to him. That would have had to remain confidential.

I spoke via phone with Son Tucker (Corbett Tucker Jr.) in late March 2006, a few days after speaking with his wife, Mildred, also via phone. I had sent him some pictures of his parents, Corbett and Daisy Tucker, when they were young, and some pictures of himself and Mildred vacationing with my parents, Frank and Judy, when they all were young. Leon's brother Corbett lived a very long life, almost ninety-two years, and died in 1991. I thought my sending Son pictures might reinforce the family connection between me and him rather than me just cold-calling him and telling him I was "Frank Tucker's son." Previously he had been very brusque with me on the phone. This time he was a bit warmer. But when I brought up the subject of Bert Mitchell's call to him regarding Nell's death, he suddenly said, "Nah, I ain't gonna get into that." I gave him another chance, asking him to recount the story for me, a chance to be the grand old storyteller that older folk enjoy being. But he stood firm and refused to talk about the subject. It didn't surprise me that the Tucker men would be unwilling to discuss this deep family secret, still feeling the loyalty and allegiance to the family name.

Even though Leon was dead for almost two decades at this point, Son still felt a loyalty to him. Even though I was a Tucker man also, just talking about the wrong done by another Tucker man somehow broke the code of allegiance. His wife Mildred of course didn't belong to the secret club and freely talked about it to Tillie and to me on the phone. I wanted to verify what Bert had told to Son personally. But Son stood his ground, refusing to talk about it. He had previously told me he didn't want any visitors. I sensed in Son a level of distrust that I would sense in others in Kentucky, as it is a part of the culture there, at least for the elderly—a distrust of even recognized family members. In a later call to Mildred, she would refuse to tell me anything further and was downright rude to me on the phone, telling me "we won't tell you nuthin'. Call somebody else!" It was as if she hated me—why, I don't know.

In the end, it wasn't critical that I get Son to tell me what he knew personally. I had enough corroborating evidence from others, and I had Son's story also through his wife Mildred repeating it to Tillie, and Tillie to me. I was concerned about how many mouths the story was passing through, and how it might have enhanced or changed from mouth to mouth, but this was the best I could get on corroborating Bert's story. I e-mailed Bert's close friend Scott Sumida, who had helped care for Bert in his final days, it becoming too much of a burden apparently on Bert's wife, Nadine, herself seventy-five years of age at the time. Scott was evidently someone Bert knew from his congregation at the church that Bert was a pastor. Scott was good with computers and sent me the Versie & Robie tape transferred to CD, plus scanned photos of the Mitchell family. He helped me communicate with Bert through e-mails. Scott also had been sending me several updates on Bert's declining medical condition, and notified me when Bert died in January 2006 at the age of eighty-two years old.

Since Scott was frequently at Bert's side during his ending months, I thought there was a good chance he might have overheard the conversation between Son and Bert about Nell's death. I e-mailed Scott to see if he had overheard the conversation in late 2005 between Bert and Son about the details of Nell's death, and how Bert knew that information. I never heard back from Scott, the lack of response being suspicious, perhaps deliberate silence. He had always responded before. But perhaps the subject matter in this e-mail was more than a Christian individual could handle, I speculated.

Using simple logic, I concluded that Son Tucker had to know something he felt in need of concealing. If he knew nothing, he would have said so. If he knew something but that it was of no consequence, he would have said that without hesitation. But to refuse to talk about the subject meant he knew something of consequence, and knew it was bad—a Tucker men secret, and he wanted to keep it buried. That's the only conclusion that makes logical sense.

I wondered why Bert didn't tell me about Leon's confession directly. I theorize it was fear. Telling someone that you knew their grandfather was a murderer to their face, and that you knew this secret for all these years and never told anyone, would give even the strongest man pause. I didn't hold it against Bert—I'm just glad he finally told the story to someone. I visited Bert's grave (in Lake View Memorial Gardens, Fairview Heights, Illinois) months after his funeral, and thanked him directly.

*   *   *

Chapter 10

THE AUTOPSY IDEA

This made the entire situation, as the British would say, "a sticky wicket." This was not going to be easy, no matter how I proceeded.

This was perhaps the hardest chapter to experience, let alone write about, in this whole journey. Exhuming Nell's remains and having them autopsied was not something I wanted to do—no one would. I hoped somewhere along the line I would find evidence making it unnecessary, or that I wouldn't find enough evidence to convince the McCracken County coroner to issue the permit for exhumation and to perform the autopsy. I knew when I pulled the death certificate from Florida that, with one glance at it, an autopsy was likely needed. The certificate said that no autopsy was performed, confirming our family memories that both Leon and Frank had refused the autopsy at the time in 1969, for two very different reasons. The medical examiner's office in Ft. Pierce, Florida, told me there was no chance of a change in the cause of death on a death certificate without conclusive autopsy results proving homicide. With no surviving medical files from the hospital emergency room from that night in 1969, the doctor who examined her remains now deceased, and only family memories and statements to go by, the prospect of an autopsy of Nell's remains now, in 2006, looked probable. I also knew that it was by no means certain I could do this just because I determined it was necessary. Getting the permission to do this, and justifying it, would be a perilous undertaking as well.

I cringed at the thought. I knew that it would be divisive for my family, and some would not agree, even be angered by my actions. I knew that ultimately it wouldn't be my choice anyway. I would have to convince other professionals in medical examiner offices in Florida and Kentucky, and in state's attorney's offices in Florida, all of whom were dispassionate and unconnected to the emotionality of the matter. They would look at the evidence I had uncovered and logically come to the conclusion that an autopsy now was warranted or was not. According to the Florida medical examiner I spoke with, it was likely that the most an autopsy could reveal is a possible broken hyoid bone proving strangulation, or a cracked skull proving a blow to the head, or a high heavy-metal concentration in her bone marrow proving poisoning.

One rationality that kept haunting my mind was this one point—the only way Nell could speak to tell her story of what happened to her is through her remains. She had no other way to communicate to me or to the living world. What secrets her remains contained, if any, would be Nell's voice in 2006 to tell her story. Nell had tried to communicate that she was in danger before she died with the postcard containing a secret signal on it to her sister Grace, and by hiding money in her brassiere that Leon didn't know about. These clearly were acts of fear, and gave Nell a voice to speak of her fear even after her death. The postcard arrived to Grace after Nell was already dead, and the mortician discovered the money in her brassiere. If she had left a journal with any fears or thoughts she was having written down in it, Leon would have found it and destroyed it. None was ever found by Frank.

I struggled with whether or not it would be worth it to disturb her remains. I struggled with whether or not it was a respectful thing to do—whether or not it was what she would have wanted—whether or not I was making a huge mistake pursuing it. I kept putting it off until I had exhausted talking with every person I could find that might know a piece of the puzzle. I put it off until I had exhausted gathering every pertinent document I could identify, and calling every government entity that might hold a piece of the puzzle. It was such a gamble.

If the autopsy results came back inconclusive, then the exhumation and autopsy would have been for nothing—huge mistakes in fact. I would look like a class A fool. But even if that result did happen, that they found nothing in the autopsy indicating a homicide, then at least I would have that answer. We would know that Nell's remains didn't contain any secrets to be known. So either way it turned out, I told myself it might be worth it—just to know the answer, one way or the other.

I had posed the arguments and ideas about the possibility of an autopsy of Nell's remains to Tillie in a meeting with her in March 2006. I needed someone else's concurrence that I was thinking right about this issue. I needed someone else close to Nell agreeing with me that this autopsy needed to be done. If Tillie didn't agree, I was prepared to abandon the idea altogether. Tillie called herself "Nell's daughter," and she really was in every way except genealogically. Technically she was Nell's niece, but in reality, she was raised like a daughter to Nell. Nell, Grace, and Grace's daughters Tillie and Mildred were all incredibly close. Nell lived with Grace and her daughters for many years when Leon had left her in Paducah alone while he worked in East St. Louis and was living with Audrey. No one still alive in 2006 could have been closer to Nell than Tillie. So it was entirely appropriate that I let Tillie's decision on this matter be the tipping point for my own decision, one way or the other.

Tillie needed time to think about it, so I let her have a couple of months until we met again in May 2006. By May, she had made her decision. She said to me, dropping her characteristic smile, lowering her voice, and speaking with emphasis denoting the seriousness of the issue, "If you are gonna do that (an autopsy), then don't . . . you . . .

tell . . . *nobody.*" She broke her words with short pauses and said the last word strongly. She was giving me her permission to pursue an autopsy of Nell's remains. She also said, "I think you'll find your answers with that. If ya don't do it, it'll eat at ya for the rest of ya' life." She was basically telling me she thought I should move ahead with the autopsy, but obviously to keep it private between us. I think Tillie wanted to have closure on this life event that had so deeply affected her also, for thirty-seven years. She wanted to know the answers for certain as much as I did.

We pretty much had proof by this time of Leon's guilt with his confession to Bert Mitchell, but that alone wasn't going to change the death certificate's cause of death. It was becoming clearer that an autopsy was necessary—no longer an option—but a requirement. Tillie was absolutely right about one thing—it would eat at me if I didn't proceed with the autopsy. I had gone too far with the investigation to stop now. I had uncovered too much to turn away and forget about it now. I was at the threshold of perhaps finding the final answer to the riddle. How could I not proceed? Still, despite finally coming to a logical conclusion to proceed with the autopsy, neither of us, Tillie nor me, relished the thought. It was an extremely hard decision to make.

I had exhausted every other avenue of finding the answer to this mystery short of pursuing the autopsy. I had sought the medical records from the Okeechobee hospital. I had contacted the daughters of the now-deceased physician (Dr. Steven Johnston) that examined Nell's remains that night in Okeechobee. From his daughters I hoped to find journals, diaries, or papers he might have left to them that might have notations about Nell's case. I had contacted local law enforcement in Okeechobee, both the city police and the county sheriff's office, searching for records. I had contacted the state agency in Florida that controlled the campground on the outside chance they might have some record of the event. I ran newspaper ads in two local Okeechobee newspapers, trying to locate hospital staff that was on duty that night in Okeechobee in 1969. I wrote to the Okeechobee hospital, asking them to research their personnel files to help me identify any employees who worked there in 1969. Through those efforts I had located one nurse that worked the Okeechobee hospital in 1969 and interviewed her. I had contacted every living relative of the Tucker family I could identify that might have a piece of the puzzle in their memory. All of my efforts were turning up either empty or inconclusive results. Some of the Tucker family knew tidbits of the story but not enough to legally establish the cause of death to change the death certificate. There simply were no records or evidence (assuming if it ever existed at all) remaining today in 2006 to solve this mystery. Leon's confession to Bert Mitchell wasn't going to change the death certificate. I had no choice left to me but the bleak, stark, and difficult fork-in-the-road decision—pursue an autopsy or walk away from all of it and never know the truth, at least for certain. So I chose my direction.

My first step on proceeding was to contact Dan Sims, the county coroner for McCracken County, Kentucky. He told me to contact a local funeral home to handle everything. I did that, contacting Wayne Carter at Roth Funeral Home in Paducah. He sounded like an elderly gentleman over the phone and listened patiently to my story.

Once I concluded, he spoke directly with Dan Sims and called me back. Both of them concluded that a court order for the exhumation wasn't necessary in this circumstance, since I was the next living descendant of Nell Tucker. The fact that Tillie, another family member, agreed to the exhumation helped avoid going to court for a court order. The "unknown" cause of death on the death certificate was strong evidence justifying the autopsy now, in 2006, to provide "closure for the family," according to Wayne Carter. He directed me to seek a local attorney in Los Angeles to swear out an affidavit of what I wanted considered as the justification for the exhumation and autopsy, and send it to Dan Sims's attention. Dan Sims would then partner with Wayne Carter, and together they would seek the Permit for Exhumation of Human Remains from the McCracken County Health Department. Wayne told me that a special forensic pathologist that the Kentucky State Police use for their toughest cases, Dr. LeVaughn, would likely do the autopsy. According to Wayne Carter, the Kentucky State Police use Dr. LeVaughn to determine the causes of death of individuals where the causes are not obvious or foul play may be suspected, and they know the determination won't be easy. Wayne Carter was confident that Dr. LeVaughn would have the necessary expertise for Nell's case. The autopsy would be performed at the Roth Funeral Home. Wayne estimated it would cost $2,500, and the exhumation and reburial would be considerably less than that amount. We would settle on the costs later when it was more firmly known what the tasks would be in this endeavor.

I wanted to make for sure of what potential legal mess I was getting into pursuing this matter. I wanted to know my legal obligations and liabilities regarding whether my siblings had to be notified or not. Some brief legal research on the Internet uncovered one possible legal authority (decided case or legal precedent in the past), *Louisville Cemetery Association v. Downs*, Ky., 45 S.W.2d 5, 6 (1931). Despite this case being seventy-five years old, it still could be used as a legal precedent in this matter, unless other cases unknown to me followed it. I'm not a lawyer, so I had no expertise in legal research. I was basically flying by the seat of my pants at this point. The decision in this 1931 case allowed "recovery," meaning allowing someone to sue, if their deceased family member's grave were disturbed if it was done "maliciously, by gross negligence, wantonly, i.e., with a reckless disregard for the rights of another . . ." It was not clear to me from this what I was contemplating fit any of those definitions. It was not clear to me that notifying my siblings of what I was attempting to do was required by this case to avoid showing "reckless disregard for the rights of another."

Looking for guidance, I contacted the McCracken County Health Department, which would be the government agency to which the permit application would be submitted. They looked through their regulations and told me that before they could approve a permit for exhumation of human remains, they would need the "written permission from all family members of the same class, or a court order." By "class" they meant the level of family relation to the deceased. Nell only had one child, my father Frank. Her siblings, husband, parents, and only child were all now dead. Her next of kin still alive in 2006 were her three legally recognized grandchildren, of which I was one.

At the time in 2006, I was estranged from all my siblings, in one form or another. With one of my half-siblings, I had a positive estrangement, meaning there was no hostility between us, just a distance from the unfamiliarity of spending the last thirty-five years apart, having only met twice in our lifetimes. I met Trent for the first time when I was six years old and the second time when I was forty-one years old. With the other, newly-discovered half-sibling, Sharon, I also had a positive estrangement, similarly from the unfamiliarity of never knowing she existed until 2005. This half-sibling was not legally related to Nell, technically, because her birth certificate showed no blood relation to Nell, despite everyone now believing the family folklore of her being Frank's daughter. Her mother had placed her first husband's name on the birth certificate as her daughter's father, not Frank's name. She never knew Nell, despite seeing her once or twice at the Noble Park swimming pool in Paducah, and not knowing she was her grandmother. (When Nell was working the ticket booth at the swimming pool, she would let Sharon in for free with just a wink and a smile, knowing she was her granddaughter, but never disclosing it to her. Nell would then call Tillie to come out the swimming pool and see "Frank's daughter.") Therefore, without medical evidence to prove it, all I had establishing her link to our family was family stories, which didn't establish the legal standing necessary for the issue at hand. This made the entire situation, as the British would say, "a sticky wicket." This was not going to be easy, no matter how I proceeded.

From all of this, I concluded that either written permission from the legally recognized siblings at the very least would be required, or a court order, to proceed. Since Sharon was just getting to know our family at this time, I decided it was best not to perhaps shock her (and perhaps scare her away) by discussing any of this matter. Any court I'm sure would first allow the legally recognized siblings to comment on their feelings on the matter before deciding to issue an order or not. Thus contacting my siblings was inevitably necessary, and something I dreaded. I think most people's immediate thought on this issue would be that the siblings had a right to be notified. But actually, when you think a little deeper, perhaps they didn't. What could they say but either "yes, I give my permission," in which case asking them was unnecessary, or "no, I don't give my permission," which would require that I take the matter to a court to seek a court order. I felt that with the evidence I had amassed, it was a foregone conclusion that I would ultimately get the court order over the objections of any sibling.

All the siblings could say was "I don't want that to happen." They would have no evidence justifying why it shouldn't happen. I had significant evidence to suggest wrongdoing—the siblings would have nothing but their preferences. It was highly likely I would win and obtain the court order. So I would waste a lot of time and money on an attorney on a judicial exercise that had a foregone conclusion to it. I suppose it was possible the siblings might try to contest the evidence I had amassed, but that would only extend their own legal costs to themselves, which they would be reticent to do. But to respect the rights of others, I prepared carefully worded letters to the two legally recognized siblings, seeking their permission for the exhumation and autopsy. I just had to pick the right time to send the letters. As in most things in life, timing was/ is everything. I put it off as long as I could, finding it an unpleasant task, and hoping some event would happen making it unnecessary. I finally sent the two letters to the siblings in August 2006. I asked in the letters that they respond to me within ten days of receipt of the letters. I provided them return FedEx airbills for them to send me back their responses at my expense.

The ten days passed without response from either of them, so I waited a bit longer. I was just about to proceed without their responses and seek a court order, but then I received a response from my half-sibling. He said that his family in Arkansas had known about the story of Nell's death for years, and from the tone of his letter, it sounded like they had their suspicions as well. He said he had no interest in pursuing an investigation into Nell's death, and that he felt the time to do this was at the time of her death in 1969. I can assume from that sentence he felt that an investigation at the time was warranted, just not now. He felt "no good would come" of investigating it now. I disagreed with that statement—I felt the good that would come of it was clearly stated in my letter to him asking for his permission. I told him in my letter that I thought resolving Nell's cause of death and getting her death certificate changed to reflect an actual cause of death were powerful motivations for good to come of an investigation. But I wasn't prepared to call him up and debate the matter with him. He stated how he felt, and he had a right to his opinions. I wasn't going to try to convince him as he likely would see that as harassing. But I wasn't going to allow his refusal to give his permission block my rights to pursue it independently, through seeking a court order.

The other sibling belatedly responded only after being prompted by a reminder e-mail from me. The response was a non-response really—no permission given, not a yes, not a no—just more questions about why I was wanting to do this. I offered to answer any questions, but I suspected this type of response wasn't really genuine—but a delay tactic. The wrap-up of Frank Tucker's estate was going on coincident in time with my request for permission for this forensic investigation into Nell's death. The estate issues weren't going entirely smoothly. I suspected the two issues would be influenced by each other. In my mind, they were entirely unrelated and should be kept separate. What made me suspicious that the non-answer was really a delay tactic was that some of the questions being asked were already answered in the first letter I sent requesting the permission. Either the first letter wasn't read closely enough before these questions were formulated, or the questions weren't genuine. Rather, they were designed to force me to waste time answering already answered questions. In offering to answer any questions, I also said eventually, without a firm decision one way or the other, I would have to proceed anyway. I would make the conservative assumption that there was opposition to what I wanted to do. I would have to state to the court in seeking the court order that neither of my siblings approved or could come to a decision on the forensic investigation of Nell's remains. That protected their rights, and me from being sued later on for infringing on those rights. They had their say, or at least the opportunity to have their say, if they didn't approve. But that didn't block me from pursuing my rights in the matter.

I thought to myself, that's why we have judges in our society. We take to them the matters we can't agree on, where both parties have rights in the matter. We present to a judge all the evidence, and let a dispassionate, disinterested, third party—the judge—decide who is right. It was a crapshoot. It could turn out either way. I could get the court order, or the judge could refuse to grant it to me. Even with the latter result, a refusal, I could have the satisfaction that I did all I could to solve the mystery of Nell's death, so at least I would come away with something. If I hadn't tried to pursue this because I couldn't get my siblings to agree beforehand, that would have left me with some culpability in the matter. I honestly felt that, with the knowledge I now had regarding Leon's probable guilt, I was becoming a part of the cover-up of Nell's death by not pursuing all I could to bring everything to light. I felt I was dishonoring my Tucker heritage, not preserving it, by keeping these secrets buried. I suspected my siblings felt the opposite—that keeping the secrets buried was the best way to honor the Tucker heritage. I simply disagreed with that. Doing that would make us knowing, willing accomplices in the cover-up, and bring the cover-up onward into the next generation. I was unwilling to do that. I wanted no part in any cover-up.

After giving the indecisive sibling a bit more time, another month, to decide, I made the decision to move forward on my own. So reluctantly, I began pursuing the harder route—the process of seeking a court order for the autopsy. Just as I began making those steps, the indecisive sibling responded, and basically said, "No." The sibling said "I won't oppose you" but refused to give the permission I was seeking. That's sort of having it both ways, isn't it? The sibling also suggested that the autopsy results might still be inconclusive even if they proved "unnatural causes" for Nell's death. The sibling inferred that Nell might have committed suicide. I found that suggestion repugnant, because I knew that there was absolutely no evidence whatsoever of suicide, not even the hint of it from anyone who knew Nell. Indeed, there was no suicide note, and logically if one was going to commit suicide, why do it on a camping trip in Florida? Nell was a deeply religious woman and knew that suicide was perhaps the ultimate wrong one could do in the Christian faith. The suicide suggestion made no sense and convinced me the sibling was having difficulty coming to terms with the dark, painful reality that Leon might have done this crime. The sibling was desperately grasping for alternate explanations to save Leon from responsibility. That the sibling would want to blame Nell for her own death rather than Leon I found offensive—especially in the face of a complete lack of any evidence pointing to Nell and overwhelming evidence pointing to Leon. The fact that the sibling was already looking for alternate explanations for a result we didn't yet have suggested to me the suspicion was already there of what this autopsy of Nell's remains would reveal. Tillie and I apparently weren't alone in our suspicions.

The sibling also said he didn't want to "desecrate her final rest." That phrase hung in the air for a moment like a stench. No sane person would want to be part of something like that, so why was that phrase used? I had previously explained to the sibling that this proposal for the autopsy would be done in the most professional manner possible—by a licensed funeral director, a licensed forensic pathologist, with a court order from a judge, and under a permit granted by the McCracken County Health Department. Therefore, I hardly think the term "desecrate" applied. I saw that term as applying to grave robbers haphazardly digging up a grave to steal jewels, which bore no resemblance at all to what I proposed in this case. I rather think the sibling used that terminology to drum up hysterical mental images in the conversation to thwart my seeking this action. Perhaps the sibling thought I could be shamed into stopping my pursuit of this action.

Moving on from the responses from the siblings, I concluded that I had done my duty, complied with the law, notified my siblings of my intent, and solicited their opinions. So long as I included their opinions in my filing for a court order, the judge would therefore consider those opinions of the siblings in his/her decision, then I was protected. My first step was to contact the McCracken County attorney, Dan Bose, for guidance on how to obtain the court order I needed. Mr. Bose basically gave me the same answer that the state's attorney in Florida, Ashley Albright, gave me. Mr. Bose had no interest in pursuing this case since the only prosecutable person for this possible crime, Leon, was already dead. It was depressing to me how little interest law enforcement had in this potential murder. Didn't anyone care about this woman being murdered except me? Mr. Bose indicated to me that I would have to engage a private attorney for this matter. Knowing that most attorneys won't do anything for you for less than $1,000, I wanted to make sure of what I was doing before I sought an attorney. I next contacted Dr. Mark LeVaughn for advice on the likelihood that an autopsy could be worthwhile in solving the mystery. The medical examiner in Florida, Merv Waldren, seemed to think it was possible it might be useful, but by no means certain, to solve the mystery. But I wanted the input of the man who would actually be doing the work.

I finally reached Dr. Mark LeVaughn by phone in October 2006 and discussed Nell's case with him. I related to Dr. LeVaughn the following facts:

the probable cause(s) of death I suspected, which were poisoning and/or smothering;

- the type of burial was in a sealed metal casket;
- the time factor since burial was thirty-seven years;
- the cause of death was unknown, death preceded arrival at the hospital as shown on the death certificate, no autopsy was performed at the time of death; and
- the statement by Leon that he had a "drug that would stop a heart with no trace left later on" and his confession to a preacher (Bert Mitchell) of smothering Nell.

After listening to my story, Dr. LeVaughn expressed a willingness to help me, if he could. He confirmed for me that he had once been the state pathologist for western

Kentucky but now was in private practice in Evansville, Indiana. He was very candid with me on the phone and did not give me false hopes. He stated that as humans age, what is actually a three-piece jointed bone called the hyoid bone fuses into one solid, C-shaped piece, making it much more likely to fracture in a strangulation. But he said a smothering wouldn't necessarily break the hyoid bone, but it might break it. Dr. LeVaughn said that petechiae (defined as minute hemorrhages in skin or the eyes, producing a redness) would be the main thing any medical examiner would look for to prove a smothering death. But after thirty-seven years of degradation, even an embalmed body in a perfectly dry, sealed casket wouldn't still show discoloration on the skin and tissues. Therefore, petechiae would be next to impossible to find after such a long time. If Nell's casket had any water leaks in it, the tissue degradation would be more pronounced, thus destroying any petechiae evidence.

Dr. LeVaughn said that if a drug was used to poison Nell, and the perpetrator knew the drug wouldn't be detectable later on, that meant the poisoning agent disassociated into compounds normally found in the body. If potassium chloride were the poisoning agent, he said I could "forget about detecting that at this point in time" because the disassociated remnants of this chemical are normally found in the body. If a heavy-metal poison, such as arsenic, were used, it might show up in the bone marrow. But that type of poisoning didn't fit the description Leon told to Charles Stevenson, that "there would be no trace of it (the drug)" later on. I was disappointed after my conversation with Dr. LeVaughn. I appreciated his candor and frankness, but what he said wasn't what I wanted to hear.

I spoke again with the coroner for McCracken County, Kentucky, Dr. Dan Sims, a forensic pathologist. I told him what Dr. LeVaughn had said to me and asked if he could refer me to another forensic pathologist to either get confirmation or other ideas. He told me he thought Dr. LeVaughn had told me accurately what the probabilities were to get the result I was seeking, which was a cause of death determined. He said that virtually all of the other forensic pathologists in Kentucky would be working for some government entity, which would bar them from doing any private autopsies. Dr. LeVaughn was pretty much my only choice for this endeavor, said Dr. Sims.

I reiterated to Dr. Sims the evidence I had; Leon's confession to Bert Mitchell of smothering Nell, Leon's statement about a drug that could stop a heart to Charles Stevenson (related by Eddie Stevenson), the anomalies on the death certificate raising the suspicion of insurance fraud motives, Leon's ultra-violent background, Leon's second wife (Audrey) being a possible motivation, etc . . . Dr. Sims agreed with me that there was probable cause to conduct the autopsy, but warned me of the significantly low probability of finding a cause at this late date. A smothering, Dr. Sims said, would not leave any signs that would be determinable now in 2006, and a poisoning with an agent like Leon described wouldn't be determinable now either.

A poisoning with a heavy metal, like arsenic, might be determinable from hair, nail, or bone marrow samples, but even that was unlikely at this late date. A death by arsenic or other heavy-metal poisoning would have been preceded by Nell appearing visibly ill to others around her, with vomiting, cold sweats, and stomach aches being exhibited. No indication of this happening was seen by Eddie Stevenson, the witness at the campsite the day Nell died. Eddie told me he didn't think Nell appeared sick in the days prior to her dying. Arsenic or heavy-metal poisoning is rarely an acute event, rather building up chronically over time. Poisoning by a quick-acting agent, such as rat poison, would be too obvious for Leon to take such a risk and then show up with Nell's body at an emergency room. For poisoning to work, Nell had to have appeared to die a natural death. Therefore, I concluded that a heavy-metal or a quick-acting poison, like rat poison, would have been unlikely for Leon to have used. Neither fit Leon's previous statement to Charles Stevenson.

Dr. Sims confirmed for me that any situation where there was an unknown cause of death would require an autopsy by law nowadays, and he suspected it was the law also in Florida at the time (1969). Therefore, Dr. Sims agreed with me that the law wasn't followed in Nell's case. Dr. Sims sounded on the phone like he was empathetic to my cause, urging me that if I had any other questions about these matters as I pursued it to call him again. He sounded like he wanted to help me, but wanted to be honest and frank with me also about the realistic probabilities of a positive outcome. I trusted his counsel.

Last, I contacted via e-mail the famed forensic pathologist, Dr. Cyril Wecht. He has appeared on many television talk shows as an expert on forensic examinations, so I looked him up on the Internet and e-mailed his office. I described in a lengthy e-mail to him all the evidence I had and asked his opinion if he thought it would be worth it to conduct an autopsy of Nell's remains now. Much to my surprise the very next day, he responded, and he said that he did not have any confidence that an autopsy now would yield a cause of death—just too much time had passed. Dr. Wecht followed up his initial e-mail with a second e-mail, telling me that the cause of death on Nell's death certificate reading "unknown (DOA)" did indeed leave open the possibility of homicide. He agreed that if the doctor examining Nell's remains at the time (Dr. Johnston) felt it was conclusive that Nell died of natural causes, he would have stated it as "unknown natural causes" or "nonspecific natural causes." Dr. Wecht stated he thought it was a reasonable inference from the "unknown" cause of death stated that Dr. Johnston wasn't sure that homicide hadn't occurred. Despite these valuable comments from Dr. Wecht, one thing was clear. I now had three forensic pathologists telling me pretty much the same thing. My initial interest in pursuing this idea generated by Merv Waldren's comments was now dissipating with the somber reality of the situation.

Dr. Michael Baden,[14] an eminent forensic pathologist and also a TV personality on HBO's *Autopsy* series, blogs on HBO's Web site for the series, and those comments provided some insight into Nell's case. Dr. Baden states that a "potassium overdose is very difficult to determine at autopsy" and that the best way to determine a potassium overdose would be by collecting a blood sample during a heart attack or immediately after death. Dr. Baden stated that an hour or two after death, the potassium level starts to rise automatically as the cells of the body are very rich in potassium, and as the cells start to decompose (or lyse and break open), this floods the bloodstream with potassium. This potassium rise in blood concentration postmortem will hide a potassium poisoning. However, Dr. Baden points out there is one area of the body that does not see this potassium rise: the vitreous humor, which is the fluid in the back of the eyes. Here in the fluid of the eyes, the potassium rise is much slower than in the bloodstream. But in Nell's case, obviously this wouldn't be possible to sample her eye fluid now. Since thirty-seven years had passed since her death, and she was embalmed, even this new information from Dr. Baden doesn't reveal a pathway to determining if Nell was poisoned with a potassium overdose. At present, I concluded, science doesn't have the technology to determine a potassium poisoning in long-dead buried remains.

One of the other comments Dr. Baden[14] posted on his blog was intriguing, and it shed light on whether or not an autopsy should have been done on Nell's remains. Initially, Frank was told an autopsy would not allow a public viewing of the remains during the funeral because of the dissection of the body that takes place, and that justified to Frank not approving the autopsy of Nell's remains the night she died when given the chance by Dr. Johnston in Okeechobee. Dr. Baden seemed to disagree with that assertion about the inability for a viewing during the funeral following an autopsy. He described an autopsy by saying that it is performed by means of two surgical incisions. First, the Y-incision is made from the chest to the abdomen, permitting the examination of the heart, lungs, and all abdominal organs. Second, the intermastoid incision is made behind each ear, permitting examination of the brain. Dr. Baden[14] states, "Once the autopsy is completed and the two incisions are sutured closed, they cannot be seen after the body has been prepared for the family viewing." I conclude Frank was not thinking correctly, or perhaps was misinformed, about an autopsy preventing a viewing of Nell's remains at her funeral. This holds true if the autopsy procedure Dr. Baden describes above is the same that would have been performed in 1969 in Okeechobee, if autopsy procedures haven't changed in that time.

I weighed the predicted possibility of a productive outcome from an autopsy against the downsides of the issue. The downsides were that my siblings did not agree to this activity, and it would likely cause additional family estrangement if I were to proceed over their objections. Costs, though a downside, were not a determining factor because I had already agreed in my mind to cover whatever the costs would be within reason. The costs, while not unattainable for me, were not insignificant. The exhumation and reburial services from the funeral home would be approximately $1,000-1,500. The legal services seeking the court order and permit would be at least $1,000. The actual autopsy would be $2,500. So I was looking at perhaps $4,500-5,000 in total expenses for this activity. This did not include my travel costs. I had already decided that if Nell was to be disinterred, I wanted to be there as a witness, out of respect. I was her grandson, her surviving descendant, and I belonged there when and if that happened.

I also counted among the downsides the possibility of an inconclusive outcome of the autopsy. I considered how that would weigh on my psyche, having disturbed

Nell's remains for nothing. The likely embarrassment I would feel from having done this action, with nothing to show for it, would be severe. Dr. LeVaughn and Dr. Sims's comments to me made me assume that it was more likely than not that his examination of Nell's remains would be inconclusive in establishing her cause of death.

I came to the sorrowful yet unavoidable conclusion that the possibility of an answer from the autopsy wasn't worth the risk of the potential downsides, when all of them were taken together. The risk was too high. If I had gotten more positive indication from Dr. LeVaughn or Dr. Sims I might have taken the risk. But I couldn't justify it now. Having made this decision, I was confronted with what that meant. I would never be absolutely sure how Nell died beyond the evidence that I had found to date. I would not be able to achieve my central goal, to get the death certificate's cause of death changed to an actual cause. It would remain showing cause of death "unknown (DOA)" for the rest of time, which bothered me greatly. I counted it less my failure than just an acceptance of circumstances out of my control.

At this point I felt that I had been impetuous, or "jumped the gun," on asking my siblings for permission for the exhumation and autopsy. If I was going to come to the conclusion that I wasn't going to pursue the autopsy anyway, then I didn't need to burden them with this issue at all. I regretted contacting them at all now. At the time I contacted them, I was positive I was going to pursue it. But with this new information, I had to make a change in direction. I guess the siblings' refusals to give their permission were factors in my decision now not to proceed with the autopsy, so perhaps it was necessary that I contacted them about it—to aid in my decision-making.

It angered me that I was being deprived of the right to prove, legally, how Nell died. I felt anger at those who didn't investigate Nell's death at the time she died when the evidence was likely there to be found. The fault for the failure to properly investigate Nell's death belonged to others, not me. That blame lay with Dr. Johnston in Okeechobee for not following Florida law and forcing an autopsy over Leon's objections, and perhaps with the local law enforcement authorities in Okeechobee for not investigating Nell's death when they had the chance. Perhaps Frank Tucker bore some of the blame also, for not seeking the investigation himself also and having the courage to defy Leon. Their failures, and thirty-seven years of secret keeping by the family relation, prevented me from having the chance to obtain the legal proof I sought. If I could solve the mystery of Nell's death, it would be with other types of evidence. I could take no solace in the fact that the fault fell elsewhere, because I desperately wanted to conclusively solve the enigma of Nell's death with medical proof. Now I would have to solve it with other types of proof, which wouldn't be enough to change the death certificate. It disheartened me.

*　　*　　*

Chapter 11

THE TRIAL

Like a jigsaw puzzle, once all of the pieces of evidence are put together,
they form a picture.

The title of this chapter is a euphemism for arguing the evidence I've outlined in previous chapters. Leon Tucker will never be tried in reality for the murder of his wife, Nell Tucker. He died in 1987, some eighteen years after Nell's death in 1969. If he did not commit the act, then many over the years have wrongly accused him. An unfair stigma has been placed over his memory, without a way for him to clear his name. Clearing his name and the removal of that stigma from his memory was my initial goal in this investigation—this journey. However, if Leon did indeed murder Nell, then he got away with it. He paid no penalty, and never will. This fact doesn't stop me from now, in 2006, analyzing the evidence to determine, at least to a reasonable level of certainty, his guilt or innocence. I can, in effect, put Leon on trial, charged with Nell's murder, at least in my mind. I can debate the evidence just as a prosecutor and a defense attorney would in a courtroom, and then render a judgment, a verdict, just as a jury would.

In assembling this evidence, then arguing it, the temptation first was to not express conclusions about the evidence and let the reader draw their own conclusions. This is desirable because I didn't want to influence the reader by expressing my opinions. I felt perhaps I might be too close to the story to dispassionately and objectively look at the evidence with a fresh set of eyes, as the reader does. But in reality, the reader will be able to decide on the validity and conclusiveness of each piece of evidence themselves anyway, whether I write my conclusions or not. To fully argue the evidence, I have to draw a conclusion from each piece of evidence—decide what it means, to be able to assemble an overall picture. That's because there is no smoking gun in this case. I found no perfect, slam-dunk piece of evidence that wrapped everything up neatly for me. Instead, I found a lot of little pieces, each pointing one way or the other, guilty or innocent. After arguing each piece of evidence, I had to draw a conclusion from that piece of evidence to fit it into the overall puzzle of assembled pieces, and then see what the revealed picture showed. I still leave it up to the reader to make their own decision on each piece of evidence, and whether my conclusions are valid or not.

Last, I should say that it might sound like I'm working to convict Leon in this mock trial in this chapter—playing prosecutor more than playing defense attorney. That is because most of the pieces of evidence I found seemed to point toward guilt rather than innocence. There simply wasn't a lot of exculpatory evidence that proved or even suggested Leon couldn't have murdered Nell. I kept hoping to find that exculpatory evidence, e.g., Leon wasn't even at the campground when Nell died, or Nell died in front of other witnesses, proving Leon couldn't have attacked her. I kept hoping to find medical evidence showing she died of natural causes, not of a poisoning or a violent attack. I just didn't find a lot of exculpatory evidence in Leon's favor when I began to look at the specific evidence. And I think if Leon were truly innocent, there would be more exculpatory evidence, naturally, just from the law of averages. I tried to play devil's advocate with each damning piece of evidence, allowing for this evidence to be questioned as to its credibility or validity. I wasn't always successful at being able to raise reasonable doubt about some of the evidence—the evidence just says what it says. I had to accept that fact also. So if it seems like I'm arguing more for the prosecution than the defense as I present the following evidence that has more to do with the nature of the evidence itself rather than a bias on my part, I honestly wish it could have been the opposite case.

DEFENSE OPENING STATEMENT: In Leon's favor, the general, not specific, exculpatory evidence in this mock trial would be the following:

- there is no direct witness to how Nell died, who actually watched Nell die, and could testify to it, that is still alive;
- there is no medical evidence from the night in January 1969 when Nell died to establish conclusively the cause of her death;
- the key witnesses to the events that took place that night in January 1969; Leon, Walter Stevenson, Dollie Stevenson, and Dr. Steven R. Johnston, are all now dead. Even Audrey, Leon's second wife, is now dead, taking to her grave whatever secrets she might have known. What firsthand knowledge these persons could have about the details of Nell's death cannot be known. It can only be theorized what they might have known.
- Leon is not here to defend himself. His knowledge of the details of that night might exonerate him if he had a chance to defend himself.

The Evidence:

MOTIVATIONS: What could Leon's motivations be for wanting Nell dead? One doesn't kill one's wife of forty years without a compelling reason to do so. The last twenty-five years of the marriage was a three-way marriage between Leon, Nell, and

Audrey. The two women definitely knew of the other, and basically accepted it—they had no other choice. Tillie told me that sometime in the last half of 1945 or first half of 1946 all of Nell's family were called up from Kentucky by Nell's doctors because they feared she was nearing death. When they got there, they found that Leon was not there with Nell, but rather was out somewhere getting drunk. Tillie said her family later found out that in his drunken state, Leon had married Audrey, but couldn't tell me how they knew that. Apparently Leon was confident Nell was dying, and he didn't see the harm in not waiting to get married to Audrey. This is contradicted by the marriage record from 1969 I found for Leon and Audrey. There could have been an earlier marriage at this time in 1946 as well, with the 1969 marriage just being a "clean-up" type marriage to create the necessary documentation of their marriage for tax and retirement benefit purposes. They would need a marriage record postdating Nell's date of death. Any marriage record predating Nell's death would reveal bigamy, and government accounting might have revealed the conflict.

But as luck would have it, Nell didn't die in 1946 when the doctors thought she would. She recovered and eventually was well enough to be discharged from the tuberculosis sanitarium in July 1946. Nell tried to divorce Leon in later years, around 1958. A gentlemen friend of Nell's, whom she dated when she was very young prior to marrying Leon in 1929, had recently lost his wife and expressed interest in Nell again. Nell was living alone in Paducah at this time, with Leon living with Audrey in East St. Louis. Tillie advised Nell to "make a life of your own" when Nell confided in her that she had this interest from this former old boyfriend from her younger years. Nell said to Tillie at the time, "If I ever tried to divorce Leon, he'd kill me." At this time, Nell was forty-eight years old. Summoning her strength and courage, Nell contacted local Paducah attorney, Joe Freeland, and began divorce proceedings against Leon that year. When Leon was notified, he bolted back to Paducah in a rage, racing around town, trying to find Nell. He fired a shotgun blast through the front door of Ila Mae's house (Nell's sister). Leon scared Nell out of the divorce action using firearms. Leon absolutely refused to be divorced. He had been living with Audrey for at least a dozen years at this point, thus establishing a common-law marriage and bigamy. It's conceivable he might have faced criminal charges if his bigamy was revealed in a divorce action, and the judge referred the evidence to a prosecutor.

Were Nell and Audrey bigamists also, being that they knew Leon was married to the other woman also? Not really, although both had knowledge of the other woman. Nell only agreed to be married to one man. Leon sought to marry two women and lied to both. We know that Audrey knew Leon was married to Nell in Kentucky when she began living with him in Illinois, so in a sense, Audrey knew she was a bigamist also. She also knew she was still married to Joe Hayden, so if Audrey and Leon did marry before the 1969 marriage, Audrey knew this was bigamy by her as well. Nell knew Leon had Audrey as a girlfriend, and from reports from Leon's sister Versie, she knew Leon was living full time with Audrey. Nell tried divorcing Leon, and was intimidated and threatened by Leon not to divorce him. So Nell couldn't be considered

The three sisters: Grace, Nell, & Ila Mae

a willing bigamist, since she never agreed to be in this situation. There is no family recollection that Audrey ever tried to divorce or leave Leon, and no recollection that he ever contemplated leaving her. Audrey clearly was waiting for Nell to either divorce Leon or die. Leon likely lied to Audrey, saying he intended to leave Nell, but never did. It is known that Audrey's grandchildren were told that Leon had divorced Nell already, thus explaining why he was living with Audrey. Either Audrey told them (her children) that but knew it was false, or that's what Leon told Audrey (that he was divorced from Nell), and she believed him at first.

This cold war went on for more than twenty-five years, with Leon's everyday wife, Audrey, living with him while he worked in East St. Louis, and his Sunday wife, Nell, living with him when he wasn't working and had returned to Paducah. Both women seemed to accept the situation as undesirable, even repugnant, but unchangeable. In 1968 Leon approached his late fifties, and he wanted to retire from the physically demanding construction laborer's work he had done most of his life. He could no longer do it as well as when he was a younger man. He had enough money in the bank to retire on and a pension from the Local 100 Laborer's Union that would be enough to live on. Leon knew his older brothers Corbett and Rob wouldn't accept him in Paducah with two wives living in different houses in different parts of the city. They had told him so. The Christian-oriented Paducah community wouldn't have accepted it either. There would have been too much gossip. So Leon must have come to the conclusion he had to resolve the Nell/Audrey situation one way or the other. Leon would need a woman to cook and clean for him in his retirement years, and Audrey was more of a working wife. Nell could cook and clean, but refused to clean the fresh-catch fish and hunting kills that Leon would bring home. Audrey was willing to do those things.

Nell was more the "dress-up for church" type of wife, for show. Audrey was physically a strong woman despite her diminutive stature, eventually living to the age of ninety years old. Nell was a lesser strong woman than Audrey was from a health standpoint. Audrey clearly would outlive Leon and so would last for his full retirement years, whereas Nell he could not be sure would outlive him. Apparently, Leon made his choice that Audrey was the more practical choice for a retirement wife. In much the same way he would choose between two automobiles he might own, considering the features and utility of each model of car, and deciding he no longer needed two, Leon made his choice.

Last, there is the possible motivation of insurance. It was known that Nell had a Prudential Life Insurance policy in her hands three months before she died. She used it as proof of her age for obtaining her delayed birth certificate, itself a mystery as to why she was seeking that certificate so late in life and eerily coincidentally only three months before her death. The altering of the birth date on Nell's death certificate to make Nell appear approximately ten years younger than she actually was at the time of her death could have been done for only one logical reason—insurance fraud. No other motivation for that action makes sense. Indeed, this insurance is another reason why Leon couldn't let Nell divorce him. If she did, that would give the rights to insure her life back to her and her next husband. Leon obviously wanted that insurance right for himself, to be the beneficiary of the insurance when Nell died.

Summing up the possible motivations for Leon to murder Nell:

- Leon approached retirement age in 1968, wanted to retire in Paducah, and couldn't do it there with two wives. Paducah was a religious town and his siblings refused to allow it.
- Leon could not divorce Nell for fear of losing respect in his family being the first to be divorced.
- Leon could not divorce Nell for fear of his bigamy coming to light, possibly bringing him criminal charges, and definitely giving him the losing edge in any divorce from Nell.
- Leon could not divorce Nell because she would get alimony from him and get half of his assets.
- Leon could not divorce Audrey or leave either for the same reasons he couldn't divorce Nell. Indeed, Audrey could have been threatening Leon to expose their bigamy if he left her.
- Audrey was healthier than Nell, so Leon thought Audrey was the better choice for a retirement wife as he likely thought she would live longer than Nell.
- Leon likely had life insurance policies or credit-life insurance on bank loans set on Nell's life, the payouts of which would provide an adequate amount of money for Leon and Audrey's secure retirement. Leon couldn't let Nell divorce him and thereby lose him the insurance rights on her life.

Taken in total, the motivations listed above were powerful for Leon to want Nell dead.

PLANNING: Now the problem was how to get rid of Nell. Leon had to get Nell away from her family and friends in Paducah that might help defend her, or be someone that Nell could run to for protection, as she had in the past. At the time around 1958 when Nell tried to divorce Leon, she took refuge at the house of her sister, Ila Mae (Freeman) Fike. Leon fired a shotgun blast through the front door of Ila Mae's house, trying to scare Nell. It worked. She called off the divorce. In 1969, Leon needed to get Nell away from her protectors in Paducah. The campground in Florida was the perfect place. It was isolated, more than five miles from Okeechobee town, with no phones. That far away from Paducah, using the campground would allow Leon to control the story of how Nell died, or at least so he thought in the planning stages. Nell didn't want to go with Leon that year to Florida, smelling that something was up. But Leon couldn't wait any longer. That's why he forced her to go that year, intimidating Nell and her family by bringing a shotgun into Grace's house and laying it on the coffee table.

MULTIPLE STORIES: Time: January 6, 1969, Place: Campground on Lake Okeechobee. There are several stories as to what took place this day. This day was significant because it was one day before Leon and Nell's fortieth wedding anniversary. Leon told people later, including his and Nell's son, my father, Frank, that Nell was eating tangelos on the way to a seafood restaurant for supper with Walter and Dollie Stevenson in the car with them. He said that Nell began to complain of chest pains. Leon said they turned the car around and raced for the hospital in Okeechobee town. Leon said they arrived at the hospital with Nell still alive. Leon said Nell was complaining in the hospital of the chest pains, went into cardiac arrest at the hospital, and died there. That's story number one, now for story number two. Walter and Dollie Stevenson always insisted Nell died in the car, with her head on Dollie's lap. Is Leon wrong or the Stevensons wrong? They can't both be right, their stories conflict directly with each other. Someone's either confused, or worse—they're lying. Let's try to figure out why Leon might have lied about the story to Frank and the family in Paducah.

If Leon told everyone in Paducah and Frank that Nell died in the car (story no. 2), then they might blame him for not getting Nell to the hospital fast enough. The campground is only five miles from Okeechobee Town, and Leon was driving the car. By saying that Nell died at the hospital (story no. 1), it offloads the blame for Nell's death from Leon's slow response to the inability of the medical staff at the hospital to save her. If she died at the hospital, no one could ask Leon, "Why didn't you get her to the hospital before she died?" Furthermore, someone might have asked Leon, "Why didn't you try giving her emergency breathing or CPR on her chest to save her?" If she died at the hospital, Leon wouldn't have been responsible for that either. Thus, Leon had a motivation to tell Frank and other family members in Paducah that Nell died at the hospital, instead of in the car on the way there. But the death certificate clearly shows "DOA," or "dead on arrival." Nell was dead before she got to the hospital—this I can know for certain as the documentation proves it. But Leon couldn't have known her death certificate would show "DOA" when he was telling Frank and the family in Paducah that Nell died after she got to the hospital. He hadn't received the death certificate yet. Leon could reasonably assume they would never know he wasn't telling them the truth.

Leon had to have settled on the story he cooked up with Walter and Dollie Stevenson that Nell died in the car (story no. 2), and told this to the medical staff at Okeechobee General Hospital that night. Only he neglected to tell Walter and Dollie to switch to the "Nell died at the hospital" story (story no. 1) when talking with Frank or other family in Paducah. Perhaps he thought they wouldn't be talking about those details, or he could dismiss it as the Stevensons being mixed up about the details, since it was such a traumatic experience for all of them. But Grace, Nell's sister, took note of the discrepancy in the stories between Leon and the Stevensons, and it prompted her to investigate Nell's death.

Leon told Frank and the family in Paducah that the doctors at the hospital definitively ruled Nell's death as caused by natural causes, specifically a heart attack.

He couldn't have known at that time that the death certificate would show cause of death "unknown" later on, as he hadn't received it yet. Perhaps he also planned on not showing the death certificate to anyone. He, as Nell's spouse, would be the only person allowed to obtain a copy of it directly from the State of Florida, at least until he died. After Leon's death, then Frank would have the right to get his own copy, but never pursued it. It wasn't until after Frank's own death in 2005 that I, the grandson, pursued getting a copy, having the rights to do so passed on to me after Frank's death.

Leon said Nell died "right as we were pulling up to the hospital" to the medical staff at the hospital (story no. 2). Grace, whom Leon told that Nell died at the hospital (story no. 1), talked with Dr. Johnston who was on duty that night in the emergency room. He told Grace that Nell's body was dead on arrival, and had been dead for at least five hours before arriving at the hospital. This five-hour time frame coordinates with the time period Leon confessed to Bert Mitchell a few years before Leon died. Leon told Bert they drove around for approximately five hours before going to the hospital, presumably getting his story straight and, we would later learn, to sober up. Leon was drunk when he left the campground for the hospital with Nell's body. Leon couldn't show up at a hospital emergency room drunk, as that might raise suspicion. His inebriation would also make it easier for him to make a mistake in his explanation of Nell's death. Waiting for his head and breath to clear of the alcohol was needed before going to the hospital.

Leon also told Bill Yates, the funeral director who embalmed Nell's body (story no. 2) that Nell died in the car on their way to a seafood restaurant before arriving at the hospital. Bill Yates doesn't remember Leon making any mention of Nell eating tangelos and that being the cause of her heart attack. Leon told Bill Yates this when he came out to the campground the following day, January 7, 1969, to give Leon the money he had found hidden in Nell's brassiere. At this point, Leon didn't know that Tillie was talking with law enforcement in Paducah that very day. Leon didn't know that soon local law enforcement would arrive at the campground to search the trailer and intending to interview him about Nell's death.

They would come at the behest of the Paducah police who called Florida, requesting such an immediate investigation before Leon left Florida and evidence could be lost. Leon told Bill Yates the same story he told the hospital staff (story no. 2), not knowing that he would have to change that story when the police arrived, and create story number three. This new third story would be that Nell died alone in the trailer at the campground. He would need to tell this story to the local law enforcement investigators that searched the camper and campsite because they also interviewed Dorothy McNeal and others at the campground. They all saw Leon and Walter carry Nell's body out of the camper. Therefore, stories numbers one and two would not work with the local law enforcement. It is not known if the police came before Leon left for Paducah for Nell's funeral or after he returned to Okeechobee four days later. But they did interview Leon at some point and searched the trailer, as this was reported back to Grace in Paducah.

Since witnesses corroborated story number three, this story appears most likely to be the truth of what happened, at least the part of it about Nell dying in the camper at the campground. Of course, this story doesn't include *how* Nell died in the camper. Leon professed not to know that detail, saying Nell died alone while he was gone, and he found her dead in the trailer. The witnesses could not know if this part of the story was true or not, only the part about seeing Nell being carried from the camper, already dead.

Initially I couldn't think of any reasons for Leon saying different stories to different people about how Nell died. I counted three separate stories that I heard in my investigation so far.

- Story No. 1: Nell died at the hospital.
- Story No. 2: Nell died in the car on the way to the hospital.
- Story No. 3: Nell died alone in the trailer at the campground.

Could it be possible that these people telling me these pointedly different stories were just not remembering correctly, having time and perhaps enhanced memory change the facts they heard at the time? That could only be true if it were not multiple people reporting each of these stories. People don't make the same mistake if they are not remembering a story correctly. I would have gotten perhaps a dozen vastly dissimilar stories from the Tucker cousins if this were the case. But I didn't. I got strikingly similar stories from each of them depending on whom they heard their information from in the first place.

It gave me great pain to realize that Leon had told so many differing stories of what happened to Nell. Clearly, Leon was lying. What could his motivation be for lying? I allowed myself to ponder that, not immediately assuming it meant he was guilty. Could it be possible that Leon didn't tell Frank and the other family in Paducah the true story to spare them the pain of thinking Nell died alone in the camper? Nell having died was bad enough—Nell dying alone compounded the pain. Could Leon have saved her if she wasn't alone when the attack happened? Could it have been that Leon was ashamed that Nell died alone—that he thought Frank or the family might think him negligent for leaving Nell alone at the camper while he went off fishing? How could they have blamed Leon for Nell's death when there was no sign of anything imminent? They couldn't have expected Leon to be psychic and know Nell was going to have an attack that day. If any of these ideas were true, then why didn't Leon tell a consistent story to others? A little deeper thought reveals the answers.

Story number one (Nell died at the hospital) covered Leon for responsibility of not getting her to the hospital quickly enough. That's possibly a good enough motivation to tell that lie. Story number two (Nell died in the car on the way to the hospital) covered Leon to the hospital staff and Bill Yates. They clearly knew Nell was dead before arriving at the hospital, so story number one wouldn't work with them. But then, why make up story number two at all? Would it have mattered to the hospital staff and Bill Yates, the funeral director, as to where Nell died, in the car or at the campground, so long as it was a natural death? Yes, it did. Because if Nell died at the camper alone (story no. 3), then there was no way to know for sure it was a natural death. That might have prompted a mandatory autopsy over Leon's objections to find out the cause of her death. Leon had to tell the hospital staff and Bill Yates that he actually saw Nell die, and that it was a natural death. He had to make it believable also, to avoid the autopsy. Walter and Dollie backing Leon up on his story helped validate it to the hospital staff.

Leon knew, or could be reasonably confident, that the hospital staff in the small, country hospital of Okeechobee General would not risk forcing an autopsy over his refusal to authorize one. The hospital staff knew if they did an autopsy against Leon's wishes and found nothing but death by natural causes, then Leon could sue them for disturbing Nell's remains without his permission, and for no apparent reason. Okeechobee General could only be protected from liability if they found that Nell died of other than natural causes. It was too much of a risk without an external "red flag" on the outside of Nell's body justifying the risk. They didn't find that "red flag," so the doctor had no choice but to believe Leon's story. The doctor didn't force an autopsy and signed the death certificate's "cause of death: unknown (DOA)." It's possible that they had an argument, and a drunken Leon accidentally killed Nell in a moment of anger. But that type of scenario most likely would have shown some signs of trauma to Nell's body on the outside. There was none. Only a planned attack could kill Nell and not leave marks on the outside of her body as "red flags" to the hospital staff.

Let's look at story number three a little closer. Why didn't Leon tell the local law enforcement that he saw Nell have the attack in the camper, just like he did in story number two say he saw her have the attack in the car? This way they could prove it was death by natural causes. The problem with this is that it raises the specter of why Leon didn't get help immediately if she indeed had an attack that he witnessed in the camper? That didn't happen. Leon went and got Walter to help him carry Nell's dead body out of the camper to the car, but they weren't rushing about it, according to witness Dorothy McNeal—she was already dead. She had to have died alone, with no one around, for story number three to work and protect Leon from any fault or suspicion. How could they suspect him if he wasn't even there when she died, Leon likely thought.

So with a detailed examination of the possibilities, it can be seen why Leon made up the three stories. Each had a different circumstance requiring that specific story. Leon gambled no one would call Florida to compare the three stories. He gambled and lost. Grace called Florida. The Stevensons not having their stories coordinated with Leon's was the giveaway to Grace. Leon gambled that by the time the Stevensons got back to Kentucky sometime in February, even if they told story number three (Nell died at the campground) to people, he would already be up in East St. Louis and not have to answer for it. Nell would be in the ground by then. The story would be over.

TIME OF DEATH: Regarding the time of death estimate by the doctor at Okeechobee General Hospital that examined Nell's body the night she died, there are a variety of ways he could have made this estimate. It wouldn't have been just a wild guess or a hunch, rather the estimate would have come from an empirical determination from signs on Nell's body. For instance, the temperature of a dead body's core drops at a fairly constant rate after death, about 1.5 degrees Fahrenheit per hour.[9, 10] This body temperature can be used to estimate the time of death. If the core body temperature reading is taken with a rectal thermometer, a rule-of-thumb formula that some medical examiners follow is the following: 98.6 minus rectal temperature and then divided by 1.5 equals the approximate number of hours since death. Using this formula, Nell's core body temperature when examined would have been 91.1 degrees Fahrenheit to yield the five-hour time estimate since death. If she had just died immediately prior to arriving at the hospital, as Leon said, her core body temperature would have been much higher—closer to 98.6 degrees Fahrenheit.

The stage of rigor mortis would have been another way the doctor could have estimated Nell's time of death. Stiffening of a corpse occurs between just thirty minutes and three hours after death. Rigor mortis is the process by which the muscles in the body begin to stiffen from a lack of blood and oxygen. Rigor mortis first is seen in the eyelids and jaws of a corpse and spreads throughout the whole body in approximately six to twelve hours. Rigor mortis recedes again after another six to twelve hours, and a corpse becomes flexible again. If the doctor noticed that Nell's body, beyond just the eyelids and jaw but the rest of her body as well, was already exhibiting rigor mortis, then he could estimate that the time of death was at least greater than three hours. There would be no way to explain significant, body-wide rigor mortis if Nell just died immediately prior to arriving at the hospital, as Leon said.

The doctor might have examined Nell's eyes to see the degree of softness as a result of less fluid pressure behind the eye. The degree to which this has occurred can be used as a measure of the time since death. Also, a thin, cloudy film develops over the eye within three hours after death. It is doubtful that Nell's eyes were examined, because if she were indeed smothered, then petechiae (minute hemorrhages of blood vessels)[4] in her eyes likely would have been present. None was mentioned to Nell's sister Grace when she spoke with the doctor on the phone. This doesn't mean it wasn't there, it just wasn't noticed, or if noticed, mentioned to Grace.

Considering the above three methods of determining time of death from the physical state of the body, I think that the body temperature technique was probably used. The other two methods provide time of death in time increments of three or six hours, whereas the body temperature method provides time of death in one-hour increments down to a decimal. For the five-hour time frame the doctor told Grace to be valid, the body temperature method would have been the most likely method used.

It is far from certain that the doctor examining Nell would have noticed any clear sign of death if Nell had been smothered. For example, crush asphyxia, the weight of another person on the chest of a victim, making it impossible for them to breath, could have been one form of smothering used to kill Nell. Kneeling on her chest while covering her nose and mouth, called "burking,"[4] could also have done the job without leaving obvious marks for the doctor to have seen. The hyoid bone, a small, horseshoe-shaped bone in the neck that supports the tongue, is normally broken in cases of strangulation, but can also be broken in cases of smothering if force is being applied to the head area. This would have not been evident on the outside of the body to a doctor examining Nell's body. It would only be revealed in an autopsy.

NELL'S FEAR: Regarding the hidden money Bill Yates found, he told me that he found the money well hidden in a secret pocket sewn into the cup of Nell's brassiere. Nell's sister Grace used to do the same thing, so it's likely a cultural thing shared by the women of the Freeman family, or something that Grace suggested to Nell. In any event, if this was a secret escape fund for both Nell and Leon to use in case they got robbed, Leon would have known about it. But Leon didn't know about it, and told Bill Yates that. "I knew she 'as a hidin' money, I jus' didn't know whar," he said. This proved that Nell was hiding money from Leon. This could only mean that she felt she needed a secret escape fund from Leon, so that she could bolt quickly in a cab, bus, or plane. She knew Leon could potentially search the entire trailer, and even her purse, but knew he would never search her undergarments. The fact Leon suspected Nell was hiding money from him and that Nell actually was hiding money from Leon proved there was a great deal of suspicion and lack of trust between Leon and Nell.

Leon used to have a saying that he taught to Frank, and then Frank taught to me. It went, "To trust is bust. To bust is hell. No trust—no bust. No bust—no hell." Nell was apparently taking Leon's advice. I think Nell had learned early in her and Leon's forty-year marriage not to trust Leon and to always be prepared to defend herself or bolt from Leon.

TANGELO STORY: Leon and the Stevensons told people that Nell had a doctor's directive not to eat citrus fruit in Florida, either from a citrus allergy, or because it would interfere with her medications that she was taking. They said they saw her eating tangelos the day of her death, with Nell saying as she ate them, "These may kill me, but they're so good, I'm gonna eat 'em anyway." Nell's sister Grace wholly disputed the existence of a doctor's order to Nell regarding eating of fresh citrus. This problem of eating citrus fruit is usually concerning grapefruits. Doctors sometimes prohibit the consumption of grapefruits, and usually grapefruits only, to some of their patients because they contain compounds that interfere with certain medications. Specifically, furanocoumarins are the compounds contained in grapefruit that interfere with the efficacy of some drugs, e.g., statin drugs for cholesterol, blood-pressure medications, etc. These drugs have difficulty being absorbed in the intestines because of an intestinal enzyme that destroys them as they are absorbed. Doctors deliberately prescribe a higher dosage of these drugs than necessary because they count on this inefficient absorption in the intestines. Grapefruit juice inhibits the intestinal enzyme from working, thus allowing the drug to be absorbed more efficiently. Therefore, a regular dose of a medication given to get a desired result might actually result in a much higher blood concentration of the drug if grapefruit juice were consumed at the same time as the medication. This could be a dangerous overdose of some of these medications.

This, in a much less technical way, was what Leon and the Stevensons were saying happened to Nell. Basically, they allege Nell had a heart attack because she ate citrus fruit that interfered with her heart medications, most probably a blood pressure medication. In the study[8] done on Florida citrus published in 2005, this issue was examined. Tangerine and tangelo fruit are hybrids that contain grapefruit parentage and, therefore, could also possibly contain the compounds that inhibit absorption of some drugs. These citrus relatives (tangerines and tangelos) of grapefruit were tested and found not to contain furanocoumarins, the problematic compounds. This study[8] provided evidence that tangerine and tangelo varieties grown in Florida are unlikely to cause any inhibition of absorption of the drugs affected by grapefruit consumption.

Leon and the Stevensons could not have known that the furanocoumarins were not present in the tangelos they said Nell was eating prior to the heart attack they said happened, since this issue wasn't studied until 2005. Leon and/or the Stevensons had probably heard that doctors warned some people not to eat grapefruit because of drug interactions, and assumed because tangelos are a grapefruit hybrid, the prohibition applied to tangelos as well. But we now know that tangelos don't have the necessary compounds to cause the problem. Therefore, Nell could not have had a drug dosing problem from eating tangelos and thereby could not have had an attack caused by that. The tangelo story of Leon and the Stevenson's falls apart when the science is examined.

This also assumes that Nell was even eating tangelos in the first place. If anyone is told by their physician not to eat grapefruit because it might endanger their lives, then anyone with half a brain isn't going to eat grapefruit, or its hybrid cousins, such as tangelos. Even if I assume Nell had this directive from her doctor about not eating grapefruit, it doesn't prove she was eating something her doctor specifically forbade her. After all, tangelos aren't irresistible enough to endanger one's life to eat. And even if Nell did eat them anyway, disregarding her doctor's warnings, they couldn't have interfered with her medications, as Leon and the Stevensons alleged. Furthermore, if Nell had an unusual and rare citrus allergy, something her sister Grace denied, then Nell certainly would not have eaten any Florida citrus and risked such an attack. Nell wasn't stupid, suicidal, or reckless.

Last, I got in touch with the Stevenson family in Ft. Meade, Florida. The Stevensons of Ft. Meade had sold property there to Leon in the 1950s or early 1960s, and he sold it back to them on April 10, 1971. Specifically, Larkin "L.A." Stevenson sold the land to Leon, and Leon sold it back to L.A.'s grandniece, Joleen (Stevenson) Harden. When Leon sold it back to the Stevenson family, the deed transfer showed "Elbert and Audrey Tucker," so this documents that Leon and Audrey were definitely married by April 1971. L.A. Stevenson's nephew Robert Stevenson and his wife, Irene, were the Stevensons in Ft. Meade that Walter and Dollie Stevenson along with Leon and Nell (and later Leon and Audrey) would stop and visit with on their way to Okeechobee. Robert and Irene Stevenson had two daughters, married names Diana (Stevenson)

Lashley and Joleen (Stevenson) Harden. Robert Stevenson died in 1999, but his widow Irene was still alive in 2006. When I spoke with all three in 2006 by phone; Irene, Joleen, and Diana; each gave me tidbits on Leon's visits to Ft. Meade, first with Nell, later with Audrey. Diana remembered that the property that Leon owned, located on the southeast corner of the intersection of Olandt and NE Seventh streets, had citrus on it when Leon owned it, but not tangelos. She said it was tangerines, grapefruits, and oranges, but no exotic hybrids like tangelos.

In fact, that property had all the citrus trees removed when houses started being built in the area and never had tangelo trees on it at all. So the tangelo story from Leon seems even less likely to have been true. Whatever citrus they picked up in Ft. Meade on their way to Okeechobee, it wasn't tangelos, at least not from their property. If they had tangelos, they were bought elsewhere. The property that Leon owned is still vacant today, with Joleen and Kenny Harden planning to one day build their retirement home on the corner lot, refusing many offers for it from developers over the years. Joleen said she doesn't want to sell it but rather build on and live on it since it is the last parcel of an entire city block the Stevenson family once owned there. The rest was sold off piece by piece over the years.

CONSPIRACY (?): Assuming that Nell actually did eat tangelos in Florida that year, the possibility of the tangelos being poisoned has been considered, as Tillie suggested she believed this happened. When Leon confessed to Bert Mitchell about 1985 to smothering Nell, he would have been confessing for himself only. Let's assume the tangelos or other food were poisoned as the first attempt to kill Nell with the smothering being the back-up plan if the first attempt didn't work. Leon only confessed to the smothering, not the poisoning. If the tangelos or other food were poisoned, or Nell's medications tampered with, then why didn't Leon confess to this part of the story also?

One logical reason to delete part of the murder plot when confessing to it would be to protect another party that was involved in that other part of the plot. That other party had to be someone of significance to Leon, someone that mattered, for him to want to protect them. By 1985, when Leon confessed to Bert Mitchell, Walter and Dollie Stevenson were both dead. Walter died in 1975, and Dollie died in 1979. So it is unlikely Leon would be deleting the poisoning part of the murder plot from his confession to Bert Mitchell to protect the Stevensons. If the Stevensons had been involved, one or both of them, then Leon would have no impediment to admitting this part of the story. This trail of logic further suggests the Stevensons' innocence. Leon had to be deleting the poisoning part of the story from his confession to Bert to protect someone that was still alive at the time of the confession in about 1985. Audrey was still alive in 1985. She didn't die until 1999.

There would have been no one else that Leon would have trusted with this great of a secret—a murder plot against Nell. He might have trusted Walter Stevenson, and he definitely would have trusted Audrey. Walter Stevenson has already been eliminated by the logic above. That leaves Audrey. Audrey had a strong motivation to participate in such a plot. She would have wanted Leon all to herself, 100 percent of the time, and to retire together with him in Paducah. She wouldn't have wanted to share him part time with Nell anymore as she had for about twenty-five years at that point (in 1969). Audrey knew the citizens of Paducah, and Leon's family wouldn't have accepted her in Paducah with Nell still alive. Dollie Stevenson had been consistently rejecting her over the years so long as Nell was still alive and Leon married to Nell. All of these circumstances established a strong motivation for Audrey to want Nell out of Leon's life. She knew Leon couldn't divorce Nell without their bigamy being exposed, and Nell possibly getting alimony and half of their mutual property from Leon. Therefore, this established a scenario where Audrey could have wanted Nell dead. Audrey could also have known of the life insurance on Nell and wanted that also for her, and Leon's retirement nest egg.

It cannot be known what participation, if any, Audrey may have had in Nell's murder—only logically theorized. Leon might have needed help gathering the poison, as this might have been outside his scope of abilities. It was known Leon elicited the help of others when he was planning a previous murder, such as when he tried to get Walter Stevenson to help him set up a "hunting accident" for Earnest Collins, but Walter refused. Audrey was a tough woman, physically and personality-wise, so I must consider it at least possible she participated in Nell's murder plot. But to be fair I must also give her the benefit of the doubt and allow her to remain innocent until proven guilty. If she did participate, she didn't reveal this to her daughter Frances, or if she did reveal it, Frances wouldn't reveal it to me. It is understandable how a daughter would want to protect her mother's memory on something like this matter. Also, if a mother were to conceal anything from her daughter, her participation in a murder plot would be it.

Eddie Stevenson told me that about a week after Nell's death, Leon arrived back down at Okeechobee with Audrey to spend the rest of January and finish his vacation. This meant that Leon had to have left the trailer behind, drove to Paducah for Nell's funeral, picked up Audrey in Paducah (Audrey having traveled from East St. Louis to Paducah by bus, which her daughter Frances said was common), and drove back down to Okeechobee. Considering his wife of forty years had just died, I think anyone would find it hard to understand how a man could resume his vacation with his second wife and not be in a grief-stricken state. The only way Leon could do this is if he had already come to terms with Nell's loss beforehand, so it wasn't a shock when it happened. This additionally suggests the murder was planned, and not an act done in the heat of the moment, or an unforeseen death by natural causes.

Leon likely called Audrey from Florida to tell her that Nell was dead and that he wanted her to come to Paducah. Audrey immediately took off from work. How could she have taken off from work on such short notice, no notice at all in fact, and left for a multi-week vacation in Florida with Leon? This suggests that Audrey had asked for the time off from work before Nell died, with enough advance notice to her employer, Hunter Meat Packing, for them to approve the time off and thus not endanger her job. This also suggests that Nell's death was pre-planned, at least by Leon. Leon had to have known beforehand when Nell would die, so he could tell Audrey when she needed to request the time off from her job.

Audrey could do the math herself about the time frame. Audrey knew when Leon was going to Florida with Nell—she knew everything Leon did. Audrey knew when Leon would want her to join him in Florida—starting in Okeechobee on the thirteenth or fourteenth of January 1969—so she could ask her employer for the time off. She had to be in Paducah by the eleventh for Nell's funeral. So therefore Audrey knew how much time Nell was going to be in Florida, only a week or less. This would have been extremely uncommon for the great distance, driving time, and cost of transport to Florida at that time. At this time in the 1960s, people took extended trips to Florida to camp and fish, with a minimum of three to four weeks being the norm. It didn't make any sense for Leon to drive all that way for only a few days with Nell in Florida—the driving time would almost equal the camping time for Nell. Therefore, it's logical that Audrey had to suspect, if she didn't already know for sure from being in on the whole plot, that something would happen to Nell in Florida to cut her time there short.

One other possibility needs to be discussed, prefaced by the fact that I have no evidence this occurred. But it makes sense, so I'll discuss it. It is possible Leon took Audrey to Florida first and left her in Okeechobee or Ft. Meade, while he went back up to Kentucky to get Nell. Leon cared little about family holidays. In all the years I knew him, totaling twenty-three years, I never remember him coming a single time to our house for Christmas or Thanksgiving or any other holiday, or our family being invited to his house for a holiday visit. Our visits to his house were almost never on a holiday. Construction work in East St. Louis in 1968 would have stopped before Christmas, not to resume until after New Year's. Leon wouldn't have had any work to do between Christmas and New Year's, and it's logical he would have taken off for his monthlong January fishing trip to Okeechobee as early as possible. The Stevensons were a family-oriented people, so it's logical they would have stayed in the Calvert City, Kentucky, area to be with their children at Christmastime and not have left to join Leon in Florida until after New Year's.

If Leon didn't arrive in Paducah until around New Year's to pick up Nell, then what did he do between Christmas and New Year's? It's logical he went to Florida early, to set up the murder scene for Nell. He wouldn't have gone alone either, as Leon hated being alone. Its logical if this happened, he took Audrey with him. If he took Audrey with him before Christmas to Florida, and returned to Paducah to pick up Nell alone, then Audrey would have been left behind in Florida, either in Okeechobee or Ft. Meade. Leon couldn't very well leave Audrey in the trailer on Lake Okeechobee and then return with Nell in the car. Leon had to have the trailer with him to keep from raising suspicions when he left with Nell. Perhaps Audrey went ahead on a bus to Florida? Audrey, if she was left behind, had to have stayed elsewhere, at a motel or perhaps with the Stevensons in Ft. Meade. Irene Stevenson, when I posed this scenario to her, did not have any recollection of Audrey ever staying with them without Leon there as well, so this appears unlikely to have happened.

Nell's funeral

What reason would there have been to leave Audrey behind in Florida while Leon went to retrieve Nell? The sack of poisoned tangelos or other food on Leon's lot in Ft. Meade needed to be set up. This could have been Audrey's assigned task. Also, Leon needed someone to help him with the drive back to Paducah for Nell's funeral. Frances, Audrey's daughter, was certain Audrey attended Nell's funeral in Paducah, as she remembers seeing a memento from Nell's funeral in Audrey's belongings that passed on to her after Audrey's death in 1999. This hypothetical scenario would have allowed Audrey to set her departure date from work ahead of time as opposed to waiting for Leon to call from Florida that Nell was dead, then leaving work on short notice to her employer. So Audrey arrived in Paducah for Nell's funeral either by bus from East St. Louis, or with Leon from Florida.

INTENTIONAL VAGUENESS: Regarding the cause of death on the death certificate, the doctor recorded it as "unknown (DOA)," and that was powerful. If he truly believed that the cause of death was of natural causes, he would have stated that on the death certificate, or some variation of that. At the very least it would have said something to the effect, "cause of death: undetermined natural cause(s)" or "cause of death: nonspecific natural cause(s)." But he didn't do this. He intentionally recorded it as "unknown." An unknown cause of death leaves open the possibility of homicide equal with natural causes. It basically says the doctor wasn't convinced it was death by natural causes, or he would have stated that.

If the possibility of homicide had not been ruled out completely, then the doctor had the responsibility to continue to investigate according to Florida law. With the possibility of homicide not eliminated, an autopsy should have been forced over the objections of Leon and Frank Tucker. At the very least, the doctor should have referred the case to local law enforcement before the body was released for embalming. Without being able to view the medical records from that night in 1969, and not being able to interview the doctor himself since he is now deceased, I cannot know for sure that bringing in law enforcement was not done. Law enforcement may have been at the hospital at the time, but I will never know. No records exist to establish this. But I can reasonably assume that the doctor did not contact law enforcement that night in 1969, or if they were, they took no action. If law enforcement were present, I believe an investigation into Nell's cause of death would have ensued if the physician hadn't eliminated the possibility of homicide.

Perhaps the listing of "unknown" as the cause of death was Dr. Johnston's flag to others who would see the death certificate later on. He couldn't know whom this might be or how long it would take for it to be seen by others. As it turned out, thirty-seven years would pass before someone other than Leon would see Nell's death certificate, and see Dr. Johnston's handwriting of "unknown" cause of death. Perhaps Dr. Johnston was signaling to those who would see it later on that he had suspicions of Nell's cause of death. I cannot know now in 2006 what Dr. Johnston's true intentions were in 1969.

DR. JOHNSTON: What motivation could the doctor have had or what circumstances could have been the cause for him not to pursue an investigation of this mysterious death before him? I initially theorized that perhaps he was incompetent. I pictured a doddering, old man who was long past his prime, and perhaps in the early stages of confusion common to elderly people. However, all of my research on the physician who signed Nell's death certificate, Dr. Steven R. Johnston, disproved my initial theory. Dr. Johnston was an eminent and prestigious physician in the Okeechobee area who was widely trusted and respected. The focus of his practice was obstetrics, and Tommy Markham of Okeechobee told me "he delivered half of Okeechobee." Dr. Johnston was fifty-six years old at the time of Nell's death. He didn't die until six years later in 1975. With all that information, it can be reasonably assumed the doctor was not incompetent at the time he viewed Nell's body.

With no medical records surviving to 2006 to consult, I tried contacting Dr. Johnston's last wife, Christine "Tina" Johnston. She was elderly and being cared for by her children, Lowery and Lee Anita Markham. Lowery worked for a real estate brokerage office in Okeechobee. I learned that Tina Johnston was not able to speak with me perhaps due to her advanced age, but her son Lowery was able to give me some information on Dr. Johnston. He said Dr. Johnston's records were destroyed at the time of his death for the confidentiality of his patients. On a hunch I asked Lowery if Dr. Johnston was a Freemason. Lowery said yes, he remembered Dr. Johnston was indeed a Freemason. This raises a possible explanation of one of the mysteries in 1969. I'll explain more on this idea in another section.

To verify this point, after a long and at times frustrating search, I located Dr. Johnston's first daughter, Venetia (Johnston) Mendoza. Women change their names when they marry, so finding them is usually only possible through government records, which are a huge pain to search through. When I found her living in Florida in 2006, she told me she didn't believe her father was a Freemason, but admitted she didn't know much about what he did after her parents divorced when she was about ten years old. Lowery Markham knew Dr. Johnston in his older years, a time when he would have been more likely to be a member of the Freemasons, not in his youth, when he was married to Venetia's mother. Venetia told me Dr. Johnston was married five times in his lifetime, which I couldn't help but chuckle at and be somewhat impressed.

I located Dr. Johnston's second daughter (by another wife) and half sister to Venetia, by the name of Kathleen (Johnston) Banks. Venetia wasn't in touch with her, and so couldn't provide any contact information. I tracked Kathleen down through property and marriage records as now living in Port St. Lucie, Florida. I wanted to see if one of Dr. Johnston's daughters had any diaries or journals their father might have kept that might shed some light on Nell's death. I had hopes maybe Dr. Johnston recorded his thoughts of what he saw that night, January 6, 1969. It was a real long shot anyway, that any diaries or journals existed, and if they did, that any notes were made about Nell. Venetia didn't have anything like that except a few letters Dr. Johnston had written to her. Kathleen told me the same thing, she didn't have any journals or diaries that belonged to her father. Kathleen also said she didn't believe her father was a Freemason, but admitted she lost contact with him when she was five years old and her parents divorced. She reunited with him when she was eighteen years old, which was in 1975, the year Dr. Johnston died.

It's possible the two daughters didn't know their father, Dr. Johnston, was a Freemason from his older years. Being a Freemason in a small town like Okeechobee for all prominent citizens, such as elected officials, doctors, lawyers, school administrators, would have been a way for networking to take place—for power acquisition and maintenance of society position. Some people have a natural suspicion and dislike of the Masons, it being such a secretive and all-male society. Therefore, without knowing it, these two daughters of Dr. Johnston may have instinctively answered "no" about their father potentially being a Freemason, when they really didn't know the answer because of the long years of estrangement from him. It was also possible Dr. Johnston wasn't a Freemason at all. Lowery Markham's brother Thomas Markham, a local historian in Okeechobee, said Dr. Johnston to his recollection was not a Freemason. So I don't know who to believe, Lowery says he was, Thomas says he wasn't. Perhaps Dr. Johnston didn't disclose this to his daughters about his history, but did disclose it to the male members of the Markham family. This is the only way I can resolve the differing answers about Dr. Johnston's potential Freemason history. This resolution only holds true if all the memories of the parties involved are accurate. I suggest that Dr. Johnston might have been a Freemason, and it might have had a role in why he did not force an autopsy of Nell's remains over Leon's objections. Perhaps he just didn't want Leon suing him, or going berserk in the emergency room that night. Perhaps when Dr. Johnston called Frank, Nell's son, in Illinois and also got a "no" from him about the autopsy, it tipped the balance to not doing it. Dr. Johnston got too much opposition from the family. All of it could have played a role.

I even ran newspaper ads in the local newspapers of Okeechobee attempting to find hospital staff employed by Okeechobee General Hospital in 1969, but got no responses from my ads at all. I wrote to the Personnel Department of the hospital in Okeechobee, now called Raulerson Medical Center, the current-day descendant of the Okeechobee General Hospital. They couldn't locate anyone who would have worked at the hospital in 1969 unless they still worked at Raulerson today or within the last five years. That's all the length they kept their records. The Okeechobee library staff directed me to the county circuit court's office, who indeed said they had some records from the old hospital. They looked for me through the records but said the records from that era were lost in a fire.

I also wrote to the Okeechobee County Historical Society and asked their help in identifying medical staff that worked at the Okeechobee General Hospital in 1969. They wrote back with a name, Pearl Godwin, who still lived in Okeechobee. Bless her heart, I hated to bother her with a call from a stranger. She was eighty-six years old when I contacted her by phone in 2006. She was still clear of speech and mind, from what I gathered. I described Nell to Pearl Godwin, gave her Nell's name and the circumstances in how she died. It didn't ring any immediate bells with Pearl. I would have been very surprised if it had from that long ago. The event wouldn't have been significant to her anyway such that she would commit it to memory. She did agree to receive some photos of Nell I would mail to her, to see if Nell's image might jog her memory. She couldn't help me identify any other medical staff from Okeechobee General Hospital in 1969 that were still alive in 2006, but she promised to give it some thought and let me know if she remembered any.

When she got the photos, it wasn't successful at jogging any memories, but she did say she thought the hospital records from that time still existed at a warehouse owned by the Markham Cannery in Okeechobee, and she would check into it for me. She told me she thought that Dr. Steven Johnston was a competent doctor, but a bit of a "skirt chaser." We shared a laugh about that, since I already knew he had been married five times in his lifetime, so had to be a bit of a "lady's man." She said she thought it highly unusual for an unknown cause of death to be left on a death certificate with no autopsy performed. She thought it was state law at the time that an autopsy would have been required, not optional. It made me think when she said that perhaps Leon threw a holy screaming fit to keep them from doing an autopsy and violate state law by doing so. It was also possible that Dr. Johnston's possible Freemason membership interfered with the proper following of state law regarding the necessary autopsy.

Pearl did have one valuable sliver of information that peeked through what she was telling me. I didn't immediately recognize it as notable, until contemplating it all later. She said the hospital was so small that they had no regular doctor except Dr. Steven R. Johnston. Other doctors from Orlando would come down on weekends, but Steven R. Johnston would have been the doctor on call that night, January 6, 1969, since that was a Monday night. The doctor that Grace (Freeman) Martinez, Nell's sister, talked to about the details of Nell's time at the hospital must have been Dr. Steven R. Johnston himself, not an intern, as had been told around inside the family over the years. Pearl Godwin said there were no interns, only Dr. Johnston, at the hospital during those years.

FREEMASONRY: I know that Freemasons, from what my father (who was a thirty-second-degree Mason, holding the title of Sublime Prince of the Royal Secret)[3] told me, had an ability to converse with each other with hand signals in such a way as other people around them wouldn't know it. Freemasons have a way of recognizing each other even without glancing for a Masonic ring on the hand, sometimes with phrases or trigger words said with certain points of emphasis that another Mason will recognize. Just the act of shaking hands in a certain way could signal from one Mason to another to recognize each other. For instance, if a Mason when shaking hands applies pressure with the thumb to the space between the second and third knuckles on the other person's hand, this signals to them they are a Mason.[2]

Freemasons will do anything for each other, they have to, as required by the blood oath they take when they join the "brotherhood." I remember my father telling me that if I was ever stranded or in trouble, and could identify a Mason by his Masonic ring, that I should say to him, "I am the son of the widow's son, and I need help." I was supposed to say it with emphasis on the words "son" and "widow's son." This statement would compel any Mason to help me, even up to the point of his own death.

If a Mason discovers a crime committed by another Mason, he must keep it secret to protect the brother Mason.[7] Leon had learned to abuse this automatic trust among Masons by pulling crooked deals on his Lodge brothers, and was kicked out (blackballed) of the Freemasons of East St. Louis because of it, according to Jim Mitchell. I can theorize that Leon might have done the same thing to Dr. Johnston that night at the Okeechobee General Hospital in 1969. Dr. Johnston couldn't have known that Leon was kicked out of the Masons in Illinois. He would have felt, seen, or heard the Masonic signals coming from Leon and recognized him as a fellow Mason. He therefore would have been more likely to believe whatever story Leon was telling him of how Nell died, and not question it. Masons, after all, were sworn not to lie to each other. Dr. Johnston couldn't have known that Leon was a lifelong, masterful liar and a world-class storyteller.

Even if Dr. Johnston suspected Leon wasn't telling him the truth, if a Mason, Dr. Johnston would be required to support Leon anyway. If Dr. Johnston suspected Nell didn't die of natural causes and suspected Leon was lying about the story he was telling to him, then he would have logically suspected Leon had something to do with the unnatural death laying before him. Why else would someone lie when delivering the body to a hospital emergency room and explaining how the person died unless they were hiding something? If he were a fellow Mason though, Dr. Johnston would have been obligated to keep this secret and support Leon anyway.

Without more specific information showing this actually happened, I can do no more than speculate. I don't for a minute suggest I know for certain that Dr. Johnston knowingly helped Leon cover up a homicide. But he didn't question Leon's story of how Nell died sufficiently, that can be known for certain. Dr. Johnston was, however, suspicious enough to write down "unknown (DOA)" as the cause of death. At least this documented Dr. Johnston wasn't entirely convinced Nell's death was by natural causes. He just wasn't suspicious enough to order the necessary autopsy over Leon and Frank's refusals. This act, stating the cause of death as "unknown," doesn't in itself betray any Masonic support for Leon. In fact, I'm surprised the death certificate didn't state cause of death to be natural causes, as Leon was stating. That would have shown complete support to Leon by Dr. Johnston. But without an autopsy, he couldn't make that determination (of death by natural causes) stick. He knew that. So he apparently found the midpoint between showing Leon support and obeying his oath as a doctor. I always wondered whether an oath of a doctor or the blood oath of a Mason would predominate in the mind of a doctor who was also a Mason and faced with a conflict of loyalties between the two oaths.

MISSING AUTOPSY: I cannot know that Dr. Steven Johnston did anything more than inspect Nell in a cursory way. To answer the question why Dr. Johnston did not overrule

Leon's objection to an autopsy of Nell's remains that night in 1969, Dr. Johnston would need to have left some notes behind. If any such notes ever existed, they are gone now. The medical examiner in Ft. Pierce, Florida, Merv Waldren, gave me one possible explanation for this lack of pursuit of the autopsy by Dr. Johnston. He told me that in that time period (1969) as well as today in 2006 in Florida, Floridians were and are weary of paying tax dollars to service the tourists. A lot of elderly tourists travel to Florida and die there. Floridians feel since the tourists don't pay property taxes, the burden of servicing their needs postmortem, such as an autopsy, should be borne by their home state. In Nell's case, that would have been Kentucky.

This argument by Floridians is flawed on many points, and here's why. Tourists bring huge amounts of money into Florida ever year. One of the main pillars of the Floridian economy is the enormous influx of dollars from other parts of the country spent by tourists visiting Florida. Those tourists pay taxes and fees not borne by other Floridians on camping sites, rental cars, hotel rooms, and entrance fees at attractions. The money spent by tourists provides jobs to Floridians, which in turn allows those Floridians to pay income taxes to the state, and pay their property taxes to local governments. Therefore, albeit through an indirect pathway, the tourists end up paying for the government services of Florida just the same as the residents do. Plus, couldn't tourists just be billed for the medical services they require, including autopsies, while in Florida? Thus the burden on the Florida taxpayer would be nullified.

Considering these facts, it follows then that my grandmother Nell deserved to be treated with the same level of service that any Floridian would have been at that hospital in Okeechobee in 1969. If she wasn't, this was negligence or incompetence. I cannot prove she wasn't treated the same, other than pointing to the glaring lack of an autopsy to conclusively establish her cause of death. At the very least, a coroner's inquest into her death should have been held in any case of unknown cause of death. Most jurisdictions require this by law. Allowing the husband of a woman whose dead body is brought to a hospital emergency room to decide whether an autopsy is done or not was not appropriate. Allowing the body to leave the hospital that night for embalming with no cause of death clearly established yet was not appropriate. Recording Nell's cause of death on her death certificate as "unknown" was not appropriate. A mistake was made there that night—and I cannot determine with the information I have whose mistake it was: Dr. Johnston's, the hospital's, or the attitudes of Floridians. Ultimately, Dr. Johnston was charged with the authority in the matter, since he was the physician signing Nell's death certificate. But Dr. Johnston may have only been following procedures common to the hospitals of Florida at the time regarding tourist deaths. Those procedures may have been influenced politically by the attitudes of Floridians at the time about paying for services for tourists.

DEATH CERTIFICATE ANOMALIES: The fact that Leon refused an autopsy in the first place is not surprising at first glance. Many people would be averse to having their loved one dissected the way bodies are during an autopsy. However, Nell died of

221

undetermined causes, and the doctor would not place "cause of death: natural causes" on the death certificate. If it were I, I would want to know how my wife died. The fact that a closed casket funeral would be necessary after the autopsy is a small sacrifice to obtain that information. But the hospital told Grace that Leon vehemently refused the autopsy offer. Frank refused when the hospital called him also the night Nell died. Clearly, the unorthodox call to Frank for permission for the autopsy indicated a heavy suspicion at the hospital that Nell may not have died of natural causes as Leon said. The call to Frank would have been unnecessary if they were satisfied with the veracity of the story from Leon. Frank's refusal to authorize the autopsy was consistent with a lifelong capitulation to Leon's dominance in their family, not wanting to go against him. Frank knew there would have been holy hell to pay if he went against Leon on something this significant.

Regarding the other anomalies on the death certificate, the changed date of birth only makes sense if insurance fraud was the motivation. If the funeral home had simply gotten the date wrong in the initial typing of the certificate, considering how important this document is, they would have started over with a new document. If the funeral home had gotten the date wrong—and Leon noticed it was wrong—he would not have called back to change the birth date on the death certificate. It would not have mattered to Leon if the death certificate were simply being placed in a drawer or file for posterity. The correct birth date only mattered if he was going to submit the death certificate to some government entity or private agency, such as an insurance company, that would check that birth date against some other source of information, like an insurance application.

The address Leon placed on Nell's death certificate, the Fifty-second Street address in East St. Louis, is pertinent to note in that it shows Leon expected to be in East St. Louis shortly after returning from Florida. He knew he would not be in Paducah long enough to wait for the death certificate to arrive in the mail at Nell's house (1603 Little Avenue, Paducah). What did it matter if he got the death certificate in Paducah? It had to matter because Leon needed the death certificate in East St. Louis right away. Why did he need it? The only reason anyone ever actually needs a death certificate is to claim an insurance payout. Mostly death certificates are just a keepsake for families. But Leon's apparent urgency at getting the death certificate shows he needed it for an insurance payout. No other reason makes sense.

Would the possibility of life insurance be enough of a motivation for Leon by itself to murder Nell? I don't believe so. I believe Leon's motivation was the situation that he wanted to retire soon and couldn't have two wives and two households in Paducah simultaneously. But if due to this "retirement in Paducah" motivation, Leon decided he needed to get rid of Nell, then it makes sense that in Leon's view, why not take out some life insurance on Nell to maximize his retirement nest egg? Why miss the opportunity to cash in on an act already decided upon for other reasons?

This therefore fits. It makes sense that he would have to reduce Nell's age on the death certificate, from fifty-eight to forty-nine years old, because he would have had to reduce Nell's age to get a new life insurance policy on Nell. An older policy wouldn't need the age reduction most likely, as a lie about her age would have been discovered beforehand. Only collecting on a brand new policy would require such an age reduction on the death certificate. At her age of fifty-eight, few insurance companies would have issued life insurance on her. At forty-nine years old, more of them would be willing to issue such a policy. This therefore coordinates and connects two of the anomalies, the birth date change and the East St. Louis address. They were tied together, both pointing to insurance fraud as an ancillary motivation for Leon to murder Nell.

This also correlates with the fact that Nell was reviewing her Prudential Life Insurance policy in September 1968, only three months before she died. She used it to document her age to get a delayed birth certificate issued, which she never had before in her lifetime. For what purpose could she need a birth certificate at the age of fifty-eight? One plausible explanation is that it had some connection to the birth date change on her death certificate, which I've previously reasoned had life insurance fraud as the motivation for that. The whole matter, the birth certificate, death certificate, and review of life insurance policies, could have been all part of Leon's plan. The coincidences are too many to ignore and say that everything was innocent.

MEDICATION MANIPULATION: Regarding the empty pill bottle found by the Okeechobee county sheriff's office that searched the camper in the days after Nell died, this appears to be one of the most revealing pieces of evidence. It cannot be known for certain without more specific information, but the inference from this evidence is that Nell's medications were being manipulated. Nell would have gotten her medications refilled at Hugg the Druggist in Paducah before she left on this trip. It is not known what medications she was on at the time, beyond Tillie's recollection that she had some Valium with her. If she was taking some kind of necessary medication for some ailment (which was unknown to Grace), and if Leon substituted a poisonous pill identical in appearance to the pills in the bottle, Nell could have been poisoning herself slowly and not have known it. Rarely are these types of poisonings acute, but chronic, taking weeks or longer to kill someone, such as arsenic poisoning. Leon couldn't make it look like a sudden death if he was poisoning her. It had to look like a natural death, as a slow weakening and eventual death from slow, low-dose poisoning would accomplish.

If Leon substituted a placebo, or fake pill, identical in appearance to the pills in the bottle, then Nell could be denying herself necessary medication without knowing it. This also would cause a slow weakening in Nell's health, eventually leading to a death that appeared natural. Either one of these occurrences is plausible. Nell just didn't weaken and die fast enough for Leon. Leon lost his patience, perhaps hastened by being drunk one night, and decided to smother her to finish her off. A weakened Nell wouldn't be able to fight back very effectively against Leon's strength, which would explain the lack of exterior marks on her body that would show resistance to a physical attack. In either of these cases, the poisoning or the placebo substitution, Leon would have to get rid of the pills after Nell died, so they couldn't be found by someone else, namely police or family members, later on. He likely flushed them down the toilet of the camper, or put them in his pocket and ditched them in the trash at the hospital, leaving the empty bottle in the camper that the police would find the next day.

If Nell was taking the Valium that Tillie insists she had, then if Leon gave her an overdose of Valium, perhaps slipping it into her food without her knowing, it would weaken her significantly eventually leading to death. An overdose of Valium could appear to a doctor or law enforcement later as perhaps an accidental overdose self-administered by Nell, or a suicide attempt by Nell. Either way, Leon wouldn't be suspected. But if the Valium overdose didn't kill her, and just made her weak and groggy, then a drunken Leon might have become impatient and decided to smother her to finish her off. This also could explain the empty medicine bottle. Nell had only been in Florida for one week of a monthlong trip. She could not have run out of any of her medications that quickly. If she had spilled them accidentally, then she would have gotten more locally in Okeechobee.

There was no indication Nell was suicidal, and would not have overdosed herself. No suicide note was found nor were there any indications from Nell's family that she was in any way depressed or suicidal in nature. If Nell had wanted to kill herself, she would have found a more effective agent than the medications she was using, which would have been difficult to overdose on. Indeed, there is evidence to the contrary—that Nell wanted to live. The fact that Nell sent a plea for help on the postcard to her sister, and was hiding money in her brassiere as a secret escape fund, indicates Nell wanted to live. She wouldn't have done those things if she were planning to commit suicide. Therefore, an empty medicine bottle one week into a monthlong camping trip had no plausible explanation other than it being evidence of foul play. I couldn't make sense of this any other way.

POISONING (?): A possible poisoning of Nell by Leon becomes more plausible when Leon's comments to Charles Stevenson are considered. Charles said Leon once told him, "I got me a drug that'll stop a heart an' after they'd be no trace of it." If Leon wasn't just blustering male bravado to another man as some men do, then this shows a state of mind of Leon that he could actually contemplate murdering someone using a poison. Indeed, Leon was smart enough to think ahead about covering up the crime by selecting a drug that was undetectable in an autopsy. A substance that fits Leon's description could be potassium chloride. This drug is a rather simple compound commonly available, sometimes used as a substitute for table salt, and breaks down in the body to just potassium and chlorine. At high enough concentrations, it is used to stop the heart of a convicted prisoner being executed in modern-day chemical-injection executions. Without knowing what to look for, which would be elevated potassium levels in the blood, a forensic examiner could easily miss this type of poisoning and rule the death as caused by heart attack. Especially if the examination didn't take place immediately after death, because red blood cells lyse (burst open) shortly after death, dumping potassium into the blood, which would mask any elevated concentrations of potassium. Only a pathologist looking specifically for this elevated potassium concentration and comparing it to normal potassium to iron ratios might discover this type of poisoning.

Epinephrine could also have been used to increase cardiac instability. Couple either one of these (potassium chloride or epinephrine) with a stress situation of being smothered, and the act of smothering wouldn't be needed to cause death. A cardiac arrest could have been instigated by the combination of the drugs weakening or destabilizing the heart, and the smothering generating the needed stress situation to trigger the heart attack. Where could Leon have gotten these drugs? Anywhere—they were commonly available without prescription. Epinephrine might have been slightly harder to obtain, but not impossible.

Other drugs that might stop a heart, as Leon described, could be the drugs used in surgery situations as muscle relaxants administered by anesthesiologists. These drugs include succinylcholine, or commonly called scoline, as well as sodium thiopental, or pancuronium. All of these compounds would paralyze muscles and, in high enough dosages, stop the diaphragm muscle from causing breathing and stop the heart. But how could Leon have gotten these types of drugs? It is less likely to believe he had access to these drugs.

That leaves potassium chloride as the drug that was commonly available and fits Leon's description of a "drug that could stop a heart with no trace later." Where could Leon have gotten the potassium chloride or found out about it? Potassium chloride was occasionally used in meatpacking operations for tanning of hides, or as a salt substitute in curing of luncheon meats. Leon had previously worked in meatpacking in 1941-1942 and could have learned about it then. Where could Leon have gotten the potassium chloride in 1968 when Nell's murder would have been planned? Audrey worked at Hunter Meat Packing in East St. Louis at that time.

STEVENSONS: I want to say clearly that I have come to the conclusion that the Stevensons, Walter and Dollie, as well as their son Eddie Stevenson and his wife Linda, did not participate in the murder of Nell in any way, at least not knowingly. All four were simply witnesses. Walter and Dollie were seen by witnesses helping Leon take Nell to the hospital after her death, and helped Leon spread the story of her dying in the car, but I believe that is the fullest extent of their involvement with Nell's death. I can assume Walter loved Leon like a brother so much that he would have done almost anything for him, including helping him out of his trouble. I say almost anything, because Walter did draw the line when Leon proposed murder at least one previous time in their past. Leon proposed to Walter for him to help Leon lure Earnest Collins, Walter's son-in-law, into the woods so that Leon could set up a "hunting accident" for Earnest—meaning Leon intended to shoot him and make it look like an accident. Walter refused. I can assume from this that participating in murder was beyond what Walter would have done for Leon.

It can be assumed that Walter was fond of Nell also, having known her for roughly forty years. Nell's gentle and feminine nature made her universally liked by everyone she met, and this would have included the Stevensons. I cannot imagine Walter would have helped Leon in any way if he knew Leon was planning to murder Nell. I can, however, reasonably assume Walter may have helped Leon out of a bad situation, if the deed was done and Walter didn't know beforehand to stop it from happening. Whether or not Walter believed Leon intentionally killed Nell, or Leon accidentally killed Nell, or Nell died accidentally on her own, or Nell died of natural causes, cannot be known for certain. The five hours of riding in the car between leaving the campground and arriving at the hospital with Nell's body had to be filled with something going on. Walter had to be suspicious of something during that period of time if he didn't know for sure already what had happened. Perhaps he knew Leon was drunk and needed to sober up before going to the hospital, or suspicious eyes there would be on Leon. Perhaps Leon needed to spend those hours convincing Walter, and then Walter convincing Dollie, to go along with Leon's stories when they got to the hospital.

After Nell's death, Leon had to leave for Kentucky for the funeral. The Stevensons stayed behind in Florida and did not attend Nell's funeral. Leon would leave his camper at the campground, to hold on to his favorite lot, because he knew it was going to be guarded by the Stevensons. Leon may have even talked them into staying behind to guard the campsites, so they wouldn't lose their spots to others when they returned, rather than the Stevensons attending Nell's funeral with Leon in Kentucky and taking their trailers back with them. It is surprising Walter and Dollie Stevenson didn't attend Nell's funeral because they had known Nell for forty years also and were close. Many who attended Nell's funeral commented on Walter and Dollie's absence.

Charles Stevenson, Walter and Dollie's son, told me he asked his father once if he thought Leon had anything to do with Nell's death, and Walter replied to Charles, "No, I don't think Leon had anything to do with it." Even the wording on the sentence is revealing, using the word "think" rather than stating with more certainty "know." Without knowing it, even Walter Stevenson left open the possibility that Leon might have had something to do with Nell's death by answering his son Charles's question in that manner. If he did believe Leon was responsible or could have been, I'm sure Walter's deep brotherly-type love for Leon would have prevented him from saying so.

Walter and Dollie's motivations for helping Leon with a concocted story that day in 1969, and the weeks and years that followed, are not clearly known. What Leon told them happened, and how he convinced them to go along with this concocted story is also unknown. I would have desperately wanted to interview Walter and Dollie for this investigation had they still been alive in 2006, or if I had begun this investigation earlier when they were alive in the 1970s. But if Leon were still alive at that time, then the Stevensons would have been intimidated into not revealing anything they knew. So it wouldn't have done any good to interview them anyway. I could only have gotten the truth from them if Leon was already dead, and even then Walter's loyalty to Leon would have likely gotten in the way of getting the truth. It can only be theorized from the statements of their children what Walter and Dollie Stevenson might have known about Nell's death. Of one thing I'm certain—the Stevensons knew more than they told to others and took the secrets of what they knew to their graves.

THE CONFESSION: Let's examine the confession by Leon to Bert Mitchell. When I first heard this, it sounded a little too convenient. Why did this piece of evidence just drop into my lap when I was investigating this event in 2006? I had contacted Bert Mitchell in the spring of 2005 when I was doing genealogy research on my family. Bert was a well-known Tucker family historian. I met with him at his home in Caseyville, Illinois, only discussed the family tree and listened to stories of the people in that family tree. Bert didn't mention anything to me about Nell's death at this time. But this visit established a rapport between Bert and I—he liked me. He invited me to return again, and I knew that I would, as I developed more questions in my genealogy research. I gave him my father Frank's phone number and address, and he called Frank sometime that summer. They had a nice phone conversation where the two first cousins caught up with each other's lives and reconnected. When Frank died in October 2005, I notified Bert, and he was very saddened to hear of Frank's passing, saying in his familiar western Kentucky drawl, "I jus' hate hearin' that. I's always fond o' Frankie."

I made an appointment to meet with Bert again in November 2005. This time I came with the specific question of what he knew of Nell's death, mainly from the stories I had heard from Tillie. I hadn't even gotten the death certificate from Florida yet, so Bert was really the beginning of my investigation into Nell's death. Bert told me, and these are his precise words, "All I can say is—I heard the same thing—that Leon smothered Nell with a pillah (pillow)—and drove 'round for five hours with a dead body in the car." Those words are very revealing, if examined closely with information discovered later added in. This visit to Bert evidently put this event back on the front burner in Bert's mind. Bert was dying slowly of a variety of illnesses and was eighty-two years old at the time of my last visit with him in November 2005.

Let's entertain the idea that Leon confessed to Bert a few years before he died in 1987. Bert told me in my November 2005 visit that he visited with Leon a number of times at Leon's home on Husband Road in Paducah. Leon lived on Husband Road from approximately 1974 until he died in 1987—or thirteen years—so the time frame is right for the confession. Leon knew a few years before he died that he was dying, as his health began to wane. Bert Mitchell was a pastor in a Christian church, the denomination I'm not aware of, in Caseyville. Leon had gotten very religious in his retirement years. I'm sure it started out as a social thing and something to fill his time. But later on Leon genuinely believed in his religion and seemed to want to redeem himself for his indiscretions earlier in life. Pete Keeling, the pastor of Leon's church, which was the Eastside Holiness Church on Husband Road in Paducah, said at Leon's funeral that he noticed Leon tithing heavily in his last years, seemingly "wanting to cleanse himself of his youthful, wayward ways, and seek forgiveness." Tillie said she sensed that Leon had confessed to Pete Keeling that he had killed Nell as well as confessing to Bert Mitchell.

So it makes sense if Bert Mitchell was visiting Leon in Paducah sometime in the eighties, that Leon might have confessed to him about murdering Nell. Leon knew that Bert as a pastor couldn't reveal anything Leon told him in the confidence held between a pastor and a sinner seeking forgiveness. Decades later, when I was sitting in Bert's living room in Caseyville in late 2005 only months before Bert would die, Bert was surprised when I asked him about Nell's death and that I had heard Leon had killed her. He looked so surprised and serious when he asked me, "Who told you that?" Bert thought for a moment before responding, and then chose his words carefully, like a surgeon. He said, "All I can say is . . ." That is very revealing in itself, the key word being "can," because it could mean that Bert felt he couldn't say all that he knew. He was telling me only what he could say, and nothing more. A pastor couldn't reveal a confession he had heard from a sinner.

But Bert told me that "I heard the same thing," which was a truthful statement, without revealing to me he heard it from the horse's mouth—Leon. His details that he told me about Leon smothering Nell with a pillow and driving around for five hours with a dead body in the car were details that corroborated the time frame the body had been judged to be dead by the doctor at the hospital that night in 1969. Only the "smothering" detail was new, no one had heard that. Only Bert knew that detail. If that were a detail that came from a rumor, then others in the family would have known that detail also. But they didn't. Only Bert knew the detail about "smothering."

Bert was a pastor of his church. He would not have lied about anything nor exaggerated anything neither. Despite being eighty-two years old, he was sharp of mind, remembering all of the Tucker history in detail. Bert's memory of how Nell died was not a creation nor enhanced memory nor rumor spreading, but had to come from some firm knowledge from someone who knew the truth. Bert simply could not have had that many details by rumors or guessing. When I asked Bert how he knew that story, whom he had heard it from, he said, "I don't remember whom I heard it from." He looked away from me when he said that, as most people do when they aren't telling the truth. I believed then, and I believe still to this day that Bert did remember how he heard that story, but couldn't reveal it to me.

If it was a pastor-sinner confession situation, then he couldn't very well say to me, "I can't tell you how I know that story, since it would break a confidence," because this statement would reveal to me that it was a confession from Leon to Bert. I could easily make that assumption from the circumstances. No other scenario would fit that statement. If it were someone else that had told him, and not Leon, then he would have readily told me, as almost all of those people from that time period are now dead. So Bert had to lie in a small, allowable way, by saying that he "didn't remember" who had told him that story. These types of small lies, fibs really, are allowed for pastors to protect the confidentiality of a sinner's confession. I'm not going to hold it against Bert for acting like he didn't remember who told him that story when I believe he did. Bert was such a genuine treasure for our family and a fantastic resource for my research that I could do nothing but hold him in the highest regard.

But my visit to Bert and my questioning him about Nell's death evidently weighed heavily on Bert's conscience. He knew he had not told the complete story he knew to me, Nell's grandson, one of the last surviving members of Leon's progeny, and a Tucker male, to whom he owed a family allegiance. With this weighing on him, Bert called Son Tucker (Corbett Tucker Jr.) in Paducah in December 2005 and told him, "Son, I'm a gonna be a dyin' soon. I got somethin' weighin' on my conscience. B'fore I die, I want someone t' know this . . ." He told Son the story of the details of Nell's death and Leon's confession. Son passed them on to his wife, Mildred, who passed them on to her sister, Tillie. Then Tillie told me. Bert was smart enough to have figured out this would have been the pathway to me getting the information, since I told him Tillie was the original source of the information I was asking him about. He knew Tillie was sister to Mildred, Son Tucker's wife. It was a safe bet anything he told to Son Tucker would eventually find its way to me. Bert, much to my sadness, passed away in January 2006. It's almost like a deathbed confession by Bert, that he knew this story, and revealed it just before dying. Bert certainly wouldn't choose to lie about something just before dying.

That's why it makes me believe it was true—it happened—Leon had indeed confessed to Bert. Is this confession by Leon conclusive proof by itself that he was guilty? Perhaps—but the totality of the evidence is really where the proof, one way or the other, should be found. Since Bert's account of Leon's confession was hearsay evidence, although powerful, it should be taken with equal weight as other evidence. Son Tucker refused to talk about what Bert had told him, saying, "I don't wanna get into that." If what Son knew was exculpatory for Leon, or he knew nothing of any importance, then he would have said so in either case. But by refusing to talk about it, he in effect confirmed he knew something significant. Indeed, he pretty much confirmed the story his wife Mildred told to her sister Tillie, and Tillie told to me, by refusing to talk about it. I can make that reasonable assumption.

LEON'S MENTAL STATE: Regarding the army medical records from Leon's time in World War II, Leon was diagnosed by two sets of doctors in two different hospitals as having "emotional instability (including inadequate personality, schizoid, cycloid, prepsychotic, etc.)." Clearly, considering the definitions of these psychiatric terms provided in a previous chapter, Leon was severely mentally ill, although still functional, such that others around him didn't know it. They mistook his abnormal behavior as just being "mean" or "coming from his hard background in Kentucky." But it wasn't—it was mental illness. This mental illness doesn't excuse Leon's behavior that stemmed from it, but it does explain it.

This now made sense—it explained the years of Leon's volatility (hair-trigger temper), his violent behavior, and his seeming fearlessness about personal combat with others, even when weapons were involved. It now explained how Leon could establish two marriages concurrently when that wouldn't make sense to any normal person, but it made sense to him. It now explained why Leon would be the enforcing muscle for the Local 100 Laborer's Union in East St. Louis, beating up nonunion workers, and driving up on sidewalks trying to run over African-Americans. It now explained why Leon would start barroom brawls with perfect strangers who hadn't done anything to him, but just happened to be in the bar at the same time as Leon. Jim Mitchell told me Leon would buy three bottles of beer, open one of them, drink it, and use the other two as clubs to strike strangers from behind to start fights.

It now explained why Leon beat his second wife Audrey within an inch of her life, threw her out of moving car, and left her for dead in a ditch. It now explained how he could have tied Audrey to a tree and, with a shotgun, shot an apple off her head. It now explained Leon throwing Audrey off the roof of the clubhouse in Grand Tower in a fight between them. It now explained how he could have beaten her another time until she was unconscious, put her in a boat, and rowed her out in a lake, preparing to dump her in so she would drown. Her waking up in the boat was the only thing that stopped him from doing it. It now explained why an adult Leon beat up his older sister Versie and put her head through a wall. Leon in a demented state wouldn't have understood limits in any of these cases—that he couldn't go beyond certain limits when fighting with another person—particularly a woman. I myself witnessed one mild instance of his hair-trigger temper even in his elderly years. Leon once was reaching into the refrigerator to get the mayonnaise and picked it up by the lid instead of the side of the jar. Someone, it could have been Audrey or it could have been Leon himself, previously just rested the lid on the jar without screwing it down. When Leon went to pick up the jar, the jar dropped from beneath the lid to the floor and spilled the mayonnaise. Leon immediately turned beet red, screwed up his face like a fist, grabbed a dish towel, and began striking Audrey with it. Our family was visiting and was sitting at the kitchen bar counter, witnessing this incident. It was a mildly violent incident, but with this information on Leon's mental health now revealed, it resonates as part of the story.

It now made sense that multiple people saw Leon repeatedly committing theft—being almost a kleptomaniac about it—at literally dozens of times throughout his whole lifetime. It now explained the Freemasons of East St. Louis kicking Leon out for crooked deals. It now explained Leon's total disregard for laws. I myself witnessed him, when driving, habitually cutting corners through gas stations in his car without even slowing down, just to avoid stoplights. He would floor his gas pedal and shoot his car across traffic on a red light, causing other cars to screech and veer wildly to avoid collision. He had total disregard for others who might have been hurt by his driving habits. He'd actually laugh at the panicked honking of the other drivers. Leon would refuse to obey limits on how many deer he could hunt and kill on public lands in a season, or how many fish he could catch at public lakes. He would take as many as he could get his hands on. This would include the use of deer stands, which are illegal platforms built in trees for a hunter to sit on and wait to ambush passing deer. Leon would also practice jug fishing, which was illegally floating hundreds of milk jugs with fish hooks dangling beneath them, always overnight so as not to be seen, to harvest large quantities of fish. Leon simply didn't think laws were worth respecting, but rather something to get around.

In an instance of a less severe nature, I can remember a time when I visited Leon on my own, during my college years, just a few years before Leon died. It was at his home at 1735 Husband Road in Paducah. I brought my new car down to show my grandfather, proud as I could be of it. In fact, it was a used car, a 1980 Buick Regal, but it was new to me, and I was eager to show it to him. When viewing it together, Leon asked me to go inside, and he would look at it alone. This confused me as to why he would want to look at it alone, but I complied. As I looked out the kitchen window to the carport, I saw Leon take out his pocketknife and begin chipping the paint off the trunk lid. I rushed to the door and said plaintively, "Papaw, don't mar up my car with your knife!" Caught in the act, he gave that characteristic half-smile, lowered-eyelid look of his and said, "I's jus' checkin' if it's repainted." To anyone else, common sense tells you that you don't take a pocketknife to chip the paint on someone else's car to check it if had been repainted. But to Leon, in his delusional mind, it made sense. I previously thought he was just jealous of someone else's new car that day, but with this new information about his mental health history, it now explained it probably was his mental illness instead that caused this behavior.

It now explained why Leon was violent with his first wife (my grandmother), Nell, as witnessed by Tillie. It now explained why he would fire a shotgun blast threw the front door of Nell's sister, Ila Mae, to intimidate Nell into not divorcing him. It now explained the deaths, either murders or self-defense killings, attributed to Leon—counting to at least five men, according to Bert Mitchell and Tillie Edwards (combined). It now explained the most important event in Leon's life, at least in my opinion, the possible murder of his first wife, Nell, in Florida in 1969. I now understood how Leon could actually have done it—to have murdered Nell. I previously didn't believe Leon was capable of it.

I had proven to myself from my talks with the Tucker cousins that Leon had a very violent upbringing and past, so violence from Leon was possible. But that didn't prove to me that Leon could have killed someone who wasn't attacking him first. It didn't prove to me Leon could attack supposedly someone he loved—his first wife, Nell. Nell was a soft-spoken, demure, and feminine woman who posed no threat to Leon or anyone for that matter. Even if they had been arguing, I can't imagine Leon ever feeling a physical threat from Nell such that a self-defense mechanism would have been triggered. That's why I couldn't understand how Leon could ever have murdered Nell. But with these severe mental illnesses factored in, I now understood how he could have done it. To a manic-depressive, psychotic, schizoid, and emotionally unstable (pardon the redundancy) individual as evidently Leon was, an act such as this, murdering Nell, could easily have been justified in his mind. To Leon, Nell was the obstacle preventing him from retiring with Audrey in Paducah. Divorce wasn't an option. So this justified killing her—at least in Leon's mind.

If Leon were ever tried for this crime, could his defense lawyer plead insanity as a defense? Certainly the army hospital documents prove that Leon was diagnosed with severe mental illnesses in the middle 1940s. However, one can be mentally ill and still be held responsible for one's criminal acts. It depends on how severe the mental illness is, and how it manifests itself in the individual. To avoid being held responsible for one's criminal acts by reason of insanity, a requisite element must be present—that the individual could not discern right from wrong, and therefore didn't know they were doing wrong when they did it. Applying this to Leon, I don't believe it could be said that Leon didn't know he was going to kill Nell, or that killing Nell was wrong. There is no evidence that this happened in the heat of a moment. No one sharing the campsite with them remembers a loud fight, nor were there any signs of struggle in the camper or signs of a violent event on Nell's body. If Leon tampered with Nell's medications or poisoned the tangelos or other food, this would evidence prior planning of the murder, invalidating an insanity defense.

For Leon to go to great lengths to cover up the murder later on, with the concocted stories and refusing the autopsy, this would indicate that Leon knew he had done wrong. He wouldn't try to cover up the murder if in his mentally ill state he didn't believe it was wrong to have done it. Leon brought Audrey down to Florida to finish his vacation immediately after Nell's funeral, having left his camper at Okeechobee with the Stevensons to hold his camping spot. This showed a gross lack of impact on Leon of Nell's passing. It couldn't have been a shock to him that she died, his wife of forty years, and have him continue his vacation with his second wife immediately after. Either this was sociopath-like behavior in Leon, or he had known beforehand Nell was going to die and had already come to terms with the loss. This also evidences preplanning by Leon, invalidating an insanity defense.

What could have caused Leon's mental illness? Some people say it can be genetic or a physical state in the body. Most assuredly manic depression, or what they called "cycloid" at the time Leon was examined, is a chemical imbalance that can be treated with medications. Some say it's environmental, being brought on by early-life traumatic experiences. It was known that George W. Tucker, Leon's father and my great-grandfather, was an extremely violent man. It was common at that time that men would beat their children into submission to make them behave. Many of the Tucker cousins told me stories of when Leon and his siblings were children, George W. Tucker would hold their heads between his knees to beat their backsides with whatever he had in his hand—a belt, a board, a pole, or a stick. He wouldn't beat them just enough to get their attention, but would beat them until they vomited, the signal they had been given enough. George W. Tucker thought that this made his children tough and strong, as was needed to survive in that rough part of rural Kentucky during the early 1900s.

His second wife, and my great-grandmother, Ruth (Keeling) Tucker, once took off chasing her husband George with an ax because he wouldn't stop beating one of their children when she told him to stop. The violence between their children was frequent also, with the Tucker boys fighting each other until one of them was injured so badly they would require a hospital visit to "git sewed up." Knife fights were common between them at this time. Leon was covered from head to toe with deep scars from all the knife fights he had been in all his life, from childhood on up.

232

I theorize that level of violence in Leon's early, formative years might have caused him the emotional instability and general mental illnesses that he carried with him the rest of his life. This early violence may have been a direct, contributing factor to Leon ultimately committing murder multiple times in his lifetime, perhaps including that of his wife of forty years. Indeed, this high level of violence in his youngest years could have caused Leon to develop the tendencies of a sociopath, as exhibited by his disregard for human life he showed in later years, such as trying to drive over African-Americans in East St. Louis.

Another explanation for Leon's schizophrenia might have been damaged genes from an older father. There have been many studies done revealing a correlation between older men having children and those children having a dramatically higher incidence of schizophrenia. The schizophrenia.com Web site has many articles on this phenomenon, with the most poignant work being done by researcher Dr. Delores Malaspina.[15] She noted in a 2006 article that for fathers less than twenty-five years old, their offspring would have a 1 in 141 chance of having schizophrenia. But for fathers fifty and older, the incidence of schizophrenia in offspring jumps to 1 in 47. George W. Tucker, Leon's father, was born in 1860, and was fifty-one years old when Leon was born in 1911.

Dr. Malaspina noted that the father's age is not connected to the risk of schizophrenia when it runs in families, only when there is no family history—terming it sporadic schizophrenia. There are no other incidences of schizophrenia documented in the family of Tucker cousins that I could ascertain, so I theorize this isn't a family trait. Dr. Malaspina goes on to say that schizophrenia is commonly considered to result from the synergistic combination of a "genetic susceptibility and environmental exposures, particularly those occurring during fetal development and adolescence."[15] This makes sense that if Leon was genetically susceptible to schizophrenia due to his father being past fifty years of age when he fathered him, combine this with the ultra-violence that Leon experienced in his younger years, this could have produced Leon's schizophrenia. Dr. Malaspina's research was replicated with similar results by researchers in England and Sweden.[17]

The mechanism by which the older father's sperm produces a greater predisposition for schizophrenia was also interesting to explore. Mullich[16] posited that sperm cells don't repair themselves like most other body cells, and that unlike women who are born with their lifetime supply of eggs, men constantly produce more sperm cells by copying the previous sperm cells. This results in copy error, just like the distortion of Xerox copies of documents that are copied multiple times getting blurry. The sperm of an older man can be somewhat imperfect, producing a somewhat imperfect child.

PROSECUTION CLOSING ARGUMENT: As I began this chapter with a list of the exculpatory evidence in Leon's favor with the defense's opening statement, similarly I will end this chapter with a list of the damning evidence against Leon, or the prosecution's closing argument:

- Leon had strong motivations to want Nell dead. He wanted to retire in Paducah with Audrey, and couldn't with Nell there.
- Leon couldn't allow Nell to divorce him because his bigamy with Audrey would come to light.
- Leon had life insurance over Nell's life. Divorce would lose him that right to insure Nell's life.
- Nell was forced to go on the trip to Florida in 1969 against her will, with the show of firearms by Leon as intimidation.
- Nell got her birth certificate issued for the first time in her life just three months before her death, and would not have needed it for any retirement purpose for years to come.
- Leon lied by telling at least three separate stories of what happened the night Nell died to different people, all in direct conflict with each other. Two of the three stories have been proven impossible to be true based upon evidence known to be true. There was no reason to lie if Nell died a natural death.
- Nell's body had been dead for five hours prior to arriving at the hospital, when the distance from the campground would have only required less than twenty minutes to drive.
- Nell expressed fear of Leon to her family before leaving for Florida. Nell sent a signal on a postcard, indicating she needed help. Nell hid money in her brassiere, unknown to Leon, as a secret escape fund. All of these acts prove Nell had fear of Leon.
- Dr. Johnston wrote Nell's cause of death as "unknown (DOA)," instead of natural causes, because he wasn't sure she died a natural death. Leon refused to allow an autopsy of Nell at the time she died. The death certificate proves Nell died before arriving at the hospital.
- No autopsy was performed on Nell at the time of her death, against Florida law at the time. Dr. Johnston asked Frank, Nell's son, if he wanted the autopsy after Leon refused it. This proves Dr. Johnston thought the autopsy was necessary but didn't want to order it without support from at least one of Nell's immediate family. Dr. Johnston's motivations for signing the death certificate in violation of Florida law may have been motivated by his possible Freemason membership, and that of Leon's.
- The tangelo story of Leon's has been proven false since tangelos don't contain any compounds that affect medication efficacy like grapefruits do. Nell had no order from any physician to avoid consuming fresh fruits.
- Nell's age on her death certificate was falsified to make it appear she was forty-nine years old and not her actual age of fifty-eight years old. The only reason making sense that explains this alteration would be insurance fraud. Leon would have been the only source for the information on Nell's death certificate. Leon was the only person at the campground that had any right or ability to insure Nell's life. Therefore, Leon would be the only person

that could possibly be motivated to conduct insurance fraud regarding Nell's death.

- Leon had a long history of hyper-violence in his youth and middle-age years, including the deaths of five men attributed to him in his lifetime. It is not known if these were murders or killings in self-defense, but it does prove Leon was capable of killing a human being, even in a violent manner. Some of Leon's hyper-violence was directed toward women, including both of his wives and one of his sisters (Versie).

- Leon nearly killed Audrey, his second wife, four times, including shooting an apple off her head when she was tied to a tree, beating her unconscious and throwing her from a moving car and leaving her for dead in a ditch, beating her unconscious and attempting to dispose of her body in a lake, and pushing her off of the roof of a house. This establishes his ability to kill a human being, including a woman.

- Leon had attempted to plan the murder of the husband of a cousin but could not complete it when other cousins objected. Leon had stated to a cousin that he "had a drug that could stop a heart with no trace afterward." These stories establish Leon's ability to plan murder.

- Police in Okeechobee that searched the camper following Nell's death, at the request of Nell's sister Grace, found one of Nell's medication bottles empty when it was filled for a month's supply just a week prior. The pills couldn't have been consumed by Nell that quickly at the prescribed rate, and were not the type of medication used for overdosing in a suicide. There is no evidence that Nell was suicidal. Evidence exists, to the contrary, that Nell wanted to live. Sending signals of fear to others and hiding escape money prove she wanted to live. There is no plausible explanation for the empty medicine bottle other than someone was tampering with Nell's medications. Only Leon had access to them.

- Leon had been twice diagnosed by U.S. Army doctors as being severely mentally ill, spent time in U.S. Army mental hospitals, and went untreated for his mental illness all his life.

- Leon exhibited erratic behavior many times in his life, e.g., attempting to run over African-Americans in his car, starting knife-fights in bars with strangers without provocation, enforcing union rules against nonunion workers through deadly violence, having bloody knife fights with his brothers, and doing pathological theft akin to kleptomania.

- Leon lied about his war experiences to hide his mental illness diagnoses.

- Leon had confessed to Bert Mitchell a few years before his death (Leon's) that he had "smothered Nell to death and rode around for five hours with the body." This five-hour period matches the time period the medical staff at the hospital said Nell's body had been dead before arriving at the hospital, validating Leon's confession. Bert Mitchell was a preacher, was clear of mind

235

until he died, and kept Leon's confession secret until he (Bert) approached his own death, and only then revealed it. Bert would have no motivation to lie about Leon's confession, or exaggerate it.

VERDICT: All of the above evidence leads me to a conclusion, a verdict if you will, that I didn't want to find. I tried very hard during this investigation to find exculpatory evidence to disprove this awful rumor that plagued my family. But I had to be a realist also and told myself I would accept whatever story the evidence told me. I considered that all of the evidence argued in this chapter came from different sources, not the same person or office. That made it impossible for this rumor to be rooted in one single error that had been blown out of proportion. All the family members and witnesses to the events got their information from different sources as well, so it couldn't be a case of error from one source just compounding as it was passed from person to person. Like a jigsaw puzzle, once all of the pieces of evidence are put together, they form a picture. Each individual piece by itself isn't conclusive of anything and can definitely be argued as reasonable doubt. But when the whole picture is examined from the assembled puzzle, reasonable doubt becomes unlikely.

Furthermore, I believe for reasonable doubt to be established, the compound probability of all these pieces of evidence must be considered. Each individual piece of evidence by itself has a probability of being true that is not high enough to surpass reasonable doubt. But combined, all of these pieces of evidence, all pointing in the same direction, establish a compound probability that certainly is high enough to surpass reasonable doubt. Either Leon is the unluckiest person on the planet to have all these pieces of evidence pointing to his guilt, but yet he was innocent, or the obvious is the true explanation. I cannot know positively that Leon murdered Nell. Even an autopsy of Nell's remains if one could have been performed couldn't have proven Leon guilty. It might, though unlikely, have proven how Nell died, not by whose hand. It was never my task to prove Leon guilty in this journey anyway. I wanted to find evidence of his innocence or guilt, and accept the result as the resolution of the matter. That is the best that can be done at this late point in time.

My conclusion from all of the evidence, my verdict, is that Leon was guilty. He murdered Nell. I believe he did confess to Bert Mitchell as Bert said. I believe Leon planned the murder of his wife of forty years when she became inconvenient. If I were on a jury where Leon was being tried for this murder, I would vote to convict him. I say that with a heavy heart, as I wish it were otherwise.

* * *

Nell and Leon Tucker circa 1935.
Frank as a toddler is peering out over Nell's shoulder.

Chapter 12

THE RECONSTRUCTION

Her birth certificate Nell obtained three months prior (to her death),
in October 1968, could have been needed at this time for the collection of
the insurance proceeds.

After viewing all of the evidence and arguing the evidence in my head in "The Trial" chapter, I can reasonably reconstruct the events that led to Nell's murder. In a few instances what I reconstruct here uses assumptions to bridge the gaps between known facts. Knowing the personalities of the people involved and the general atmosphere of the time and place of these events, this can be done with reasonable accuracy. For instance, if a city directory shows a person living at a certain address in one year, and then again at the same location five years later, I can reasonably make the assumption they were living there at that address continuously during that stretch of time.

The events that led to my grandmother Nell's death actually started sometime in the early 1940s, approximately thirty years before she was murdered. Leon and Nell met in Graves County, Kentucky, in the late 1920s, and married in January 1929. Nell was only eighteen years old; Leon was merely seventeen years old. They had their first child, Frank Leon, in 1931. Some of Leon and Nell's movements can be traced using the city directories of East St. Louis and Paducah from the 1900s. They would sometimes list themselves in those directories, which were compiled by door-to-door census takers each year, as "Leon and Nell" together, or sometimes they would list themselves individually. Because they would be listed together does not necessarily indicate they were both living there at that time, because in some years they would be listed in both cities. This likely meant they were living apart, with Leon in East St. Louis working and Nell living alone in Paducah, usually renting houses owned by her siblings. For instance, the Paducah city directories for 1934-1936 show Nell living alone in Paducah, working for the Paducah Box & Basket Company, and living on Rural Route 5. Leon is not mentioned, indicating they were likely living apart at this time. Frank would have been just a toddler during these years. In 1937, Nell and Leon purchased a life insurance policy on Nell's life. It is not known if a policy was also purchased on Leon's life. Being that Leon and Nell were very poor at this time, it is a curiosity why life insurance on Nell's life was a priority for Leon and Nell at this time.

In around 1938, Leon and Nell left Kentucky together for East St. Louis, Illinois, to find work. Frank told me that he, Leon, and Nell arrived in East St. Louis with only fifty cents in Leon's pocket. They stayed in a one-room shack with a dirt floor for a year to get started, likely at 729 N. Fifty-ninth Street, as this is the first address Leon and Nell together have in any East St. Louis city directory. There was literally no work in Paducah, Kentucky, at that time, so many in the Tucker family were doing the same thing and heading for East St. Louis. At least three of Leon's siblings, Versie, Robie, and Rob, and many more cousins, Stevensons and Burgesses, all left Paducah and headed for East St. Louis at that time, all looking for work. East St. Louis was booming at the time, hiring anyone who applied, as many meatpacking operations had opened near the riverfront, many construction projects on bridges were ongoing, and just building the infrastructure of the city and the housing to support the many new residents kept everyone working steady.[13]

By the early 1940s, Leon worked many types of jobs—meatpacking, metal casting, construction, etc.—and Nell kept house and raised their young son, Frank, until he was old enough for school, then Nell took clerical jobs during the school days. They had enough money by then to get a regular place, upgrading from the one-room shack with a dirt floor, and moved to 5009 Bunkum Road for the period of time of 1940-42. Leon had a wandering eye, and Nell and my father, Frank, both looked the other way about it. It could have been because of fear of Leon's explosive temper and his lack of control over becoming violent, or it could have been for fear of not being able to support oneself. My father was a child at this time, not even in his teens yet, and entirely unable to support himself. Nell was an uneducated woman, capable at that time of doing nothing more than sales clerking or something similar. There weren't even good social services from government entities at this time to support women with children on their own. Nowadays Nell would have many more options at supporting herself and her son independent of Leon, but at that time, women relied upon their men much more, and therefore that limited their options.

At sometime in the early 1940s, Leon sent Nell and Frank from East St. Louis back to Paducah to go live with family there. There would have been no clear reason to do this other than Leon wanted the freedom to be with a new, permanent girlfriend, Audrey Hayden. Born Audie C. Marshall, nicknamed Audrey, she had married twice by the time she met Leon. First, she married Michael Reed in 1925, having two children, Frances and James Harold (known as Harold). The marriage didn't last as Michael Reed was a heavy drinker and suicidal. He abandoned Audrey and his kids in 1933. Audrey didn't divorce Michael Reed until 1939 when she was ready to marry again, this time to Joe Hayden, in 1940. That marriage lasted a year and a half. Joe Hayden abandoned Audrey in 1942. Audrey was available again when she met Leon at the Hunter's Meat Packing factory in East St. Louis in 1942. They could have met earlier, like in 1941, since the 1942 abandonment date comes from Audrey. There is no documentation of it.

Strangely, Audrey never divorced Joe Hayden, would keep his last name and her legal marriage to him intact for almost thirty years until 1969, when she was ready to marry Leon legally and in the open. When Leon got his draft notice in early 1943 to serve in the U.S. Army and fight in the then-burgeoning World War II, Audrey likely bothered Leon to marry her, so she could have his benefits if he were killed in action. Audrey probably knew he was still married to Nell because she had met Nell accidentally on a bus. Nell and Audrey rode the same bus route on Bunkum Road in East St. Louis for a long time without knowing each other. They only lived about ten blocks apart. Audrey's residence was at 1132 N. Forty-second Street starting around 1941, an address she started with her second husband, Joe Hayden, and then kept living there after he abandoned her in 1942. She would remain there, sharing it with Leon, for approximately thirty years.

The meeting between Nell and Audrey on the bus on Bunkum Road occurred before Nell was sent by Leon back to Paducah, and may have been the reason for it. Audrey may have told Leon to get Nell out of East St. Louis after she found out he was still married. Before Audrey found out about Nell, Leon likely lied to Audrey about his married status. She couldn't hold that against him, since she likely lied to him also about her being still legally married to Joe Hayden. On the bus that fateful day, sitting next to each other by accident, the two women began talking and sharing stories about their men, Nell about her husband "Leon," Audrey about her boyfriend "Leon," until they both had the grim realization they were both talking about the same man. Audrey would joke about this chance encounter decades later, recounting it to Dollie Stevenson in the years after Nell's death.

Leon went away to war in early 1943, heading to Camp Shelby in Mississippi to join the Antitank Company of the 339th Infantry of the U.S. Army. Leon sent from Mississippi to Audrey in East St. Louis certain items, like souvenir silk pillowcases, photos, and notes, professing his love for her. No such items were sent to Nell in Paducah, to anyone's recollection. To Leon, he already had Nell in the bag. Audrey, however, still needed to be wooed. Their relationship wasn't that old before he had to leave for the military. Leon would periodically return to Paducah and East St. Louis when he would get leave from his training, as photos of Leon in his military uniform with his preteen son Frank were taken. Leon would be stationed at Ft. Sheridan, Illinois, near Chicago, in the summer of 1944, departing for Europe at the end of August that year. Leon stopped through New York, either going or coming back from Europe, likely going, and drank heavily with his army buddies at Bartley Madden's bar near Times Square.

Souvenir photo of a drunk Leon at Bartley Madden's
bar in New York sent by Leon to Nell

Leon arrived in Europe in the first days of September 1944. Leon's unit was assigned to the Twenty-eighth Infantry Division, which was already fighting across France and was one of the divisions that liberated Paris, and paraded through the city famously in late August 1944. Leon missed this parade by only a few days. Apparently as this unit left Paris, L-Company containing Leon joined them, and they advanced through the Forest of Compiegne in France. The division with Leon in it went into Belgium, averaging advances of seventeen miles a day against German resistance.[11] After the city of Arlon, Belgium, fell to the American Twenty-eighth Infantry Division, they spread out into Luxembourg. The 110th Infantry Regiment liberated the northern part of Luxembourg and on September 11, 1944, entered Germany. The division with Leon in it moved north and cleared the Monschau Forest of Germans near Elsenborn, Belgium, then advanced up to the Siegfried Line again. The division with Leon in it made another move northward to the Hurtgen Forest, attacking on November 2, 1944, the cities of Vossenack, Kommerscheidt, and Schmidt. Savage fighting ensued, and losses were heavy, but by November 12, 1944, they had completed their Hurtgen Forest mission. The division with Leon in it returned to the area of their initial entry into Germany along the Our River, near the northeastern tip of Luxembourg.[11]

The bulk of the 110th was deployed along the St. Vith-Oiekirch Highway,[11] called by the Americans as the "Skyline Drive." The Skyline Drive was a hard-surface road that ran parallel to the Luxembourg-German border. It overlooked the Our River and Germany to the east and the Clerf River and Luxembourg to the west. Along this road, L-Company (Leon's) held the city of Holzthum, in Luxembourg.[11] Somewhere along this time period, the middle of November 1944, is when Leon left his company and was admitted to an army hospital in Europe, possibly in England, for treatment of mental illnesses. It can only be theorized as to why this happened, as the records do not show why he was admitted. It is logical to assume that Leon was exhibiting aberrant behavior that made his commanding officers suspect he was mentally ill, such as excessive combativeness with his fellow soldiers. Leon was known all his young life to have a hair-trigger temper and to become hyper-violent, like flicking a light switch on. He would remain in this mental hospital in Europe, likely England, for approximately four months time, until the end of March 1945 when he was shipped home to the U.S. He received no combat injuries in the war, as he would later tell family he had.

What happened to Leon between the middle of April 1945 and the beginning of June 1945 is undocumented and cannot be known for certain. Leon may have gone directly to Ft. Sheridan, Illinois, resuming active duty, or may have been given leave to return to East St. Louis to be with Audrey. Nell was still in the tuberculosis sanitarium at this time, so he couldn't have returned to be with her. It is known that in June 1945, Leon was at Ft. Sheridan because he was readmitted to an army hospital there—again for mental illness. He would be diagnosed twice by two different sets of doctors at two different hospitals, one in Europe and one at Ft. Sheridan, as having "emotional instability (including inadequate personality, schizoid, cycloid, prepsychotic, etc.)." The medical records showed these were preexisting conditions Leon had before entering active military service, and did not stem from some trauma experienced during the war. This severe mental illness evidently went untreated, as Leon was honorably discharged in July 1945 for "inaptness," meaning inability to perform at a level of use to the military, and he returned to East St. Louis. Leon was categorized by the military as "unable to reenlist." Nell was still in the tuberculosis sanitarium when Leon was discharged. Leon's mental illness would be left untreated for the remainder of his life, as he never revealed these diagnoses to anyone. He likely thought the diagnoses were nonsense.

In April 1944, Nell was diagnosed with tuberculosis. At that time, tuberculosis was thought to be a highly contagious disease, and the law required isolation of the infected patient. The infected person wasn't given a choice about their quarantine. Nell was quarantined at the tuberculosis sanitarium at Fairview Heights, Illinois, about ten miles from East St. Louis. This made sense, so family would be nearby. Frank was sent to various family members, the Tucker cousins, in the Paducah area to live, since Leon was gone off fighting in the war and Nell was institutionalized. Thirteen-year-old Frank had no parent left to care of him. Frank would take a five-hour bus ride, then walk several miles from the bus station, once per month, to wave at Nell from the courtyard of the sanitarium, Nell waving back from a third-floor window. Frank was not allowed inside the sanitarium to see his mother face to face. Nell's home address at the time she went into the sanitarium, according to the records held at the St. Clair County Health Department, was 1018 North Fifth Street in East St. Louis. There's no record Leon ever lived there—he could have—there's just no record of it.

Upon returning to East St. Louis in July 1945, Leon resumed his relationship/marriage to Audrey. Nell still had a year in the tuberculosis sanitarium before she would be released. Despite having separate addresses for looks, Leon lived with Audrey at 1132 N. Forty-second Street in East St. Louis. Leon would defend Audrey's nineteen-year-old daughter, Frances, from her fiancé's infidelity by crashing his car in 1946, at this address. At sometime during Nell's infirmity in the tuberculosis sanitarium, Nell was close to death, and her family was summoned by her doctors to Fairview Heights to visit her before she died, or so they thought. During this visit, Nell's family noticed that Leon was absent. Tillie Edwards said they later found out that upon hearing Nell was dying, Leon got drunk and married Audrey, although no record of this 1946 marriage has been found. If true, this most likely occurred in the winter of 1946.

Tuberculosis sanitarium in Fairview Heights where
Nell was interred for more than two years

Frank's high school graduation photo from 1950

When Nell was discharged from the sanitarium in July 1946, Leon set her up initially to live in her place on Fifth Street. But Audrey was angry and jealous that Nell lived in the same town she did and didn't want the chance she would run into Nell at the supermarket. She pestered Leon to move Nell out of town and back down to Paducah, saying she would "shoot Nell" if he didn't. Audrey would taunt Nell also, driving by her house on Fifth Street and telling her taxi driver to honk the horn until Nell came to the door and then stare at Nell. (Even in her older years when I knew Audrey, she had an evil stare. It made me shiver to wonder what was behind those eyes as they stared at me, a stare that was like someone saying to themselves, "I could cut your throat before you could block my hand.") Leon moved Nell back down to Paducah, where she would usually live with her sisters or in a house by herself that was owned by one of her sisters, Ila Mae (Freeman) Fike and Grace (Freeman) Dotson (later married name Martinez). The 1947-49 Paducah city directories shows Leon and Nell both in Paducah, and no listings are in the East St. Louis directories. This likely meant that Leon was living with Audrey on Forty-second Street, and Nell was with Frank in Paducah. Frank is listed in the 1949 directory as a "student" living with Nell on Morton Street in Paducah. For sure Leon wouldn't have returned to Paducah with Nell because he had no work there.

Leon was being employed as a construction laborer in the Local 100 Laborer's Union of East St. Louis at the time, which was heavily infiltrated and controlled by organized crime. Violent enforcement of union rules was practiced. Beatings, murders, and destruction of projects not built with union labor were common practice at this time. Leon was used as an "enforcer" by the union. One of the union representatives still with the Local 100 in 2006 was Walter Abernathy, and he remembered "Big Tuck," as he called Leon. He said Leon put a couple of nonunion electrical workers from out of town in the hospital for doing nonunion work in their region. This is not surprising since Leon had so much violence in his past from his upbringing in Kentucky in the early 1900s, he probably was immune to pain and completely fearless toward fighting other men. He would have been the perfect choice for the union's muscle. He also belonged to the Freemasons of the area, which, despite being more like a religion, were connected to the labor union at the time simply because so many belonged to both organizations.

Nell occasionally returned to East St. Louis after her son, Frank, began living and working there. Frank began marrying and producing grandchildren for Leon and Nell. Leon interfered with Frank's first relationship with his high-school sweetheart, Nadine, and forbade Frank from marrying her when she got pregnant, with the threat of cutting off his college support money if he did. Leon didn't like Nadine. Frank abandoned a pregnant Nadine, and with the exception of one isolated and incognito meeting some three decades later, would never know his daughter Sharon, born to Nadine. Frank would marry in December 1953 another woman, Maudine Pruitt of Arkansas, and they would begin living behind Leon's house at 1225 N. Fifty-second Street in East St. Louis. Leon had a trailer in the front part of the property, and Frank converted a garage in the back into a bungalow. Frank and Maudine gave Leon and

Nell their first (official) grandchild in July 1955, so this likely was the time Nell would have left Paducah for East St. Louis.

It was known that Nell had her own apartment in 1957 in East St. Louis, watching Frank's son Trent during the daytime while Frank worked. Maudine and Frank had separated by this time and were divorcing. Leon lived elsewhere in East St. Louis then, likely with Audrey. On Christmas Day 1957, Nell and Leon would "play house" at Leon's trailer, which neither lived at, to provide a meeting point for their son Frank's ex-wife, Maudine Pruitt, to visit her son Trent, of whom Frank had custody. I say that neither lived at this residence, since a stranger named George Hubert also listed himself as living at that trailer during that period of time. It's logical that Leon was renting the trailer to George Hubert, and Leon and Nell lived separately elsewhere. But for appearances purposes, so as not to provide anything negative the Pruitts could point to in a custody battle for Trent, Leon and Nell set up a "pretend" house at the trailer for Maudine's Christmas visit with Trent. At that fateful meeting, Trent was stolen back by Maudine when Leon went to the bathroom, and lost for the Tucker family for good. Maudine ran Leon down with her car in her frantic escape with Trent. Leon tried to block her escape, and she ran him over, flipping him over the hood. Leon would later file a hit-and-run report against Maudine, but she had already successfully escaped to Arkansas with Trent.

By 1959, with Trent gone, Nell returned to Paducah and lived alone at 1603 Little Avenue, an address she would keep continuously for roughly ten years, from 1959 until she died in 1969. Nell began to heed the advice of her sisters, Grace and Ila Mae, and contemplated divorcing Leon. It's almost certain she knew by that time if Leon had illegally married Audrey, at least in a common-law marriage if not in a legal one. She knew he was openly living with her full time in East St. Louis. Leon's sister Versia "Versie" (Tucker) Nowak kept Nell informed of what Leon was doing in East St. Louis, and if he was staying at Audrey's or showing up at family events with Audrey. Leon once beat Versie nearly to death, putting her head through a wall, for telling Nell about his time spent with Audrey.

Sometime in the early 1960s, Nell engaged the highly respected Paducah attorney, Joseph Freeland, to handle her divorce. Tillie has said it might have been prominent Paducah attorney, Thomas Garrett, but Joe Freeland was more likely the one Nell used. Joe Freeland would later be instrumental in advancing civil rights legislation in Kentucky, and was considered one of the most powerful attorneys in western Kentucky. Nell chose well. But even as powerful a man as Joseph Freeland was, he was no match for Leon Tucker. No man could intimidate Leon. Leon had been through too much in his life already, and survived it. Leon probably thought of himself as invincible. He definitely thought of himself as omnipotent from laws, as he pretty much did as he pleased, e.g., bigamy. According to a search by the circuit clerk's office in McCracken County, no divorce papers were ever filed by Nell through the time period ending in 1969, so the divorce action never advanced beyond the stage of discussions with a lawyer. When Leon got either a call from Nell, saying she wanted a divorce, or received a letter of intent to divorce from Nell's attorney while he was living in East St. Louis at Audrey's, he immediately drove back to Paducah to face Nell down.

If there was a marriage between Leon and Audrey that predates the 1969 record I found, then Leon knew that in a divorce action brought by Nell he would be exposed as a bigamist, and possibly arrested and jailed for that bigamy. Tillie was confident Leon had married Audrey legally as early as 1946, and surely Nell knew this and could prove it. He couldn't allow Nell to divorce him, never mind his probable feelings of machismo that no woman should ever divorce him, and that Nell was his property. A divorce meant for Leon a loss of face to his brothers and sisters that he would be the first of the Tuckers to be divorced. At this time and place, divorce was simply unthinkable—the ultimate in humiliation. Leon would lose insurance rights over Nell's life if she divorced him, plus he might have to pay her alimony. Those thoughts probably contributed to his rage, but the fear of being exposed as a bigamist, or at least an adulterer, was what primarily motivated Leon's enraged visit to Paducah that year.

Leon raced around Paducah like a madman looking for Nell, fully intending on beating her into submission, as he had done many times before. No woman should ever stand up to a Tucker man, according to Leon. Nell was hiding from him, but not at her home or her sister's homes. Leon fired a shotgun blast through the front door of the house of Nell's sister, Ila Mae (Freeman) Fike, because he thought Nell was inside. Fearing Leon was going to vent his rage at her sisters instead of her, Nell eventually allowed Leon to find her. Leon threatened her (or physically-forced her through a beating more likely) to drop the divorce moves. According to family members, Leon told Nell he would kill her if she didn't drop the divorce action. Faced with that choice, drop the divorce or die, Nell called off the divorce. Nell told her niece Tillie at the time, "Leon isn't married to me—Leon owns me."

Nell certainly didn't call off the divorce because Leon wooed her, or promised her he would leave Audrey. Leon couldn't divorce or leave Audrey either because of the potential for his bigamy and/or adultery to be exposed. Also, Leon knew Audrey's brother Claud Marshall was in a controlling position in the East St. Louis Local 100 construction union, and that union being basically the same thing, at that time, as organized crime. Not only did Claud control Leon's access to work in East St. Louis, Leon's very life may have been in danger if he tried to divorce or leave Audrey. He may have not wanted to be rid of Audrey in any case. After all, the only thing any Tucker man has ever been afraid of is being alone. After Nell called off the divorce, Leon went back to Audrey in East St. Louis and resumed the bizarre situation of having two wives in two cities. This cold peace, an impasse or stalemate really, would continue for about another eight or nine years, until Nell's death.

Evidently things were patched up between Nell and Leon periodically, at least for "looks" purposes, by the mid-1960s. I have photos of Nell and Leon visiting the parents of Judy, their new daughter-in-law. Frank's second wife, Judy (Bond), was very close with her parents, Glen and Ruth Bond, and they all lived in East St. Louis from when Judy was finishing high school in the late 1940s until about 1962. At that time

Glen and Ruth Bond moved back home to Chesterfield, which was a very rural, small town in Macoupin County, Illinois. Frank and Judy had married in 1958 and began having children in 1961. When Nell would make the journey north from Paducah to East St. Louis periodically to see her son and new grandchildren, she and Leon would pretend to be a happily married couple for "looks" purposes in front of the Bonds. One time it is known that Leon and Nell visited Chesterfield in 1964. Frank and Judy were living in Chesterfield themselves for one year, 1964-65. This visit by Leon and Nell to Chesterfield likely occurred just after I was born. At that time, in February 1964, Leon and Nell were vacationing in Florida. Leon again was fishing on Lake Okeechobee, and they camped nearby in Palmdale, Florida. When they returned from Florida, they likely made the journey to Chesterfield to see their newborn grandson.

During this year in Chesterfield, Frank was trying his hand at opening a used car dealership in nearby Reeder, Illinois. After a year, the used car dealership failed when, according to Frank, all the car engines were sold out of the entire lot of cars by one of Judy's first cousins, Jim Dawson. Jim had partnered with Frank in starting the business. When Frank left for a vacation out of town, he came back to a lot of cars with no engines, and Jim Dawson was nowhere to be found. Jim could sell the engines out of the cars and any other parts without transferring the titles to the cars, which would have required Frank's signature. The cars were obviously junk at this point. Faced with that loss, Frank and Judy moved back to East St. Louis with two young children, again to find work. Their newborn son Dwain was only an infant of less than one year at that time.

I remember as a toddler, probably in 1968, visiting Nell in Paducah, and even at that young age of four wondering why "Papaw" (Leon) wasn't there with her. At that age I couldn't understand this complicated situation of Leon in East St. Louis with Audrey, and Nell in Paducah alone. During this 1968 visit, I remember Nell and I riding on the kiddie train ride together at Noble Park, and me giving her a nickname, "Peepeyes," which caught on with the family. Other photos during this time record Leon and Nell visiting their preteen grandson Trent in Osceola, Arkansas. Also, photos show them taking trips almost every winter to the Lake Okeechobee area of Florida.

From the late 1940s until Nell's death in 1969, Leon would spend most of the year in East St. Louis working, returning to Paducah a couple of times per month and spend a weekend with Nell when she was there. According to family cousins who witnessed these visits, Nell and Leon were like any other married couple in the way they treated each other. Apparently they would refer to each other as "hon," short for "honey." Leon would alternate years, one year taking Nell to Florida for vacation with him, then the next year take Audrey. Leon would sometimes take both women only weeks apart in the same year to Florida. We have no family remembrances that Nell was ever at the clubhouse at Grand Tower, Illinois, on Rattlesnake Ferry Road, but many family members remember Leon taking Audrey there. Leon was apparently unashamed to show Audrey to his other family members, freely displaying her as his wife, or at least as his companion. Everyone knew that Nell was still his wife, living in Paducah, but no one ever challenged Leon on it—no one, except Dollie Stevenson.

When Leon would show up at the Stevenson's farm near Calvert City, Kentucky, not far from the Kentucky Dam, Dollie, Walter's wife, would tell Leon to leave Audrey in the car. Only after Nell had died was Audrey allowed out of the car, and begrudgingly accepted by Dollie. Dollie apparently was fond of Nell. The Stevensons were the most common companions for trips to Florida with Leon and Nell, and Leon and Audrey as well. Leon was known to have first taken Audrey to Florida for a trip, leave for a week while he drove Audrey home to East St. Louis, then drive back down to Florida, picking up Nell in Paducah on the way. Leon and Nell also partnered with Stella and Uvil Taylor for Florida trips during this period of time. Vacations to the clubhouse at Grand Tower were usually accompanied by Versie (Tucker) Nowak and her husband Frank, and Elmer R. D. Burgess with his wife and their adult children. All of these names—Nowak, Burgess, Taylor, Stevenson—were all Tucker cousins. Evidently the Grand Tower clubhouse trips were basically sloppy weekend-long drinking parties, entirely inappropriate for Nell. That's probably why Leon never took Nell to Grand Tower, but he would take Audrey there. Also, hunting was one of the primary activities for the men during these Grand Tower trips, so Audrey was needed there to clean the kills that the men brought back, which Nell would have refused to do.

Going to Florida was the most common trip Leon would take because he owned an orange grove (sold to him by the Stevensons) that he leased out in Ft. Meade. Fishing on the Lake Okeechobee was Leon's favorite pastime. The photos of this time of Nell and Leon in Florida appear to show a happily married couple, both smiling and embracing each other as they posed for photos in front of some tourist site. Accompanying them to Florida sometimes were some of Nell's church friends from Paducah, such as Dorothy McNeal and her husband. One can suspect that Nell may have invited others from Paducah along on the trip to Florida as an insurance policy against Leon trying anything against her. If he did, she likely thought, at least there would be witnesses.

This bizarre three-way marriage between Leon, Nell, and Audrey continued until the late 1960s when Leon approached his retirement years signaled by his physical strength beginning to wane and his body wearing out. Forty years of hard construction labor had burned Leon's body out early. Leon knew he had only a few years of work left and needed to come to a conclusion with the three-way marriage situation. He had been waiting for either Nell or Audrey to die of natural causes, but neither did. Nell, being the weaker of the two women physically, was naturally expected to be the one to die first of natural causes. She apparently wasn't dying fast enough to fit Leon's retirement schedule. Leon knew he couldn't divorce Audrey, couldn't leave her behind in East St. Louis and build his retirement home in Paducah, and couldn't move Audrey to Paducah and set her up in a household with Nell already in a separate household in Paducah. Paducah was a small, heavily religious city at that time. Leon's brothers Rob and Corbett made it clear to Leon he had to resolve this situation with his two wives, or he wasn't going to be accepted in Paducah—by the city folk or his kin.

Nell and Leon embracing

Nell posing in front of an orange tree on the lot she and Leon owned in Ft. Meade, Florida. Their Rambler stationwagon with Leon's fishing boat on top and the Shasta camper behind it can be seen in the background.

Thus, the plan was born to get rid of Nell—a wife that had become inconvenient. Leon thought he had no choice but to help Nell along on her way to dying. I'm sure, to him, he rationalized it wasn't that bad of a thing to do at all. She would have died within a few years anyway, at least in Leon's mind. In September 1968, Nell got a delayed birth certificate issued for the first time in her life at the age of fifty-eight years old. It is unknown for certain why she did this, only three months before she would die in Florida. One of the possible explanations for her seeking her birth certificate was because Leon wanted it. Leon may have pestered Nell in September 1968 to review the life insurance policy she had on herself since 1937 with Prudential Life Insurance Company of Baltimore, Maryland. He may have pestered her to get her birth certificate issued, which she never had since birth. Nell complied, probably confused as to why Leon was so adamant about getting it. Another possible explanation as to why Nell was getting her delayed birth certificate issued was because, with Leon behaving strangely and asking to see the insurance papers on Nell, Nell suspected something was up. She may have suspected Leon might be planning to kill her. Nell may have decided to document her true age and leave a trail for others to follow by getting her delayed birth certificate issued without Leon knowing. On that birth certificate, she stated her life insurance policy number, a highly unusual thing to do. There are many ways she could have documented her age on the birth certificate, but to use a life insurance policy was highly suspicious. She must have done that for a reason.

Nell was living at the time, in 1968, at 1603 Little Avenue in Paducah, in a house owned by her sister and brother-in-law, Ila Mae (Freeman) and Carl Fike. Nell for a time had lived with Ila Mae and Carl in their home, but moved to one of the houses they rented out because evidently Carl had made a pass at Nell. Nell didn't feel comfortable living in the same house with Carl anymore. Leon would rarely contribute to Nell's support in Paducah. She was basically on her own about paying the rent. This year, Christmas 1968, Leon may have taken Audrey to Ft. Meade or Okeechobee, Florida, over the Christmas holiday and left her behind. He then would have driven to Paducah to pick up Nell to take her to Florida. If he did this, left Audrey down in Florida, he did this knowing he could pick her up in a week or two after Nell was dead. It makes sense since he knew he would want to take Audrey to Okeechobee after Nell's funeral and wouldn't have wanted to drive the seven hours roundtrip to East St. Louis just to pick up Audrey. Audrey could also have come to Paducah for Nell's funeral from East St. Louis by bus, as her daughter Frances said it was common for her to drop her mother at the bus station in Belleville, just east of East St. Louis, for the trip to Paducah during the years Audrey was with Leon. Leon could also have sent Audrey to Florida by bus in advance of needing her there when he arrived with Nell.

This is thought to be the last photo of Nell alive,
taken at Tillie's less than a week before the Florida trip.

Leon told Nell in December 1968 that he wanted her to go to Florida with him just after Christmas that year. Nell told her sisters Grace and Ila Mae that she didn't want to go. Nell said to Grace she was afraid of Leon, that he was acting funny to her, and she suspected something was up, but didn't know what. Nell had a sense of foreboding about this trip. Nell and Grace worked out a signal system where Nell was to send a postcard to Grace with the circle above the *i* in her last name, Martinez, instead of a normal dot. That was a signal to Grace that Nell felt in trouble and needed help. Nell knew the campground had no phone at it, so postcards would have been the only way to communicate a plea to Grace without Leon being tipped off.

Despite Nell's constant statements of not wanting to go on the trip, Leon would hear none of it and insisted she go. On the day of their departure, Nell still hadn't completely agreed to go yet. Leon showed up at Grace's house and began cleaning his shotgun on the front porch. Clearly this was intimidation, so no one there at Grace's house would oppose him. Finally, Leon came into the house, laid the shotgun on the coffee table, and told Nell to get in the car. Nell was crying when she got into the car and waved good-bye for the last time to her beloved sister Grace, telling her, "I don't think I'll eva' see ya again." Grace's daughters Tillie and Mildred witnessed this statement by Nell.

Leon and Nell arrived in Ft. Meade, Florida, after about two days of driving on or about January 2, 1969. They visited with Robert Stevenson and his wife Irene, and camped on the lot Leon owned nearby, which had a mixed citrus grove on it. Leon and Nell loaded up bags of citrus before leaving for Lake Okeechobee to the south. If some of the citrus, tangelos it was said to be, were poisoned, this is likely where they were picked up. If Audrey was remaining in Florida, waiting for Leon, it's possible she could have prepared the poisoned tangelos and left them in an arranged spot for Leon to find when he came through town with Nell. Nell must have mailed a postcard to Grace immediately upon arrival, perhaps under the ruse to notify Grace that she and Leon arrived safely in Florida. Leon wouldn't have suspected anything unusual in that. Nell must have sensed she was in danger on the ride down to Florida, since on the very first postcard she sent, she dotted the *i* in Grace's last name with a circle. The secret distress signal was sent. Because postcards are handled the slowest by the U.S. Postal Service, it took about a week for this postcard to make it to Kentucky, arriving on or after January 7, 1969.

Walter and Dollie Stevenson were already down at the campground in Florida waiting for Leon and Nell's arrival. Leon and Nell arrived about January 4, 1969. Walter and Dollie's son, Eddie, and Eddie's wife Linda were also there before Leon and Nell arrived, by only one day. All began what was intended to be a normal fishing vacation on Lake Okeechobee—nothing out of the ordinary. But evidently Nell felt she was in danger because she began to hide money from Leon, approximately $200 in small bills like tens and twenties, in a secret pocket she had sewn into the cup of her brassiere. Nell felt she needed an emergency escape fund to grab a taxi to a bus or plane on short notice, if she felt in imminent danger from Leon and needed to flee.

Nell knew that Leon could search the entire trailer and even her purse for any hidden money she had, but would never have thought to search her brassiere. Perhaps the pocket in the brassiere was sewn so well that it wasn't obvious in a casual search. He would have had to do a thorough search of the brassiere to find it, which was highly unlikely.

Sometime in the first week of January 1969, Leon may have tampered with Nell's prescription medications. He may have poisoned some of the tangelos that they picked up at Ft. Meade as well, although in this scenario Leon would have had to guard against others besides Nell eating the tangelos without him around to prevent it. Leon did these acts to weaken Nell's health, so she would either die naturally or make her weaker at self-defense for an attack later on. It cannot be known if placebos or poisonous pills were substituted for the real medications, or if he just emptied the containers out, so she would have to stop taking the medications. These can be the only logical explanations for the empty medication bottle found by the police in a few days. Without written prescriptions from her doctor with her, she would have had to wait until they returned to Kentucky to refill the prescriptions at Hugg the Druggist in Paducah, unless a phoned-in prescription to a pharmacy in Okeechobee was achieved.

January 6, 1969, arrived, and as best as can be known, it was a usual day. It was one day before Leon and Nell's fortieth wedding anniversary. They were married on January 7, 1929, in Kentucky. Leon and Walter would have gone fishing in the morning when it was cool. Nell and Dollie would have stayed at the campground cooking, cleaning, relaxing, and reading. Eddie and Linda Stevenson may have joined the older folks in their activities, or did their own thing, being so much younger. When the sun got too hot for fishing in the afternoon, Leon and Walter returned to the campsite for their lunch and planned on relaxing in the shade for the rest of the day. That afternoon, after lunch, Leon and Walter began their usual heavy drinking. This time, Leon had a purpose for getting particularly drunk. He needed the courage the liquor provided to do what he came to Florida this year to do—get rid of Nell.

The tampering with her medications or the poisoned tangelos hadn't done the trick yet of killing Nell, but it had weakened her—making her sluggish and sickly. Leon was impatient and didn't want to wait for the poison or the pills to do the job. Sometime in the middle of the afternoon, Leon went into the camper in a drunken state. He found Nell taking a nap. Perhaps he woke her and began an argument, or perhaps he just attacked her as she napped, attempting to smother her. The act of smothering would have kept her screams for help muffled, so no one heard. The action possibly triggered a heart attack in a weakened Nell, or she may have asphyxiated from the smothering. Either way, he succeeded. She was dead. Leon then went to get Walter Stevenson to help him carry her body out of the Shasta camper.

Dorothy McNeal, a church friend of Nell's from Paducah, had a nearby campsite and witnessed Walter and Leon carrying Nell's body from the Shasta camper to Leon's car. Dorothy said she hadn't seen Nell all day that day and was worried about her. She said she saw Leon and the Stevensons take off for the hospital with Nell's unconscious (albeit she didn't know Nell was likely already dead) body in the car in the afternoon. She would later tell Grace about witnessing these events upon her return to Paducah, as she knew Grace as well from the same church. Eddie and Linda Stevenson witnessed his father and Leon carrying Nell from the camper as well. Leon, Walter, and Dollie took off with Nell's body in the car for the hospital, or at least that's what they told the others at the campground. Eddie and Linda Stevenson did not join them. Walter directed his son to stay behind. Leon and the Stevensons drove around for five hours, sobering up and perfecting what story they were going to tell at the hospital. The lie of Nell dying in the car on the way to dinner at a seafood restaurant, instead of in the camper at the campsite, was born. The detail of Nell eating tangelos was scripted at this time.

When the group arrived at the hospital in the middle of the evening, Leon and Walter carried Nell's body to a stretcher and into the hospital emergency room. The physician available at the time briefly examined Nell's body in a cursory way and pronounced her "DOA" or "dead on arrival." The physician, Dr. Steven Johnston, would later sign the death certificate. He spoke with Leon briefly. Dr. Johnston was likely a Freemason, as Leon definitely had been in the past. If they recognized this in each other, as most Masons do, an immediate kinship or brotherhood would have been established between the two men. Dr. Johnston would have been more willing to believe anything Leon told him about Nell's death since it was coming from a fellow Mason. Leon knew how to use this, or rather abuse this, to his advantage.

Leon told Dr. Johnston the story of how he, Nell, Walter, and Dollie were on their way to a seafood restaurant for dinner, and Nell was eating tangelos. Leon's story was that Nell said of the tangelos, "These may kill me, but they're so good I'm gonna eat 'em anyway." Leon said her doctor told her not to eat uncooked food, but she did anyway. This established that Nell died of her own doing, not of anyone else's fault. This was a lie, as Nell's sister Grace said no such doctor's order existed. But then again the whole tangelo story detail was a lie anyway. Leon told Dr. Johnston that Nell began to have bad chest pains in the car. Leon said he turned the car about and began racing for the hospital. Leon said Nell died in the car of a heart attack just before arriving at the hospital. Leon said her head was lying in Dollie's lap in the backseat of the car when she died. Walter was there at the emergency room, likely backing up what Leon was telling Dr. Johnston.

Not knowing any better since he wasn't there at the time and could only go on what Leon was telling him, Dr. Johnston asked Leon if he wanted an autopsy of Nell's remains. Leon vehemently refused. This sounded suspicious to Dr. Johnston. After concluding his conversation with Leon, he waited until Leon had phoned his son, Frank, in Illinois to notify him of Nell's death. Then Dr. Johnston placed his own phone call to Frank in Illinois and offered him the opportunity of an autopsy. Frank also refused, not wanting to go against his father, and saying he didn't want his mother "cut up like that." Frank was terrified of Leon most of his life, as most people were who knew what Leon was capable of in his younger years. There were no "red flags" on Nell's body—no signs of trauma, no puncture wounds, no blood—so the cause of Nell's death was categorized by Dr. Johnston as "unknown (DOA)."

With the lack of any compelling reason to override Leon's refusal of an autopsy, and perhaps feeling compelled to show the loyalty to a fellow Mason, Dr. Johnston didn't pursue the matter further. He did, however, leave the door open for an investigation in the future of Nell's death. He left the cause of death as "unknown," not as "natural causes," as Leon stated. He knew from Nell's body temperature that she had been dead at least five hours prior to arriving at the hospital, so Leon's story of her dying just as they arrived at the hospital could not be true. It can only be speculated about the fact the two men, Leon and Dr. Johnston, were both Freemasons, and if this played a role in Dr. Johnston's lack of pursuing the cause of Nell's death. Dr. Johnston's nurse, Pearl Godwin, who worked at the hospital in 1969, said an unknown cause of death would have required an autopsy by state law. Therefore, Dr. Johnston's act of not insisting on one may have been illegal.

Leon, Walter, and Dollie Stevenson left Nell's body at the hospital after the funeral director, Bill Yates of Yates Funeral Home in Okeechobee, arrived to remove the body. Bill Yates spoke with Leon for a few moments, gathering the personal information on Nell, contact information for Leon, and the destination for the body to be shipped back to Kentucky. That destination was the Kennedy Funeral Home in Paducah. Leon gave Bill Yates his East St. Louis address of 1225 N. Fifty-second Street to send the death certificate. Bill Yates collected her body that night and began the embalming process right away. He discovered the hidden money in her brassiere when he began to disrobe Nell for the embalming. Being an honest man, Bill Yates drove out to the campground the following morning, January 7, 1969, and found Leon to give him the money. Leon said to Bill Yates, "I knew she was a hidin' money on me, but I didn't know whar." Leon told Bill Yates the story of Nell dying in the car on the way to the hospital. Bill Yates completed his work on Nell's remains, placed them in a metal casket, and drove her remains to Palm Beach Airport, a few hours' drive from Okeechobee. It was the closest major airport with an air connection to Evansville, Indiana, the closest major airport to Paducah, about an hour's drive away. Nell's remains were shipped via Eastern Airlines with a connection in Atlanta, and were picked up by representatives of Kennedy Funeral Home for her final return to Paducah.

Nell's sister Grace received the call on the evening of January 6, 1969, from Frank that Nell had died, and immediately told her daughter Tillie that "Leon killed her." In the next few days, with Grace distraught over the loss of her sister, Tillie was staying with her to help her through it. Tillie checked Grace's mail and discovered a postcard from Nell in Florida. Nell must have mailed it immediately upon arrival in Florida for it to been delivered in Paducah on or about January 7, 1969. The *i* in Grace's last name was dotted with a circle, which was the signal from Nell she was in trouble. Tillie thought the sight of that card would cause Grace to have her own heart attack, so she didn't show it to her. Tillie took the card to the authorities in Paducah, and the Paducah authorities called the Okeechobee County sheriff's office, requesting an investigation before any evidence at the campsite was lost. The Okeechobee County sheriff's office arrived at the campground, interviewed Leon, and searched the Shasta camper. They found nothing to indicate a crime had occurred, no blood or signs of a struggle were apparent. But they wrote down in their notes that Nell's prescription bottle was empty. Leon had either emptied it earlier before Nell died, denying her the pills she needed, or emptied it early on the morning of January 7, 1969, to dispose of the fake pills (either ineffectual placebos or an actual poison) he had substituted for the real ones earlier in the week.

Leon left the campground late in the day on January 8, 1969, to attend Nell's funeral planned for three days later. The drive from Okeechobee to Paducah takes a little over fourteen hours when driven straight through, so it can be reasonably assumed it took Leon one whole day of driving to get back to Paducah. All four Stevensons, Walter and Dollie as well as Eddie and Linda, remained behind to continue their vacation. It's surprising that Walter and Dollie didn't leave with Leon to attend Nell's funeral, having been close to Nell for forty years. Leon left his Shasta camper behind so as not to lose his favorite camping spot, knowing the Stevensons were there to guard it. Leon arrived back in Paducah about January 10, 1969, one day before Nell's funeral on Saturday, January 11, 1969. Audrey attended Nell's funeral in Paducah with Leon, to the surprise of Nell's family. Audrey either came from Florida with Leon if she was already there, or came by bus from East St. Louis and met Leon in Paducah.

At the funeral, Leon would tell everyone the story of how Nell had died at the hospital pleading for help. This made Leon look like a hero because he got her to the hospital before she died, and her death therefore was the fault of the hospital staff, not Leon's. Leon was the only person there to tell the story of what happened to Nell, as the Stevensons, the only other witnesses, were still down in Florida. It is a curiosity as to why the Stevensons did not join Leon on the trip to Paducah for Nell's funeral. They too had known Nell for forty years, and the couples were close, particularly Dollie and Nell. Perhaps Leon directed the Stevensons to remain in Florida—that he would be back in less than a week anyway? It's logical that Leon would have wanted them to remain in Florida so as to not contradict his storytelling at Nell's funeral of what happened to Nell in Florida. With only Leon to tell the story, he could tell whatever story was he liked—whatever was convenient. The confusion as to how Nell died sent red flags up to many people at the funeral, but none would confront Leon about it, knowing Leon's previous history of violent rage. Grace was so suspicious and grief-stricken that she tried to pry open the mouth on Nell's corpse as it lay in the casket during the viewing at the funeral home. She wanted to see if there was anything inside Nell's mouth that was evidence of foul play. Clearly, she wasn't thinking straight in her moment of overwhelming grief.

Leon left Paducah immediately after Nell's funeral with Audrey in the car and proceeded back down to Okeechobee to continue his vacation for the remainder of January 1969. His wife of forty years had just died, he had just buried her, and he was continuing a vacation with his second wife in Florida. The lack of grieving at this time revealed that Leon had already come to terms with Nell's death before it happened, as it wasn't a shock when it occurred. To others, this type of loss would have required a time of recovery from grief. Leon did no grieving and left immediately for Florida after the funeral. If Audrey was not prepositioned in Florida waiting for Leon, and rather was in East St. Louis when Nell died in Florida, then she must have known beforehand it was going to happen, or at least had to suspect it. Audrey was working full time at Hunter Meat Packing in East St. Louis at the time and had to have requested the time off from work to head to Florida. She couldn't have done this at that last minute, like after Nell's death, if Leon suddenly asked her to join him in Florida as a replacement for Nell on his Florida vacation. Audrey must have had advance knowledge from Leon of when Nell would be leaving Florida. If Audrey didn't know already from Leon that Nell was going to die, she had to be suspicious as to why Nell was spending such a short time, only a few days in fact, in Florida with Leon.

When Leon arrived back at the campsite in Okeechobee with Audrey in the car, he immediately asked the group, both Stevenson couples, to move upstream from their favorite campsite with the campers. Eddie Stevenson said Leon did this because he felt that the other campers nearby saw him leave to bury his wife and then immediately returned with another woman, and it looked bad. They moved the campers upstream for that purpose only. Leon and Audrey finished January in Okeechobee.

In February 1969, when Walter and Dollie Stevenson returned from Florida, they apparently were not coordinating their stories with Leon. They did not back up Leon's story that Nell died at the hospital, and instead told people in Kentucky that Nell died in the car just before arriving at the hospital, with Nell's head in Dollie's lap in the backseat of the car. That was the cover story they told the hospital staff in Okeechobee, and Leon hadn't told them he had changed the cover story to tell the family in Paducah. Despite the fact that the Stevensons were Leon's cousins, not Nell's, and they didn't really know Nell's side of the family, the word got back to Grace through mutual friends of the story that they were telling of how Nell died. Paducah was a small town at that time, and everyone was either related or had mutual friends.

The conflicting stories between Leon and the Stevensons confirmed to Grace that Nell had been killed. Grace called the hospital in Okeechobee and spoke with the doctor that received Nell's body that night. This doctor had to be Dr. Steven Johnston. He told Grace that Nell arrived "DOA" at the hospital, and from his examination of her body, that she had been dead at least five hours before arriving at the hospital. Armed with all this evidence, Grace went to the local district attorney, called the "commonwealth's attorney" since Kentucky is not a state but a commonwealth. This commonwealth attorney was named Albert Jones. Albert Jones was only a few years older than Nell and Leon's son, Frank, and had played football with Frank at Paducah's Tilghman High School. Albert Jones would go on to an illustrious career, becoming mayor of Paducah, and serving in the state legislature as well. He knew G. Gordon Liddy and Mark Felt, the infamous "Deep Throat," both from Watergate fame, during his law school years, and would be asked to comment on them in later years.

Evidently there was never enough evidence to warrant a prosecution of Leon, but there was enough for a preliminary investigation. At the very least a few phone calls were made to the authorities in Florida, and that contributed to the decision by the police to search Leon's trailer in Okeechobee. The Stevensons were interviewed, as were many others, including Leon. Grace, in her anger, called Pood Roberts, the supervisor over the Local 100 Laborer's Union in East St. Louis, and tried to get Leon in trouble by relating the story of Nell's death. Frustrated and out of options for justice, Grace sat with a pistol in her purse at the Farmer's Market in Paducah, intending to shoot Leon when he came there for his usual lunch during one of his later visits to Paducah. Leon had to return to Paducah to sell Nell's belongings and pack up what he wanted to keep from them. Leon was lucky that day, as he had unexpectedly left early for East St. Louis, and therefore never showed at the Farmer's Market where Grace laid in wait for him—armed. Leon wouldn't return to live in Paducah again until 1974, after more than a five-year absence. Of Nell's two sisters, Grace would die in March 1977, and Ila Mae would die in June 1970 (a year and a half after Nell died).

Sometime after Leon had left Florida, he phoned back to the Yates Funeral Home to correct the date on Nell's death certificate. He changed it from August 10, 1910, to July 17, 1919. This made Nell appear to be forty-nine years old at the time of her death, not fifty-eight years old, which she actually was. Nell's actual birthday was July 17, 1910, a combination of the two dates Leon gave to Bill Yates. It is not known why Leon changed this date on Nell's death certificate, but there had to be a motivating force to do so. Insurance fraud is one possible explanation. Leon would have collected on Nell's life insurance with Prudential Life Insurance Company sometime in February 1969. Her birth certificate Nell obtained three months prior, in October 1968, could have been needed at this time for the collection of the insurance proceeds.

Nell was buried in Paducah at Mt. Kenton Cemetery, the first to be buried in a plot of four graves originally purchased by Leon's brother, Rob. Rob had purchased the plot of four graves for himself, his wife Gertrude (known just as "Gert"), and their two infant sons who had died many years prior. Both of those infant sons were buried at the Old Concrete Church Cemetery, now known as the Carter's Mill Cemetery, near Symsonia, Kentucky. They were buried next to Rob and Leon's parents, George W. and Ruth (Keeling) Tucker. Rob had intended to relocate the caskets of his dead sons to Mt. Kenton Cemetery, but found the bureaucratic red tape was too difficult to do so and gave up. He gave the other two graves at Mt. Kenton to Leon, and Leon ordered that Nell be buried there. When ordering the gravestone, Leon and Rob together split the cost of the stone, an upright four-foot wide by three-foot tall piece of pink granite, because all four names at the grave site would be placed upon it. It would be centered over the plot of four graves, Nell and Leon's names on one side, Rob and Gert's names on the other side. Leon for certain knew the right date of Nell's birth at this point, as the gravestone is correctly marked with her birth year of 1910. Leon would have been the only source for this, so it additionally confirms Leon knew he was giving the wrong birth date to the Yates Funeral Home in Florida for Nell's death certificate.

Nell's and Leon's gravesite

Leon resumed his life with Audrey in East St. Louis upon returning from Florida in February 1969. Audrey sought a divorce from her last husband, Joe Hayden, filed in May of 1969, and got the final divorce decree in absentia, since Joe Hayden could not be found in July 1969. Audrey actually had to advertise in the local newspaper of her divorce action, to notify Joe Hayden if he was still in the area. It is not known if Leon knew of Audrey's divorce action or if Audrey did this on her own. It can be reasonably assumed Leon knew Audrey was still married to Joe Hayden for the previous approximately thirty years that Leon and Audrey were together as a couple, but it is also possible he never knew she was still married. This might have been a deep secret of Audrey's, since her daughter, Frances, didn't know Audrey was divorcing Joe Hayden in 1969. She thought they divorced back in the 1940s when Joe Hayden abandoned Audrey. I asked Frances about this issue in 2006, and she didn't recall it.

Leon and Audrey formally married in Chester, Illinois, located in rural southwestern Illinois in Randolph County, on September 19, 1969, nine months after Nell's death. Only they knew if this was their first marriage to each other, or the second "clean-up" marriage to create the necessary documentation of a legal marriage that was dated after Nell's death, for the purposes of tax and retirement benefits. Leon and Audrey bought the house at 1524 N. Forty-sixth Street in East St. Louis, which was immediately next door to Frank and Judy's at 1530 N. Forty-sixth Street, on October 2, 1969, two weeks after they married. They would live there for just four years. Leon would sell the vacant lot in Ft. Meade, Florida, he had purchased earlier from the Stevensons back to another member of the family, Jolene (Stevenson) Hardin and her husband Kenny, in 1971. Oddly, Leon had saved Jolene's life approximately eight or nine years prior, about 1961, at a public swimming pool in Ft. Meade, by jumping in and pulling her out when she was drowning.

In the early seventies in East St. Louis, there was dramatic social upheaval going on, with the major meatpacking operations of Armour, Hunter, and Swift closing down and taking with them all the jobs that supported the city. East St. Louis began a steep decline in living quality, government services began to fail, crime skyrocketed upward, and the white population began moving out of the city in a mass exodus. Houses were being sold for small fraction of what they were worth. Frank and Judy's house at 1530 N. Forty-sixth Street was a two-story brick home with three bedrooms, two bathrooms, a dining room separate from kitchen, a full basement, a large extra lot attached, a large backyard, an enclosed front porch, a fireplace, a two-car detached garage, wood floors, was well landscaped, and had significant curb appeal. It was sold to an educator for only $12,500, according to Frank's memory.

East St. Louis began shrinking in population from a high above one hundred thousand people in the first half of the 1900s to today's population of around thirty thousand people. Perhaps half of the city's houses today are abandoned, are burned-out shells, or empty lots where houses used to stand. The demographics of the city changed also from what was before a mixed-race city to today almost 100 percent African-American. When Frank and Judy left East St. Louis to move to the suburb of

Cahokia in the summer of 1973, Leon began building a brick, ranch-style home at 1735 Husband Road in Paducah for his retirement. He had purchased the lot for his retirement home in September 1970, roughly a year and a half after Nell's death and a year after he had married Audrey (married formally, at least openly). With insurance proceeds from Nell's death likely, Leon began to set up his retirement. Property records reveal the lot in Paducah only cost $3,800 at the time it was purchased. The construction costs of the new home for Leon and Audrey would be significantly more, $18,500 for the two-bedroom, two-bath, nine-room, ranch-style brick home on the two-acre lot. Audrey told others she "matched Leon dollar for dollar" on the construction costs of the house on Husband Road, but few believed that. When their house was complete, Leon sold his house in East St. Louis on Forty-sixth Street in November 1973 and moved Audrey to Paducah to begin his retirement. He was accepted by his brothers Rob and Corbett, the Paducah community, and his extended family (the Tucker cousins), because he only had one wife now—Audrey. Frank focused on his own career development and his life with his wife Judy and their kids in Cahokia, putting Nell's death and the East St. Louis years behind him. Later, Frank and Judy moved to the small, rural town of Morrisonville in central Illinois to raise their children. Nothing more would happen with the mystery of Nell's death until many years later after Frank and Judy divorced in 1985, after Frank had remarried to Audra Lance in 1986, and after Leon had died in 1987.

Leon's death in June 1987 caused Audrey to rethink her life, and she sold the house on Husband Road for $44,000 in 1988. She left Kentucky for the final time, never to return. She moved in with her daughter Frances in Caseyville, Illinois, to be near her grandchildren. In 1990, Frances got Audrey to sign a power of attorney over medical decisions and finances over to her, and in a few years Frances would place Audrey in a nursing home. Audrey would spend the rest of her life there, dying in 1999.

Frank, reunited with Tillie after many years apart, learned of many of the things that Grace and Tillie found out about Nell's death. He had never been told these pieces of evidence before. Frank began to have his own suspicions about how Nell had died. His previous suspicions he had voiced to his wife Judy over the years together were never solid enough to pursue. But this information from Tillie was solid enough, and it made Frank ponder the unthinkable. Could his father have actually murdered his mother?

Frank planned a trip in the late 1980s, the exact year I cannot be certain of, to Florida. His third and last wife, Audra, would tell of him driving out of their way, not a logical path on their itinerary for their vacation at all, to the campground on Lake Okeechobee. He examined the campground for clues to see if what Leon had told him had happened in 1969 was true. Frank went to the hospital in Okeechobee town intent on searching for the emergency room records from that night in 1969. It apparently didn't occur to Frank to seek a copy of Nell's death certificate, or if it did, he never mentioned it to anyone, not even Tillie, his confidante and secret keeper. No one in the family thought to seek a copy of the death certificate, as Tillie saw a copy of it for the first time when I gave her one in 2006. At the hospital, Frank stopped himself before entering the hospital and stood in front of it smoking cigarettes for an hour. Returning to the car, he told Audra he didn't want to know if his father killed his mother. It would be too horrifying to know that. Frank stopped his investigation of his mother's death, getting perhaps a little too close to a terrible truth he couldn't bear to learn, and turned the page on history.

I can remember once when Leon and I went to visit Mt. Kenton Cemetery when I visited him in Paducah, alone, without my family, during my college years. This most likely would have been 1984 or 1985, about two years before Leon died in 1987. Standing over the grave of Nell, Leon said to me in his familiar western Kentucky drawl, "Ya know, thar's the only woman I ever really loved. That other'n, nah, I don't love her." He waved his hand like he was shooing away a fly, signaling he was disregarding Audrey as his wife, and not even mentioning her by name. He continued, "Ya wanna talk 'bout really *lovin'* (he placed emphasis on that word) somebody—thar she is." He pointed down to Nell's grave when he said that. He continued, almost like he was repenting or confessing, "Ya know, she'd see me on the street with my arm 'round 'nother woman. She'd jus' turn her head away, n' look down t' the ground, never say nothin'." I asked him in a calm tone without accusation, "Well, why did you do that then, Papaw?" He shrugged his shoulders, smiled his charming smile, that same charming smile he used all his life to get what he wanted, and here he wanted out of the focus of my question, and said, "I 'as young." Apparently he thought that was a sufficient excuse.

I now understand the look on Leon's face that day in 1985, when I didn't at the time. He had a look on his face like he wanted to say something to me, to reveal a deep secret, perhaps confess to me about Nell. He tensed his lips, squinted his eyes, and looked up to the sky, like he was summoning courage. But he couldn't tell me the secret—he knew that. He couldn't reveal that to me for fear that I would repeat it to Frank. He couldn't risk what Frank's reaction might be at learning the truth of his mother's death. That look on Leon's face that day, as we stood over Nell's grave, is burned into my memory. I understand it crystal clear now. I'm positive of that.

Near that time around 1985, Bert Mitchell, a nephew of Leon's by his older sister Robie, came to visit Leon, as was his habit. Bert loved his Tucker family history and turned himself into a family historian by the end of his life, collecting all the stories and photos of his Tucker grandparents, aunts, and uncles. He would often go to Paducah from his home in Caseyville, Illinois, (located just outside of East St. Louis) and stay with the many Tucker cousins, aunts, and uncles he had in Paducah. He did this so often that he acquired the accent that western Kentuckians had, despite his brothers and sisters speaking more closely to that of the dialect and accents of East St. Louis area. Bert was a religious man and a pastor of a church.

During Bert's visit, Leon, attempting to clear his conscience before he died, confessed to Bert that he had smothered Nell to death. He told Bert the details of what happened that night, minus the part where he had previously tampered with Nell's pills or had poisoned the tangelos or other food. He knew Bert would never reveal what he was confessing to him because Bert was first a pastor and thereby obligated to keep confessions a secret, and second because he was a Tucker man, and had the strong allegiance to the family name. Bert Mitchell's name was the first name signed on the signature book (which Frances Lemanski, Audrey's daughter, gave to me in 2006) for attending Leon's funeral in 1987. It was Bert's habit to attend all the funerals of the Tuckers, be the first one to arrive, and the last to leave, not wanting to miss anybody who showed up.

Leon in his older years, as he neared death and knew it, became a deeply religious man, attending church as many times in the week that service was held. He tithed to the church for the first time in his lifetime. As frugal as Leon was all his life, learned from the time when he was young, dirt-poor, and starving, this was an amazing development. To get Leon to give money for something and not get something immediately in return would be totally inconsistent with Leon's whole lifetime of behavior. But he did give to his church at this time. This was attested to by the pastor at Leon's church in Paducah, Pete Keeling, himself actually a distant cousin to Leon. Pete said he sensed Leon "wanted as much religion as he could get in his last years, attempting to redeem himself for his wayward behavior as a younger man." That sentence of Pete's sticks out in my memory from when I attended Leon's funeral in 1987 and listened to Pete's eulogy for Leon. It now makes sense that if Leon had the guilt on his mind of Nell's murder, he would want to try to make up for that somehow before dying and meeting his Maker. Fear of having to atone for his misdeeds in the afterlife made Leon want to cleanse himself if he could, thus yielding his good deeds of tithing to the church in later years and his confession to Bert Mitchell. Tillie believed Leon had confessed to Nell's murder to Pete Keeling also. If so, Pete Keeling took that secret to his grave, not even sharing it with his wife, Grace. I asked Grace Keeling in 2006 if she knew anything about this, and she said no. Pete Keeling left behind no journals, nor shared anything about Leon with his sons, as I spoke with one of them in 2006 as well.

And so I bring this story full circle, back to the beginning. The rumor of Nell's death being a murder instead of a natural death would resurface at family events over the years—funerals, weddings, family reunions, etc. It would be until Frank's funeral in 2005 that the rumor of the mystery of Nell's death would trigger any more action on it. Tillie spoke to me about it, and with the concurrence of others, it began to congeal with me as a feasible possibility, not just a silly rumor. I began my own investigation into Nell's death, intent on putting to rest this rumor once and for all, and removing the stigma of suspicion from Leon's name and the Tucker family as a whole. My investigation, however, didn't accomplish the original goal. My investigation, instead, led me to believe in Leon's guilt.

*   *   *

Proposed location for Nell's final resting place, next to her father, Allen Freeman

Chapter 13

THE RESOLUTION

It haunted me that Nell was lying, menacingly to her at least in my mind, next to her murderer.

One of the things I needed to resolve in this matter was the final resting place for Nell's remains. Before pursuing the autopsy, I had suggested to Tillie that Nell's remains should not be resting next to Leon's if we came to the conclusion that Leon had murdered her. It just wasn't right to leave it like that. I felt confident Nell wouldn't have wanted her remains to spend eternity lying next to the man that murdered her. After thinking about it for a while, Tillie agreed, saying she would check the Clark's River Cemetery in Symsonia, Kentucky, where Nell's entire family is buried, if there were any available spaces near any of Nell's family. I already knew there was, immediately next to her father, Allen Freeman. That would be an entirely appropriate place for Nell's final resting place, next to her father, and in the same cemetery with her mother Annie Ford, her sisters Grace (Freeman) Martinez and Ila Mae (Freeman) Fike, and her brother, Melvin "Ernest" Freeman. It haunted me that Nell was lying, menacingly to her at least in my mind, next to her murderer.

I envisioned placing Nell next to her father at Clark's River and placing a tasteful, elegant, medium-sized, above-ground, and slanted-face granite stone, selected in a feminine color, on her grave, with the inscription as follows:

IN LOVING MEMORY

NELL ANNIE

FREEMAN TUCKER

"PEEPEYES"

JULY 16, 1910-JANUARY 6, 1969

BELOVED WIFE, MOTHER & GRANDMOTHER

When exploring the legalities of exhuming Nell's remains, I discovered there are two entirely separate and different procedures to follow. One tract was followed for exhuming for the purposes of autopsy and reburial in the same location. Another tract was followed for exhuming and relocation of remains to another burial location. They were not one and the same processes. Getting my siblings, the McCracken County Health Department, and perhaps a court judge to agree to the exhumation and autopsy was one hurdle to cross. Getting all those parties to agree to a relocation of her remains to another cemetery was another hurdle, and a higher one than the first. Ideally it would have been best to do the exhumation, autopsy, and reburial at Clark's River (not the original grave site next to Leon at Mt. Kenton Cemetery in Paducah) all in one step, so Nell's remains wouldn't have to be disturbed more than once.

I came to the conclusion that without some support from my siblings for the reburial at Clark's River, I could not justify seeking the reburial alone. I was told by the Health Department that reburials were normally only allowed in the case where the original burial location was being destroyed by development or construction, or flooded, or not being tended and cared for by the cemetery. Family unification was normally not sufficient justification to allow relocation of remains. Also, I would have to show that Nell would have wanted this relocation, and it was not just my wish alone. Even the agreement of all my siblings wouldn't be sufficient to gain the necessary approval. I could not prove with any documents where Nell would have wanted to be buried, since she died before writing a will. She never stated to anyone where she wanted to be buried. She didn't leave any letters, diaries, journals, or anything else in writing indicating where she wanted to be buried. For all the Health Department knew,

269

Nell was buried exactly where she wanted to be, next to Leon in Mt. Kenton Cemetery. They wouldn't allow that to be changed without a compelling reason. My preference wasn't a compelling reason. Family unification wasn't a compelling reason. Leon would never be tried and convicted of her murder, and therefore I couldn't establish legally the compelling reason. I had to accept what I could not change.

To try to determine what Nell might have wanted for a burial location if she could have expressed her wishes before dying, I examined what remained of Nell's life. Did Nell still love Leon at the time of her death, such that she would have wanted to be buried next to him, or did she merely fear him, such that she couldn't leave him? While it was known Nell tried to divorce Leon once in the late 1950s and was scared out of it by Leon, there is one physical piece of evidence surviving today that might indicate Nell's feelings at the end of her life. We found in Nell's jewelry box, which Frank had kept all his life as a keepsake memento of his mother, a small heart-shaped locket. When the locket was opened, it revealed a black-and-white photo of Frank in his teens on one side, and a black-and-white photo of a middle-aged Leon on the other side. They were the two men Nell loved in her lifetime (outside of her father, Allen Freeman). It was known that Nell wore the locket frequently even into her older years. The fact that she kept Leon's picture with her on a day-to-day basis might reasonably indicate that she still loved him, despite all he had done to her. Leon had basically abandoned Nell after World War II to support herself at a time when it wasn't easy for single women without an education and with a child to support themselves. He did this while he was shacked up with Audrey for the next twenty-four years. Leon was violent to Nell at times. Despite all of that, she likely still loved him, as perhaps evidenced by the photo in the locket she wore.

It is possible I may revisit the autopsy idea in the future, should technology develop such that I believe a reasonably good chance of determining her cause of death would be achieved by doing an autopsy, or I get other opinions from other forensic pathologists that contradict the two I spoke with (Dr. Sims and Dr. LeVaughn). I would just endure whatever family repercussions that came about by pursuing it if there was a good chance of achieving my goal, medically determining the cause of death.

I felt like I wanted to do something for Nell. In a strange way, I felt I wanted to try to make it all up to her. I certainly bore no responsibility for the injustice that happened to her. I was not even five years old at the time. But I just couldn't get over the naked injustice of it all. I felt saddened that I never got to do anything for Nell before she died. I never got to tell her I loved her to her face—not that I remember. If I did, it was likely at the prompting of my parents, like usually happens with little kids. I never got to buy her a birthday or Christmas gift, or make her something at school. I never got to do something for her around her house, like a grandson might do, such as mow her lawn, shovel her snow, move heavy furniture, or even just bring in her groceries for her. It saddened me that not only was Nell cheated out of her older years by being murdered at fifty-eight years old, but so many others were cheated out of what we had coming also. I had years of opportunities coming to me to have encounters creating memories with my grandmother, and I got cheated out of those. Leon took so much from our family when he murdered Nell. He didn't just take from Nell herself, but from all of us.

Except for two memories that I've made a point to permanently burn into my mind (described in the first chapter), I hardly remember Nell in person, just from photos. I couldn't fill this void left behind by Nell's passing—her absence was noticeable. That's why I wanted to try to do something for her. Perhaps solving the mystery of her death was enough. Letting the family and the world know how she died was perhaps enough. I contemplated the relocation of her remains to Symsonia as one of the last things I could do for Nell—to please her—to do something she would have wanted. But alas, I had to face the reality of the legal restrictions keeping me from doing so. Yet it still haunts me.

This journey I went on in late 2005 and almost all of 2006 wasn't something I had planned or foreseen. It just kind of dropped in my lap at Frank's funeral in October 2005. Just as I discovered I had a half-sister I never knew, and I rediscovered a half-brother I knew existed but thought I would never see again, additionally getting the spark to start on this journey made that funeral of my father's the most bizarre single event of my life. In addition, my father's passing was the tipping point for the final separation between me and another feuding sibling. The events surrounding my father's death and his estate tipped that precariously perched relationship into estrangement. This significant amount of events all happening as a result of one man dying couldn't have been just coincidence—it had to be fate.

I didn't want to find what I found on this journey. I wanted very much to find the opposite. I set out with the intention to clear my grandfather's name of suspicion, clear my family's name of any related stigma, and harness the needed armaments to do battle in the future against this recurring, insidious rumor. Every step of the way, as I found out more evidence, it seemed to open more doors. There seemed to be a trail of crumbs to follow, almost as if someone were leading me along to find the evidence. I wondered to myself, was it possible that Nell was guiding me on my journey of discovery? I'm not a spiritual person at all, and I have difficulty believing in the occult. But it was eerie how the crumbs of evidence just kept falling in my lap, trailing in a direction for me to follow to keep finding more and more. If was like some force was wanting me to find this truth that was so deeply buried.

Considering this event I was investigating was thirty-seven years old, and little to no documentation was done at the time about it, it was amazing I was able to find anything at all about it. Furthermore, it was amazing that after thirty-seven years, there would still be people alive that remembered the events, in some cases were witnesses to the event, and could tell me what they saw or remembered. That I could find all of those people, most of whom I was related to yet had never met, was also amazing.

How did I feel about Leon now? After coming to the conclusion that he was guilty of Nell's murder, I had a heavy heart about my grandfather for several months. I resisted the urge to hate him—hate his memory. How could he have done such a thing? It just didn't make any sense. It was such an evil thing to have done. The frustration I felt that he got away with it was palpable. I know one of the first things parents teach their children is that life isn't always fair. But this seemed to be over-the-top unfairness—a gross injustice—that a gentle, lovely woman was murdered, and no one cared enough to investigate it (except her sister Grace). How could my father not have investigated this more? I know he feared Leon until Leon died. He feared learning the truth even after Leon died because he thought it might be too hard to take. He feared it might have driven him crazy had he discovered the truth.

I still remember the good times with Leon during the years I knew him. Nothing will ever erase those memories. In a way I'll always love Leon in my memory—despite what he did. After all, he was my grandfather. Just the kinship feelings alone are enough to keep me from hating Leon's memory. But I cannot deny that my memory of him has been forever changed—denigrated to some extent. I now recognize so many moments in my memory of times I looked at him, saw a look on his face, and I now understand that look in a completely different way. I now know what he was thinking, when before I didn't. He was concealing this huge secret. He had to have thought about Nell every time he was around our family—every time he was around Frank, for the rest of his life. Perhaps living with the guilt of what he did was his punishment—who knows?

Can I temper my feelings of condemnation for Leon for what he did with the recognition that he was diagnosed as mentally ill? While this doesn't excuse what he did, it does explain it. I believe Leon still knew right from wrong, proven by his repentance late in his life. If he was mentally ill in 1969 when he did this act, it might be a mitigating factor in deciding his punishment, but I don't believe it excuses the act such that he should not be held responsible for it.

This journey has been an emotional one. I started with irritation, segued into curiosity, moved on to determination, continued on through shock and amazement, then experienced incredulity, next felt anger well up in me, and finally arrived at feeling resoluteness and acceptance. That was quite a roller coaster of emotions to feel, some overlapping along the way. It's almost akin to the emotions felt when there is a loss in a family, and specific steps are followed to reach final acceptance. Only this journey took almost a year to complete those steps. Writing this book not only was useful for me as an organizational tool to make sense out of all the disparate pieces of evidence, but also was actually therapeutic and cathartic in that it allowed me to vent what I was thinking and feeling. Imagine me trying to keep all that is in this book bottled up inside myself—I would have exploded.

On this journey I also accomplished a few side things that I hadn't expected. I discovered a family I never knew I had. I traced my family's history as far back as the middle 1800s. I visited locations where my family's history took place, such as Kentucky, Florida, and Arkansas. I uncovered the culture of rural Kentucky in the 1900s, and how it explained so much of my grandfather's and my father's behaviors.

I couldn't close this book without addressing the disturbing revelations about slave ownership in my family's past. Never had anyone mentioned to me in our family lore that there was slave ownership by our ancestors. I don't think anyone entertained the possibility because our ancestors were known to be poor farmers, not wealthy landowners, or even the middle-class. My great-great-grandfather, Levi Tucker (Leon's grandfather), inherited "one Negro slave" from his father-in-law, and moved to the then-slave state of Arkansas (pre-civil war). My great-great-grandmother, Sally Rose (grandmother to Peepeyes), was pictured being held as an infant by what we assume is a slave girl. I certainly take no pride in these findings. At the same time I feel no shame in them either. I had nothing to do with any of it. I personally find the idea of slave ownership repugnant and unthinkable. But that doesn't make me believe these people that lived at this time were all fundamentally bad people because they owned slaves. Rather, they were a product of a place and time—a culture where slave ownership was considered normal. Agreed, there were those who opposed slavery on moral grounds even at the time in question here, the mid-1800s. But the culture of the southern states at that time accepted slavery as normal, and my ancestors were brought up in that culture. I suspect our descendants living a hundred years from now might find some of our present-day customs and culture to be shocking, such as the persisting discrimination we see against certain segments of our population even today.

I now put this issue of my grandmother's death to rest. I've done all I could to resolve this mystery in my family's history. I hope Nell can rest in peace, knowing that her family—the world in fact—now knows the truth of how she died. I close by wondering aloud, directly to Nell—"Did I do right, Peepeyes? Was it what you would have wanted?" I can never know her answer.

*   *   *

Three generational picture; Frank, Leon & Dwain Tucker, circa 1984.
Frank is standing, Leon is at left, and a rather bored looking Dwain is at right.

Epilogue

What's the future for the Tucker family? I hate to say it, but demise for the Tucker name appears likely. Out of the ten children that my great-grandfather George W. Tucker had, only four were boys to carry on the Tucker name—Corbett, Remus, Rob, and Leon. All six women married and changed their last names, so the Tucker line stopped there. Corbett Tucker had four children, two boys and two girls, Corbett Jr. known as "Son," Owen known as "Blue," Dorothy, and Bertie Lee. Of Corbett's two sons, only Owen had sons himself, named Owen Jr. and Leonard. Both of them don't have sons themselves and are too old now to have any more children. So the Tucker line stops there with them. Remus Tucker had only daughters.

Rob Tucker had two sons, but both died in infancy. Leon, my grandfather, was the only one who produced a male offspring lineage that continues on carrying the Tucker name forward. Leon had one son, my father Frank, and my father had three sons. Of those three, one had a son, who is my nephew, Spencer Tucker. Spencer is eighteen years old as I write this, and I'm already encouraging him to strive to have at least one son in his lifetime. He's the end of the line for the Tucker name, at least this branch of it, the descendants of George W. Tucker. It's sort of amazing out of that many descendants, it all comes down to resting on one pair of shoulders, Spencer's, to perpetuate the Tucker name.

Of the people in this book, most are elderly, and I would suppose plan to just finish their lives in quiet retirement. Tillie Edwards fills her time with her gardening and decorating her home. Her progeny still living, which are her daughter, Pam, and the children of her son Brad (deceased) help care for Tillie. I still visit Tillie whenever I am in the Midwest, and I stop by to say hello to Eddie Stevenson as well. Eddie still goes to Okeechobee for fishing now and then. Eddie keeps saying he wants to have a pig roast with beer one of these times when I visit and invite all the relation in the area. I told him I'd take him up on that offer one of these days.

Frances Lemanski still encourages me to visit her in Caseyville, Illinois, when I can, and each time I do, she seems to remember some new tidbit of family history that she hadn't told me before. I shared with her some video we had of my father's last wedding to Audra Lance, which Leon and Audrey attended. She told me that was the only video of her mother, Audrey, that her family had ever seen. Audra Lance fills her time taking care of her many grandkids and now great-grandkids, and living a peaceful retirement in Red Bud, Illinois.

I visit Illinois and Kentucky less frequently nowadays. Since both my parents are gone, I have less reason to go there anymore. However, I'll one day be buried in Illinois, in a cemetery in the small central Illinois town of Chesterfield. That is where my mother's parents, Glen and Ruth Bond, are buried. My mother Judy is buried there also, beside her father. My father Frank is buried there also, at his request, a few feet away from his beloved Judy. Our family has more plots adjacent to these available for future use by me and my relatives. I hope I won't need it for forty or more years, but it's reassuring to know my place with my family is already reserved.

The relationship I have with my half-brother Trent is still distant but cordial, and I hope to keep those lines of communication open in the future. The same goes for my newly discovered half-sister, Sharon, with whom I've now established contact. I'll make the effort with both of them, with realistic expectations. I plan on putting this writing habit aside for a while, having spent a couple of years writing this effort as well as my own autobiography. I'll continue with my work in engineering, planning to retire in about fifteen years when I'll be in my late fifties. I love to travel internationally, and do so almost every year. I'll also continue my pursuit of an acting career, still striving for my big break that is long overdue.

I always tell people that are retiring that they shouldn't worry about finding something to do when they're not working full time anymore. I tell them that everyone has at least one book to write, one song to compose, one sculpture to sculpt, one painting to paint, etc. I've at least checked off one of those on that list with this book. At the risk of being immodest, I think I did more than just that. I contributed something real and valuable to my family's history. I solved a mystery that had stigmatized our family for close to four decades. I didn't remove that stigma, but rather focused it onto one person—Leon. Rumor no longer plagues our entire family. I feel the rest of the family have been cleansed by this book.

It's been a fascinating ride for me. I hope it was interesting for the reader coming along.

Dwain S. Tucker
Venice, California
2006

*   *   *

STATE OF FLORIDA

OFFICE of VITAL STATISTICS

CERTIFIED COPY

STATE BOARD OF HEALTH
BUREAU OF VITAL STATISTICS

CERTIFICATE OF DEATH
FLORIDA

STATE FILE NO. 69-004662

REGISTRAR'S NO.

1. PLACE OF DEATH a. COUNTY	CODE NO.	2. USUAL RESIDENCE (Where deceased lived. If institution: Residence before admission) a. STATE	b. COUNTY
Okeechobee	57-027	Kentucky	McCracken
b. CITY, TOWN, OR LOCATION	c. IS PLACE OF DEATH INSIDE CITY LIMITS? YES☐ NO☐	c. CITY, TOWN, OR LOCATION	d. IS RESIDENCE INSIDE CITY LIMITS? YES☐ NO☐
Okeechobee		Paducah	
d. NAME OF HOSPITAL OR INSTITUTION (If not in hospital, give street address)		d. STREET ADDRESS	
Okeechobee General Hospital		Unknown	RR-16

3. NAME OF DECEASED (Type or print)	First Nellie	Middle Annie	Last Tucker	4. DATE OF DEATH	Month January	Day 6,	Year 1969
5. SEX female	6. COLOR OR RACE White	7. MARRIED☒ NEVER MARRIED☐ WIDOWED☐ DIVORCED☐	8. DATE OF BIRTH 7/16/19 August 12, 1919	9. AGE (In years last birthday) 49	IF UNDER 1 YEAR Months Days	IF UNDER 24 HRS Hours Min.	

10a. USUAL OCCUPATION (Give kind of work done during most of working life, even if retired) House Wife	10b. KIND OF BUSINESS OR INDUSTRY HOME	11. BIRTHPLACE (State or foreign country) Kentucky	12. CITIZEN OF WHAT COUNTRY? U.S.A..
13. FATHER'S NAME Allen Freeman		14. MOTHER'S MAIDEN NAME Annie Ford	
16. SOCIAL SECURITY NO. Unavailable	17. INFORMANT'S SIGNATURE Elbert Tucker 1225 N. 52thStreet Address E. St. Louis, Ill.		

18. CAUSE OF DEATH [Enter only one cause per line for (a), (b), and (c)]		INTERVAL BETWEEN ONSET AND DEATH
PART I. DEATH WAS CAUSED BY: IMMEDIATE CAUSE (a)	Unknown (D.O.A.)	
Conditions, if any, which gave rise to above cause (a), stating the underlying cause last.	DUE TO (b)	
	DUE TO (c)	
PART II. OTHER SIGNIFICANT CONDITIONS CONTRIBUTING TO DEATH BUT NOT RELATED TO THE TERMINAL DISEASE CONDITION GIVEN IN PART I(a)		19. WAS AUTOPSY PERFORMED? YES☐ NO☒

20a. (Probably) ACCIDENT☐ SUICIDE☐ HOMICIDE☐	20b. DESCRIBE HOW INJURY OCCURRED (Enter nature of injury in Part I or Part II of Item 18)	
20c. TIME OF INJURY	Hour a.m. p.m.	Month, Day, Year	
20d. INJURY OCCURRED WHILE AT WORK☐ NOT WHILE AT WORK☐	20e. PLACE OF INJURY (e.g., in or about home, farm, factory, street, office bldg., etc.)	20f. CITY, TOWN, OR LOCATION	COUNTY	STATE

21. I attended the deceased from 1/6/69 to 1/6/69 and last saw her alive on DOA Death occurred at DOA	Degree or title:	22b. ACCIDENT	22c. DATE SIGNED 1/9/69
22a. SIGNATURE Steve R. Johnston, M. D. Okeechobee, Fla			

23a. BURIAL CREMATION REMOVAL (Specify) Removal	23b. DATE 1-7-69	23c. NAME OF CEMETERY OR CREMATORY MT. KENTON CEMETERY	23d. LOCATION (City, town, or county) Paducah, Kentucky	(State)
24. FUNERAL DIRECTOR'S SIGNATURE YATES FUNERAL HOME OKEECHOBEE, FLORIDA	25. DATE REC'D BY LOCAL REG. Jan. 9, 1969	26. REGISTRAR'S SIGNATURE Geneva Ruckle, D.R.		

C. Meade Grijji , State Registrar

Date Issued: NOV 02 2005

HEALTH

DH FORM 1046 (08-04)

B2203066   CERTIFICATION OF VITAL RECORD

2203066

Nell Tucker's death certificate

THE FACE OF THIS DOCUMENT HAS A COLORED BACKGROUND - NOT A WHITE BACKGROUND

1364023

PLACE OF BIRTH

County McCracken

City of ____

DELAYED COMMONWEALTH OF KENTUCKY

NOTE—All facts must be given as of the Date of the Birth being recorded.

STATE BOARD OF HEALTH
OFFICE OF VITAL STATISTICS

Special Certificate of Birth and Affidavits
(For Use in Recording Births Occurring Prior to 1911)

No. ____ St. ____

File No. 48822

2 FULL NAME OF CHILD *Nellie Annie Freeman*

3 Sex of Child	4 Legit—more?	5 Twin, Triplet or other	6 Number in order of birth	7 Date of Birth
Female	Yes			July 16 1910

8 FULL NAME FATHER	14 FULL MAIDEN NAME MOTHER
Allen Franklin Freeman	Annie Gertrude Ford

9 POST OFFICE AT TIME OF THIS BIRTH	15 POST OFFICE AT TIME OF THIS BIRTH
Symsonia, Kentucky	Symsonia Kentucky

10 COLOR OR RACE	11 AGE AT TIME OF THIS BIRTH	16 COLOR OR RACE	17 AGE AT TIME OF THIS BIRTH
White	38 (Years)	White	23

12 BIRTHPLACE	18 BIRTHPLACE
Graves County	Graves County

Affidavit: I hereby declare upon oath that the above statements are true. (to be signed by registrant)

Signature *Nellie Annie Tucker* 1603 Little Ave. Paducah Ky. 42001

Subscribed and sworn to before me September 28 1968

(SEAL)

My Commission Expires March 12, 1972

(APPLICANT—DO NOT WRITE BELOW THIS LINE)

Abstract of Supporting Evidence

	Name and Kind of Document	Date Original Document Was Made
1	Affadavit: Thomas S. Fike Non-relative Age 86	9-28-68
2	McCracken County, Kentucky School Census record	9-10-23
3	Policy # 7118508 Prudential Life Ins. Co. Baltimore, MD.	6-12-37
4		

Information Concerning Registrant As Stated in Documents

	Birth Date or Age	Birthplace	Name of Father	Maiden Name of Mother
1	X	X	X	X
2	July 16, 1910		X	
3	26 next birthday			
4				

Additional Information: ____

Signature *Lewis C. Bush* State Registrar, Reviewing Official

Date Filed Oct. 3, 1968 (over)

Form YS-18-2

THE BACK OF THIS DOCUMENT CONTAINS AN ARTIFICIAL WATERMARK - HOLD AT AN ANGLE TO VIEW

Nell Tucker's delayed birth certificate.

SERVICE NUMBER: 36782720

CATEGORY:	CODE:	EXPLANATION:
RANK:	2	Enlisted Man (includes Aviation Cadet or Student)
AGE:	33	33
RACE:	1	White (includes Mexican)
YEARS OF SVC:	4	6-12 mo.
ARM OF SERVICE:	99	Unassigned and Assignments (Not Elsewhere Classified)
AAF STATUS:	0	Neither assigned nor attached to AAF (includes all unassigned, and all Arm or Service known with no mention of AAF)
ADMISSION STATION:	6188	Ft. Sheridan, Illinois
ADMISSION MO/YR:	7 5	July 1945
LAST TREAT FACILITY:	6	Regional Hospital
SPECIAL CLASS:	0	None
TYPE OF CASE:	J	Disease
TYPE OF ADMISSION:	x	Readmission case, Same diagnosis, EPTS (Existed Prior To entry on active military Service)
FIRST DIAGNOSIS:	4632	Emotional instability, cycloid, inadequate personality, prepsychotic, schizoid
LOCATION:	-	Not Found
OPERATION:	-	Not Found
SECOND DIAGNOSIS:	-	Not Found
LOCATION:	-	Not Found
OPERATION:	-	Not Found
THIRD DIAGNOSIS:	-	Not Found
CAUSATIVE AGENT:	-	Not Found
CIRCUMSTANCES:	-	Not a traumatism
FINAL RESULT:	000	Discharge/retirement: med reasons--but not for any residual condition w/ a code
NON-EFFECTIVE DAYS		
Total Days:	000	Carded for Record Only
Overseas Days:	000	Case admitted in US
TYPE OF DISPOSITION:	3	Discharged or Retired for Inaptness, etc. (includes all discharges under old Section VIII, new ARs 615-368 or 369 for CPS, etc.)
FIELD OF CAUSE OF DEATH OR DISCHARGE:	1	First Diagnosis field
DISPOSITION MO/YR:	7 5	July 1945
HOSP DAYS (GH/CH):	000	Carded for Record Only
DAYS IN LAST GH/CH:	-	Unknown
SPEC TREAT:	-	Not Found
G/C HOSPITAL:		No entry made
SAMPLE SIZE:	7	Not Found

Source: This information was obtained from the Hospital Admission Card data files (1942-1945; 1950-1954), created by the Office of the Surgeon General, Department of the Army. During 1988, this secondary source material was made available to the National Personnel Records Center by the National Research Council, a current custodian of the data file. The file was originally compiled for statistical purposes; therefore, name identification does not exist and sampling techniques were used with the result that not all hospital admissions are included. Veterans on the file are identified by service number and other data related to hospital admission.

Leon Tucker's military hospital discharge report

Appendix

How to Investigate a Family Mystery

In preparing to market this book, I took a class on writing query letters to literary agents. In that class, a fellow writer, April, suggested the missing component to my book was to explain how I did the investigation. She suggested that the readers might be curious as to how I uncovered all these stories and records in this investigation. I needed to include this information, so the readers could investigate their own family mysteries be they suspected murders, genealogy, secret siblings or relation previously unknown, or just old family stories.

There are several methods I used to do this investigation, and I must say I discovered them all by accident. I didn't have a guidebook to follow on any of this and just stumbled my way through it over the course of about two years. The easiest way for me to explain how I did this is instructively, rather than describing my recollections, which are already detailed in the book.

Recovering Your Own Memories

The easiest place to start investigating a family mystery is to write down what you already know. You'll be surprised at how much you already know but just don't know how to dig it out of your memory. To trigger your memories, dig out old photos albums, and any family mementos. Try to recreate the scenes inside those photos in your head. Try to recreate the path that each of these family mementos took in their existence as they passed from person to person. Write down all the places you have lived, worked, and went to school in your lifetime, and where your family members have lived, worked, and went to school. Go revisit those locations if possible. You'll be surprised at how many memories come flooding back when you physically visit the places of your youth, or where your family members lived and worked during their lifetimes.

Finding People

The next step investigating is to contact family members, especially ones you didn't even know you had. To locate all of your relation, as that's where the detailed information on the family history would be, use the following Web sites:

Genealogy Research: *www.ancestry.com*
Phone Number Search: *www.whitepages.com*
People Search: *www.zabasearch.com*

These three together, using them to cross-reference each other, is a great way to locate a long-lost family member. Ancestry.com can help you find listings of the person by their family connection, which helps you eliminate them down from the hundreds of others in the country that share their name. That usually leads to the city that they live in, if not their direct telephone number. But some of the data on Ancestry.com comes from sources that are out of date, so I would double-check the information or seek further information from www.whitepages.com. If the person has an unlisted phone number or no longer has a landline phone and relies only on cell phones, a last resort is www.zabasearch.com. I don't know what databases zabasearch.com pulls from, but it's uncanny how it can find someone who even has an unlisted phone number. When using Zabasearch, you will get a long list of names and addresses found within the state you specify. You can search within that list with the Find feature under the pull-down menu of Edit under most Internet browsers. Enter any city you are looking for in particular, and it will advance to that city within the listed results. Zabasearch also provides extra information, like birth years, if available. That will aid you in deciphering between many similar names. Once you've eliminated it down to just a few people that might be the person you are seeking, then you have to just cold-call all the numbers listed until you find the person you're seeking. Note that the Zabasearch results are somewhat alphabetical, but if you scroll down, you will find more results that are not alphabetical. Also, sometimes people list their names by initials or spouse names, not their own first names.

One additional note on Ancestry.com, that it is a subscription service, so I recommend you decide early on how long you think this investigation will take. If it will take a year, then purchase a yearly subscription at a much lower price than the monthly rate. But if the project is of a relatively short duration, then a monthly rate would be the better choice. Another helpful pointer on Ancestry.com is that you should quickly construct your family tree with their software, Family Tree Maker, and then upload it to Ancestry.com database. This allows other people researching their family trees to find yours, and then e-mail you. I can't tell you how many people contacted me after I uploaded my extensive family tree to Ancestry.com, most of whom were distant cousins I never knew I had. They gave me even more information and photos of my family history, and it definitely aided me in the investigation detailed in this book.

Interviewing Relation

Once you've located family members to contact and then interview, start preparing how you will conduct the interviews. Lay the groundwork on what you will ask about. Plan how you will approach these family members, many of whom will be strangers to you, and more importantly, you being a stranger to them.

APPROACHING FAMILY ELDERS: Seek out family elders first, as they will have the longest memories and the most information for you. Visit them in person, but first call them to clear the way. Tell them how you are related to them if they don't immediately recognize your name, and prime their memory of you by offering a few general family memories to establish the family connection. Clearly outline the family tree relation—how you are related to them—so they can feel comfortable accepting a visit by you. Make reference to old photos that you have that they might be interested in, photos of their parents or of them when they were very young. Your possession of mysterious photos will be irresistible to the relation and will peak their interest in having you visit them. It also helps prove you are who you say you are if you have photos of people they will recognize, thus establishing a trust level. Offer to deliver the photos in person and make a brief visit to ask them some questions on family history. If you sense any resistance, don't press them on it, instead offer to mail them the photos. This allows the family member, usually an elderly person, to first receive the photos to prove you are not a con artist but are actually a family relation.

You can even offer to meet the family elder at a restaurant and offer to buy them a meal. Offer to meet with them in a group of other family relation they already know if you sense they feel awkward or fearful of meeting you alone. Meeting with a person they've met only by phone and don't know personally, although they know they are related to you, is sometimes daunting, particularly to a frail, elderly person. The family elder may feel fearful to have you come to their home directly, so offering to meet them at a public place may make them feel more at ease. This worked for me with the Mitchell cousins, but I failed to do this with some of the Stevenson cousins, as a few of them (but not all) refused to meet with me in person and would only allow me to interview them by phone.

Once you've obtained their permission to visit them, make copies of photos from your family albums already in your possession to take with you to your visits with your relation. Most of these photos are from long before digital photography or even 35 mm negative photography, so you'll need to scan these old photos with your computer. Upload these scanned photos to a photo printing Web site, then pick them up or have them mailed to you, but picking them up in person speeds your investigation. Costco (www.costco.com) is cheapest on a per print basis, and you don't need to me a member of Costco to use their online photo service. Walmart (www.walmart.com) is also good and cheap. Walgreens (www.walgreens.com) will allow you to pick up photos at any of their locations nationwide. This last point is important, the versatility of picking up the photos anywhere nationwide, because you may be traveling at a location not near your home and need to retrieve some photos you forgot or need extra copies. Having them already uploaded to a national chain's Web site, so you can pick them up anywhere they have a store, is very convenient. You can use the Internet connection at any local library you are near, go on the photo Web site, order the prints, and pick them up locally where you happen to be traveling.

In going to visit your family relation, bring extra photos that have not been identified yet to ask the family elder you are visiting to help you identify the people in the pictures. Also take with you a portable photo scanner with your laptop computer. This allows you to scan and copy their photos that they have without having to ask to borrow them, which most people will be reluctant to permit. When arranging the visit, you could suggest to them that they have their own photo albums retrieved, out, and ready for you to examine when you get there.

When beginning the interview, if you fear you may lose something in note-taking, you can always ask the family member if they mind if you tape record the interview. It may intimidate them, but you can also point out that their children may like to get a copy of this tape for a record of their parent's voices and stories. Remark to them how these recordings are treasured later on by descendants—especially videotaping the interview. Offer to provide copies to their children, so they can hear the stories of the family history also. This usually will soothe any nervousness about being recorded by the family elder. These recordings will also greatly aid one in getting the stories down on paper completely.

Tell the family elder of the stories you remember or have already uncovered, and ask them to give you more details of the stories you already know. All of this, the family photos you are sharing, the stories you are sharing, will "prime the pump" of their own memory. After doing all of this, the family elder will feel very comfortable with you and be open to discussing anything else you might want to ask them.

Invariably you will uncover in your discussions some deep, dark family secret that is unsavory or unpleasant, or even shameful or embarrassing for certain individuals. This can include illegitimate children, criminal records, violence in families, substance abuse problems, or family bitterness and estrangements. When you have to ask about something that is uncomfortable, like a surly reputation of a family member in the past, such as Leon and his brothers in this book, you might first state that you already know these facts and are simply asking for confirmation from them. Tell them these people are already gone, nothing they say about these deceased people matters now, and that you won't be insulted or hurt at all if they are candid with you. Tell them you are eager to hear the "good, the bad, and the ugly" truth, all of it, with no reservations. Tell them that nothing they tell you now that might be unsavory about a family member in the past will change your positive memories of them now—it's just harmless history to retell and record for posterity. When discussing with a family member any information that is uncomfortable, you might want to change topics over to something positive or neutral—at least temporarily—so that they don't withdraw from you. You can even say that you will come back at another time if you feel they are beginning to get weary. In conducting my own interviews, I always remembered that these people were in their elder years and tired easily. Usually with an elderly person, two hours of conversation was the maximum time possible before one's welcome begins to wane.

Tell the family member that you believe it's important that the accurate history be written down before the "old-timers" are all gone, and that should be sufficient for these family elders you are interviewing to pour out what they know. Elderly folk seem to have a commonality—they want to preserve the memories of their time, the age in which they lived, and are usually eager to tell those stories to anyone interested in recording them for posterity. You can also point out that we here in this time don't judge what people did in the past because we don't know what agreements they had with each other, such as open marriage agreements or what motivations people had for doing what they did. They aren't here in the present to defend themselves, so we really can't judge them fairly. Repeat this line of reasoning to the family elder that is displaying reticence about telling you something negative about another family member, and this may smooth the path for them to continue with the details they know.

When talking about something that might embarrass a family member, like violence reported by their parents in the past, don't mention it first, let them tell their story and bring it up. If you mention something too personal like that, the family member may feel embarrassed and cut off the conversation. You'll not get information on other subjects. If you must ask about it, delay asking about the sensitive subjects until you've exhausted all other areas and the conversation is closing, then ask about the sensitive subjects. Realize you may compromise your ability to get further information down the road. As you discover more details from other sources on these family stories, you may want to contact these previous sources again to verify the stories or use these new details to jog their memories. If you've previously "burned the bridge" by asking about sensitive material that either embarrassed or offended them, then you won't be able to contact them again in the future if need be. So it's a judgment call and a gamble if it's worth asking about something sensitive in your early meetings.

Even though the family elder that you are interviewing may have the beginnings of dementia or Alzheimer's, you might be surprised that long-term memory appears to be the last thing to go. Short-term memory is the first to go, but people seem to remember with remarkable clarity the details of old family history that occurred decades earlier.

One caveat to remember—when evaluating what the family elders are telling you, always remember to ask if they saw this firsthand or heard it from another. Word of mouth tends to inflate stories to bigger than they actually were, as each storyteller adds their own level of intensity to the story to make it more interesting. If you are hearing it firsthand, it's a good bet there is little amplification. If it's a story handed down through many people, you might be getting a greatly exaggerated story. Only corroboration from many sources will lead you to a story you can feel confident is the truth of what happened.

In summary, people want to tell their story. Most family elders love to be the "Great Storyteller"—to recount the family history as they know they are the only ones who can. For a brief moment, these family elders get the respect they feel they are due because people are asking them for what they know, so most are eager to share. Ask them for telephone numbers of other family members or the cities where they are located. Be sure to ask for married names of female relatives or maiden names of women that married into your family, as women in the past almost always changed their maiden names when they married, which nowadays isn't always the case.

PHOTO SHARING: One final note on photo scanning and printing—Walmart and most major drugstore chains now have stand-alone photo scanning and printing devices in their stores that come in excellent for reproducing photos. You can borrow photos from a family member and return them before you leave town, or the family member can come with you to the store for the scanning and printing if they don't wish to loan out their photos. This assumes you can't afford a portable scanner and laptop computer to do the scanning of their photos at their home. A portable photo scanner (a flatbed scanner is best as some photos you will be scanning are not small, some will be in photo frames, and some will be tin-type photos from the 1800s) can usually be purchased for around $100 at most electronics stores or on the Net, and basic-level laptop computers are under $500 currently.

Scan the old photos into your computer and print out your own copies later. You'll be surprised that in the backgrounds of these old photos, you might find more clues to the lives that these ancestors lived, such as locations, storefronts, uniforms, and even the body language of the people in the pictures. For instance, is the couple in the photo embracing, indicating a close relationship, or do they appear to be strangers in the picture, just merely standing next to each other? Do the facial expressions reveal anything about the mood of the people in the pictures? The old adage of a picture being worth a thousand words will be proven true in this investigation.

Government Records

Searching government records takes time, patience, diligence, and a wee bit of ingenuity. I say ingenuity because each government office operates in a different way—there is no standard format that you can learn and then apply to each office you go to. You have to be open to learning each new format. The good news is that the records you seek are almost always there to be found—you just have to be persistent, dogged, and unflinching when you hit the initial roadblocks you inevitably will run into. Don't allow yourself to become frustrated as this will only delay you, and likely alienate the "counter people" at these government agencies you encounter such that they will not help you. Making friends with these "counter people" is essential if you are to get from that office what you seek. A few compliments their direction or a friendly comment about the weather outside goes a long way to establishing a pleasant rapport with these people who are likely bored witless at their jobs. Also, don't allow an initial negative result to deter you from looking further, as you might not be looking in the right area of their records. Ask for help—tell them in detail what you are seeking—and if the right rapport has been established at the beginning, you will usually get the help you need.

In general, I discovered when you are talking with a person at a governmental agency that is not related to you, you can make the call personal by revealing you are searching for information to solve a family mystery that has some importance to you. Usually that will be enough to engage the person on the other end of the phone or the other side of the counter. I found that people love to help in solving a problem or unraveling a mystery. Don't immediately burn a bridge by asking to speak to a supervisor. Only resort to that if you can't get a solid answer from the frontline person answering the phone at that office, or sense they don't know the answer to your question and are faking like they do. Try not to offend them by asking to speak to a supervisor, rather couch it in terms such as "Thanks for trying to help me, but perhaps you weren't trained or exposed to the issue I'm asking about? Is there someone else there, an old-timer, that might be able to help me, or perhaps a supervisor as a last resort?" That'll go down a lot easier than acting like you aren't respecting the frontline person by early on asking to speak to their supervisor.

Here's a brief rundown on some of the government records I sought in this investigation:

- BIRTH & DEATH CERTIFICATES: Seeking birth or death certificates can be done nationwide through www.vitalchek.com. You will have to pay a fee, and it's not cheap (usually under $25 for the record and $20 for overnight mailing). However, you can minimize your costs by requesting standard mail rather than overnight mailing of the documents. Also, you might request a simple photocopy, not an official, stamped version, of the document if you are only seeking the information on it. That might lower the cost, and also speed the processing and delivery of your order.

  When examining birth and death certificates, look at all the boxes on the document. See if every single piece of information on it is accurate. A death certificate must be signed by the physician or medical examiner examining the remains of the deceased. Try to contact the physician or medical examiner if they still live. Contacting the hospital that they worked at in the location where the death occurred is a great starting point. Ask them if any medical records exist of the examination of the deceased. You'll have to be a family member if you want access to these records—so it isn't exactly lying to say you are a "family member" and not advertise that you aren't an "immediate family member," if that's the case.

  If the doctor or medical examiner doesn't work there anymore, ask to speak to the hospital's Personnel Department or Human Resources

287

Department, and ask for their current contact information. Be honest—don't lie about why you want to contact them. You may get the information or you may not. If the Personnel Department refuses to give you the current contact information for the person you seek to talk to because of privacy concerns, then ask that they forward a letter from you to the party you seek in lieu of giving you their current address. This protects their privacy, but still allows you to contact them.

Another way of contacting medical professionals is through professional associations. Each state has medical licensing boards, usually located in their state capital cities. You can contact these licensing boards for the current work location of the professional unless they are retired. If retired, you can ask for their last work location, and that might give you a city where to search for them. I believe in most states, the current contact information of professionals licensed by the state—medical professionals, lawyers, etc.—is a public record, and therefore merely a request for this information compels them to provide it to you.

Death certificates usually list where the decedent was buried and to which funeral home the remains were released. Try contacting that funeral home and ask for a copy of their records on the funeral. See below for dealing with funeral homes. Also, state archives of each state, usually located in their capital city and sometimes at the state university of that state, have birth, death, and marriage records amassed for as far back as any record ever existed in that state.

Lastly, if you are attempting to get a birth or death certificate, or any government record not of an immediate ancestor and you run into resistance in getting it because of your lack of direct relation, then you can always write to a local judge. The family court of circuit court of any local county within that state has the authority to release a government record, even if not in their immediate jurisdiction but elsewhere in the same state. Write to a judge that presides over family issues, explain you are doing genealogy research, and ask for permission to access a government record not of your own family. Chances are, you'll get it. You won't need to hire a lawyer to write to this judge for this purpose, a simple, detailed letter will suffice.

One other note on birth and death certificates—if they have been changed or altered for any reason over the years, the original will still be on record, with the subsequent changes and documentation establishing the changes all will be kept on file. I know this because I changed Nell Tucker's birth date shown on her death certificate to the correct birth date, and reflected her true age at the time of her death. At the very least, if I couldn't change her cause of death from "unknown," I could at least change her age to accurately reflect how old she was at death.

- MARRIED & DIVORCE RECORDS: County clerk's offices are the locations where marriage records are kept. Circuit court offices are where divorce files are kept, since it's a legal action to dissolve a marriage. Most of their databases are searchable by groom's last name and bride's maiden name, in addition to dates. When contacting them, one should first ask if they can take your request by phone or e-mail. Most operate on the old system of requiring a letter to them. Compose a standard letter giving all the information you have assembled, and there is usually a small fee they require for their search. Ask for the cheaper type of documentation to be sent instead of an "official" copy, stamped and embossed, to save some money. Marriage records can reveal who the parents of the parties were, maiden names if not previously known, and potentially addresses at the time of marriage. Divorce records can be lengthy with all the letters from attorneys and court orders kept. These divorce files are a veritable treasure trove of information regarding violence in marriages, infidelity, money issues, assets owned by the parties, and even documenting behavior as it pertains to character assessment for child-custody disputes. There usually is no fee for a copy of these files, which are usually held on microfiche. Ask for copies of all of them, they can reveal quite a lot and yield many avenues for further research.

   Both marriage and divorce records are usually public documents, though there may be some issues with the divorce records having to be held a certain time before they can be released to the public. Your being a relation, particularly if you are a descendant, and your stating that you are doing research usually smoothes the way to getting the entire divorce file (a copy) sent to you. Birth and death records are not public documents, and usually are only available to immediate descendants or parents of the individual you are researching. Therefore, and I can't advise anyone to lie, but pointing out that you are the next-in-line descendant, all others closer to the decedent are already dead, helps gain you the access you may need. The information you provide on your right to access the information is not verified, it's the honor system, so it's up to the individual how honorable they choose to be pursuing this information. My feeling is, if the person is gone now, their rights aren't infringed upon by the release of their documents now.

- OLD OR FORMER ADDRESSES: Looking for old addresses no longer currently listed on directories on the Net is a bit of a challenge, but here's a good strategy. Go to the city library of any city and ask to see their old city directories or phone books. They are usually kept by the public library of that city. If you can't visit the library in person, you can e-mail from their Web site to the reference librarian and ask politely if they can copy the information for you. They may charge you for the research work or the copying, or if your request is not voluminous, they might not. Be patient—give them time to do it because your request will likely be handed off to volunteer research librarians who will do it when they get around to it, without any urgency. It may take months before you hear a response, but it is perfectly acceptable to call or e-mail a status check within four to six weeks after you make the initial request if you haven't heard a response.

When making your request to them, be as specific as you can with all the information you need. Give names and dates or time frames for them to check. If you give them a wide time range, like "all of the 1900s," that's too large of a time frame, and they will not take it seriously. If you can tighten up the time frame, the volunteer researcher won't view it as that big of a task and be more willing to do it. Always ask for suggestions from them about how you might further your research with what they have in their collection. They might have a local book of interest that you didn't know existed and therefore couldn't have known to ask for the pertinent information to be copied for you. Tell them your goal—what you are trying to achieve—and they might have great suggestions for you. After all, they know their library best. Even do this when you go to a library in person—ask the reference librarian what resources they have that you don't already know about.

- LAW ENFORCEMENT: If a suspected crime occurs in a rural area, the law enforcement agency with jurisdiction over the matter is the county sheriff's office, not the city police of the nearest town. The county sheriff is usually located in the capital city of that county, or what's called the county "seat."

District attorney's offices keep extensive files of any investigation into people's deaths, whether criminal charges are ever filed or not. In some states, they are called commonwealth attorneys in states that identify themselves as commonwealths, such as Kentucky. Various Web sites for criminal background checks can provide leads as to where records are kept. The convicting court that handled a criminal matter, superior court, would have the records of what someone was convicted of, and what their sentence was. The state's Department of Corrections would have a current record of where a criminal inmate is being currently held at, or a released inmates records as well. All of these are public records with no limitations on access.

Doing a criminal background check on anyone, alive or dead, can be purchased rather cheaply and quickly on a variety of Web sites easily found with a simple Google search under "criminal background check." I used these sites:

http://www.criminalsupersearch.com/contact.asp

www.publicbackgroundchecks.com

www.criminalcbs.com

- UNIVERSITIES: College transcripts are with the registrar's office at any university. They are usually only available to family members of deceased former students unless a signed permission slip from a former student that is still alive is provided. You'll need the social security number of the student, see below for that.

- SOCIAL SECURITY: Social Security Administration keeps records of when a name was changed to help document a marriage date, and might even have the records submitted, like a marriage certificate, to document the name change. Their Web site is www.ssa.gov. After a person dies, their SSN becomes a public record, and is searchable on Ancestry.com.
- MILITARY RECORDS: The Veteran's Administration keeps records of applications for military benefits, and will copy them to family members. Their Web site is www.va.gov. You can submit applications for their records directly through their Web sites without having to mail in an application. To get the service number of the family member you are investigating, sometimes these are listed on Ancestry.com, but an even easier method is to just look through old family relics, like dog tags (this is how I found Leon's service number) or discharge documents. With their birth date and full name, you might be able to get the military to find it for you. Some sources helpful in investigating military histories of decedents are:

http://www.genealogical.com/index.php?main_page=product_info&ref=1308&item_number=FH84

National Archives:
http://www.archives.gov/genealogy/index.html
http://www.archives.gov/st-louis/index.html

- National Personnel Records Center
Military Personnel Records
9700 Page Avenue
St. Louis, MO 63132-5100

- Department of Veterans Affairs
Louisville Regional Office
321 W. Main St.
Suite 390
Louisville, KY 40202

- MEDICAL EXAMINERS & EXHUMING HUMAN REMAINS: Each county has a county medical examiner office, and each one of those has an investigator that looks into potential criminal cases. These offices also keep meticulous files, even for cases that never develop into an actual criminal court case. Each county government lists these offices in the phone directory, and they usually have posted Web pages you can use to find the names of the individuals to call.

In talking with medical examiners, don't get emotional, just stick to facts. Also, don't exaggerate, as they can see through that, and they won't take you seriously. Stick to only what you know for a fact. You can state you suspect something, but clearly label it as a suspicion, not a fact. Be patient, polite, and express gratitude for their help. Always give the medical professional respect by referring to them by their earned title, "Dr.," if appropriate, and never by their first name or equally offensive to some physicians, "Mr." or "Ms."

Exhumation of human remains for either reburial elsewhere or belated autopsy can only be done with a permit from the Health Department of the county where the remains are buried. Those seeking a permit must either be next of kin, all of them of the same familial link to the deceased must agree, or an order from a circuit court judge must be obtained. Obviously the easiest route is to ask for written permission from family members and a letter will suffice—be sure to get it notarized. Having a document that is signed by someone notarized validates it to a judge reviewing it later on.

Failing getting family members to agree and sign their permission, pursue the exhumation through the courts. This will likely incur hiring a lawyer to write the motion, as this is too serious to handle with simply a letter to a judge. To avoid the lawyer fees, you might try writing a letter first, but I doubt something this serious could be handled without a court hearing, thus requiring the presence of a lawyer representing you. Obviously, getting a judge to agree to order an exhumation is not something that can happen just by you asking for it. You will have to have compelling reasons justifying it, such as the strong suspicion of foul play in the death, substantiated by evidence that you've compiled and not merely family rumors. Have documents ready to prove your case, such as records you've uncovered, or signed affidavits from family members that remember events you wish for the judge to consider when reviewing your request.

Once the permit for exhumation is obtained, you can hire any local funeral home to perform the exhumation, and they can engage the services of a forensic pathologist for the actual autopsy.

One of the contact people for information in this book was Dr. Cyril Wecht, http://www.cyrilwecht.com/.

- TAX RECORDS: Property tax records are kept at county tax assessor's offices and are open to the public. They might not be searchable over the phone or through the mail, and most are not searchable through their Web sites. You have to physically go there and search their records. Surprisingly they are usually well indexed and can be searched rather quickly once you learn their system of organization. The front counter staff will be willing to explain that to you. Tax records can help you find a family member that is elusive through other avenues. If they own property, like the house they live in, the county will have a public record available for you to find of it. It won't list their phone number, but it will give you an address to write to (suggested as a first contact) or show up and knock on their door (last resort). These records will also give you the current-day owners of property owned by your ancestors, in case you wanted to contact them for any information they might have on the history of the property, like whom they bought the property from and when.

Obituaries

Obituaries can be a great resource for finding names and cities where people lived of the family of the deceased. Obituaries normally appear in the main cities of the area that the decedent lived in their lifetimes, not necessarily the local paper closest to the location where they died. Also, if the deceased didn't have a long history in the city where they were living at the time they died, then the newspaper where they lived most of their lives and have the most family or friends located at will run their obituary. The purpose of an obituary is to notify others who can't be notified directly by the deceased's family members of the death, and the time and place of the funeral/burial. For instance, in this story Nell's obituary appeared in Paducah's newspaper, not Okeechobee's.

There are various Web sites where obituaries have been amassed and can be retrieved for a small fee—usually a few dollars. It isn't worth paying the yearly subscription to these sites unless you plan on retrieving enough obituaries such that the individual cost of each sums to more than the yearly subscription rate. You can usually search these sites for free to see if they even have the obituaries you seek—and then will charge you to download them. Most of these sites will allow you to preview the obituary—usually read the first few sentences to make sure it's the one you seek, so you don't buy an obituary record mistakenly. So it's best to make a list of all the obituaries you think you will need, check to see if they are all available on the site before purchasing any of them, then make the decision on the subscription purchase versus the individual purchases.

The most complete obituary Web sites are www.obitcentral.com and www.newspaperarchive.com/obituary. Some newspapers have obituaries on their Web sites for free, with searchable databases, particularly if the death occurred within the last few years, since the newspaper has had a Web site. Ancestry.com also has a significant database of obituaries already in their collection for no additional fee. Obituaries list also the burial locations, and any details known at the time of the cause of death if appropriate to be published.

One caveat I should mention about obituaries—they are only as accurate as the person reporting the information to the newspaper. Obituaries are not verified for accuracy by the newspaper prior to publication. This means the reporting family member of the deceased can alter the deceased's history—and they often do. Sometimes family members try to clean up or aggrandize the deceased's life story in their obituary, like deleting illegitimate children or a criminal history, or even the manner in which they died if it was viewed as disrespectful to mention it, such as suicide or drug overdose. They'll merely report that the person died without mentioning the cause.

An example of this in my own family is when a sibling decided to aggrandize, I theorize, my father Frank's life in his obituary by mentioning grandchildren and great-grandchildren he never had. As a researcher myself, I know that researchers want clear distinctions in obituaries as to who is a biological child, adopted child, or a stepchild. Most people honor these distinctions and don't infer any disrespect from mentioning the clear family relation to the deceased. My recently discovered half-sister Sharon, upon viewing Frank's obituary that I sent to her, queried me on the listing of various grandchildren and great-grandchildren in his obituary, confused by it. She knew, as I had previously told her, that Spencer Tucker was Frank Tucker's only biological grandchild from his legally recognized children. Sharon herself has a child that Frank never knew about but who technically is/was his biological grandchild.

In Frank's obituary, which I had no part in writing nor was I consulted with about it before it was published, the sibling chose to list his own stepchildren and stepgrandchildren from his second marriage as Frank's grandchildren and great-grandchildren (with no "step" identification included at all). I question if there is even such a thing as stepgrandchildren or step-great-grandchildren. Doesn't the "step" identification stop at some point in distance outside the marriage that created the "step" relation? Neither Wikipedia.com nor Dictionary.com have entries defining "stepgrandchild," therefore I have to assume from a genealogical standpoint, it doesn't exist. It makes sense since the individual marrying and acquiring stepchildren is making that choice, but their parents, grandparents, and siblings aren't joining in that choice. They aren't choosing to marry into this other family, so why should they be forced to acknowledge step-relation they technically have no blood connection to?

These "step" progeny mentioned in Frank's obituary, albeit referred to as actual blood progeny, are actually of no blood relation (or adopted relation either) to Frank. I can only theorize this was done by the sibling either to aggrandize Frank by creating the illusion he had greater progeny than he actually did, or perhaps to aggrandize the sibling himself by making it appear he had greater progeny than he actually does. I guess it's also a possibility it was done to score points with the sibling's spouse—by creating the public illusion of greater family "oneness" by deleting the "step" references—but that's just a guess.

It wasn't a slight that Sharon and her child were not mentioned in Frank's obituary since none of our family even knew of Sharon's existence at the time of Frank's death in October 2005. Tillie revealed Sharon's existence to me one day before Frank's funeral, and I hadn't begun my search to find Sharon yet. If we had known about her before the funeral and intentionally left her and her child's name out of the obituary to conceal the fact that Frank had a child outside of marriage, that would have been a serious and hurtful blunder. But that wasn't the case here. I'm tempted to republish an accurate version of Frank's obituary to correct the omission of Sharon and her child (only with their permission, of course) and insert the accurate "step" references, or delete progeny that wasn't actually Frank's, to correct the permanent record on Frank's life. I'm concerned future Tucker family researchers will be confused by this grossly inaccurate obituary of Frank Tucker's, but perhaps this book will help clarify the true history.

The moral of the above example is that a researcher shouldn't rely on what appears in obituaries, as they can be notoriously inaccurate, but can be good reference points to further one's investigation.

Cemeteries

Once you find out the location where family members are buried, go visit the cemeteries if possible. Most cemeteries have a phone number to contact about future burials, and you can contact them to find a location of where in the cemetery your family member(s) are buried. If the cemetery is a rural, small cemetery, then contact a local church nearby the cemetery, and usually they know who takes care of the cemetery and has the cemetery's records. Once in the cemetery, record the data on the headstones of your family members, such as birth and death dates, and full names including middle names or initials. Photograph the headstones if possible—it might help you if you question the accuracy of your transcriptions later on. This information will help you when you go looking for obituaries and birth or death certificates.

When at the graves of family members, look in the immediate vicinity around the graves for other family members you didn't know were buried there. They should be within close proximity to the family members you did know about. If you have the time and the cemetery is relatively small, you might want to walk the entire cemetery, row by row, looking for last names you recognize. It's common families seek to bury their kin in the cemeteries where they have other relation buried, instead of the most convenient local cemetery to where they currently lived. For example, we had transported my mother Judy's remains from Chicago (where she was living at the time of her death) a four-hour drive to Chesterfield, Illinois, for her burial near her parents. We had transported my father Frank's remains a five-hour drive from Kentucky (where he was living at the time of his death) to Chesterfield for burial near his beloved Judy. My grandmother Nell's remains were flown back from Florida to be buried in Kentucky in a family plot Leon had purchased in Paducah.

Whomever you contact that operates the cemetery nowadays should also have the cemetery records. They would have to consult those records to tell you where your family member is buried, so you can ask them if there are other people buried in the cemetery with the same last name as the ones you are looking for. That may reveal even more family you didn't even know you had. If you cannot travel to the cemetery, the cemetery caretaker can copy the data from their records and send it to you if you ask politely. Most people are eager to help you when you tell them you are doing research. There exist many volunteer groups that "walk," as they call it, cemeteries to record all the data on grave markers. They are usually willing to photograph the headstone of the person you request information on and e-mail it to you. They then publish this information in books or nowadays on the Internet. A Google search on the cemetery usually can pull up this information rather easily. Using the Find in Top Window feature under the Edit pull-down menu of most Web browsers then can search inside the posted records for your family name.

Some good Web sites to consult on cemetery searches are:

www.findagrave.com
http://www.obitcentral.com/cemsearch/il-cem.htm

Funeral Directors

Funeral directors are the one of the best starting points to investigating a death. They can help you understand all the aspects of death certificates, and how each state records them. Funeral homes are usually a family-run business, as was the case with the Yates Funeral Home involved in this book. Funeral directors can direct you as to who in coroner's offices to talk with further because of the many interactions they have with them. Often they have a friendly relationship with coroners.

Funeral directors can give you information on the embalming process, autopsies, decomposition rates, rigor mortis, on all things related to what happens to human remains postmortem. They can also tell you the telltale signs they look for in a suspicious death—assuming no autopsy was performed. In many cases, funeral directors are who report to coroners that they suspect foul play in a body they have been given to embalm. They discover evidence that doctors, family members, and emergency medical personnel may have missed, such as the case examined in this book—the hidden money discovered in Nell's brassiere.

When requesting a copy of the funeral home's file on a funeral they handled, make clear you are a family member doing family history research. Since these businesses usually want to establish a good relationship with you to sell you services in the future, it might help facilitate getting the information from them if you also ask for pricing and literature from them for "advance funeral planning," which these businesses thrive on. Indicate that your seeking this information about your deceased family member has made you think about your own funeral planning, and wanted to get information to start planning life insurance needs, etc., thus your request for the additional information as well. This should accomplish your goal.

Unions, Private Clubs or Secret Societies

FREEMASONS: Investigating Freemasonry is nothing more difficult than going to the library and checking out books on the subject. I invested in a few books easily found on Amazon.com, even purchasing them used to save a few bucks (great used book search engine is www.addall.com, it searches multiple used book listing services at the same time). I listed the ones I found that were better and more illustrative in my bibliography for this book. There are also various Web sites that can list the worldwide network of Freemasons and how to contact their lodges.

Freemasons are a secret society, and when contacting their various offices to verify the Freemason history of my father and grandfather, I found them sometimes unwilling to give me much information. I couldn't tell whether this was a lack of available records to search, or just an unwillingness to divulge member information. Even after I had identified myself as a son of a Freemason, that didn't seem to help. In some cases, I utilized the "secret saying" my father Frank had taught me, "I am the son of the widow's son, and I need help," which Frank said would compel any Freemason to aid. But even that didn't seem to get me information from an uncooperative, hypersensitive-about-secrecy Freemason. One office I contacted was the Okeechobee Masonic Lodge through their Web site at:

http://www.30thmasonic.com/Okee.html

LABOR UNIONS: Investigating labor union records is as easy as calling the local union hall. Identify yourself as a researcher and family member of a former union member, and they usually can put you in touch with people that remember your family member. Records can be sparse at a union hall, so don't expect much. A national union office for each labor union usually exists in Washington DC for lobbying purposes. Google searches or asking the local union hall where their national offices are located is the way to find any records of union work of your family member. The labor union office I contacted is:

Laborers' International Union of North America
905 16th St., NW
Washington DC
20006

Additional Resources

Some additional Web sites and contact addresses I used in my investigation are below:

Web sites:
Genealogy
http://www.familysearch.org/Eng/Search/frameset_search.asp
http://www.gencircles.com/globaltree/
http://www.cousinconnect.com/p/a/101042
http://usgenweb.org/
http://www.cyndislist.com/lds.htm
http://www.larfhc.org/

http://www.mygenealogist.com/
http://www.quintinpublications.com/familygenealogies_tr.html
http://www.gencircles.com/globaltree/
http://www.familysearch.org/Eng/Search/frameset_search.asp
http://www.rootsweb.ancestry.com/~ilsgs/
www.legacy.com

Illinois Death Index
http://www.cyberdriveillinois.com/departments/archives/idphdeathindex.html

Illinois Archives
http://www.cyberdriveillinois.com/departments/archives/databases.html

Mississippi State Government
http://www.mississippi.gov/frameset.jsp?URL=http://www.co.forrest.ms.us

Federal Land Records
http://www.glorecords.blm.gov/

St. Clair County, Illinois County Recorder's Office
http://www.co.st-clair.il.us/ElectedOfficials/Recorder+of+Deeds.htm

St. Clair County, Illinois County Government
http://www.co.st-clair.il.us/

Tennessee Department of Health
http://health.state.tn.us/

Illinois State Comptroller
http://www.ioc.state.il.us/office/ccbt/iocfeedinsert.cfm

Tennessee State Library and Archives
http://www.tennessee.gov/tsla/

Kentucky Vital Records
http://ukcc.uky.edu/vitalrec/

Illinois Vital Records
http://www.worldvitalrecords.com/illinois-vital-records.htm

Kentucky Libraries
http://www.kdla.ky.gov/

Kentucky Genealogy
http://www.kygs.org/
http://www.history.ky.gov/

Macoupin County, Illinois Genealogy
http://www.kindredtrails.com/IL_Macoupin.html

Tennessee State Library
http://www.tennessee.gov/tsla/

Belleville Public Library
http://www.bellevillepubliclibrary.org/

Michigan Vital Records
http://www.michigan.gov/mdch/0,1607,7-132-4645—,00.html

Illinois Vital Records
http://www.idph.state.il.us/vitalrecords/index.htm

Illinois Death Records
http://www.deathindexes.com/illinois/
http://www.cyberdriveillinois.com/departments/archives/death.html

Mental Illness
www.schizophrenia.com/prevention/older.htm
www.schizophreniaforum.org/for/curr/malaspina/default.asp
www.schizophrenia.com/sznews/archives/002592.html
www.msnbc.msn.com/id/17937814/print/1/displaymode/1098/
http://news.bbc.co.uk/2/hi/health/3760844.stm

Copyright Basics
www.ucop.edu/ott/crbasics.html

Newspapers
www.paducahsun.com

McCracken County Sheriff
http://paducahky.gov/county/sheriff_department/sheriff_department.php

State of Florida contacts:

Florida State Government Records
https://www.myfloridacounty.com/serv/MyFloridaCounty/ORI/Order?

Polk County, Florida—Property Records
http://www.polkpa.org

Florida State Attorney General's Office
http://sao1.co.escambia.fl.us/links.htm

Florida State Attorney's office
http://sao1.co.escambia.fl.us/links.htm

Raulerson Hospital, Okeechobee, Florida
http://www.raulersonhospital.com/PhoneDir.asp

Other Mail Contacts:

Cyril H. Wecht and Pathology Associates 1119 Penn Avenue Suite 404 Pittsburgh, PA 15222	Arkansas Department of Health Vital Records 4815 West Markham St., Slot 44 Little Rock, AR 72205-3867
C. Barney Metz Clerk of the Circuit Court St. Clair County P.O. Box 8445 Belleville, IL 62222-8445	Amy Villines Circuit Court Clerk Webster Circuit & District Courts Webster County Courthouse PO Box 290 Dixon, KY 42409-0290
Anthony P. Libri Clerk of Circuit Court, Sangamon County Room 405 200 S. 9th St. Springfield, IL 62701	Mike Lawrence Circuit Court Clerk McCracken Circuit & District Courts McCracken County Courthouse PO Box 1455 Paducah, KY 42002-1455
White County Courthouse Searcy, Arkansas 501-279-6223	McCracken County Public Library 555 Washington St. Paducah, KY 42003

Mount Carmel Catholic Cemetery 10101 W. Main St. Belleville, IL 62223-1407 618-397-0181	Belleville Public Library 121 E. Washington St. Belleville, IL 62220 618-234-0441
Prudential Financial Insurance Company Customer Service Office PO Box 7390 Philadelphia, PA 19176 (800) 778-2255	St. Clair County Health Dept. 19 Public Square, Suite 150 Belleville, IL 62220-1624 (618) 233-7703
St. Clair County Historical Society (618) 234-0600	Fairview Heights Public Library 10017 Bunkum Road Fairview Heights, IL 62208 618-489-2070
Barnes Hospital 216 S. Kingshighway Blvd. St. Louis, MO (314) 362-5000	Nancy Book McCracken County Property Valuation Administrator 621 Washington St. Paducah, KY 42003
Kentucky Transportation Cabinet Division of Motor Vehicle Licensing PO Box 2014 Frankfort, KY 40622	Community Title & Escrow 1207 Thouvenot Lane, Suite 400 Frank Scott Parkway East Shiloh, IL 62269 (618) 234-1400
Richard M. Weiss Clerk of the Courts Official Records Dept. Drawer #CC-8 PO Box 9000 Bartow, FL 33831	Dale K. Thompson Desoto County Circuit Clerk 2535 Highway 51 South Hernando, MS 38632
Commonwealth of Kentucky Department for Public Health Vital Statistics 275 East Main St., 1E-A Frankfort, KY 40621-0001 502-564-4212	Commonwealth of Kentucky McCracken County Family Court McCracken County Courthouse 301 South 6th St. Paducah, KY 42003
Cabinet for Health and Family Services Office of the Secretary 275 E. Main St., 5W-A Frankfort, KY 40621 (502) 564-7091	Murray State University Registrar's Office 113 Sparks Hall Murray, KY 42071 (270) 762-3741

Missouri Dept. of Health & Senior Services Bureau of Vital Records PO Box 570 Jefferson City, MO 65102-0570	Illinois Regional Archives Depository c/o Special Collections Morris Library-6632 Southern Illinois University Carbondale, IL 62901
Mississippi Vital Records 571 Stadium Drive Jackson, MS 39216	Tennessee State Library and Archives 403 7th Avenue North Nashville, TN 37243-0312
Office of State Attorney 19th Judicial Circuit Court of Florida Okeechobee Judicial Centre 312 N. W. 3rd St., Suite 260 Okeechobee, FL 34972	Okeechobee Public Library 206 S. W. 16th St. Okeechobee, FL 34974 (863) 763-3536
Okeechobee Historical Society PO Box 248 Okeechobee, FL 34973	

Glossary of Names

Abernathy, Walter	Laborer's Union Local 100 coworker of Leon Tucker
Albright, Ashley	Assistant State Attorney, Okeechobee, Florida
Baden, Michael, Dr.	Forensic pathologist, television personality
Banks, Kathleen (Johnston)	Daughter of Dr. Stephen Johnston
Barker, John	Former County Coroner for Paducah, Kentucky, current-day funeral director for Milner & Orr Funeral Home in Paducah
Bell, Carrie (Reed)	Granddaughter of Audrey (Marshall) Tucker, daughter of Harold Reed
Billy Joe	Husband of Nadine (name changed), who was high-school sweetheart of Frank and mother of Frank's daughter, Sharon (name changed)
Bond, Adam	First cousin to author, son of Donald Bond, nephew to Mary Judith "Judy" Bond Tucker
Bond, Donald	Brother to Mary Judith "Judy" Bond Tucker, brother-in-law to Frank Tucker, father of Adam Bond
Bond, Glen	Grandfather to author, father of Mary Judith "Judy" (Bond) Tucker (second wife of Frank L. Tucker)
Bond, Ruth	Grandmother to author, mother of Mary Judith "Judy" (Bond) Tucker (second wife of Frank L. Tucker)
Bose, Dan McCracken	County Attorney, Paducah, Kentucky
Brooks, Arnold	Long-lost son of Allen Freeman, half-brother to Nell (Freeman) Tucker

Brooks, Nettie (Tucker)	Sister to Leon Tucker
Brown, Frances (Stevenson)	Daughter of Tommy Stevenson, cousin to Leon Tucker
Bryant, Paul "Bear"	Football coach of University of Kentucky, coached Frank L. Tucker
Burgess, Ardie	See Elmer Ardie Burgess
Burgess, Elmer Ardie	Son of Vera (Tucker) Burgess, nephew to Leon Tucker
Burgess, Elmer G.	Son of Elmer Ardie Burgess, cousin to Leon Tucker
Burgess, Eugene	Grandson of Vera (Tucker) Burgess, cousin to Leon Tucker
Burgess, Richard	Grandson of Vera (Tucker) Burgess, cousin to Leon Tucker
Burgess, Tom	Cousin of Leon Tucker, grandson of Vera (Tucker) Burgess, son of Elmer Ardie Burgess
Burgess, Vera (Tucker)	Sister to Leon Tucker, grandmother of Tom Burgess
Carter, Wayne	Funeral Director, Roth Funeral Home, Paducah, Kentucky
Chapman, Sarah	second great-grandmother of author, grandmother to Leon Tucker
Chapman, Thomas	third great-grandfather of author, father-in-law to Levi Tucker, father of Sarah (Chapman) Tucker
Cole, Joyce	Descendant of James Young Tucker (uncle to Leon Tucker), cousin to Leon Tucker, church friend of Nell Tucker
Collins, Earnest	Husband of Freeda (Stevenson) Collins
Collins, Freeda (Stevenson)	Daughter of Walter and Dollie Stevenson, cousin to Leon Tucker
Dawson, Jim	Cousin of Judy Tucker, owned car dealership with Frank L. Tucker
Donovan, Shirley (Stevenson)	Daughter of Walter and Dollie Stevenson, cousin to Leon Tucker

Eders, Mary Ann	First wife of great-grandfather of author, George W. Tucker (name may have been Jane Pierce), but not the mother of Leon Tucker
Edwards, Mary Ann (Tucker)	Nicknamed "Aunt Molly," Sister to Levi Tucker, raised George W. Tucker (father of Leon Tucker)
Edwards, Tillie (Dotson)	First cousin of Frank L. Tucker, niece of Nell Tucker, daughter of Grace (Freeman) Dotson.
Felt, Mark	CIA employee, infamous "Deep Throat" of Watergate fame
Fennel, James	Husband of Wanda (Taylor) Fennel
Fennel, Wanda (Taylor)	Daughter of Uvil Taylor, descendant of James Young Tucker (uncle of Leon Tucker)
Fike, Carl	Husband of Ila Mae (Freeman) Fike (sister to Nell Tucker)
Fike, Thomas	Father-in-law of Ila Mae (Freeman) Fike (sister to Nell Tucker), witness attesting to Nell's age on her delayed birth certificate
Freeland, Joe	Attorney handling Nell Tucker's divorce attempt
Freeland, Murray	Wife of Joe Freeland
Freeman, Allen	Father of Nell (Freeman) "Peepeyes" Tucker, Grace (Freeman-Dotson) Martinez, & Ila Mae (Freeman) Fike
Freeman, Earnest	Brother to Nell (Freeman) Tucker
Freeman, Grace Lily	See Grace Martinez
Frick, Martha	Wife of Remus Tucker, mother of Virginia and Ruth Tucker, sister-in-law to Leon Tucker
Garrett, Thomas	Prominent Paducah attorney
Gillison, Bertie (Mitchell)	Cousin to Leon Tucker, daughter of Robie (Tucker) Mitchell
Godwin, Pearl	Nurse to Dr. Stephen Johnston at Okeechobee Hospital in 1969 when Nell Tucker died
Green, Larry	Friend of Leon Tucker
Griffith, David	Second and last husband of Maudine Pruitt (first wife of Frank L. Tucker)

Griffy, Ben	Friend of Remus Tucker
Griffy, George	Friend of Remus Tucker
Harden, Joleen (Stevenson)	Daughter of Robert and Irene Stevenson, wife of Kenneth Harden, bought land in Ft. Meade, Florida, from Leon Tucker
Harden, Kenneth	Husband of Joleen (Stevenson) Harden
Hayden, Audrey	See Audrey Tucker
Holmes, Wilma (Keeling)	Twin sister to Pete Keeling, church friend of Nell Tucker, cousin to Leon Tucker
Howe, Bertie Lee (Tucker)	Niece to Leon Tucker, daughter of Corbett Tucker Sr.
Hubert, George	Renter of property from Leon Tucker
Huckabee, Tantie	Settler of Okeechobee, Florida
Johnston, Christine	Fifth wife of Dr. Stephen Johnston
Johnston, Steven, Dr.	Physician in Okeechobee, Florida, who signed Nell Tucker's death certificate
Johnston, Tina	See Christine Johnston
Jones, Albert	Former commonwealth attorney (local district attorney) for Paducah, Kentucky
Keeling, Coon	"Coon" was a nickname, formal name unknown, cousin to Leon Tucker
Keeling, Grace	Wife of Pete Keeling
Keeling, Hard	Cousin to Leon Tucker
Keeling, Pete	Pastor of Eastside Holiness Church in Paducah, Kentucky, cousin to Leon Tucker, twin brother to Wilma (Keeling) Holmes
Keeling, Ruth	See Ruth (Keeling) Tucker
Lance, Audra	See Audra (Nichols-Lance) Tucker
Lance, Billy	Grandson of Audra (Nichols-Lance) Tucker
Lance, Mark	Son of Audra (Nichols-Lance) Tucker
Lance, Mike	Son of Audra (Nichols-Lance) Tucker
Lemanski, Frances (Reed)	Daughter of Audie "Audrey" (Marshall-Reed-Hayden) Tucker, stepdaughter of Leon Tucker

LeVaughn, Mark, Dr.	Medical examiner, former state pathologist for Western Kentucky
Liddy, G. Gordon	Watergate figure
Malaspina, Delores, Dr.	Author of article on schizophrenia
Markham, Lee Anita	Wife of Lowery Markham
Markham, Lowery	Okeechobee, Florida resident, son of Christine Johnston (wife of Dr. Stephen Johnston)
Markham, Tommy	Okeechobee, Florida, resident, local historian, son of Christine Johnston (wife of Dr. Stephen Johnston)
Marshall, Claud	Twin brother of Audrey Tucker, nicknamed "Smitty"
Martinez, Grace (Freeman-Dotson)	Sister to Nell "Peepeyes" Tucker, mother of Tillie (Dotson) Edwards and Mildred (Dotson) Tucker
McKay, Jim	Resident of Romance, Arkansas
McNeal, Dorothy	Church friend of Nell Tucker, witness at campground in Florida in 1969 when Nell died.
Meemaw	Nickname for grandmothers in Kentucky
Mendoza, Venetia (Johnston)	Daughter of Dr. Stephen Johnston
Meredith, George	Second husband of Martha Frick
Mitchell, Bert	Cousin to author, son of Robie (Tucker) Mitchell, nephew to Leon Tucker
Mitchell, Jim	Cousin to Leon Tucker, daughter of Robie (Tucker) Mitchell
Mitchell, Robie (Tucker)	Sister to Leon Tucker, mother to Bert Mitchell
Mitchell, Vera (Burgess)	Granddaughter of Vera (Tucker) Burgess, cousin to Leon Tucker, daughter of Elmer Ardie Burgess
Murray, Dennis	Current-day caretaker of the "Tucker farm" once owned by Levi Tucker in Romance, Arkansas
Nadine	High-school sweetheart of Frank L. Tucker and mother of Sharon (name changed), wife of Billy Joe (name changed)
Nichols, Beedie (Merritt)	Mother of Audra (Nichols-Lance) Tucker

Nichols, James	Father of Audra (Nichols-Lance) Tucker
Noe, Jessie	Descendant of James Young Tucker (uncle to Leon Tucker), cousin to Leon Tucker, church friend of Nell Tucker
Nowak, Versie (Tucker)	Sister to Leon Tucker, mother of Katherine (Nowak) Taylor
Overstreet, Eloy	Paducah area gambling saloon owner, friend of Leon Tucker, nicknamed "Eli"
Papaw	Nickname for grandfathers in Kentucky, commonly used for Leon Tucker
Payne, Charles	Renter of property from Leon Tucker
Peepeyes	Nickname for Nell Tucker, instead of "Meemaw" or "Grandma"
Phelps, Ethyl Lee (Stevenson)	Daughter of Walter and Dollie Stevenson, cousin to Leon Tucker
Pierce, Jane	Possible name of first wife of great-grandfather of author, George W. Tucker, but not the mother of Leon Tucker, name may have been Mary Ann Eders
Price, Louise (Burgess)	Cousin to Leon Tucker, daughter of Vera (Tucker) Burgess
Pruitt, Inez	Mother of Maudine Pruitt (first wife of Frank L. Tucker)
Pruitt, Jess	Father of Maudine Pruitt (first wife of Frank L. Tucker)
Pruitt, Maudine Celeste	First wife of Frank L. Tucker, mother of Trent Tucker
Pruitt, Patsy	Younger sister of Maudine Pruitt (first wife of Frank L. Tucker)
Pruitt, Teddy	Brother of Maudine Pruitt
Range, Captola	Aunt of Maudine Pruitt (first wife of Frank L. Tucker)
Reed, Gloria	Wife of Harold Reed
Reed, Harold	Son of Audrey (Marshall-Reed-Hayden) Tucker

Reed, Joe	Son of Harold Reed, grandson of Audrey Tucker
Reed, John T.	Paducah attorney used by Frank Tucker, no relation to Audrey (Marshall-Reed-Hayden) Tucker
Reed, Tammy	Daughter of Harold Reed, granddaughter of Audrey Tucker
Richardson, Dorothy (Stevenson)	Daughter of Walter and Dollie Stevenson, cousin to Leon Tucker
Roberts, Pood	"Pood" was a nickname, formal name unknown, union chief of Local 100 Laborer's Union in East St. Louis, Illinois, and boss to Leon Tucker
Rose, Sally	second great-grandmother of author, grandmother to Nell (Freeman) Tucker
Rose, Vickie	Daughter of Frances Lemanski, granddaughter of Audrey Tucker
Russell, Ollie	Wife of Tommy Stevenson
Sanderson, Cynthia	Judge, McCracken County Family Court
Schadt, Debbie	Granddaughter of Remus Tucker (Leon's brother)
Sheffield, Peggy (Pruitt)	Sister of Maudine Pruitt (first wife of Frank L. Tucker)
Sharon	Daughter of Frank Tucker and high-school sweetheart Nadine (name changed)
Sidecar	Baby rabbit kept as pet by Frank and Judy Tucker
Sims, Dan	County Coroner for McCracken County, Kentucky
Snooks, Ted	Man killed by Leon Tucker
Stamps, Betty (Nowak)	Cousin to Leon Tucker, daughter of Versie (Tucker) Nowak, wife of Marion Stamps
Stamps, Marion	Husband of Betty Stamps
Stevenson, Annie (Tucker)	Half-sister to Leon Tucker, daughter of George W. Tucker and first wife, Mary Ann Eders, mother of Walter Stevenson

Stevenson, Arlie

Son of Annie (Tucker) Stevenson, brother to Walter Stevenson, cousin to Leon Tucker

Stevenson, Barbara (Collins)

Daughter of Freeda (Stevenson) Collins, family historian for Stevenson family

Stevenson, Charles

Cousin to Leon Tucker, son of Walter and Dollie Stevenson

Stevenson, Clifton

Son of Tommy Stevenson, cousin to Leon Tucker

Stevenson, Dollie

Wife of Walter Stevenson, mother of Eddie, Charles, Glenda, Ethel Lee, Freeda, Dorothy, and Shirley Stevenson. Witness at campground in Florida in 1969 when Nell Tucker died

Stevenson, Eddie

Cousin to author, son of Walter and Dollie Stevenson, witness at campground in Okeechobee, Florida, at time of Nell Tucker's death

Stevenson, Edison

Nicknamed "Doodle," son of Tommy Stevenson, cousin to Leon Tucker

Stevenson, Irene

Wife of Robert Stevenson, Florida resident

Stevenson, James

Son of Tommy Stevenson, cousin to Leon Tucker

Stevenson, Larkin

Cousin of Leon Tucker, father of Robert Stevenson

Stevenson, Linda

Wife of Eddie Stevenson, witness at campground in Florida in 1969 when Nell died

Stevenson, Milton

Son of Tommy Stevenson, cousin to Leon Tucker

Stevenson, Robert

Cousin of Leon Tucker, son of Larkin Stevenson

Stevenson, Rudell

Son of Tommy Stevenson, cousin to Leon Tucker

Stevenson, Thomas, Jr.

Nicknamed "Tinker," son of Tommy Stevenson, cousin to Leon Tucker

Stevenson, Tommy, Sr.

Son of Annie (Tucker) Stevenson and nephew to Leon Tucker

Stevenson, Walter	Cousin to Leon Tucker, son of Annie (Tucker) Stevenson, husband to Dollie Stevenson, father of Eddie, Charles, Glenda, Ethel Lee, Freeda, Dorothy, and Shirley Stevenson. Walter was a witness at the campground in Florida in 1969 when Nell Tucker died.
Stoner, Aileen (Burgess)	Daughter of Vera (Tucker) Burgess, niece to Leon Tucker, mother to Robert Stoner
Stoner, Robert	Grandson of Vera (Tucker) Burgess, cousin to Leon Tucker, son of Aileen (Burgess) Stoner
Stoner, Shirley	Wife of Robert Stoner
Sumida, Scott	Friend/caretaker of Bert Mitchell
Sharon	Half-sister to author, daughter of Frank L. Tucker and high-school sweetheart Nadine
Taylor, Katherine (Nowak)	Cousin to Leon Tucker, daughter of Versie (Tucker) Nowak
Taylor, Lizzie (Tucker)	Half-sister to Leon Tucker, daughter of George W. Tucker and first wife, Mary Ann Eders
Taylor, Stella	Wife of Uvil Taylor, mother of Wanda (Taylor) Fennel
Taylor, Uvil	Cousin to Leon Tucker, frequent Florida travel companion with Leon and Nell Tucker, father of Wanda (Taylor) Fennel
Trouble	Golden retriever, family pet of Frank and Judy Tucker
Tucker, Audra (Lance)	Third wife of Frank L. Tucker, stepmother to author, friend of Tillie Edwards
Tucker, Audrey	Second wife of Leon Tucker, maiden named Audie C. Marshall, married twice before to Michael Reed and Joseph Hayden, commonly known as "Audrey"
Tucker, Corbett Jr. "Son"	Cousin to Frank L. Tucker, son of Corbett Tucker, Sr., husband to Mildred (Dotson) Tucker, brother-in-law to Tillie (Dotson) Edwards, commonly called "Son" instead of "Junior"
Tucker, Corbett Sr.	Brother of Leon Tucker

Tucker, Daisy — Wife of Corbett Tucker Sr., mother of "Son" Tucker

Tucker, Dorothy — Daughter of Corbett Tucker Sr., niece to Leon Tucker

Tucker, Dwain S. — Author, son of Frank L. Tucker, grandson of Leon Tucker and Nell "Peepeyes" (Freeman) Tucker

Tucker, Elbert Leon — Grandfather of author, father of Frank L. Tucker, commonly called "Leon"

Tucker, Frank L. — Father of author, wife of Mary Judith "Judy" Bond Tucker

Tucker, George W. — Great-grandfather to author, father of Leon Tucker, husband to Ruth (Keeling) Tucker

Tucker, Gertrude — Wife of Robert Tucker, sister-in-law to Leon Tucker, commonly known as "Gert"

Tucker, James Young — Brother to George W. Tucker, uncle to Leon Tucker

Tucker, Judy — See Mary Judith "Judy" Bond Tucker

Tucker, Leon — See Elbert Leon Tucker

Tucker, Leonard — Son of Owen Tucker Sr.

Tucker, Levi — second great-grandfather of author, grandfather to Leon Tucker

Tucker, Mary Judith (Bond) — Mother of author, wife of Frank L. Tucker, commonly known as "Judy"

Tucker, Mildred (Dotson) — Sister to Tillie (Dotson) Edwards, wife of Corbett Tucker Jr. (Son Tucker), niece to Nell Tucker

Tucker, Nell Annie Freeman — Grandmother of author, father of Frank L. Tucker, wife of Elbert Leon Tucker, nicknamed "Peepeyes"

Tucker, Nell — See Nell Annie (Freeman) Tucker

Tucker, Owen, Sr. — Cousin to Frank L. Tucker, son of Corbett Tucker Sr., nicknamed "Blue"

Tucker, Owen, Jr. — Son of Owen Tucker Sr.

Tucker, Remus "Reem" — Brother to Leon Tucker, nicknamed "Reem" or "Badeye"

Tucker, Robert	Brother to Leon Tucker, husband of Gert Tucker
Tucker, Ruth (Keeling)	Great-grandmother to author, mother of Leon Tucker, wife of George W. Tucker
Tucker, Ruth	Daughter of Remus Tucker, niece to Leon Tucker
Tucker, Spencer	Nephew of author, great-grandson of Leon Tucker
Tucker, Trent	Half-brother of author, son of Frank L. Tucker, and first wife Maudine Pruitt
Tucker, Virginia "Dink"	Daughter of Remus Tucker, nicknamed "Dink," niece to Leon Tucker
Walden, Merv	Investigator, Florida Medical Examiner's Office
Walsh, Elizabeth (Mitchell)	Cousin to Leon Tucker, daughter of Robie (Tucker) Mitchell
Wecht, Cyril, Dr.	Forensic pathologist, television personality
Yarborough, "Old Man"	Owner of property in Paducah that Leon wrongly built a house on, then burned it down
Yates, Bill	See Joseph W. Yates
Yates, Joseph W.	Mortician/Funeral Director that embalmed Nell Tucker's remains in 1969, also called "Bill"

Notes

1. Tucker, Judy Bond. *Tales of Old Paducah.* Page 17. Spectator Books, Decatur, Illinois, 1976.
2. Schnoebelen, Wm. *MASONRY: Beyond the Light.* Pg. 126-8. Chick Publications, Chino, California. 1991.
3. Schnoebelen, Wm. *MASONRY: Beyond the Light.* Page 142. Chick Publications, Chino, California. 1991.
4. Definitions from the Web site www.dictionary.reference.com.
5. Janosky, Jim. *Okeechobee: A Modern Frontier.* Pg. 15-16. University Press of Florida, 1997.
6. Gregware, Bill & Carol. *Guide to the Lake Okeechobee Area.* Pg. 83. Pineapple Press, Inc., Sarasota, Florida, 1997.
7. Schnoebelen, Wm. *MASONRY: Beyond the Light.* Page 92. Chick Publications, Chino, California. 1991.
8. Widmer, W.W. 2005. Journal of Food Science. 70(4):c307-C312
9. Green MA, Wright JC. Postmortem interval estimation from body temperature data only. Forensic Science International. 1985; 28: 35-46.
10. Knight B, Nokes L. Chapter 2: Temperature-based methods I. Pages 34-35. IN: Henssge C, Knight B, et al. The Estimation of the Time Since Death in the Early Postmortem Period. Arnold Publishers. 1995.
11. Schreckengost, Gary. January 2001. *World War II Magazine.* "Battle of the Bulge: U.S. Army 28th Infantry Division's 110th Regimental Combat Team Upset the German Timetable"
12. Rudwick, Elliott M. *Race Riot at East St. Louis July 2, 1917.* Page 4. Meridian Books, Cleveland, Ohio. 1966.
13. Yelvington, Rube. *East St. Louis—The Way It Is.* Page 238. Top's Books, Mascoutah, Illinois. 1990.
14. Baden, Dr. Michael. Cable television network HBO, Web site Q&A for series "Autopsy."
15. Malaspina, Dr. Dolores. Schizophrenia Research Forum Web site, March 28, 2006, "Schizophrenia Risk and the Paternal Germ Line."
16. Mullich, Joe. "His Biological Clock is Ticking, Too," MSNBC.com Web site, June 27, 2007.
17. Unknown author, BBC News online Web site, "Older Father Schizophrenia Link," October 22, 2004.
18. Mayfield Daily Messenger newspaper, Mayfield, Kentucky, October 18, 1906, "Hidden Gold Found."

Index

About the Author

Dwain S. Tucker lives and works in Los Angeles. He resides in Redondo Beach, enjoying the beach city atmosphere and the southern California lifestyle. He works as a licensed professional civil engineer designing wastewater treatment plants for a large municipality in Los Angeles County. He holds a Bachelor of Science degree in Civil Engineering and a Master of Science degree in Environmental Engineering, both degrees from the University of Illinois at Urbana-Champaign. He also holds a Master of Business Administration degree from Loyola Marymount University in Los Angeles. Last, he also works as an actor in television and film projects, is represented by a talent agency, and is a union member of the Screen Actors Guild and the American Federation of Television and Radio Artists. He is an avid international traveler, having visited all six continents and forty countries to date. He is single with no children.

Dwain S. Tucker

CPSIA information can be obtained at www.ICGtesting.com
Printed in the USA
BVOW061139040312

284381BV00001B/2/P